PELICAN BOOKS

A285

THE LEGACY OF THE ANCIENT WORLD

VOLUME TWO

W. G. DE BURGH

THE LEGACY OF THE
ANCIENT WORLD

BY

W. G. DE BURGH, M.A.

LATE PROFESSOR EMERITUS OF PHILOSOPHY IN
THE UNIVERSITY OF READING
FELLOW OF THE BRITISH ACADEMY

*

VOLUME TWO

*

PENGUIN BOOKS

Penguin Books Ltd, Harmondsworth, Middlesex

U.S.A.: Penguin Books Inc., 3300 Clipper Mill Road, Baltimore 11, Md

CANADA: Penguin Books (Canada) Ltd, 47 Green Street,
Saint Lambert, Montreal, P.Q.

AUSTRALIA: Penguin Books Pty Ltd, 762 Whitehorse Road,
Mitcham, Victoria

SOUTH AFRICA: Penguin Books (S.A.) Pty Ltd, Gibraltar House,
Regents Road, Sea Point, Cape Town

—

First published 1923
New and revised edition 1947
Published in Pelican Books 1953
Reprinted 1955

Made and printed in Great Britain
by The Whitefriars Press Ltd
London and Tonbridge

CONTENTS OF VOLUME TWO

*

CHAPTER NINE

CHRISTIANITY

I *The expansion of Christianity*: Christianity as a revolutionary force in world-history; its origins in, liberation from, and obligations to, Judaism; its expansion and development in the Roman world during the first two centuries; policy of the empire – the persecutions of the second century; the persecutions of the third century and the establishment of Christianity by Constantine; the cause of its success   319

II *Pagan religions and Greek philosophy*: character of pagan religious life in the third century; Mithraism; the religion of the Stoic philosophy; Neo-Platonism and the philosophy of Plotinus; the principles of casuality and of restitution – the theory of emanation; the way of salvation for the human soul; the structure of the supersensible world – the triad of *hypostases*; affinities and divergences between Neo-Platonism and Christianity   337

III *The Catholic faith*: the faith of the first Christians; individual salvation and membership of the kingdom; the development of dogma in the early church; Origen and Christian Platonism; the controversies on the Trinity and the Incarnation; significance of the Trinitarian controversy; Athanasius of Alexandria; western theology – Augustine of Hippo; the Christian synthesis of historic fact and ideal value   355

IV *Conclusion*: influence of the Roman empire on the Christian church – the spread of secularization and intolerance; the effects of Christianity on the disintegration of the empire   382

CHAPTER TEN

THE DECLINE AND FALL

I *Introductory*: the date of the beginning of the decline and fall; Rome's educative function in the period of the decline and fall; scheme of the present chapter   388

II *The reconstruction of the empire*: the need for reconstruction; the work of Diocletian and his successors; their significance, and failure to preserve Graeco-Roman civilization   390

III *The Roman and the Teuton*: policy of the empire towards the barbarians on the Rhine and the Danube; the main streams of invasion – Franks, Visigoths, Vandals, Huns, Ostrogoths and Lombards; impression made by the empire on the Teutonic invaders; their Romanization; the idea of the sacrosanctity of the empire; growth of the Papal power, its alliance with the Frankish kings, and the restoration of the empire in the West in the person of Charles the Great   395

IV *The Roman, the Slav and the Saracen:* the character of the empire in the East; the problem of the European frontier – the Slavs and other immigrants; the Persian wars, the rise of Islam and the struggles against the Saracens; the Mediterranean world at the close of the eighth century   412

V *The empire in the East:* organization of the empire in the East in the sixth century; Justinian's code of law; the church in the East – the Monophysite and Iconoclastic controversies – the schism between East and West; Byzantine art and literature   420

VI *Conclusion:* the varying fortunes of the Byzantine empire; the decline and fall of the empire in the East before the Turks; retrospect and anticipation   432

CHAPTER ELEVEN

THE LEGACY IN THE MIDDLE AGES

I *Introductory:* intention and scheme of the present chapter; what we mean by the Middle Ages; factors determining the mediaeval view of life – Germanic and Scandinavian custom, the Christian church and its theology, and the tradition of Graeco-Roman culture; chronological limits and divisions of the Middle Ages   437

II *The reception of Greek philosophy:* the value and aim of mediaeval thought; its central problem that of a synthesis of religion and philosophy; respect for the authority and other-worldliness in mediaeval thought; the reception of a process of fusion between (*a*) the thought of the western Christian schools from the ninth to the thirteenth centuries, (*b*) that of the Arabian philosophers at Baghdad and in Spain, and (*c*) the continuous Byzantine tradition; the influence of Platonism and of the rediscovery of Aristotle; Aquinas' philosophy as the fruit of the reception; Aquinas' distinction of faith and reason; his doctrines of the being of God as Creator; and of the *analogia entis*   443

III *The reception of Roman law:* influence of Roman law in the barbarian kingdoms; the revival of Roman law in the eleventh century and the school of Bologna; influence of Roman law on mediaeval ethics; Aquinas' doctrine of law; influence of juridical ideas on political theory; the mediaeval theory of monarchy, illustrated from Dante; derivation of sovereignty from the popular will; significance of the reception for later political thought   464

IV *The Renaissance:* contrast between the thought and life of the fourteenth and seventeenth centuries; faith in reason the motive-force of the Renaissance; the fruits of the new impulse in the sciences of nature and of man; the rebirth of science due to the legacy of ancient Greece; the revival of learning and the apotheosis of erudition; Erasmus of Rotterdam as the central figure in the age of humanism   481

v *Conclusion*: the creative energy of Hellenism as evidenced by the rise and growth of modern science   496

CHAPTER TWELVE

ON PROGRESS; AND ON THE LIVING INTEREST OF ANCIENT CIVILIZATION

I *On Progress*: the problem of progress – alternative solutions; neither simple progress, nor simple retrogression, nor cyclical revolutions, in the history of western civilization, but a relatively coherent development; progress not to be measured in terms of material comfort; signs of progress in science and speculative thought; purpose in history not demonstrable empirically, but the object of a reasonable faith   498

II *On the living interest of ancient civilization*: the historical and the living interests of ancient civilization; nature and appeal of the latter; Israel as a present force in the world; the present interest of Hellenism (*a*) for education; (*b*) for life; the value of the Roman legacy for the world to-day; the enduring inspiration of classical antiquity   511

III *Concluding remarks*: history as the revelation, alike of facts, and of their values   524

APPENDIX I. ON CIVILIZATION AND HISTORY

Further consideration of the problems (1) of the relation of value to fact; and (2) why the scope of history is coterminous with that of civilization; sense in which the historian does, and does not, take cognisance of ideal values; supernatural agency, if admitted, lies beyond his power of explanation; as in the case of the Founder of Christianity; the historian's criterion of importance is purely humanistic   528

APPENDIX II. ON HISTORICAL GREATNESS AND MORAL GOODNESS

(i) Diversity of ideal values; problem of the distinction between greatness and moral goodness; (ii) this problem cannot be solved by subordinating either greatness to goodness; or goodness to greatness; (iii) what the historian means by greatness; Alexander's account of greatness fails to solve the problem; greatness means more than representative of an age; and more than efficiency of adaptation; consideration of the case of moral greatness; Croce's distinction of economic and ethical value throws light on the problem; (iv) moral goodness implies an other-worldly criterion; but historical greatness is judged by a this-worldly standard of culture   538

APPENDIX III. ON HUMANISM AND THE WORLD-CRISIS

I The problem raised in ch. XII of intellectual and moral progress; the Renaissance ushered in an age of rationalism and secularist humanism   554

II *The Abuse of Knowledge*: how the logical advance of scientific knowledge has placed power in the control of governments; which may be utilized beneficially or abused. Signs of its abuse, (i) the growth of governmental authority, (ii) the mechanization of life to the detriment of personality, (iii) the spread of ethical and religious relativity at the expense of popular freedom, and consequent moral degeneration. The remedy lies, not in education; nor in secularist morality; but in a theistic faith inspiring to religious worship 556

III *The Idol of Humanism*: The humanistic faith of the eighteenth century; its secularism still lives, despite its practical refutation by recent events; man's claim to self-sufficiency belies his nature, which indicates an other-worldly goal; whereas a theistic world-view gives full scope for humanistic culture; and alone gives meaning to the concepts of fraternity, personality and humanity; so that Christian theism offers the sole security for civilization 566

IV *Conclusion*: The Christian religion as the synthesis of the Hebraic and Hellenic legacies 575

BIBLIOGRAPHICAL APPENDIX 579

INDEX 589

CHAPTER NINE

CHRISTIANITY

*

I. THE EXPANSION OF CHRISTIANITY OVER THE ROMAN WORLD

§ 1. A GENERATION had not passed since the establishment of the Roman empire by Augustus when the founder of Christianity was born into the world. *Imperante Augusto natus est.* The significance of this fact in world-history cannot be measured solely by the influence wielded by the Christian church on the religious and social life of Christendom. The church, like all other institutions, was but the outward embodiment of the living faith from which it drew its energy. The foundation of that faith was the personality of Jesus. The spirit of his life passed into the lives of his immediate followers and through them into the world around, transforming men's hearts and minds with a suddenness and swiftness without parallel in history. A new power was at work, which revolutionized the entire fabric of Mediterranean civilization.[1] At the moment when Jesus died on the cross by sentence of a Roman procurator, his mission had to all appearance ended in failure; only a handful of unlettered rustics, mostly women, remained faithful to the last. Three centuries later, Constantine, in establishing Christianity as the uniform religion of the empire, was simply acknowledging an accomplished fact. It was not merely that the old cults were supplanted by a new, but rather that the entire substructure of Graeco-Roman society, from which those cults

1. This assertion is perfectly compatible with the recognition of the historic continuity between Christianity and pre-Christian Jewish and Hellenic thought. A fair mind can hardly fail to be impressed by the disparity between the Christian faith, as we find it working in the world in the early centuries, and any other philosophical or religious creed known to history. Affinities in points of detail would not be so arresting, were not the differences of spirit and influence so profound. Effects demand adequate causes. No combination of causes is adequate that excludes, as a predominant factor, the personality of Jesus.

had sprung, was undermined, and that in its place there was arising a new order, permeated by the spirit of Christianity, which was reflected, not only in the field of religious faith and worship, but in morals and law, in art and literature, in the treatment of slaves and women, in men's whole outlook upon life. When we ask, as the student of history needs must ask, for the grounds of this transformation, they are to be found in the unique quality of the faith that Jesus inspired in his disciples. The question is not one of the speculative value of Christian dogma. Christianity was not a new philosophy, but a new religion. Jesus bade men believe, not in an idea, but in a person, who had lived and died as a man amongst men. He claimed that in this person the Son of God from love of man had taken human form, and been born on earth, at a definite moment of history, to found the kingdom of heaven and bring salvation to mankind. Idea and actuality, fact and value, were indissolubly conjoined in the person of Jesus. It was only after Christianity had won its empire over the Graeco-Roman world, that its speculative implications were disengaged from this core of concrete religious faith, and formulated, under the influence of Hellenic thought, in a system of theological doctrine. It was the overpowering impression of Christ's personality and sacrifice that gave life to the instruments of church and dogma, and won for the Christian gospel the allegiance of the Mediterranean world.

§ 2. Christianity arose and spread in relation to a historical context. In its origin, it was rooted in the soil of Judaism; its advance was conditioned by the culture of the Graeco-Roman world. Born a Jew, observant in all points of Jewish ceremonial, circumcised on the eighth day in accordance with Mosaic prescript, Jesus declared that he came not to destroy the law, but to fulfil. His first mission was 'to the lost sheep of the house of Israel'. His teaching is reminiscent at every turn of the Jewish scriptures and of the religious tradition and practice of the Jewish race. Preaching in the synagogue at Nazareth, he took for his theme a passage from the Servant-songs of the Second Isaiah.[1] The kingdom which he proclaimed to be at hand was the natural fulfilment of the vision of the prophets.

1. Is. lxi. 1: see Luke iv. 16 ff. and Vol. 1, c. iii, § 15 *ad fin.*

When those who, like the Pharisees, looked for the coming of the kingdom and the resurrection from the dead, failed to recognize in him the promised deliverer, it was not he that rejected Judaism, but Judaism that rejected him.[1] In their very refusal they were treading in the steps of their forefathers who had killed the prophets and stoned those who had been sent unto them. For Christ's doctrine of the kingdom, founded on the larger hope of Hebrew prophecy, stood in sharp contrast to the patriotic aspirations of his contemporaries. While they expected a Messiah who should achieve a secular liberation from the hated yoke of Rome, and establish in Zion a nationalist theocracy over the princes and peoples of the earth, he broke for ever with these particularist ambitions, and, resisting the temptation to institute an earthly sovereignty, declared that his kingdom was not of this world. Herein lay the incompatibility between the old faith and the new. Henceforward their severance could only be a question of time. The rapid spread of Christianity in Jerusalem in the years following Christ's death provoked the bitter hostility of the Jewish ecclesiastical authorities, to whom the Roman government allowed a wide measure of autonomy.[2] The propagation of the gospel among the Gentiles brought the issue to a crisis. Already before the conversion of Saul of Tarsus it had won adherents among the non-Jewish population in Syria and Cyprus.[3] Were

1. The Pharisees (= 'separated') combined devotion to the law with its interpretation in the light of later tradition, which was often of a liberalizing tendency. They were strongly nationalist and had a large popular following; they looked for a restored kingdom under a secular prince of Davidic line, and opposed the priestly ideal of the Sadducees. The Sadducees were aristocratic and sacerdotal, and very conservative in their adherence to the law as opposed to later tradition; e.g. they denied the resurrection (Acts xxiii. 6–8; Matt. xxii. 23–33). Christianity made many converts among the Pharisees; the Sadducees were bitterly hostile (Acts v. 17). The future of Judaism rested with the Pharisees, whose view of the law as supplemented by tradition lay at the root of the Rabbinical teaching in the early centuries of our era.

2. See the Additional Note to c. iii above, on the Roman administration of Judaea. For the Jewish persecutions of the Christians, see Acts viii. 1–4 (before 42); xii. 1–2 (in 43–4); they were directed against the tendency to liberalism and Hellenism among Christian Jews of the dispersion (e.g. Stephen), rather than against Christianity as such.

3. Acts xi. 19–21; especially among Gentile proselytes to Judaism, who were very numerous in the eastern provinces of the empire; there were many

these Gentile converts to be subjected to the rite of circumcision and the manifold rigours of the Mosaic law? Was it not possible to be a Christian without also being a Jew? It was on the morrow of his first missionary journey that St Paul, despite strong opposition without the Christian community and his own strong Jewish attachments, carried the day with his policy of emancipation.[1] He proclaimed the watchword of his mission in his letter to the Galatian churches: 'For in Christ Jesus neither circumcision availeth anything, nor uncircumcision, but faith working through love.'[2] The die was cast. From this time onwards Christianity, though still confounded with Judaism by the outside world, developed as a free and independent faith. The dispersion of the Jews after the destruction of Jerusalem by Titus (70) and the still more terrible subjugation under Hadrian (136) struck a fatal blow both at Jewish nationalism and at the Judaizing party within the church. Jerusalem ceased to be regarded as the religious centre of Christianity, and the Judaizing Christians, who survived for many generations under the name of Ebionites or Nazoraeans in the region east of the Jordan, had no influence on its subsequent history. By the reign of Trajan the distinction of Jew from Christian was recognized throughout the Roman world.[3] In that larger world, and not within the narrow pale of Judaism, lay the future of the new religion. But, long before the process of emancipation was complete, Christianity had been impregnated with the spirit, and, to a certain extent, the letter, of the

who accepted Judaism in everything except circumcision and certain other ceremonial practices.

1. Acts x, xv. 1–31 (decision of the church at Jerusalem); xxi. 17 ff.; Gal. ii. In the Epistles to the Galatians and the Romans, St Paul, in face of opposition from Judaizing Christians in Asia, defines his attitude towards the Jewish law. The result was the rising at Jerusalem after his return from his second journey in 58, fomented by Jews from Asia (Acts xxi. 17 ff.).

2. Gal. v. 6.

3. The Ebionites (= 'poor') were separated from the church by the end o the second century, but survived, especially in Egypt and Arabia, till the fourth. The Jews found it to their interest to make the distinction clear to the Roman authorities, for, while Judaism was officially tolerated, Christianity was not. In the second century the Jews ceased to proselytize actively, and Judaism has remained a separate religion ever since. As Judaism recoiled from the West, so Christianity has never struck root on Semitic soil.

parent faith. From Israel it inherited the belief in one God, the creator and ruler of the universe, the father of mankind, who, as a spiritual person, demanded from his children the personal service of a righteous life.[1] It inherited also the Old Testament scriptures, which were accepted as a divine revelation, while they were divested of their particularist implications and interpreted in the light of the conviction of Jesus' Messiahship. Therewith was received into Christian practice a code of moral precepts, unique in purity, and applicable to the homeliest concerns of daily life. Moreover, the worship of the early church was largely modelled on the simple service of the Jewish synagogue with its prayers, its hymns, its reading and exposition of the scriptures. Christian spiritual experience found expression in prophetic vision, like that of the seers and prophets of ancient Israel. The vivid expectation of Christ's second coming (the *parousia*), and the whole circle of beliefs and hopes associated therewith – in the resurrection, the divine judgement and the age to come – took shape in imagery and language that present a close analogy to Jewish apocalyptic literature.[2] The conceptions of Satan, of angels and evil demons, of an earthly millennium, of the condemnation of the wicked to physical torment, were but a few of these Jewish survivals which left an abiding impress on Christian eschatology. Finally,

1. This belief stood in striking contrast to the Graeco-Roman cults, which were never predominantly ethical, and often definitely immoral. Judaism and Christianity stood alone in grounding morality on religion, yet without reducing religion to terms of an ethical rule. These two religions realized that worship is more than discipline, though involving discipline as an inherent factor. Mithraism, which never took root on Hellenic soil, is an exception to the general rule (see below, § 8). Greek philosophers attained to a spiritual monotheism; but its groundwork was scientific rather than ethical, and they failed to establish a society on its basis. It remained the belief of individual thinkers or, at most, of a philosophic school.

2. See Charles, *Eschatology*, cc. ix–xi. There were numerous early Christian apocalypses, of which that ascribed to St John alone found admission into the New Testament canon. Hatch (*Hibbert Lectures* for 1888, Lect. viii) points out how, while Greek ethics reflected the civic life and government of the *Polis*, Jewish ethics reflected the rule of the eastern sheikh, the paymaster and judge of his dependants. The ideas of wages for work done and of retributive justice, of atonement for sin and of remission of the debt owed by man to God, figure prominently in early Christian literature. Further, it should be noted that the belief in the resurrection of the body connects with Jewish antecedents, that in the immortality of the soul with Hellenic; Christianity taught both.

the record of God's dealings with the Jewish people was regarded from the first as a preparation for the gospel. Yahweh was the one true God, who 'spake by the prophets' to the Christian as aforetime to the Jew. The ever-widening gulf between the society of Christ's followers and orthodox Judaism served but to enhance this consciousness of the spiritual obligation that the Christian faith owed to the religion of Israel.[1]

§ 3. The Roman empire furnished the field for the expansion of the Christian faith. Of progress beyond its borders little is known, and that little is of slight moment. St Paul, the apostle of the Gentiles, and himself a Roman citizen, headed straight for the Hellenic provinces, founding churches in the chief centres of trade and culture, such as Ephesus, Thessalonica, Philippi, Corinth, and Athens. His first appeal was to his co-religionists in the synagogues. Among his auditors were many who, though not professing Jews, were conversant with the Jewish faith and well disposed towards it; the hostility of the orthodox and the ready adhesion of these Gentiles led swiftly to the preaching of the gospel beyond the Jewish pale. Carried a prisoner to Rome in 61, St Paul found a Christian community already in being; three years before, he had written to them a letter, commending their faith as known throughout the world.[2] On his acquittal by the imperial tribunal two years later, he resumed his missionary labours, returning to Rome to perish, with St Peter, in the persecution under Nero in 64. In

1. Both Christian monotheism and Christian ethics developed under Hellenic influences in ways for which Judaism afforded no precedent. The belief in the person of Jesus took shape in language and ideas akin to those current in the Graeco-Oriental mystery-religions. Much is being done by scholars at the present day to throw light on this difficult and extremely interesting question. While Jewish Christians accepted Jesus in the light of apocalyptic Messianism, Greek Christians accepted him in the light of the mystery-cults, with their sacramental teaching. See Kennedy, *St Paul and the Mystery-Religions*.

2. St Paul's chief missionary activity in Asia Minor, Macedonia, and Greece, dates from his second journey (52–8); see Acts xv. 36 to xxi. 16. The epistles to the Thessalonians, Corinthians, Galatians, and Romans date, probably in this order, from the same period. The epistles to the Ephesians, Philippians, and Colossians were written during his captivity at Rome (61–3). On the church at Rome, see Acts xviii. 2, Rom. xv. 24, where St Paul speaks of it as having been in existence for some time before the date of his letter (58). On the faith of the Roman church, see Rom. i. 8.

less than twenty years since St Paul first set sail from Antioch, Christianity had taken firm root throughout the empire, alike in east and west, in congregations organized under chosen elders (*presbyters*) or bishops.[1] Of its history in the half-century between Nero and Trajan there is scanty record; but the results show that the period was one of unbroken and vigorous activity. The two chief centres of Christian life were the churches of Rome and Antioch, which worked in close co-operation. The story of the persecutions in the second century reveals the presence of Christian communities, not only in Italy, Greece, and Asia, but in Africa and Gaul, in Britain, and in the wilds of Dalmatia. The converts, though drawn in the main from the proletariat, included men and women of

1. In the apostolic age, the general supervision of the churches was in the hands of the Apostles, who travelled from church to church, exercising the higher functions (e.g. ordination and confirmation) which afterwards devolved on the bishops. The local ministry had but a limited and subordinate scope. The two features, of local self-government of each church and general supervision of all the churches, were thus present in germ from the outset. The former received definite shape earlier than the latter. Government of each church by a single bishop, presbyters, and deacons was the rule at Antioch in the time of Ignatius (early second century), and was general throughout Christendom in the third century. At first, the terms 'presbyter' and 'overseer' (Greek, *episcopos*) or 'bishop' were identical in usage; gradually the bishop's office was separated from that of the presbyters. In the early third century, the bishop was still elected by the laity, with whom he stood in close personal relations as the shepherd of his particular flock; but in the chief towns there grew up during that century a large body of presbyters and deacons, between the bishop and the laity. The presbyters became the spiritual, the deacons the administrative, intermediaries of the bishop. In the fourth and fifth centuries the gulf between the bishop and the laity widened, the clergy (with many new grades of offices) were alone in close touch with the bishop, and the election of the bishop passed from the people into their hands. In place of popular election followed by approval by the clergy, clerical election was followed by popular confirmation. The same two centuries saw also (*a*) the vindication by the presbyters of the right to celebrate the eucharist and to preach, i.e. the rise of a sacerdotal conception of the priesthood, and (*b*) the parochial system, with a presbyter in charge of each parochial church. All these changes came about slowly and naturally; they were not the result of any deliberate policy, though maintained by deliberate policy when once established. See C. H. Turner, on 'The organization of the church', *Camb. Medieval History*, vol. i. c. 6. The institution of a priesthood, entered voluntarily, open to all, and independent of civic and political institutions, was peculiar to Christianity; the first two features distinguish it from Judaism, the last from Graeco-Roman cults.

wealth and station.[1] Christians had risen to high rank in the army and the civil service; some were appointed even to provincial governorships. 'We are of yesterday,' wrote Tertullian as the century drew to its close, 'but we have filled your whole world, cities, islands, country towns and settlements, even the camps, the tribes, the decuries of judges, the palace, the senate, the bar. We have left you only your temples. We can count your armies: the Christians of a single province exceed them in number.'[2] Christianity had become a force to be reckoned with in society and in the world. Philosophers and men of letters took note of its existence. The government was alarmed at the rapid spread of an unlicensed confraternity, and issued stern decrees for its suppression. The Christians felt the necessity of championing their faith in the face of popular calumny and official persecution; and the abler minds among them composed apologetic writings in its defence. Meanwhile, disruptive tendencies were at work within the church. The prophets and prophetesses of Montanism, voicing the revolt of personal inspiration against ecclesiastical discipline, spread the menace of anarchy from Phrygia to Africa and the west; while, in the eastern provinces, Gnostic teachers threatened to dissolve the faith in a historical Christ into a phantasmagoria of speculative abstractions. On the one hand lay the danger of antinomianism, on the other, that of absorption into Hellenic metaphysics. The nucleus of dogmatic theology, of which we shall speak presently, is discernable in these second-century controversies. They called into play the intellectual weapons that had been forged by the genius of Greek philosophers. Side by side with the intellectual legacy of Hellenism, Christianity began also to absorb the political legacy of Rome. Need was felt for a regu-

1. Christianity first took root among the workers in industrial and commercial centres; e.g. the oldest church at Alexandria was beside the wharves; and, even at the height of its world sovereignty, it never lost the democratic impress stamped upon it by its founder and his disciples. Through its influence, the poor acquired a status denied to them by the best thought and practice of Greece and Rome. Prior to Christianity, the Greek word employed in the New Testament for 'poor' (*ptóchos*) was used always in a depreciatory sense, to mean one who cringes and begs. See Bosanquet, *Theory of the State*, p. 297, and Liddell and Scott's *Lexicon* (s.v. πτωχός).

2. *Apol.*, 37, tr. Bigg, *Origins*, p. 258.

lating authority, alike in faith and practice. Though each church as yet preserved its local independence, there prevailed throughout Christendom a strong consciousness of unity, which was bound to issue in the establishment of a central regulative organ. The world had long been habituated to look to Rome as to the fountain of law and justice. Her secular vocation and authority had been recognized by St Paul, who taught with no uncertain voice the duty of obedience to the civil government.[1] To 'render unto Caesar the things that are Caesar's' was an accepted part of the Christian rule of life. It was inevitable that the imperial system should set its mark deep on the structure of the Christian community. As in the secular economy of the empire all roads led to Rome, so the Roman church and its bishop formed the natural centre of ecclesiastical intercommunication for the other churches of Christendom. Not that there was yet any question of the formal recognition of the primacy of the Roman see. The Roman bishops claimed no right to override the autonomy of local churches. Such authority as they possessed was *de facto* rather than *de jure*.[2] But Rome felt from early days an instinctive consciousness of oecumenical responsibility. The first epistle of Clement, written at the close of the first century, expresses the active interest of the Roman church in the spiritual welfare of other Christian communities. These in turn viewed the Roman

1. See Rom. iii. 1–7, and compare 1 Peter ii. 13–17. These passages define the Christian position in opposition both to Jewish nationalism and to anarchical tendencies among early Christians. The duty of obedience to the 'powers that be', as 'ordained of God', is insisted on uniformly by the Fathers of the first six centuries.

2. In theory, all bishops were equal; each stood for the unity of his particular church. But, in practice, a hierarchy arose naturally within the episcopate. The provincial system of the empire gave the metropolitan an authority superior to the other bishops of the province. The greater the see, the greater the *prima facie* claim of its bishop to a commanding dignity. Rome, Alexandria, Antioch, and (after Constantine) Constantinople were rivals for eminence in the fourth century. The same period saw the definite assertion of papal claims to appellate jurisdiction and to legislative authority, especially by the worldly and able pope Damasus (366–84). The council of Sardica (343) had recognized the pope as judge of appeals, under reservations. Pope Liberius (352–66) had been the first to issue decretals. Papal authority was largely extended by the greatest of the early popes, Leo I (440–61). See C. H. Turner, *loc. cit.*, and Davis, *Mediaeval Europe* (Home University Library), p. 125.

church with natural veneration. Her illustrious apostolic tradition, gathered round the martyrdoms of St Peter and St Paul, the numbers and influence of her members, the bounty which their wealth enabled them to dispense to less favoured congregations, and, above all, her unquestioned orthodoxy and sobriety of judgement – these combined with her central position and the prestige of the imperial metropolis to strengthen her growing authority as the leader of Christendom. Irenaeus, a Gallic bishop of Asiatic birth, and the foremost champion of orthodoxy in the closing years of the second century, spoke of her 'superior sovereignty' (*potentior principatus*) as the exponent of apostolical faith.[1] In all the most important developments in the life of the church, such as the organization of the episcopal hierarchy, the fixing of the New Testament canon, the formulation of the baptismal confession as the apostolic rule which served as the nucleus of a creed, and the regulation of internal discipline, Rome played a leading part. '*Dans la pratique,*' writes a modern scholar, '*on s'inspire partout des idées romains.*' Especially in the handling of such delicate questions as moral offences among Christians, the treatment of apostates in times of persecution, and the growth of ascetic practices, her sound judgement and instinct for ecclesiastical statesmanship were of incalculable service to Christianity.[2] Nor was the Roman church merely a disciplinary and legislative power. Her constancy amid persecution gave evidence that her zeal for ortho-

1. Irenaeus, iii. 3, 1; see Harnack, *History of Dogma*, ii. p. 157, note 3.
2. Duchesne, i. 519. Marriage in particular was strictly regulated; religious marriage with episcopal sanction was usual by the end of the second century, though the church recognized civil marriages. Slavery was viewed in a new spirit of humanity; Christian masters were expected to instruct their slaves, slave-marriages were encouraged, and, at the close of the second century, a slave, Callistus, became bishop of Rome. The term slave is never found in Christian epitaphs. Christian thought readily assimilated the teaching of the Roman jurists, that all men were by nature free and equal; the existence of slavery was explained as due to sin, and its legality was justified as a form of remedial punishment. But the influence of the church was strong in favour of manumission. Christianity set itself from the first against infanticide, abortion, and the sexual aberrations characteristic of Hellenic practice. Moral discipline extended to minor details, e.g. manners at table, women's dress, mixed bathing, the wearing of cut flowers and jewellery, attendance at theatres, etc. Rome was careful to control ascetic practices; the home of monasticism and of the anchorites (third century onwards) was Egypt.

doxy and order was inspired by a grasp of the spiritual essentials of the faith. In matters of doctrine, Rome stood consistently for the apostolic tradition.[1] She held to Christianity as a religion, resisting firmly all tendencies to reduce it to a speculative theory of the schools. To Rome it was chiefly due that the impulse towards the unity of Christendom crystallized into definite shape as the conception of a single visible church, catholic (i.e. universal) and apostolic, the earthly embodiment of the invisible kingdom of God, and the necessary instrument of man's salvation. Thus many of the salient phenomena in the church's history – the multitude of its adherents, its growth in wealth and secular influence, its organization through episcopal synods, the severance of clergy from laity and the rise of sacerdotalism, the multiplication of heresies, the concentration of interest on doctrinal problems, and the progressive assimilation of the heritage of Graeco-Roman philosophy and law – appear as the progressive unfolding of germs that were already alive in the early Christianity of the second century.[2] There is no break in continuity from the apostolic age to that of Constantine.

§ 4. The general policy of the empire towards the religions of its subjects was one of mingled toleration and uniformity. Throughout antiquity religions were national, the citizen being under obligation to the gods of his community. As the peoples of the Mediterranean world were absorbed politically into the

1. E.g. the apostolic writings, the apostolic succession to the episcopate, the apostolic rule of faith. In the second century, the Roman baptismal confession had expanded into the rule of faith virtually identical with what is known as the Apostles' Creed (see later, § 17). Rome was the sole arbiter of tradition in the West; in the East, Antioch, Jerusalem, and Alexandria all claimed to be authoritative depositaries. On the respect for oral tradition and its causes, see Davis, *Mediaeval Europe*, pp. 120 ff. Literary records could be allegorized in very various ways; tradition was employed to test the text. Distrust of literary skill and reluctance to publish the highest truths to the profane also tended to strengthen the influence of oral tradition.

2. Provincial synods were common, especially in Africa and Asia, in the third century. We find Italian, and ninety African, bishops in attendance at their respective synods. The chief instrument of intercommunication was by letter from one bishop or group of bishops to another. There was no oecumenical council before that of Nicaea in 325. The church councils became the organ through which federated Christendom developed both its creeds and its canon law.

Roman state, their local cults continued to be recognized side by side with that of Rome. No inconsistency was felt when a Roman pontiff worshipped Cybele or Mithra, or when an Egyptian devotee of Isis offered incense at the altar of Augustus. Only in rare cases and on grounds of morality rather than of religion were particular rites prohibited by the Roman government, such as those of the Druids in Gaul with their accompaniment of human sacrifice, or the casting of children into the flames before Moloch among the Semites of Africa.[1] On the other hand, all alike were expected to pay honour to the *genius* of Rome and of Augustus, the religious symbol of the political unity of the empire. This tribute involved no renunciation of other divinities and no profession of religious faith; it was but a formal act of allegiance to Caesar on the part of Caesar's subjects. That anyone should boggle at it on religious grounds was incomprehensible to the Roman mind. In fact, associated as it was by skilful policy with the autonomy of the provincial councils, it was accepted everywhere, not merely without a murmur, but even with ardour, save by Jews and Christians. Their refusal to bow in homage to any god save one, perfectly intelligible to us to-day, excited in the Roman only irritation and contempt. In the case of the Jews, whose faith was national, the authorities were prepared to compromise, sanctioning their worship as a *religio licita*, though they forbade under heavy penalties the conversion of Roman citizens to Judaism.[2] So long as Christianity was undistinguished from Judaism, it

1. In 186 B.C. the *Bacchanalia* were prohibited at Rome on moral grounds. The account, given by Livy, xxxix, 8–17, is the chief precedent for the later Roman policy towards Christianity. It must be borne in mind that religion, which to us means a direct contact between the soul and God, and is consequently a matter of conscience, was for the Roman primarily an affair of the individual in his relation to the state (the gods of the city). Conscience had little to do with it; the all-important thing was worship (*cultus*). Neglect of due observance was a political crime. There was no place for the conscientious objector. See Hatch (*Hibbert Lectures*, 1888, p. 21). On the worship of the emperors, see above, p. 280.

2. Hadrian prohibited circumcision and instituted Graeco-Roman worship at Jerusalem. Despite the terrible vengeance enacted for the revolt that ensued, the Jews retained their rites and worship. Early in the third century, Severus penalized conversion to Judaism, but by this time the Jews had ceased to proselytize.

CHRISTIANITY331

shared in this official toleration; Gallio, in the *Acts*, viewed the outcry of the Jews against St Paul as a petty internal squabble, and, with the indifference of a modern civil servant, confronted with a sectarian dispute among the natives of India, 'cared for none of these things'. It was not his business to wrangle over technicalities of the Mosaic code, but to repress crime and keep the peace.[1] The persecutions at Rome in the first century under Nero (64) and Domitian (96) were not due to an official policy of suppression, but arose out of local and temporary circumstances, in connexion with allegations of specific crime. The historian Tacitus thus describes Nero's attempt to divert from himself the odium caused by the great fire of 64. 'Consequently, to get rid of the report (that Nero had ordered the fire), Nero fastened the guilt and inflicted the most exquisite tortures on a class hated for their abominations, called Christians by the populace. Christus, from whom the name had its origin, suffered the extreme penalty during the reign of Tiberius at the hands of one of our procurators, Pontius Pilatus; and a most mischievous superstition, thus checked for the moment, again broke out, not only in Judaea, the first source of the evil, but even in Rome, where all things hideous and shameful from every part of the world find their centre and become popular. Accordingly, an arrest was first made of all who pleaded guilty; then, upon their information, an immense multitude was convicted, not so much of the crime of firing the city, as of hatred against mankind. Mockery of every sort was added to their deaths. Covered with the skins of beasts, they were torn by dogs and perished, or were nailed to crosses, or were doomed to the flames and burnt, to serve as a nightly illumination, when daylight had expired. Nero offered his gardens for the spectacle, and was exhibiting a show in the circus, while he mingled with the people in the dress of a charioteer or stood aloft on a car. Hence, even for criminals who deserved extreme and exemplary punishment, there arose a feeling of compassion; for it was not, as it seemed, for the public good, but to glut one man's cruelty, that they were being destroyed.'[2] It was in the reign

1. Acts xviii. 12–17.
2. Tacitus, *Annals*, xv. 44; *tr*. Church and Brodribb.

of Trajan that Christianity was first proclaimed an illicit religion, the existence of which contravened the law of the empire. When in 112 Pliny as Governor of Bithynia reported to the emperor for instructions, the answer was in strict conformity with imperial tradition. There was no desire to persecute, and Trajan showed evident reluctance to take proceedings; but the law must be obeyed. Every inducement was offered for recantation; and, above all, charges must rest on definite and responsible information. The rescript approving Pliny's action was brief and incisive. 'You have adopted, my Secundus, quite the right course in examining the cases of those who were denounced to you as Christians. For indeed no general rule can be laid down which might afford what may be called a fixed form of procedure. They must not be sought out: if they are denounced and convicted, they must be punished, yet with this limitation, that any one who denies that he is a Christian and proves his denial by deed, that is to say by adoring our gods, however suspicious his first conduct may have been, shall earn pardon by repentance. But anonymous placards ought not to be regarded in the case of any crime; for that would be a very bad example, unworthy of our time.'[1] The hostility of the crowd, such as St Paul had faced in earlier days at Ephesus, vented itself frequently in charges of immorality, to which a confraternity that holds secret meetings is always liable.[2] The Roman administration was studiously careful not to take action on such irresponsible evidence. Christians, if proved to be such, were condemned as Christians, for the 'name'. But Trajan's successors were not invariably so indifferent to the public clamour. The martyrdom of Polycarp at Smyrna under Antoninus Pius (155) and the Lyon persecution under Marcus Aurelius (177) were fomented by the mob. In the course of the second century the churches of Asia, Greece, Gaul, and Africa all suffered under the strong arm of the Roman state. Its policy alternated

1. Pliny, *Letters*, x. 97 (tr. Bigg, *Origins*, p. 95). Pliny applied three tests; the accused must repeat a prayer to the official Roman deities, burn incense at the emperor's statue, and disavow Christ. The second was the most serious in Roman eyes; to refuse it was treason (*ib.* p. 93).

2. The fact of secrecy rendered Christianity a natural object of suspicion and misconstruction not only to the vulgar but to the government.

between active repression and tacit tolerance. The most conscientious emperors were the most rigorous to enforce the law. Commodus indeed might be wheedled into indulgence by the entreaties of his Christian mistress, and Hadrian's sceptical indifference might incline him to discount the political danger of an illicit confraternity, but the very loyalty of Marcus Aurelius to his Stoic creed served but to blind him to the faith which led the slave girl Blandina to face with joy the beasts in the Lyon arena, or the aged Pothinus to answer the legate's question, 'Who is the god of the Christians?' with the proud words, 'If thou art worthy, thou shalt know.' 'Sheer obstinacy' -- such was the Stoic emperor's reflection in the *Meditations*; and for all his Hellenic wisdom he bade the terrors of the arena to be added to those of death.[1]

§ 5. The persecutions of the second century brought thousands of adherents to the gospel. 'The blood of the martyrs was the seed of the church'. The spectacle of their constancy stirred even the bureaucrats and the legionaries to pity. Epictetus showed a truer insight than Marcus Aurelius when he observed how the Galileans were disciplined to despise tyrants, and that the demonstrations of the schools were impotent to generate such a faith.[2] Doubtless the Christians were often provocative in speech and action, and courted death by their contumely towards heathen worships. Such displays were hardly calculated to move their enemies to admiration. It was their devotion to their Master that was compelling and conclusive. When Polycarp was bidden to curse Christ, he answered: 'Eighty and six years have I served him and he never did me wrong; how then can I curse the King my Saviour?' Their love one towards another and their simple purity of life refuted more effectively than all the literary efforts of the Apologists the current allega-

1. Marcus Aurelius, *Meditations*, xi. 3. On the Lyon martyrs, see the letter from the churches of Lyon and Vienne to those of Asia in Eusebius, *H.E.* v. i. and Bigg, *Origins*, pp. 175 ff. For the martyrdom of Polycarp, Bigg, *Origins*, p. 155. The wonderful story of the *Acts of Saints Perpetua and Felicitas*, martyred at Carthage in 203, has been edited by Armitage Robinson, and is sketched by Bigg, pp. 293 ff.
2. Epictetus, iv. 7. 6.

tions of debauchery and treason. But it was inevitable that as the faith grew in influence and favour, the resolve of the government to enforce the law should become more pronounced. Its attitude was that of the practical man in all ages; appealing to commonsense and reasons of state, it pursued a vacillating policy of kicks and kindness, and called it justice. The more capable among the third-century emperors saw instinctively that Christianity was a dissolvent agency, alien in spirit to the culture of which the empire was the guardian. The political unity of the state required expression in a uniform worship, and the hour had not yet come when that function could be fulfilled by the new religion. Above all, the eyes of the rulers were fixed on the need of defending the frontiers against the tide of Teutonic barbarism, and the spread of Christianity in the army seemed a menace to military discipline. For this reason they favoured Mithraism, a soldier's creed, and in no wise irreconcilable with the official worship of Augustus. Hence we find that two deliberate attempts were made, one by Decius in the middle years of the third century, one by Diocletian and his colleague Galerius at the opening of the fourth, to exterminate the Christian faith. The last-mentioned was the most terrible that the church was ever called upon to endure. For two years it raged with full blast throughout the empire. It formed the crowning struggle between paganism and Christianity. In the West, the rigour of the persecution abated on Diocletian's abdication in 305, but in the East, the ancient nursery of Christianity, it continued with increasing ferocity till the eve of Galerius' death in 311. Its failure carried with it the final triumph of the new religion. The event came swiftly. In 312, Constantine, master of the West by the victory at the Milvian bridge, entered Rome under the Christian banner. In the following year, conjointly with his eastern colleague Licinius, he proclaimed liberty of conscience and restored to the church its confiscated buildings and lands. In 324 the overthrow of Licinius laid the Roman world at the feet of Constantine; and, the year after, the Christian bishops who had gathered at his summons passed into the council chamber at Nicaea amid the salutes of the imperial soldiery. Christianity was officially established as the religion of the Roman empire.[1]

§ 6. The efforts of the Roman government to crush Christianity claim notice for two reasons. In the first place, the nature and methods of its religious policy reflect the deep cleavage that parted the old order of society from the new. It is quite true that the persecutions, save those of Decius and of Diocletian, were neither persistent nor universal, and that in the intervals the church enjoyed comparative tranquillity and was recognized in practice, though not in theory, as a property-holding and autonomous corporation.[2] But in principle the empire could only be hostile, seeing that its roots were planted in the soil of a Hellenism to which the Christian gospel appeared as foolishness. Secondly, the story of the persecutions throws into relief the spirit that was the driving-power of early Christianity. The annals of ecclesiastical institutions and doctrinal controversies are apt to blind our eyes to the presence of

1. Constantine's motives in recognizing Christianity as the religion of the empire were doubtless in part political. But his family were pro-Christian, and there is no reason to question the sincerity of his preference. The emperors of this age, whether pro-Christian or anti-Christian, and despite moral short-comings, were often sincerely devout. This is equally true of Diocletian, Galerius, and Constantine. It was an age of soldier-princes, and soldiers are not wont to be freethinkers. Rationalist scepticism was out of keeping with the times. Constantine was not baptized till just before his death in 337; but there was nothing unusual in this. In considering his recognition of Christianity, we must banish entirely the modern ideas associated with an 'established' church. Decius and Diocletian tried to exterminate Christianity because, not being a state-religion, it had no right to exist. Constantine solved the difficulty by declaring it to be the state-religion. His action was doubtless advantageous to the imperial government, but it was a disaster of the first magnitude for Christianity. For (a) secularism invaded its domain, and (b) in Duchesne's words (iii. 1), the church 'épousait un malade, qui devient bientôt un moribond'. The baneful results which Dante attributed to the unhistorical 'Donation' of Constantine had their real source in the establishment of Christianity as the state-religion (see Dante, de Monarchia, iii. 10 and 13; cf. Inf., xix. 115 f., Par., xx. 55 ff.). (The Donation was a forgery, purporting to be the grant by Constantine to Pope Sylvester of temporal authority over Rome.)

2. Thus Severus Alexander decided that certain ground belonged not to the Roman innkeepers but to the Christian community, while Gallienus restored sacred buildings and property to the churches after the Decian persecution, and Aurelian adjudicated at Antioch in an internal dispute among Christians, and ordered that the cathedral should be placed in the hands of the bishop nominated by the bishops of Rome and Italy. In all these instances, drawn from the third century, the existence of the Christian church as a corporate body was implicitly recognized.

this essential force. Christianity, as a faith working in the world for its redemption, had of necessity to objectify itself in a visible framework of institutions, documents, and creeds. These outward embodiments must needs appear inadequate when measured by the living experience which they struggled to express. The hierarchical church of Irenaeus and Cyprian, with its liturgy and canons, its authorized title-deeds and rule of faith, its property and buildings, its severance of clergy from laity, its growing secularization, and, above all, its claims that membership of a visible society is a prerequisite of salvation (*extra ecclesiam nulla salus*), might easily be thought a derogation, when compared with the life of the primitive confraternity of the apostolic age. The atmosphere seems more clouded than that in which moved the first disciples, united in brotherly love as members of an invisible kingdom, and awaiting in hourly expectation the second coming of their Lord. The record of the martyrs serves to remind us of our error. Behind the visible institution the living faith endured. But, side by side with its message of hope and salvation to the individual, it had taken shape as an organized community, bearing witness to the conviction that Christ, though ascended into heaven, was still present among his followers on earth. There was no inherent contradiction between the faith and its visible embodiment. Christianity was never merely an institutional religion.[1] Neither was it the religion of a book. Even the New Testament scriptures were a means and not an end. Nor, finally, was it the religion of a creed. Dogmas, like documents and institutions, were but instruments of its mission. The Greek word for creed is *symbolon*, a 'symbol'. Not these alone, but the faith that gave them life, enabled Christianity to emerge victorious from its

1. This statement must not be taken to imply that Christianity, as a missionary faith working for the redemption of the world, could dispense with embodiment in a visible church. It means merely that the visible institution, which was a necessary instrument of this mission, was the outward symbol of the spiritual body of Christ and, as such, was a means and not an end in itself. Moreover, no rigid line of demarcation can be drawn between the earthly institution (the Church militant), which derives its origin and authority from Christ Himself, and the heavenly community, the 'mystical body of Christ, of which His faithful followers are "very members incorporate"'. The visible church is not, like the State, a merely earthly society.

warfare with the Roman state and with Hellenic culture. It was the love of Christ, informing the lives of his followers, that overcame the world.

II. PAGAN RELIGIONS AND GREEK PHILOSOPHY

§ 7. Christianity in the third century was confronted, not only by official persecution, but by the conflicting claims of a variety of philosophic and religious faiths. The times were favourable to a revival of religious enthusiasm. The empire presented a melancholy spectacle. Without, there was the barbarian menace; within, financial exhaustion and civil discord; and in men's hearts, mingled apathy, world-weariness, and fear. To pagan and Christian alike the wrath of heaven seemed to have fallen upon the world. In their distress they sought salvation, not from the emperor, the great Leviathan or mortal god, but from supernatural powers. The crying need was for direct communion between the soul of the individual and the gods. To satisfy this need was the common profession of the hosts of faiths, Hellenic and Oriental, that jostled together in the disordered panorama of the third century. They appealed to both sexes and to every rank in society, with the voice now of reason, now of sensuous emotion. Neo-Platonism had its gospel for the philosopher, Mithraism for the legionary, the cults of ancient Egypt for the jaded *femme du monde* of the capital. On the one side, the crudest superstitions, the practice of magic, black and white, the belief in daemons, oracles, and omens, in mysteries and purifying ceremonial, in astrology and occult probing of the future, spread mushroom-like over the empire from the imperial palace to the frontier camps in Britain and Mesopotamia. Early in the century, the empress Julia Domna, wife of Severus, had striven to blend the traditions of Pythagoras with Christian accretions in a new cult, which gathered round the memory of Apollonius of Tyana, a first-century Pythagorean.[1] At the opposite pole stands the speculative system of

---

1. See the *Life of Apollonius*, written by Philostratus at the empress's request. It is accessible with a translation in the Loeb series. On the Egyptian cult of Isis,

Plotinus, the supreme effort of the Hellenic genius to realize philosophy as religion. Between these two extremes, on varying planes of spiritual endeavour, a diversity of creeds flourished in an atmosphere of mutual toleration. The prevailing temper of the public mind was towards syncretism, the conscious effort to force all varieties of thought and worship into harmony. An admirable example of this tendency is furnished by the amiable and learned Plutarch, who lived at Chaeronea in Boeotia under the early empire (48–120). A man of sincere piety and warm affections, he varied his tranquil literary labours with the punctilious discharge of official duty as mayor and priest of his native borough. Plutarch was the foremost man of letters of his day, and a thorough conservative, whose mind lingered, as we have already seen, on the history, thought, and religion of the past. Convinced of the value of religion to the maintenance of social order, and of the necessity of satisfying the claims both of the vulgar and of the educated, he set himself to show how the polytheistic cults of Greece, Egypt, and the East were all alike symbolic accommodations of a reasonable faith in God to the popular intelligence. The method of allegory furnished him with a facile instrument. Greek philosophy in this age showed itself more tolerant of magic and superstition than did Christianity with its insistent championship of truth. Plutarch was not a powerful thinker, and his adaptation of Platonism hardly supports the doctrines which he erected on its basis. But he was representative of the temper of his age, in his Platonism, in his endeavour after a *rapprochement* between reason and faith, and above all in his insistence on the problem of evil, and his belief that philosophy can lead the

---

see Apuleius' description in the *Metamorphoses* (xi. 5): he wrote as a convert. From Asia Minor came the worship of Cybele, from Syria that of the Dea Syra. All these religions taught a gospel of salvation for the soul from bondage to the material world, a 'way of return' to God by immediate contact with him in trance or ecstasy. Cybele, Isis, etc., were regarded, when worshipped in the Hellenic atmosphere, as diverse manifestations of one supreme divinity. The mystery-cults of Oriental origin differed from the Hellenic in their tendency towards pantheism and in the plasticity of their deities, whose characters and acts could easily be adapted to suit the needs of different races. They were also distinguished by the proselytizing zeal of their adherents.

soul to union in ecstasy with God.[1] There were many of lesser note in the ensuing age who strove, as he had done, to mediate a compromise between religion and philosophy. Where all came to the same thing in the end, it was easy for anyone to believe anything; the Stoic or the Platonist could solace his soul by initiation at Eleusis, and an emperor could reconcile devotion to Mithra with the respect due to the ancient gods of Rome. Atheism alone found no favour, and the followers of Epicurus, who denied providence and immortality, had fallen into general discredit. Lucian, *railleur* and rationalist, the Voltaire of an un-Voltairean age, who let his irony play freely with all forms of sophistry and superstition, has left on record his appreciation of the simplicity and geniality of the Epicurean rule of life. For the rest, it was an affair of live and let live, save always for the Christian, in whose eyes all pagan faiths alike were false and idolatrous.[2]

§ 8. Of the third-century religions other than Christianity the most widespread was Mithraism. Its ancient home was among the primitive Aryans of Iran, who worshipped Mithra, as did also their kinsmen in India, as the deity of light and truth, warring against the powers of darkness. In the teaching of Zoroaster, Mithra held a subordinate place among the gods,

1. Of Plutarch's fame as a biographer we have spoken in the preceding chapter, § 24. There is an excellent account of his speculative and religious views in Bigg, *Neo-Platonism*, c. v. His treatises *On Isis and Osiris* and *On the Failing of the Oracles* (a circumstance which caused him much anxiety) should be consulted. An unbridled freedom in the use of allegory and a recognition of the value of myth (cf. Plato) prevailed in Hellenic thought from the early days of Stoicism (see Murray, *Five Stages*, pp. 146 ff.). Christianity made free use of the allegorical method. On the problem of evil Plutarch is loyal to Hellenic thought in rejecting the Oriental solution that evil is due to matter, the creation of an evil god. He follows Plato in holding that it is due to the evil soul, and that, while positive, it is not ultimately real; the way is open, by aid of the gods, for moral struggle and victory. He misinterprets Plato when he identifies the evil soul with the soul of the world and asserts that God created the world in time. Boeotia, it may be noted, was an ancient home of oracles and divination.

2. On religion in the third century see Inge, *The Philosophy of Plotinus*, vol. i, Lect. ii, iii; Cumont, *Oriental Religions in Ancient Paganism*; Kennedy, *Saint Paul and the Mystery-Religions*. The Christians were popularly classed with atheists even late in the second century; compare the proclamation at the mysteries in Lucian's parody: 'If any atheist or Christian or Epicurean has come as a spy upon the festival, let him flee' (Luc., *Alex.*, 38).

but his worship, fostered by the Persian kings and modified by Semitic influences from Babylon, took root in the east of Asia Minor under the successors of Alexander, and had the Romans not conquered Mithradates of Pontus, its expansion westwards might have preceded the foundation of Christianity. Actually, its hold on the West dates from the close of the first century A.D. The chief instrument of its dissemination was the army, which was recruited in large numbers from the eastern Asiatic provinces and spread the cult in the second and third centuries to the remotest frontiers of the empire. A bas-relief, with the familiar image of Mithra plunging his dagger into a bull, dedicated in London by a discharged veteran of the Britannic army, may be seen to-day in our national museum. Sixty chapels to Mithra are known to have existed in Rome. The chief centres of the faith were the camps along the Germanic and Danubian frontiers. In the Hellenic provinces, the chosen field of Christianity, it took no root. Its virile code, the quasi-military organization of its churches with their strong *esprit de corps*, its doctrines of resurrection, immortality, and final justice were well calculated to stir the devotion of soldiers.[1] But it failed to appeal to the intelligence and developed no theological or sacred literature. The nerve of its teaching was the belief in Mithra as the mediator between the supreme deity and man, and the redeemer of the human race from the powers of evil. He was the unconquered warrior, identified often with the sun-god, eternally young, under whose banner men could fight victoriously against evil passions within and evil daemons without. Mithraism was a purely practical creed, in which the life of contemplation (*theoria*) found no place. It had many points in common with Christianity; beside the faith in a divine mediator and the hope of resurrection, it taught the efficacy of prayer, sacramental union with God, and his providential presence in all events of daily life. Certain of its rites were analogous to the baptism, confirmation, and eucharist of the Christians.[2] Many

1. The neophyte's oath was analogous to that of a conscript; the rite of full initiation, admitting to the grade of *miles* in the Mithraic church, was called by the military (and old legal) term *sacramentum*. Women had a very subordinate place in Mithraic worship, which was always masculine and military.

2. Sunday was observed as a holy day and December 25th as the festival of

of these affinities, e.g. baptism, were due to a common Oriental tradition, others, such as the adoration of Mithra by shepherds, and his ascension, were probably borrowed from Christianity; in a few cases, chiefly of ritual, Mithraic usages may have passed into the practice of the church. But the divergencies cut deeper than the likeness. The fact, noted above, that Mithraism failed to take root on Hellenic soil, is sufficient of itself to mark the difference. A religion that appealed to the heart to the exclusion of the head could not conquer the world. Above all, the Mithraic redeemer had no historical foundation. The worshipper of Mithra felt no contradiction between his belief and that of the other faiths surrounding him.[1] To the Christian the two were irreconcilable. The one absorbed polytheism, the other uncompromisingly rejected it. Hence while Christianity flourished amid persecution, Mithraism died peacefully of inanition. The patronage of the third-century emperors who, valuing its influence on the tone of the army, adopted the Mithraic style '*pius, felix, invictus*', and dreamt thus of sanctioning their authority by divine right, and of an alliance between throne and altar, did not avail to save it from extinction. The successes of the barbarians hastened its decay, and in the fourth century it had yielded to Christianity even in the ranks of the legions. Its last surviving adherents seem to have been absorbed in Manichaeism.[2]

§ 9. Mithraism, for all its vogue, was not a formidable rival of Christianity. The real issue lay between the religion of the gospel and the 'way of life' of the Hellenic schools. At the moment the church thought otherwise, and, recking little of

the rebirth of Mithra. Mithra, too, had his ascetics. Mithraic architecture and art certainly influenced the Christian.

1. Mithraism as practised in the Roman empire shows many signs of syncretism, e.g. with the cults of Cybele in Phrygia (this gave women a place) and of the Celts in Gaul. Certain attempts were made at a synthesis with science and philosophy on a crude plane, especially in astrology. But Mithraism never showed any real capacity for fusion with western speculation. The attempt, for instance, to identify the sun with the supreme intelligence of the universe does not imply a serious philosophy.

2. On this section, see Cumont, *La réligion de Mithraisme*. Our knowledge of Mithraism is derived almost entirely from archaeological sources: no Mithraic liturgies or other writings have survived. On Manichaeism, see below, § 22, p. 377, *note* 2.

the speculations of the cultured, marshalled her forces against the polytheism of the multitude. But she had evinced from the first a capacity to enlist the intelligence in the service of the faith. The time was not far distant when she would have to meet the philosophers on their own ground. We shall see presently how already in the third century the Christian Platonists of Alexandria were absorbing the intellectual inheritance of Hellas into the structure of catholic theology. But though Greek philosophy had value for Christianity, Christianity had none for Greek philosophy. To minds trained in the atmosphere of the schools, its historic revelation and its democratic message of salvation were alike contemptible; what to the Jews had proved a stumbling-block was foolishness to the Greek.[1] The bitterest opponents of the new religion were to be found among those who, like the emperor Marcus Aurelius, were most eminent in wisdom and virtue and most deeply permeated with the thought and ideals of Greece. It was because such men realized so fully the worth of Hellenic culture that they were the least willing to renounce it for a faith whose spirit was alien to all that they prized most dearly. Happiness, or the chief good for man, lay for them, not, as for the Christian, in a heavenly fruition, to be attained by renunciation of the world and self, but in the perfection of man's natural powers in a life of specifically human activity. Nor was it a goal to which the way was open wide to all mankind; the good life was only for those endowed with the Hellenic character and qualified in the wisdom of the schools. Sacrifice was indeed requisite for its achievement; but the sacrifice was that of the lower passions in the service of philosophic reason. 'Sei vornehm' – 'ensue distinction' – was the animating principle of Graeco-Roman culture, and the distinction it enjoined was that of the philosopher realizing a rich personality in a life of human interests which to the Christian were branded with the stamp of sin. This divergence of spiritual outlook is most evident when we

1. 1 Cor. i. 23. The early Christians instinctively felt the danger of alien ideas *within* the church; see especially St Paul's epistle to the Colossians. The fact that the church did not regard Greek philosophy as a serious opponent in the third century is quite compatible with the view taken in the text that it was a most formidable antagonist.

set the teaching of Christianity beside that of the philosophic
school which, as we have seen in an earlier chapter, appealed
most forcibly to the cultivated Roman in the first two centuries
of our era. The Stoic and the Christian codes of ethics had much
in common – the recognition of the unconditional command
of duty and of the intrinsic worth of virtue, austerity of moral
discipline and the ideal of a spiritual commonwealth embracing
all mankind. But the differences are more radical than the
resemblance. For the Stoic, human nature was all-sufficient for
salvation. His faith was only for the wise and strong, who could
attain by effort of their own wills the mastery of their souls. It
offered a gospel, not of confident hope, but of resignation and
detachment. The Stoic sage was an intellectual and moral
aristocrat, self-centred even in the discharge of obligation towards his friends. 'So far as words go,' wrote Epictetus
explaining the right attitude towards one oppressed with grief,
'be not slow to fit thyself to his mood and even if so it be to
lament with him. But have a care that thou lament not also
from within.'[1] There was no room in the system for forgiveness; every man had to take the irremediable consequences
of his acts. Stoicism, indeed, taught men to face the storms and
disillusionment of life with the unruffled calm of self-respect,
and at the close to meet death, if need be by their own hand,
with a melancholy fortitude. It was the creed of those who had
little to learn or to unlearn, and who did their duty with their
gaze fixed on the great things of the past. Its strength lay in its
realization of the meaning of suffering; its weakness in its ignorance of the meaning of love. This is why it failed to hold its
ground on the rise of Neo-Platonism.[2] Its last great teacher was

1. Enchir., 16.
2. The Neo-Platonists, as we shall see, absorbed much of Stoic doctrine
into their system. Stoicism was a dying creed when Christianity, in the course
of its development, came to settle its account with Greek philosophy.
'Stoicism throve, because, like Christianity, it is a philosophy of suffering; it
fell because, unlike Christianity, it is a philosophy of despair' (Bigg, *Christian
Platonists*, p. 288). The Cynics, on the other hand, who were imbued with the
missionary spirit and appealed to simple folk, were still numerous in the days of
Augustine. Cynic ethics influenced Christian practice; the word 'anchorite'
is derived from their term (*anachôrein*) meaning 'to go into retreat'. Stoicism,
too, left its mark both on Christian theology (e.g. the doctrine of the *logos*) and
on Christian ethics. The conception of life as warfare, the practice of self-

the emperor Marcus Aurelius. His *Meditations*, penned in camp upon the Danube, are a strange comment on Plato's dream, now visibly realized, of a philosopher who should be king. They reveal a noble spirit, tirelessly busied with the duties of his office in peace and war, bearing the burden with a practised cheerfulness, uncomplaining and unresentful, friends with his own soul, but without hope and without joy. He knew nothing higher than himself save the abstract order of the universe, whose inexorable law he studied to follow with loyal resignation. We bow in admiration before this high embodiment of pagan culture, yet with a sense that it was powerless to inspire the world or to recreate its youth. The *Meditations* stand for ever, in the phrase of Renan, as the gospel of those who are without religion.

§ 10. The third century saw the rise of Neo-Platonism, the final utterance of the speculative genius of Greece. Though rooted in Platonic soil, fertilized and enriched by the inheritance of Aristotle and the Stoics, Neo-Platonism was no mere republication of traditional doctrines, but a union of old and new. For more than three centuries the Hellenic mind, reflecting the temper of the world in which it moved, had been thinking its way towards a closer fusion of philosophy with religion.[1] This led naturally to a revival of Pythagorean and Platonic teaching, in which stress was laid on the hope of salvation from the ills of earthly life by means of intellectual love of, and mystic union with, the divine principle. The supersensible world, where Plato of old had sought and found true being, was conceived in more concrete form as the dwelling-place of a God who stood in intimate relationship to the souls

examination, and the recognition of man's dependence upon God, are familiar to the Stoics. 'Can any one', asks Seneca (*Ep.* 41, 2), 'rise superior to fortune save with the help of God?' St Ambrose (late third century), by education a Roman official, popularized in his sermons Cicero's paraphrases of Stoic ethics (in the *de Officiis*). There was much in Stoicism, despite its Hellenic dress, that tallied with the lofty moral code of Judaism. The early Fathers adopted also the theories of natural law and of a state of nature, prior to the institution of civil government, which had passed from Stoicism into Roman law.

1. On the precursors of Neo-Platonism from the first century B.C. onwards, see Bigg's *Neo-Platonism* and *Christian Platonists*, and Inge's *Philosophy of Plotinus*, vol. i, Lect. 4 and 5. Numenius of Apamea (flor. 160–80) was perhaps the most important, but little is known of his teaching.

of men. Herein lies the intrinsic interest, the distinctive appeal, of Neo-Platonism. The time is past when its doctrines could be dismissed by critics as a fantastic thaumaturgy, or as a hybrid of Hellenic metaphysics and Oriental superstition. The loyal child of Greek philosophy, its mysticism, like that of Plato or of Spinoza, was grounded on reason. It aimed at a synthesis of experience by the method of scientific logic. Plotinus, the first and greatest of its masters (204–70), came indeed from Alexandria, the historic meeting-place of East and West; but he taught and wrote his *Enneads* at Rome, and his mind was the mind of Greece. Other thinkers followed in his steps, but the *Enneads* form the best approach to the study of Neo-Platonism.[1] They claim our attention here, both for the reasons we have just indicated, and also for their lasting influence on the structure of Christian theology.

§ 11. Plotinus' philosophy, like that of Plato, appears to start from the contrast of two worlds, the sensible and the spiritual. In fact, its whole purport is to overcome the dualism. The spiritual alone has true being; the sensible is no alien reality, but an image begotten by the spiritual in its likeness, in accordance with a universal law.[2] 'It is necessary that each principle should give of itself to another; the Good would not be Good, nor Spirit (*Nous*) Spirit, nor Soul Soul, if nothing lived dependent on the first life.'[3] This law, with its implica-

---

1. The *Enneads* are in six books, each containing nine (Greek *ennea* = nine) treatises. They were thus arranged by Plotinus' pupil Porphyry, whose life of his master should be read. For works on Neo-Platonism and translations, see the *Bibliographical Appendix*.

2. Reality or true being (*ousia*) belongs to soul and that which is above soul; such defective being as is possessed by things of sense is derived from the supersensible. Soul creates the sense-world after the pattern which it contemplates in Spirit (*Nous*). I follow Dean Inge (ii. 37, 38) in translating *Nous*, the second person of the Plotinian trinity, as 'Spirit', rather than as 'mind', or 'thought', or 'reason', not because *Nous* does not mean these, but to avoid confusion between *Nous* and the lower faculty of discursive, logical intelligence (*dianoia*). *Nous* is intuitive vision, i.e. reason at its highest grade; there is no opposition between *Nous* and reason, no short cut to the Absolute, which can be reached only by way of speculative thought. I have, however, used the phrase 'spiritual world' (in contrast with the world of sense) of the *whole* supersensible world, including Soul universal, which is below, and the One, which is above, *Nous*.

3. *Enn.*, ii. 9, 3, *tr.* Inge i. 195.

tions, especially for the human soul and its salvation, is the keystone of Plotinus' system. The universe, from its highest principle, the One or the Good, to its lowest limit in indeterminate, non-existent matter, presents a continuous scale of being and perfection.[1] The whole is a harmony; only the fragments, in their isolation, sound a discordant note. The world of sense is real, after its kind; it may be called a world of appearance, if by appearance we mean, not an illusion that is actual only in the mind of the thinker, but a partial manifestation of reality. Its being, like that of all else, is neither mental nor non-mental; just as, in the spiritual world, mind and its object form inseparable moments in a single reality. Here, as elsewhere, Plotinus set his face firmly against dualism.[2] Mind both makes and finds its object. Complete thought and complete reality are one and the same. On the lower planes, e.g. in perception of sensible things, imperfect apprehension is in strict correspondence with the imperfect being of the object. The sense-world is real, not because it is known by mind, but by grace of the creative soul informing it. It is the mirror that reflects, though 'in a glass darkly', the world of spirit. 'All things that are *here* ' – we are reminded of the *di là* and the *di quà* of Dante – 'are also *there*.' For, 'whence else', asks Plotinus, 'could they have come?' And, if we include soul among things of earth, 'all that is *there* is also *here*'.[3] Thus our experience of the sense-world points us to its source in the supersensible. It bears upon it the marks, not only of imper-

1. On the One, see below, § 13. Matter (as for Aristotle) is bare possibility of being, a limiting point, devoid of all quality, at which the creative activity, that flows forth through all things, is finally exhausted. Plotinus' 'matter' must not be understood in the current sense of the word; it is prior to space and to body, and there is also supersensible matter. That it is somehow positive, and a cause of defect and evil, is a difficulty which Plotinus' concept of matter shares with that of Aristotle. For Plotinus, the scale of existence is one with the scale of value; hence positive disvalues, such as evil, give a positive character to matter, which, on the scale of being, is merely negative (non-existent). See Inge, i. 131 ff., 162; ii. 77 ff.

2. There is hardly a trace in Greek philosophy of the familiar modern doctrine, known as subjective idealism, that things have no reality independent of the percipient or thinking subject, that they exist only as ideas in the mind, that, in Berkeley's phrase, their *esse* is *percipi*.

3. *Enn.*, iii. 2, 4; v. 9, 13; Inge, i. 197–9.

fection (plurality and change), but of its ideal archetype. Here Plotinus' thought is in line with the high tradition of Greek philosophy. Grades of perfection and imperfection imply the existence of a perfect standard; plurality and change the existence of an unchanging One. Grades of reality are discernible also within the supersensible world, which contains diversity, though it transcends time and change. Thus all things are linked together in an unbroken chain of being. In this conception, Plotinus finds at once the cause of their existence and their hope of restitution. For everything that is is active, in proportion to its grade of being; to be is to act and to produce. The higher its place in the scale, the richer and the more pervasive is its causal efficacy. The One, the supreme source of being, overflows of its plenitude, generating in a timeless act an offspring, inferior to, yet like, itself, which in its turn gives forth of its being to another, that is likewise creative, until, in the series of successive emanations, the stream of energy is wholly spent. This conception of the causal process contrasts sharply with that of modern evolutionary science.[1] For Plotinus creation, as the act of spirit or soul, is not in time, though the timeless causality is mirrored in the sense-world under the form of a temporal history. The cause, again, is of necessity more perfect than the effect; the relation is one-sided, and the agent suffers no degradation through any reaction from the effect. The complement of this downward process is the return of all things towards their primal source. Since every product bears the impress of its cause, there is that in its nature which has its true home above. Like is known by like, and draws like to itself. The creative source is also the final goal. The One is the beginning and the end, the Alpha and the Omega, of the universe. The whole creation 'groaneth and travaileth together' in a desire which rest in the One alone can satisfy.

1. The Neo-Platonists were of course aware that *historically* the more imperfect is prior to the more perfect, and Proclus in particular stressed this repeatedly (see Whitaker, *The Neo-Platonists*, on the *Commentaries* of Proclus). But this recognition of obvious facts was always subject to the cardinal principle that the temporal process is dependent on the timeless reality of the perfect archetype, apart from which the whole upward development is inconceivable. Here lies the difference between their doctrine and that of evolutionary science.

§ 12. Plotinus shared to the full the craving of the age for release from bondage, and dwelt at length on the upward pilgrimage by which the soul may regain its true fatherland. In essence, the soul is immaterial, and abides, without loss of individuality, but free from the trammels of the body, in the supersensible world. 'There', united with all other souls in the tranquil life of Soul universal, it has its eternal home.[1] 'Here', in the world of time and change, it is coupled with a material body. But its essential nature, though obscured thereby, is not obliterated; even when most deeply sunk in the slough of material accretions, it hungers for its source. 'He who has learnt to know himself will know also whence he is.' The soul is a 'wanderer from God', leading an 'amphibious' life, an immortal nature clad in the garment of mortality.[2] Its impulse to mount leads, first, to habituation in political or social virtue, then to purification by means of ascetic discipline, the moral preparation for the theoretic 'way of life'. The ensuing stages represent a progressive illumination. The exercise of the discursive intellect, in scientific and philosophical studies, enables the soul at length to rise to the consummation of the life of contemplation, in the immediate vision, transcending the bounds of knowledge, in which it attains union with the supreme unity.[3] The process is one of detachment, first, from

1. See *Enn.*, vi. 4, 14; iv. 3, 12. The statement in the text refers to the higher soul within each individual soul; it is not the whole soul that thus has its abiding-place above. On the universal soul, see below, § 13; it must be conceived, not as a collection or society of souls, but as the individual source of all soul; particular souls, e.g. of men and women, are not its parts, but its offspring. Plotinus is quite definite in asserting that individuality is preserved in the supersensible world (*Enn.*, iv. 3, 5); the timeless element in the soul is the man's true self. More than any other Greek philosopher, he recognizes the importance of personality; but it was left to Christian thought to give full expression to its claims. 'Soul' (*psyché*) includes all 'life', animal and plant life as well as human; all nature is informed with 'soul' in varying measure.

2. See *Enn.*, iv. 7 for Plotinus' masterly argument to prove the immateriality and immortality of the soul. He realizes, of course, that the immortality is timeless. The whole doctrine may be profitably compared with that of Spinoza's *Ethics*, Part V. The soul is 'of the same essence' (*homo-ousios*) with the divine (*Enn.*, iv. 7, 10).

3. There is comparatively little in the *Enneads* about this 'ecstasy'. Porphyry (*Life of Plotinus*, c. 23) tells us that Plotinus experienced it only four times during the years of their association. It came suddenly, and was attended by

the body and all things of sense, then from every object of thought that claims independence of our consciousness, till the seer and the seen are one. 'Strip thyself of everything', is Plotinus' bidding.[1] 'In this state, the seer does not see or distinguish or imagine two things; he becomes another, he ceases to be himself and to belong to himself. ... We ought not even to say that he will *see*, but he will *be* that which he sees. ... If then a man sees himself become one with the One, he has in himself a likeness of the One, and if he passes out of himself, as an image to its archetype, he has reached the end of his journey. And when he comes down from his vision he can again awaken the virtue that is in him, and seeing himself fitly adorned in every part, he can again mount upward through virtue to Spirit (*Nous*) and through wisdom to the One. Such is the life of gods and of godlike and blessed men; a liberation from all earthly bonds, a life that takes no pleasure in earthly things, a flight of the alone to the Alone.'[2]

§ 13. The supersensible world is no blank unity, but an ordered diversity of structure, continuous with its offspring, the world of time and change. It consists of a triad of *Hypostases*,[3] or substantial realities, graded in an ascending scale of unity and perfection. At the lower limit is Soul universal, the world-soul of Plato and the Stoics, where abide in union the formative principles (*logoi*) that are the generative causes of sensible nature.[4] But the universal Soul points upwards to a

complete suspension of self-consciousness; the soul did not even know whether it was in the body or no (cf. St Paul's vision, 2 Cor. xii). It was an experience of unspeakable joy. Self-consciousness, involving the distinction of subject-self from object-self, is transcended in this immediate vision; see Inge, i. 236 ff., and ii. 125–62 (where the whole question of mystic union with God is reviewed).

1. *Enn.*, v. 3, 17.
2. *Enn.*, vi. 9, 10 and 11, *tr.* Inge. (I have substituted 'the One' for 'God' in the rendering of the last sentence but one; Plotinus says 'to itself', meaning the One). The whole passage, *Enn.*, vi. 9, 7–11 should be read (Inge, ii. 135–42). Cf. *Enn.*, i. 6, 7; v. 5, 3 and 8.
3. *Hypostasis* was a Stoic term; the implications are self-dependence, individuality, concreteness. On the use of the term in Christian theology, see Bigg, *Christian Platonists*, pp. 203–4, 299 *note*, and below, § 19.
4. Individual souls have their home (as we have pointed out) in Soul universal; but they abide *also* in Spirit (*Nous*) and in the One. Compare Dante's conception of the souls of the redeemed in Paradise, who, pending the Day of

higher grade of unity. For it generates the world of sense in the light of the Forms, the intelligible archetypes of things of sense. Where have these Forms their being? At this point, Plotinus deviates from his master's teaching. Whereas for Plato the Forms were substances, independent of the mind that thinks them, Plotinus, insisting that 'the objects of Spirit (*Nous*) do not exist apart from Spirit', held that they had their being in indissoluble union with *Nous*. *Nous*, the divine mind of spirit, is the second *hypostasis*, which thinks in one timeless act of thought the eternal truths, that constitute its own being, and are thus one with, not other than, itself.[1] But even on this high plane of unity, difference is still discernible, both in the objects of Spirit and in its relation to them. The distinction of thinker and thought implies, even in perfect self-consciousness, a difference of aspect, and points to a yet higher principle of absolute simplicity, called by Plotinus the One, the Father, the Good. As the One, it is the source of unity throughout the supersensible and sensible worlds; as the Father, it is the primal cause of all existence, outpoured from its plenitude of being; as the Good, it is the supreme object of desire, the goal at which all things aim. In Plato's phrase, it 'is beyond all existence (*ousia*) and all knowledge'.[2] Plotinus is no pantheist; the absolute One transcends being and all that is. It also transcends knowledge, and can be characterized only by negation; it is '*not* this', '*not* that'. Yet it is truer to affirm of the One, than to deny; for though excelling all assignable perfections, it

Judgement, are at once operative in different spheres and have their true abode with God in the non-spatial empyrean. The entire supersensible world in Plotinus is, of course, non-spatial; there is diversity, but no local separation.

1. Spirit (*Nous*), the objects apprehended by Spirit (the spiritual realities), and the act of spiritual apprehension, are one and the same; Spirit apprehends itself as the world of Spirit in a single intuition. *Nous*, as Inge points out, is really the 'God' of Plotinus' system.

2. *Rep.*, vi. 509 (see Vol. 1, c. v, § 20). The One is thus the source of all existence and of all value; a transcendent Absolute. Plotinus, true to the main Greek tradition, keeps well clear of Stoic pantheism. The conception of the One as above being and above knowledge deeply influenced Christian speculation, especially through the pseudo-Dionysius (see § 14, note 4). The 'way of negation' (*via remotionis*), viz. the view that, in strict truth, positive predicates can only be denied, never affirmed, of God by the human mind, has its origin in Neo-Platonism.

includes them in the richness of its super-being, and is not less than they, but more. Only by *being* it, in the vision of communion, can we experience the One as it is. For the rest, attempts after description must be couched in analogies drawn from the imperfect imprint visible in its effects. The image, of which Plotinus never wearies, is that of light, which streams in parted rays from the sun, illuminating and giving life to the utmost verge of creation, where it is lost in the darkness that is mere privation. The simile was Plato's; through Plotinus and his Christian followers it has furnished an unfailing inspiration to the theology, the metaphysics, and the poetry of the western world.[1]

§ 14. The three *hypostases* that form the Plotinian trinity illustrate how this great thinker gathered up into an original synthesis the rich deposit of earlier philosophy. In the Soul universal we trace the divine world-soul of the Stoics, in Spirit (*Nous*) the self-thinking God of Aristotle's *Metaphysics*, in the One the Platonic Form of the Good.[2] Plotinus came nearer than any of his precursors both to the fusion of religion and metaphysics, and to the reconciliation of the claims of the one and of the many to a place in the system of reality. He was the first to give coherent form to a philosophy of emanation. The school he founded flourished for more than two centuries and

1. Light was conceived by Plotinus as an incorporeal energy, issuing forth from the luminous body. This simile is found at every point in Dante's *Paradiso*. The following stanza (liv) from Shelley's *Adonais* is in the spirit of Plotinus:

'That Light whose smile kindles the Universe,
    That Beauty in which all things work and move,
That Benediction which the eclipsing Curse
    Of birth can quench not, that sustaining Love
Which through the web of being blindly wove
    By man and beast and earth and air and sea,
Burns bright or dim, as each are mirrors of
    The fire for which all thirst; now beams on me,
Consuming the last clouds of cold mortality.'

2. From the first century B.C., or even earlier, the materials for the concept of a supersensible trinity were shaping themselves in Hellenic and Jewish-Hellenic thought (e.g. in Philo). The distinctive teaching of Christianity fitted naturally into the triadic mould; and early Christian speculation, nursed at Alexandria in the atmosphere of later Platonism, developed on lines parallel to Neo-Platonism. There is no one-sided dependence of Christian on Neo-Platonic thought.

was still in being when Justinian closed the pagan academies in 529.[1] From that time onwards the history of Neo-Platonism falls almost wholly within the pale of Christian thought. It was in fact the gate through which Hellenic philosophy went forth to permeate Christian theology and the mediaeval schools. It influenced the western church through Augustine, the eastern through the Greek fathers of the fourth and fifth centuries and, later, through the writings of the pseudo-Dionysius.[2] Thus we find ourselves at one of the critical moments in the history of civilization, when the religious development that culminated in Christianity was brought into direct contact with the speculative system that had gathered in the full harvest of Hellenic philosophy. We are impelled to ask why it was that, instead of Neo-Platonism absorbing Christianity, Christianity assimilated Neo-Platonism. To answer this question, we must indicate the differences that underlay their manifold affinities. (1) Neo-Platonism, like Christianity, opened a way of salvation through knowledge of God; but the knowledge was the fruit of scientific study, and the way could be traversed only by an intellectual and moral aristocracy. Its message, like that of the Stoics, was for the wise; the ignorant and the vicious were objects of a compassion that scarcely concealed contempt.[3] While the Christian held that man was by nature sinful, and his redemption possible only by grace of God, Plotinus, faithful to the Greek tradition, taught the inherent perfectibility of the human soul. The ideal of the self-sufficiency (*autarkeia*) of the wise man haunted Hellenism to its close. It is most conspicuous in the Plotinian rule of detachment. The nearer the individual approached to God, the more absolute was his isolation from

1. The last great name is that of Proclus, who taught at Athens in the fifth century. He was the main channel through which Neo-Platonism influenced mediaeval thought.

2. These writings of a Christian Neo-Platonist of the sixth century were ascribed to Dionysius the Areopagite, one of St Paul's auditors at Athens (Acts xvii. 34).

3. *Enn.*, ii. 9, 9. 'The wise man ... knows that there are two sorts of life, that of virtuous people, who can rise to the highest degree of life, that of the spiritual world; and that of vulgar and earthly persons, which is itself double; for sometimes they dream of virtue and participate in it to some small extent, and sometimes they form only a vile crowd, and are only machines, destined to minister to the first needs of virtuous men' (*tr.* Inge, ii. 188).

his fellows. The law of vicarious suffering, with its implication of the mutual responsibility of each for all, had no place in Neo-Platonism. An individualist creed could not hope to prevail against a society bound together by a common ideal of self-sacrifice, and inspired with a democratic fervour to save the souls of men.[1] (2) The appeal of Christianity was strengthened by the belief in a historic revelation. Neo-Platonism, though not avowedly hostile to revelation, treated it as mythical and symbolic, and relegated it to a subordinate place in its economy.[2] Its heart was set on the realm of ideal values, not on that of temporal events. Metaphysics counted for more than history, and in metaphysics there is no room for revelation. The tenacity with which Christian theology strove to weld together these two aspects of fact and value will come before us in a later section. The issue was not merely one of speculative theory, but involved questions that vitally affected the religious life, such as the value of human personality, the nature of the body, the belief in particular providences, moral responsibility, and the origin of evil.[3] (3) The last-mentioned problem weighed heavily on the mind of the third century. Plotinus discussed it frequently, and his statements were not always consistent; but his prevailing view was that matter is the source of evil. This doctrine, if pressed to its logical

1. We can see here the principle that underlies 'institutional' religion and missionary effort. The slight significance attached by Plotinus to political institutions and the structure of society is a striking difference between his system and those of Plato and of Aristotle.

2. Certain Catholic modernists furnish a parallel: to say that only values matter, not facts, is an easy way out of scientific and historical difficulties. For Neo-Platonism, temporal events were not illusory, but on a low plane of reality, and therefore unimportant. A curious but logical result was that Neo-Platonism was more tolerant to magic and popular superstitutions than was Christianity; these things did not matter much either way. It is only fair to Plotinus to observe that he managed the worldly estates of his wards with remarkable sagacity (see Porphyry's *Life*, c. 9).

3. The belief, derived from Judaism, in the resurrection of the body, saved Christianity from many aberrations. If the body is 'the temple of the Holy Spirit', it cannot be regarded merely as an encumbrance to the spiritual life. Neo-Platonism denied particular providences (*Enn.*, iii. 2, 1), and it is difficult to follow Plotinus in his vindication of freedom of the will; both those convictions are cardinal in Christianity, which saw in the course of history the working-out of a divine purpose (see below, § 23).

conclusion, would lead to the condemnation of physical nature and the human body as intrinsically corrupt. Moreover, it lands the mind in a hopeless dilemma; for, if matter be real, we are confronted by a dualism of good and evil principles; while, if the reality of matter be denied, that of evil also vanishes. There is, in fact, no solution to be found along this oft-trodden path. For Christianity, on the other hand, evil has its root in the soul of man, who in self-will abused his power of free choice.[1] (4) We pass, finally, to the nature of God and his relation to man. Of the difference between the graded *hypostases* of the Plotinian trinity and the Catholic doctrine that the three persons are consubstantial and co-equal, we shall speak presently, in connexion with the theological controversies of the fourth century.[2] The crucial divergence of the two faiths lies not here, so much as in the scheme of redemption by which man achieves union with God. Neo-Platonism claimed to furnish a mediation between God and man on a principle of one-sided dependence. Man, the effect, could rise in knowledge and love to his divine original. But God could not stoop down to man. The cause abides, in bleak aloofness, unconscious and heedless of what transpires beneath. The student of Plotinus can hardly fail to be troubled by the difficulty of understanding this fundamental principle of his philosophy. How can the One pour forth of its fullness to beget a world of which it has no consciousness and for which it has no desire? Plotinus' answer that 'all things, so far as they are perfect, beget', that it is a primal law of being thus to give itself, and that 'the One could not be alone', is intelligible only on an interpretation which he would have indignantly repelled, that the One is moved to show forth its glory in a creation with which it can

---

1. Plotinus at times has recourse to a similar explanation (see *Enn.*, iv. 8), where, after experiencing the ecstatic vision, he marvels why the soul is imprisoned in the body. Three suggestions are offered: the soul is not fully actual till it has found creative expression in the world of sense; it is impelled thither by necessity of spiritual law, in order to reproduce the spiritual order (iv. 7, 13); it chooses to fall by an act of selfwill (*tolma*, pride), or is forgetful (v. 1, 1) and bewitched (iv. 3, 12). But the last suggestion is inconsistent with Plotinus' main doctrine (i. 8), that matter is primal evil (see Inge, i. 254 ff.).

2. See below, § 20.

be bound in love.¹ The Christian doctrine of the Incarnation, that God gave himself to the world in love, would have been anathema to a thinker impregnated, as was Plotinus, with the spirit of Hellenic culture. To ascribe to God an act of voluntary humiliation that would have shattered the cherished self-respect of a Greek philosopher must have seemed impiety. The view that evil had its source in matter made such a belief still more inconceivable. We can no longer feel surprise at the deep antipathy with which the Neo-Platonists viewed the progress of the new religion. Other of its doctrines were acceptable and familiar; that God was one and a moral personality was taught by Judaism; that man could rise to union with him was taught, in their several ways, by the mystery-cults and by philosophy. But that 'the Word (*Logos*) was made flesh and dwelt among us', that God for man's salvation became man, was original to Christianity, and marks the point of irreconcilable cleavage between the faith of the gospel and the religion and philosophy of Hellenism.²

III. THE CATHOLIC FAITH

§ 15. The faith of the first Christians cannot be expressed in formal propositions. The difficulty is not primarily due to the critical problems, of authorship and interpretation, arising out of the study of the four gospels and other early Christian

1. *Enn.*, iv. 8, 6. The generation of the effect is not of the *essence* of the One, but is necessary to its *manifestation*. This law, that being overflows in creation of what is other than, and inferior to, itself, is accepted by Plotinus apparently without any misgiving; but, as stated by him, it remains brute fact, admitting of no rational explanation. No philosophy can be expected to demonstrate its ultimate grounds; we can claim only that they should be such as can account for facts. But the Christian belief that 'God so loved the world', though far from solving all speculative difficulties, goes a long way further towards an intelligible solution. It enables us to build on the analogy of our own experience of creative love, instead of falling back on a blind impulse of emanation.

2. See St Augustine's statement of the difference between Christian and Neo-Platonic teaching. 'In the books of the Platonists, which I read in a Latin translation, I found, not indeed in so many words, but in substance and fortified by many arguments, that "In the beginning was the *Logos*, and the *Logos* was with God, and the *Logos* was God; and the same was in the beginning with God; and that all things were made by him, and without him was nothing made that was made; in him was life and the life was the light of men; and the light shineth

literature.[1] It lies in the fact that Christian theology was gradually elicited, and attained definite form only in the fourth and
fifth centuries. Yet it was implicit in Christianity from the
first; for Christ imparted to his disciples no ecstatic vision, but
communicable knowledge and truth. His revelation and rule of
life appealed to the reason as well as to the heart and will.[2] The
object of this knowledge was no idea or abstract dogma, but
a person. 'I am the way, the truth, and the life.' Christ and
Christ crucified was the nerve of the apostolic preaching.
Ignatius answered the Docetists of Philadelphia, when they

in darkness and the darkness comprehended it not." Further, that the soul of
man, though it bears witness to the light, is not itself that light, but God, the
Logos of God, is the true light that lighteth every man that cometh into the
world. And that "he was in the world, and the world was made by him, and the
world knew him not". . . . Also I found there that God the *Logos* was born
not of flesh, nor of blood, nor of the will of a husband, nor of the will of the
flesh, but of God. But that "the *Logos* was made flesh and dwelt among us",
this I found not there.' *Conf.*, vii. 9, *tr.* Inge, ii. 206, 207.

1. We cannot here enter upon the mass of problems connected with the
critical study of the New Testament. During the past half-century a vast literature has accumulated on this subject, and the results of scholarly research have
constantly been published in a form accessible to the general reader. It must be
carefully borne in mind that the prevalent opinion of the learned on these
matters is apt to swing now to the left, now to the right, and that latterly
the dominant tendency has been in a more conservative direction than was the
case a generation or so ago. The once familiar antitheses, for example, between
the Christ of the Synoptics and the Christ of the Fourth Gospel, or, again,
between the Pauline and Johannine interpretations of Christianity, must be
considered with reserve; as also that between ideas of Palestinian and those of
Hellenistic derivation. Our concern is rather with the essentials of the faith
that inspired the Apostles and their immediate followers in the first generations
of missionary activity. On this the reader is referred to Professor C. H. Dodd's
concise and masterly summary in his book, *The Apostolic Preaching*, where he
shows how the teaching of the Apostles as recorded in St Paul's Epistles (the
earliest documents of the Apostolic age), in the Synoptic and the Fourth
Gospels, and in the earlier chapters of the Acts, displays a remarkable consistency in the fundamentals, outlined in this and the following section. He adds
at the close some very instructive comments on the development of the views
of the first Christians on the *Parousia*.

2. The goal of spiritual experience is declared to be knowledge both in the
Pauline and in the Johannine writings, e.g. John xiv and xvii. 3, Col. ii. 2, 3,
and *passim* (*epignôsis*). 'I will pray with the Spirit', writes St Paul, 'and I will
pray with the understanding also, (1 Cor. xiv. 15). Widely different as are the
knowledge of the Christian religion and that of the Platonic philosophy, they
are at one in that for both (*a*) the supreme good is the supreme reality, (*b*) this
supreme good is knowable, (*c*) this knowledge is indissolubly bound up with
love.

objected: 'If I find it not in the archives, I believe it not in the gospel', with the words 'My archives are Jesus Christ.'[1] This faith had its source not merely in Christ's assertion of his divine sonship; his whole life, lived in unity with the Father, was the compelling revelation that took shape in the simple confession of the church of the first century, 'Jesus Christ, the Son of God, the Saviour'.[2] Jesus was, first, the Christ, the Messiah of Jewish expectation, who had come to found, and would return to accomplish, the kingdom of God. He was also the Son of God, who had come forth from and ascended to the Father; the divine mediator who by his incarnation, death, and resurrection had 'broken down the middle wall of partition' between God and man.[3] To all minds familiar with the Hellenic tradition, this assertion of Christ's sonship implied essential unity with the Father as divine. Thus the thought of God's fatherhood, heralded by Jewish monotheism, acquired a wholly new significance; God was the Father, no longer of the Jewish nation in its exclusive collectivity, but of Jesus Christ, and, through him, of each and all among mankind.[4] Thirdly, Jesus Christ was the Saviour, who by the sufferings of the cross had redeemed the world, and reconciled fallen humanity to God. 'God so loved the world, that he gave his only-begotten Son, that whosoever believeth on him should not perish, but have eternal life.' Henceforth all members of the human race, liberated from bondage, were entitled to share, as adopted children, in Christ's inheritance of the glory of God.[5]

1. Ign. *Phil.*, 8; see Bigg, *Origins*, p. 110, who explains that by 'archives' were probably meant the Old Testament and the evangelic records. The Docetists held that Christ's human form, sufferings, and death were only a semblance; in other words, that God did not *really* become man in Christ.

2. In Greek, $Ιησοῦς \ Χριστὸς \ Θεοῦ \ Υἱὸς \ Σῶτηρ$, forming the anagram $ΙΧΘΥΣ$, meaning 'fish', a common symbol among the early Christians (Duchesne, i. 44).

3. Eph. ii. 14 ff. Here is the point of contact between the new faith and the Graeco-Oriental mystery-cults. St Paul already uses language analogous to theirs.

4. See Harnack, *History of Dogma*, i. 64, 65.

5. John iii. 16; Rom. vii. St Paul was well aware that in Roman law the adopted son was in every respect the equal of the son born of the father's body. In Rom. viii. 19–22, he conceives the redemption as embracing the whole created universe.

§ 16. We saw in an earlier chapter how the hopes both of the individual and of the community found utterance in the religious life of Israel, and how Judaism failed to effect their reconciliation. In Christianity, they stood in inseparable union as moments of a single process. On the one hand, the new faith recognized the infinite worth of each human individual in the sight of God. It declared the redemption through Christ of his entire personality, both soul and body; as God had been made flesh, so man's body would share in the resurrection unto life. Thus decisively did the Christian gospel part company with the thought, persistent among eastern races, and issuing in extravagant asceticism, that matter is evil and the body by nature corrupt.[1] On the other hand, only through membership of Christ's kingdom could the individual find salvation. In forgoing his private selfhood, and identifying his will, after Christ's example, with that of the Father, he won peace and joy as a member of Christ and of his kingdom. Here again we remark the divergence between the teaching of Christianity and that of many religions of the East. Self-discipline is not the means to an absorption of the individual in the Absolute; the Christian does not gain his soul in order that he may lose it, but loses it that he may gain it, in union with Christ and with his brethren. The antitheses of individual and society, egoism and altruism, self-expression and self-sacrifice, cease to bear a meaning on the plane of this inner, interpenetrative union of minds and wills in the love of Christ. At the same time, the scope of the kingdom is inevitably broadened to include the whole human race. Membership of the kingdom and eternal life are one and the same. Moreover, the kingdom, being eter-

1. See, especially, 1 Cor. xv. St Paul would say 'body, soul, and spirit'. (On this tripartite psychology see Charles, *Eschatology*, pp. 467–72.) Early Christianity had to struggle hard against the Oriental dualism referred to in the text. It appeared in Docetism, Gnosticism, and (later) Manichaeism. Marcion, a very important second-century figure, cut the knot of the problem of evil by positing a second divine power, the creator, subordinate to and derived from the supreme God, yet his rival. Our knowledge of this, as of other early heresies, is defective, for it is mainly based on the statements of orthodox opponents; in Hatch's (*Hibbert Lectures*, p. 10) phrase: 'when catholic Christianity had routed the enemy, it burnt the camp'. The orthodox solution of the problem of evil was in terms of free will (Irenaeus, Origen).

nal, is conceived as both present and future, as both in heaven and on earth. Though not, like Caesar's empire, of the world, it yet works in the world for the world's redemption. This temporal process is likened by Christ to the grain of mustard-seed growing into a tree whose branches overspread the earth, and to the leaven that leavens the whole lump.[1] The church is a spiritual society, whose members, whether living or dead, form one communion of saints under Christ's kingship. It is the living body of which he is the head.[2] In it, and in the hearts of its individual members, dwells the Holy Spirit, continuing the earthly mission of Christ until the full accomplishment of his kingdom. Finally, the conditions of salvation are spiritual; repentance, entailing through Christ immediate forgiveness, the hunger and thirst after righteousness, faith in Christ's saving power and love. Only against the unloving and the self-satisfied are the doors of the kingdom closed. Even for such, there is the hope of forgiveness; for their sin is ignorance of the truth, they 'know not what they do'.[3] Thus the early faith of the first century, rooted in the person of Christ, the Son of God and Saviour of the world, harmonized implicitly the mani-fold claims of man's nature. Historic fact and ideal values, the temporal and the eternal, nature and spirit, reason and revela-tion, *gnosis* and *praxis*, the individual and the community, human responsibility and divine grace – all these seeming con-tradictions in religious experience found their synthesis in a faith, which meant for the Christian the reasonable service of Christ as God and man.

§ 17. Christian dogma, like the institution of the visible church, was a necessary and natural development of the primi-

1. The temporal form of the kingdom was doubtless dominant in the minds of the first Christians; but even when thus conceived, it was never, despite the vivid expectation of Christ's second coming, *merely* future. Christian thought soon realized that the temporal form was inadequate to express the eternity of the kingdom (e.g. Origen saw this clearly). But it held firmly to the reality of temporal happenings, handling thus with rare judgement one of the most difficult of speculative problems, the relationship of eternal truths to events in time.

2. Rom. xii. 4, 5; 1 Cor. xii; Eph. i. 22, 23; ii. 11 ff.; iv and v.

3. For the gist of the apostolic preaching, see Matt. xxviii. 19, 20; Luke xxiv. 47; Acts ii. 38, x. 34–43, xvii. 30, 31, xx. 21, 25, xxvi. 16–23, xxviii. 31.

tive faith. Doubtless it is a far cry from the sermon on the mount to the creeds of the fourth-century councils. Hellenism, with all that this term stands for in religion and science, had come in between. But the appropriation of Hellenism was the logical outcome of the impulse towards universalism that Christianity received from the teaching of its founder. The knowledge imparted by Christ was a living growth, the significance of which was destined to evolve in the minds of successive generations of his followers. 'When he, the Spirit of truth, is come, he shall guide you into all the truth.'[1] In the words of a great modern philosopher, 'It was not till the feast of Pentecost that the Apostles were filled with the Holy Ghost. To the Apostles, Christ as living was not that which he was to them subsequently as the Spirit of the church, in which he became to them for the first time an object for their truly spiritual consciousness.' Thus the articles of belief, which set forth in explicit form the essential implications of the Christian revelation, were rightly regarded as the deposit of apostolical tradition. The rule of faith, formulated in the Roman church and accepted throughout Christendom in the course of the third century, was couched as follows: 'I believe in God, the Father Almighty; and in Jesus Christ, his only Son our Lord, born of the Holy Spirit and of the Virgin Mary, crucified under Pontius Pilate and buried, raised from the dead the third day, ascended into heaven, seated on the right hand of the Father, from whence he shall come to judge the living and the dead; and in the Holy Spirit, in the Holy Church, in the remission of sins, in the resurrection of the flesh.'[2] This simple creed, comprising three articles which answer to the three terms of the primitive baptismal confession 'in the name of the Father, the Son, and the Holy Spirit', together with a brief summary of the gospel history, represented the faith of the Christian church at the

1. John xvi. 13. The quotation that follows is from Hegel's *Philosophy of History*, Part III, Sec. 3, c. ii.

2. Duchesne, i. 504, 505, who points out that this formula, known certainly to Tertullian, dates probably from the first years of the second century. The points embodied are all to be found, though not in formal shape, in the letters of Ignatius (c. A.D. 110). C. H. Turner, *Camb. Mediaeval History*, vol. i, c. 5, suggests that the origin of the primitive creed may be found in the teaching handed over by St Paul to his converts at Corinth, 1 Cor. xv. 3 ff.

dawn of the epoch of doctrinal controversy. It formed the basis for the edifice of speculative theology that arose in the fourth and fifth centuries. The product of Palestinian Christianity, it as yet bore little, if any, impress of Greek philosophical influence. It was not long, however, before that influence inevitably made itself felt. The church found itself confronted with the task of interpreting its faith in terms of reason. If Christianity were to justify its claim to redeem the whole nature of man, the demand of the intellect to think out its teaching could not be denied. From the earliest times four motives combined to foster the growth of a reasoned theology. There was, first, the necessity of presenting, especially to Hellenic converts, an intelligible account of the new religion. The Greek asked questions, and wanted to know how and why. Signs and wonders, even the personal magnetism of the preacher, were not of themselves sufficient to satisfy his mind. He required to know the logic of the gospel, and to have it explained in terms of the inheritance of Hellenic thought. Secondly, the objections raised on grounds of reason by writers hostile to the faith had to be met with intellectual weapons. The Christian apologists of the second century did much in this way to lay the foundations of speculative theology. Thirdly, as has been already noted, conflict of opinion made itself heard within the Church as to the meaning and relative value of different tenets of the faith. Already St Paul, in the epistles to the Galatians and the Romans, had been forced to combat Judaism and to define the Christian conception of justification and the relation of the gospel to the Mosaic law. In his epistle to the Colossians, he had expounded the theory of Christian *gnôsis* (= knowledge) against the precursors of second-century Gnosticism.[1] Lastly, though not till later in the day, the voice of reason itself stimulated the more speculative minds in the church to think out the articles of the revealed faith as a coherent system of theo-

1. Since the dogmas of catholic Christianity were formulated in view of prevalent heresies, they are often more significant in what they deny than in what they affirm. The doctrine, e.g. that the world was created *ex nihilo* by a free act of the divine will was intended to ward off (*a*) the dualistic theory of a pre-existent matter, (*b*) the Neo-Platonic theory of necessary emanation (see Pringle-Pattison, *The Idea of God*, Lect. XVI).

logical knowledge. The outcome of these processes was the appropriation by Christian thought of the intellectual legacy of Hellenism.[1] A scientific theology required an equipment of philosophical ideas and a medium of philosophical language such as Greece, and Greece alone, could furnish. At every stage in the speculative discussions of the fourth and fifth centuries we can trace the influence of Hellenic thought working its way with pervasive subtlety into the structure of the Christian faith. Everywhere it brought light, clarity of thought and diction, the sane voice of reason. Informed by the Hellenic spirit, Christianity stood firm against the wild fantasies of Oriental mysticism. But it remained faithful to its apostolic credentials. It never degenerated from a religion into a theory of the schools. The rejection by catholic Christianity of the Gnostic theosophies of the second century meant the decisive refusal to be absorbed in Hellenism.[2]

§ 18. The catechetical school of Alexandria formed the nursery of Christian theology, and the greatest name was that of its master, Origen.[3] Alexandria, with its museum and university,

1. The synthesis with Greek philosophy began in the apostolic age at Ephesus (see above, § 3), and was continued later at Alexandria (see the next section).

2. The centre of Gnosticism was Alexandria. It was the religion of a philosophic school, and had its origin before Christianity. (On pre-Christian *Gnôsis*, see Murray, *Five Stages*, p. 143.) There were many varieties of Gnostic opinion. The chief teachers, Valentinus and Carpocrates, were men of remarkable speculative ability, and are at one (*a*) in rejecting the creator-God of the Old Testament and referring the creation of the material world to an inferior divine power (dualism, condemnation of the sense-world as evil), (*b*) in asserting the unknowableness of the supreme God, (*c*) in interposing a multitude of abstract powers, organized in a hierarchy of mediators, between God and the created world, (*d*) in denying the reality of Christ's life in the body, his passion and resurrection, (*e*) in grouping men in rigid castes, of which the highest, the 'pneumatics' (spiritual *illuminati*) possessing *gnôsis*, were alone capable of full salvation. Free will and the worth of the practical life (*praxis*) were discountenanced. The tendency to interpose a plurality of mediating powers between God and man reacted on Christianity, practically in the worship of saints, theoretically in the belief in an angelic hierarchy, developed later by the pseudo-Dionysius (see Webb, *History of Philosophy*, Home University Library, pp. 96, 97). The serious issue between Gnosticism and Christianity was this: Is the gospel a record of historic fact or an edifying myth?

3. On this section, see Bigg's Bampton Lectures on *The Christian Platonists of Alexandria*, and the shorter and more popular account by the same author, in his *Neo-Platonism*, c. x. The Alexandrian Church in the second century

was the crucible in which the thought of the East fused, in manifold combinations, with the philosophy of Greece. There had studied the Jewish Platonist Philo, the chief Gnostic teachers, and Plotinus. Late in the second century the catechetical school was presided over by Clement, the first of the Christian Platonists of Alexandria, a Greek convert with an enthusiasm for *belles lettres*, who found in Christianity the coping-stone of Hellenic philosophy. When Clement, who had little zest for martyrdom, fled before Severus' persecution in 203, Origen, at the age of eighteen, took his place as leader in the school. His nature was cast in a very different mould. To a fiery zeal for the faith he united depth of learning and a genius for daring speculation unique in the annals of the early church. In ascetic practices, which he carried to immoderate lengths, he was the forerunner of St Anthony and the Egyptian anchorites of a later generation. The son of a martyr, he thirsted passionately for martyrdom. But it was his erudition and the ardour with which he probed the problems of religion to their first principles that determined his pre-eminence in the germinating epoch of Christian theology. His literary activity was enormous. Aided by a workshop of stenographers, he produced, we are told, six thousand rolls of manuscript. Following in the steps of the Alexandrian editors of Homer under the Ptolemies, he applied himself to the text of the scriptures, collated manuscripts, and in his *Hexapla* published in parallel columns six versions of the Old Testament, including the Hebrew and the Septuagint. On the basis of this textual criticism, Origen composed commentaries on every book of both Testaments, appending to each passage a threefold interpretation, in its literal, ethical, and spiritual significance. The method of allegorism, though carried to extremes, enabled him to present a harmony of the Scriptures and, above all, to develop from them a coherent speculative theory of God, man, and the universe.

enjoyed great prosperity, and had escaped persecution: the catechetical school stood in close relation to the university – the curriculum embraced the sciences, philosophy (especially ethics), and Christian theology. Porphyry said of Origen that, though a Christian in his manner of life, in his views on God he was a Greek; but this statement (quoted by Eusebius) ignores the fact that the conception of God as love is the centre of Origen's theology.

In these commentaries, together with the earlier treatise on
first principles (*peri archôn*) and the refutation of Celsus' attack
on Christianity, Origen raised and discussed, with uncompromising audacity, the burning issues of later theological controversy. God, the supreme and transcendent good, communi-
cates through his Son, the Word (*logos*), of the plenitude of his
being to the universe, which, as the effect of his creative
activity is – here Origen is at one with Neo-Platonism – of
necessity inferior to its cause. All nature, informed by his
presence, furnishes a symbolism of the divine purpose, a 'divine
visual language', in Berkeley's phrase, which whoso runs may
read. Man, like the evil angels, fell by misuse of the gift of
freedom; Christ, the *logos*, is the means to his recovery and
eventual restitution.[1] In the divine economy, Father, Son, and
Spirit form a perfect and timeless harmony of three distinct
hypostases or individual subjects, coeternal, and, though Origen
mistrusts the term, as one current in Gnostic writers, consubstantial. But they are not coequal; though Origen fights
hard against subordinationism, he gave a handle to those of a
later generation who, after the manner of the Neo-Platonists,
affirmed the inferiority of the second and third persons of the
Trinity to the first.[2] The entire history of the universe is inter-

1. The history of the term *logos* is very instructive. It means 'word' and also
'argument', 'reason'. (1) Aristotle used it to mean the formula of definition,
which expresses the essential 'form' of each of the various kinds of beings
(e.g. triangle, horse, man). (2) The Stoics used it to signify the active force
inherent in physical nature, as a whole and in its different parts. (3) Philo of
Alexandria gave it a theological application, to mean 'the whole mind of God
as travelling outside itself and expressing itself in act', and also the mediator
through whom man attains knowledge of the Father. (It is disputed whether the
use in the Fourth Gospel is derived from Philo or from Palestinian Judaism,
where it was also current.) (4) Plotinus employed the term with a meaning
analogous to the Stoic. The *logoi* are spermatic powers, breathed into the
sensible world by the universal soul. (5) In the fourth gospel, esp. John i. 1–14,
and in Origen, it is applied to a historical person and means Christ, the Son
of God, being associated for the first time with the belief in the Incarnation.
Origen conceives it as immaterial power stretching forth into the material
world.

2. Subordinationism, as the name implies, means the inferiority of the Son
and the Spirit to the Father. Origen must not be regarded as heralding
Arianism; had he lived in the fourth century, he would probably have joined
hands with Athanasius. He was broaching a new question that was not yet
ripe for settlement. The danger in his day was in the other direction, viz. of

preted by Origen as a progressive process of redemption, from
the law of nature to that of Moses, from Judaism to the Christian gospel, from the gospel of apostolic tradition to the eternal
gospel, when the veil of symbolism shall be wholly done away,
and men shall share in a purely spiritual communion with God.[1]
Origen ever presses behind the letter to the spirit. As the
temporal gospel is the shadow of the eternal, so is the temporal
church of the eternal; it is not the act of ordination that makes
the priest, but the spirit of Christ; Christ's presence in the
bread and wine of the eucharist is not corporeal but spiritual.[2]
Heaven is no place, but a spiritual condition, for God's being
knows no temporal or spatial limitations; the creation of the
world and the generation of the Son are alike timeless operations of his activity. Following in Plato's steps, Origen reconciled divine justice with the reality of evil by the doctrine of
the soul's pre-existence; while, after the death of the body, it
will pass to a state of purification, and in the end all souls,
cleansed by fire, will share in the universal restitution.[3] Thus
all nature is a revelation; what men deem miraculous is but the
working of a spiritual law to which the whole creation is subordinate.[4] Origen's Platonism found expression also in the

Sabellianism, which blurred the distinction of the three members of the Trinity
into mere modes or aspects. Origen was consequently insistent on the reality
of the distinction.

1. The Scriptural basis for the 'eternal gospel' is Rev. xiv. 6. The idea constantly recurs, especially in Joachim of Flora, a Calabrian abbot of the twelfth
century. Origen grasped clearly that eternity transcends time.

2. See Bigg, *Origins*, c. xxiii, where he refers to the partiality of the Reformation theologians for Origen. Origen held that a pious layman was a true
priest, while absolution pronounced by a bad priest was invalid. Erasmus, too,
said that he learnt more Christian philosophy from a single page of Origen
than from ten pages of Augustine. It was the tribute of one great scholar to
another.

3. Origen grounded this belief, partly on the divine love, partly on the
presence of a spiritual element in human nature (Platonism). Immortality
implied pre-existence to the Greek mind. Origen criticized trenchantly the
current materialistic view of the resurrection and the expectation of temporal
rewards for virtue in the life to come. His vindication of the purely spiritual
nature of God was decisive in the struggle against Christian materialism.

4. Origen was critical on the question of miracles. The crowning miracle
of Christianity, in his judgement, was its acceptance by a multitude of believers.
Here he anticipates the noble argument of Aquinas, *Summa contra gentiles*, i. 6.
He attached more weight to the evidence of prophecy.

ascription of a higher grade of goodness to those who had achieved intellectual enlightment. His faith, it must be owned, was that of a school rather than of the church. Of his system, part was absorbed in the body of catholic theology, part explicitly rejected as erroneous. Even during his lifetime a suspicion of unorthodoxy gathered round him. He died at Tyre in 254 from sufferings endured in Decius' persecution, in communion with the church. The impression which the grandeur and tenderness of his character and his incomparable learning made on his contemporaries lingered long after his death. Origen was one of those who belong less to their own age than to the future, whose thought, through its high originality, foreshadows the ruling ideas of after times.

§ 19. It would carry us too far to attempt a survey of the doctrinal controversies that raged throughout Christendom from the fourth to the seventh century. We shall select for illustration that which gathered round the teaching of Arius and received its definitive solution in the catholic doctrine of the Trinity. It was not a mere question of words or even of philosophical conceptions, but one that concerned the very being of the Christian faith. The gospel declared that Christ was both God and man; the fact had been accepted without question from apostolic times; but how – this was the disturbing problem – was this fact to be conceived?[1] The difficulty was twofold. In the first place (a), in what relation did Christ, the Son, stand to the Father? Is the Godhead that was manifested in human form identical with the creator of the universe? If so, how were their unity and their distinction to be held together in thought? On the one hand, unless there be a real unity, either Christ is not divine, or two gods must be affirmed, at the cost of a relapse into pagan polytheism.[2] If, on the other hand, the reality of the distinction be questioned, Christ's mediation becomes chimerical, the divine and the human fall asunder as in Judaism, and the hope of union with God through Christ

1. The triple name (Father, Son, and Holy Spirit) was used in the formulae of baptism and of benediction from the earliest times, though its meaning and implications were diversely conceived until the fourth century.

2. The latter alternative, if the problem be extended to the Holy Spirit as well as to the Son, is tritheism – the assertion of three gods.

must be renounced. Hesitation on any of these points imperilled the gospel of redemption. Each party to the controversies felt that he was contending for an essential truth. The full bearings of the issue were not evident at the outset; and a great variety of opinions, both extreme and moderate, were put forward on either side. There were those who, like the Sabellians of the third century, in their anxiety to safeguard monotheism, blurred the distinction of Father, Son, and Spirit into one of attributes or aspects of the one God. Others, like Arius, whose intellect rebelled against the admission of real distinctions within the divine unity, denied that the Son was consubstantial, coeternal, or coequal with the Father.[1] Arius maintained that the *logos* was created in time, that 'there was a time when he was not', and that Jesus, having as man by his free will chosen the good, was adopted by God as his Son and endowed with the divine, though created, *logos*. Here arises (b) the second aspect of the difficulty. How were the divine and human natures in Christ united in a single personality? Did God enter into a real union with human nature, thus raising that nature to the plane of the divine? Otherwise, redemption is chimerical and the hope of the Christian vain. Yet the distinction of the two natures must equally be recognized; for, if Christ were merely divine, his human manifestation and bodily sufferings were phantasmal (Docetism, Gnosticism); if he were merely human, the gulf between man and God remained unbridged. In the event, both problems found their solution in the doctrines of the Trinity and of the Incarnation. Of the latter, which was not defined till after the theological disputes of the fifth century, we shall speak in the ensuing chapter.[2] The trinitarian dogma that emerged as the fruit of the Arian controversy suffered doubtless from the inherent defects of language and the inadequacy of speculative thought to express the convictions of spiritual faith.

1. Sabellianism (early third century) was thus the earlier danger. Arius, an Alexandrian priest, was not a thinker of great ability, though he gave his name to the controversy. His position was based on that of two far more remarkable theologians, Paul of Samosata and Lucian the Martyr, who taught at Antioch 'adoptionism', i.e. the view that the man Jesus was adopted (at the incarnation, or at the baptism, or after his death) by the Father as Son of God, and endowed with the *logos*.

2. See c. x, § 19.

368 THE LEGACY OF THE ANCIENT WORLD

Western Christendom, guided by the practical Roman mind, early reached a definition – one substance and three persons – and would have been well content to evade the metaphysical problem of what it really meant. The serious discussions centred in the Hellenic East. The Greek did not cease to be a Greek when he became a Christian; he went on asking questions until he found an answer. It was the great triad of Cappadocian Fathers – Basil of Caesarea, and the two Gregories, of Nazianzus and of Nyssa – who probed the heart of the problem, and furnished the speculative ground-work for its solution. The concepts round which the controversy gathered, of *ousia* (essence) and *hypostasis* (individual substance), had long been familiar to Greek philosophy.[1] Was the Son (and the Spirit) of the same essence (*homo-ousios*), or of like essence (*homoi-ousios*), or of different and unlike essence (*an-omoios*), with the Father? These and a multitude of alternative formulas were put forward by various parties in the course of the long debate. In the event, the victory lay with those who affirmed one *ousia* and three *hypostases*. The Greek theologians, with much hesitation, admitted the Latin formula, 'one substance, three persons' (*una substantia*, *tres personae*) as the equivalent of this doctrine.[2] Arianism was condemned as heretical, and the term *homo-ousios*, carrying with it the assertion of equality of the Son with the

1. *Ousia* goes back to Plato and, especially, Aristotle (see above, c. vi, § 13); it means both individual substance and the essential nature of a thing. On *hypostasis*, see above, § 13. The two terms were used as equivalents as late as the fourth century, e.g. by Athanasius. When they were distinguished, *ousia* was taken to express the essential nature, *hypostasis* to express individual personality.

2. The Greek bishops complained (with some reason) of the poverty of the Latin tongue to express philosophical ideas. *Ousia* and *hypostasis* were both rendered by *substantia*; the term *essentia*, the natural equivalent of the former, not being yet in current use. Seneca (Ep. 58, 6) tells us that Cicero used to render οὐσία by *essentia*; but this equivalent did not establish itself. Augustine, at a later date, translates the Greek formula as '*una essentia*, *tres substantiae*'. *Substantia* was the natural equivalent of *hypostasis*; but since it was used to translate *ousia* at the time of the controversy, another word had to be found. The Latins put forward *persona*; this, however, suggested to the Greeks the taint of Sabellianism, for Sabellius had spoken of *tres personae*, using *persona* in its familiar meaning of 'status'. In the end, they accepted *persona* as the equivalent of *hypostasis*. So Augustine (*de Trin.*, v. 9) observes that as *essentia* normally = *substantia*, it is best to say '*una essentia* or *substantia*; *tres personae*'. See also p. 374, note 1, and Aquinas, *S. Th.*, i. q. 29, art. 1

Father, was incorporated into the creed of the catholic church.[1]

§ 20. The dogma of the Trinity, if we consider its metaphysical bearings, is the point where the Christian revelation comes into closest contact with the problems of Greek philosophy. The Hellenic schools, before the days of Plato, had set their minds to work out the question of the One and the Many, with the result that an abstract monism (reality is ultimately One, not Many) and an abstract pluralism (reality is ultimately Many, not One) were alike discredited. Philosophy pointed, for the Greek thinkers, as for Hegel in modern times, to a synthesis of unity and plurality, in which each factor should be recognized as real. A unity that does not unify is no true unity, and to unify there is needed a manifold as real as the unifying principle. A plurality, again, must, if real, be a plurality of 'somewhat', and the 'somewhat' constitutes a common nature that serves as a real principle of unification. This reasonable conviction, that a bare unity of being is inconceivable, was embodied by Christian theologians in their interpretation of the divine nature as a Three in One. Such a conception might thus claim to be in closer accord with the demands of speculative reason than the unequal *hypostases* of Neo-Platonism.[2] The

1. The creed known as the Nicene (from the fifth century) asserts 'being of one substance (Greek, *homo-ousios*) with the Father'. This confession was adopted, not, as its familiar title suggests, at the countil of Nicaea (325), but at that of Constantinople (381). The earlier creed adopted at Nicaea, before the Arian controversy reached its height, certainly implied the same doctrine. The title 'Nicene' creed is, therefore, not entirely a misnomer. The actual creed of the council of Nicaea was the first expression of the faith that was stamped with the official sanction of the church: it was based on that in use in Palestinian Caesarea. The creed of Constantinople (our 'Nicene' creed) resembled it closely enough to pass muster as an expanded edition. It was adopted in the East from the fifth century, both in the liturgy and in the baptismal rite; in the West, it never superseded the primitive baptismal creed, but passed into liturgical use in the sixth century in Spain under the Visigoths, and thence in Rome (see C. H. Turner, *loc. cit.*). The full bearings of the doctrine of the Trinity are brought out in the so-called 'Athanasian creed', which may be dated from the sixth century, or even earlier.

2. The philosophic reader may bethink himself of an obvious solution of the problem of the One and the Many, irreconcilable with Christian theology, viz. the doctrine of an Absolute immanent in its diversity of manifestations, which in their unconditioned unity form the universe, as held, e.g. in modern times by Hegel. But no advocate of this solution will be blind to the philosophical difficulties that beset it. Christianity stood, indeed, for a transcendent God, the creator of the universe, a belief which it took over from the religion

Arians, on the other hand, defined the relationship of the Son to the Father in terms of the narrow, formal logic which has proved the bugbear of serious metaphysics in every age.[1] Moreover, the synthesis of unity and plurality within the divine nature is the natural complement of the Christian belief in man's redemption to unity with God, conceived as involving no annihilation of human personality, but as a real union in which the individual achieves the full crown of his perfection.[2] It would, however, be a grave error to suppose that the doctrine of the Trinity was developed primarily as the solution of a speculative problem. Its motive was religious rather than metaphysical. Like the belief in the Incarnation, which carried with it the assertion of a real diversity in the Godhead, its roots were planted in the ethical monotheism inherited by Christianity from Israel. The reconciliation of divine transcendence with divine immanence was asserted, not as a metaphysical inference, but as a moral fact.[3] The primary significance of the doctrine lay in its bearing on the Christian gospel of salvation for all mankind. It was, for Athanasius and later for Augustine, more than a credal formula; for it formed the keystone of a speculative world-view, which enabled Christians to face and to answer metaphysical problems to which Hellenic philosophy offered no satisfactory solution. This was the reason why the controversy was not confined to the doctors and political leaders of the church, but evoked intense party-feeling in the mass of the Christian community. Theological songs, composed by Arius, were sung by Alexandrian dockers, and introduced on

of Israel; but it affirmed, also, his immanence in the human soul. The problem of reconciling God's transcendence and his immanence is a living problem for modern philosophic thought.

1. Arianism affords an excellent illustration of the method of the 'abstract understanding', the relative value of which, and its limitations, are emphasized by Hegel in his *Logic*. Its weapons were scholastic; its logic appealed to, while it degraded, that of Aristotle; and its temper was anti-Platonic.

2. The highest human experiences, of intellectual insight, and, above all, of love, point unmistakably to the conclusion that individual personality is realized, not in isolation from, but in union with, that of others (see Shakespeare, *The Phoenix and the Turtle*).

3. See W. R. Matthews, *Studies in Christian Theology*, pp. 54, 55. The fathers maintained the unity of substance against Hellenic polytheism, the distinction of persons against the purely transcendent unity of the God of Israel.

the theatrical stage; if you ask a baker at Constantinople, says Gregory of Nyssa, the price of a loaf, he will answer you that the Father is greatest, the Son subordinate. One of the sects was nicknamed the Pastrycooks, after the trade of their Syrian chief.[1] Arianism spread like wildfire among the barbarian immigrants; its profession by East Goths and West Goths, Burgundians, Suebes, Vandals, and Lombards, disturbed the unity of Christendom for centuries. The storm of theological controversy among the peoples of the empire constituted an urgent political problem for the government. The emperors intervened, now in a hopeless endeavour to allay the agitation by artificial compromise, now to employ the secular arm in defence of Arianism or of orthodoxy. The baneful, if inevitable, results of the close alliance between church and state were exemplified at every turn of the struggle.[2] We have here something more than an illustration of the influence of speculative ideas on practical life. The heart of the public was touched by a sound instinct that the issue under debate was one that threatened the very existence of Christianity as a religion.

§ 21. The protagonist in this theological drama was Athanasius, bishop of Alexandria (c. 296–373). Born, like Origen, in Egypt, but a Greek in race and mind, he was present, though under thirty and a deacon, at the council of Nicaea (325), and three years afterwards succeeded to the episcopal throne. The Alexandrian bishop wielded an almost absolute sovereignty over the church in Egypt and enjoyed a prestige second only to that of Rome in Christendom. Without the erudition of Origen, or the *flair* for metaphysical speculation of the Cappadocian triad, Athanasius was enabled to dominate the church for half a century by his force of personality, his clear and resolute grasp of the essentials of the faith, and his indomitable will. A vigorous and incisive style, the expression of a keen

1. The Bathyrians: Duchesne, ii. 578.
2. Constantine imposed a premature settlement at the council of Nicaea (325); several of his fourth-century successors actively favoured Arianism; Theodosius (sole emperor from 395) finally determined the triumph of orthodoxy, under the guidance of St Ambrose. The brief pagan reaction under Julian excited little more than amusement, being regarded by most sensible people as a Quixotic anachronism. For the eventual suppression of Arianism among the Lombards in the eighth century, see c. x, § 12.

and lucid intellect, gave to his writings a compelling power; the pamphlets which poured from his pen at each stage of the theological crisis sounded a clarion call in defence of the catholic and apostolic faith. He stood firm as a rock amid the tempests that engulfed the world. Five times he was driven from his episcopal throne, once for as long as six years; condemned by successive councils and synods and by the imperial government, he fought single-handed – *Athanasius contra mundum* – for half a century against the combined ecclesiastical and political forces of the empire.[1] His own Egyptian church, the populace of Alexandria, and the anchorites of the desert, remained staunch in his support through the darkest hours. The cells of St Anthony and his followers afforded a sure retreat from persecution. In the event he triumphed, after weathering alike the Arian policy of Constantius and the pagan reaction under Julian (361–3). His victory was due to the fact that he stood unswervingly for the apostolic tradition, to which, after transitory and devious distractions, the mind of the church always returned. Athanasius was far more than a partisan of orthodoxy; uncompromising in essentials, he cared little for niceties of formulas, and strove with rare statesmanship to rally all shades of catholic opinion round the standard of the faith. He battled for the gospel of salvation, for the conviction that 'God himself became man that we might be made God'.[2] Faith in the Incarnation was the single watchword of his life. The doctrine thus resolutely championed by Athanasius against the Arians became in his hands the first principle of a new metaphysical synthesis, in the strength of which the Church could fearlessly confront the pagan classical tradition on its own ground. Nothing was further from his mind than to offer a refuge in irrationalism from the imbroglio in which that tradition had found itself entangled. Rather he claimed by the aid of a reasonable faith to save the intellect from the menace of

1. His episcopate lasted from 328 to 373; the five exiles were in 335–7, 339–46, 356–62, 362–4, 365–6.

2. *De Incarnatione verbi Dei*, § 54, and very frequently elsewhere. This conviction was traditional at Alexandria: Clement (*Protrept.*, i. 8) had written: 'The word of God became Man, in order that thou also mayest learn from Man, how man becomes God ' (*tr.* Bigg). It is found also in Irenaeus.

obscurantism and superstition that endangered it on every side. It is significant that Athanasius applied to the doctrine of the Trinity the term ἀρχή which Greek philosophers from Thales onwards had used to denote the ultimate principle of metaphysical explanation. While on the one hand that doctrine affirmed God's infinite transcendence as Creator of all existence save His own, and His consequent incomprehensibility to the human mind; it proclaimed on the other hand His knowability for all men through His self-revelation in Christ. The divine 'economy', displayed in the creation of the world and in its redemption from the evil wrought by man's self-will and fulfilled in the person of the Incarnate Word, was henceforward the presupposition of any intelligibility that reason could find in man and nature. Thus the ghost of the two-world philosophy that was the stumbling block of Platonism was finally laid, when the invisible things of God were declared to be made manifest for faith in the visible processes of nature and history, and the spiritual order to be immanent in the temporal. We do not naturally look to Gibbon for a eulogy of even the most illustrous of the defenders of the Christian faith; and his tribute to 'the immortal name of Athanasius' is a striking illustration of the standing judgement of history.[1]

§ 22. The thought of the West, in theology as in the problems of law and government, was always directed to the satisfaction of practical rather than of speculative interests. It left metaphysics to the East, and viewed with some impatience the persistent efforts of the Greek thinkers to express the doctrines of the Trinity and the Incarnation in terms of philosophical exactness. The Westerns did not understand that the history

1. See Gibbon, c. xxi, where we read constantly of the 'great' Athanasius, of his 'intrepid' nature and 'calm courage', of 'the ascendancy of his genius', and how 'in the various turns of his prosperous and adverse fortune, he never lost the confidence of his friends, or the esteem of his enemies'. 'Athanasius displayed a superiority of character and abilities which would have qualified him, far more than the degenerate sons of Constantine, for the government of a great monarchy.' He was, in fact, free from many of the weaknesses that often tarnish the characters of great leaders of men. He disdained all exhibitions of vanity and took no pleasure in vulgar flattery. A born fighter, he struck hard at the living among his opponents, but spared the memory of the dead. He carried loyalty to his friends to the verge of rashness; and the austerity of his life was tempered by a saving grace of humour.

of the world, in the long run, is largely determined by ideas.
As against any attempt to convert the Christian faith into a
theory of the schools, they were entirely in the right, and, as
the story of Athanasius makes clear, had the best minds of the
East on their side. It is difficult to overestimate the service rendered by the Roman church in this particular during the centuries of doctrinal controversy. But when full allowance has
been made for the practical insight and strong faith of the
Western church, it remains true that it was prone to rest exclusively on the voice of apostolic tradition, and, if ever it did
grapple with questions of speculative principle, to resolve them
on the plane of juristic rather than of metaphysical thinking.
Tertullian, whose fiery, intolerant, and gloomy spirit clouded
the dawn of the third century, was a conspicuous instance of
this defect; his keen, legal intellect defined indeed the doctrine
of the Trinity in words which forestalled the decision of a later
generation, but which were drawn from the vocabulary, not of
philosophy, but of jurisprudence.[1] All the more remarkable
is the fact that a century later there appeared in Africa a theologian with a genius for metaphysics. Augustine, bishop of
Hippo (*b.* 354), deserves to rank in the annals of Christian
theology beside and even above Origen and Athanasius. The
story of his wild and passionate youth, his inner conflicts, his
intellectual ardour, his early eminence as a rhetorician, his
'spiritual *Aeneid*' among many schools and creeds, and his conversion through St Ambrose, consummated by the experience
in the garden at Cassiacum, is familiar from the pages of his
Confessions. His own tumultuous and intense soul was ever his
absorbing interest, colouring, and at times distorting, his
vision of religious and philosophic truth. Self-consciousness was

---

1. It was Tertullian who introduced the formula '*una substantia, tres
personae*' into Christian theology, borrowing both terms from Roman law,
where *persona* meant an individual subject capable of holding property and
substantia the property held (cf. our phrase 'a man of substance'). He conceived
God as analogous to a single property held by three persons, and the two
natures in Christ as analogous to two properties in the possession of a single
person. Such juristic fictions might pass muster in the West, but could not
satisfy a serious philosopher. See Bigg, *Christian Platonists*, pp. 202 ff.;
Harnack, iv. 131 f., 144 f., and above, p. 368, note 2.

the dominant note of his philosophy and life. For him, as for Cardinal Newman, there were two and only two indubitable realities, himself and his Maker.[1] That he should have anticipated by twelve hundred years the *cogito, ergo sum* ('I think, therefore I am') of Descartes is a startling but characteristic instance of the originality of his thought. He was the first philosopher to recognize the claim of human personality to a central place in the metaphysic of experience. Both Plato and Aristotle had found in reason the real man and had taught that to follow reason was the road that led to self-realization; but both had failed to reach an adequate concept of personality. Plato left unsolved the problems of the integration of reason with the inferior powers of the soul and of the union of soul and body in the individual; Aristotle, in answering these problems, had been driven to separate the higher power of reason from the soul defined as the form of the organic body, and to posit an impersonal cosmic intellect with which the individual soul entered into a mysterious contact that baffled the comprehension alike of his Greek and mediaeval interpreters. Augustine was the first to give the concept its full extension. He anticipated the researches of Freud and Jung. By his inclusion of instincts and unconscious impulses (*irrationabiles motus*); in his emphasis on the will in opposition to the classical traditions (*quid sumus nisi voluntates?*), he may be regarded as the precursor of William James, who called him 'the first modern man', and of many recent advocates of voluntarism. As a believer in the doctrine of the Word made flesh, he could not but question the Platonic view of the bodily organism as irrelevant to man's true selfhood. The same faith secured the objectivity of personality and disproves the charge of an exaggerated subjectivism to which Augustine's philosophy at times gives a certain plausibility. He is never weary of insisting on the soul of man as fashioned in the likeness of the Creator and of dwelling on the many analogies it presents to the Trinity, which, for him as for Athanasius, is the basic principle of the world-order. The con-

---

1. See Newman, *Apologia*, c. i. Augustine was fully conscious of his originality as a psychologist. 'What I have found, I have found in my own mind and nowhere else' (*de immort. animae*, iv. 6).

stitution of the soul is in his view indissolubly bound up with the divine 'economy'. Of special note are his analyses of memory, of self-consciousness, and of spiritual contemplation. As bishop of Hippo in his native province from the age of thirty-one (395), he played an active part in the affairs of the church, reconciling the Donatist schismatics to the orthodox faith, contesting heresy, prodigal of speech and writing, devoting his rare gifts of intellect and personal charm to the cause of union and internal peace. But it was his speculative genius that wielded so powerful an influence on the later religious thought of Latin Christendom. Both during the Middle Ages and at the epoch of the Reformation, Augustine's writings were the mine wherein theologians, both Catholic and Protestant, delved for gold. No other of the Fathers left so deep and enduring an impression on the fabric of Christian thought. This was due, not to the coherence of his speculations, which were diffuse and often inconsistent, but rather to his learning, his power of exposition, his wide range of intellectual interests, and, above all, to the distinctive impress of his many-sided personality. Augustine was at once a mystic, possessed by a longing for the infinite, and an ecclesiastical statesman, jealous for the maintenance of authority and of the unity of the catholic church.[1] That his mysticism implied no disparagement of reason is evident from his ascription to God of truth as an essential characteristic, and on his insistence on the argument to God's existence from the capacity of the finite intellect to apprehend eternal truth in the light that radiates from the splendour of the divine mind. *Deus illuminatio mea* is the cardinal principle of his epistemology. Faith, so far from being opposed to reason, is its complement, being itself an act of intellectual apprehension and, as *fides quaerens intellectum*, provocative of intellectual effort after full clarification of its mysteries. Augustine was the resolute foe of the irrationalism and superstition which, under the guise of fortune, chance, or circumstance, had, throughout the classical tradition, been posited over against the power of human character as one of the two forces that co-operate to shape the destiny of the individual and the course of history. In his view,

1. On Augustine's mysticism see Dom Cuthbert Butler's *Western Mysticism*.

the sole source of the evils that condition and limit man's effort after the infinite lay in the sinfulness of his will, and the sole remedy in the gift of divine grace. By this gift he was enabled to rise to the higher plane of intellectual perception which Augustine distinguished as *sapientia* from that of *scientia* or philosophic knowledge, such as was attainable by the methods of discursive thinking canonized in the writings of Greek philosophers. Thus humanistic learning first found its due place in man's life, enjoying its full rights under the aegis of a Christocentric metaphysics. This is what Augustine meant when he spoke of Christ as 'the foundation for a new physic, a new ethic, and a new logic'.[1] The ἀρχή and the categories of the gospel furnished at once the transformation and the justification of those of Aristotle. Every word he wrote is the outcome either of personal feeling or of the pressure of a practical crisis. Controversy with the Manichaeans, the Donatists, or Pelagius, is blended with the outpouring of Christian aspiration, and the love, which never deserted him, for the great teachers of the pagan world. Through the medium of his mind, the spirit of Plato passed into that of the western church. Under the influence of Victorinus, he had been led from Manichaeism, which appealed early to him by its insistence on the reality of evil, to the doctrines of Plotinus; and when, like his teacher, he embraced Christianity, the new loyalty perfected rather than displaced the old.[2] His Christian faith was engrafted on a Neo-Platonic stock. In his eyes, Plotinus was the halfway house to the true faith. We have quoted above the passage from the *Confessions* where he marks the point of divergence between Neo-Platonism and Christianity.[3] 'That "the Word (*Logos*) was

---

1. Cochrane, *Christianity and Classical Culture*, p. 417.
2. Manichaeism was the religion of Manes of Ctesiphon (the capital of the Persian kingdom), in the middle of the second century. It taught a dualism of two eternal divine powers, of light and darkness, and ascetic renunciation of the body and of the material world as belonging to the realm of evil. Manes was probably unacquainted with orthodox Christianity, and his religion was not a heresy, but a rival. Despite persecution, it survived in the East till the Mongol invasion, and traces are found even in the West for several centuries. It had many adherents in Turkestan, India, and China, and is one of the most important phenomena of religious history.
3. *Conf.*, vii. 9. On what follows, see Bigg, *Neo-Platonism*, pp. 330 ff. The

made flesh and dwelt among us'', this I found not there.' To Augustine, as to Athanasius, the Incarnation was the cardinal message of the gospel, God's free gift of suffering love to sinful man. This grasp of the divine love, as taught by St John, and of divine grace, as taught by St Paul, working on Augustine's vivid sense of personal sin, was the nerve of his polemic against Pelagianism. Pelagius, a British monk, who, after a long sojourn in Palestine, appeared at Rome early in the fifth century, taught that each man was solely responsible for his own virtue or vice, the maker, as a free agent, of his own spiritual destiny. He denied the inheritance of original sin, disparaged the efficacy of prayer, and relegated divine grace to the position of an external adjunct to human effort. The issue, raised clearly for the first time in the history of thought, was that of the relation of morality to religion. Pelagius voiced a popular and belated Stoicism, the doctrine that man can be saved by his own strength. To Augustine such a tenet was intolerable. If true, the need of Christ's redemption vanished. He searched the problem to its depths in the light of his own spiritual experience. Building on the epistle to the Romans (especially on Rom. v. 12), he affirmed that all men were born in Adam's sin and could be saved only by the free and irresistible grace of God, developing the doctrines of sin and grace to extremes in which catholic theology has declined to follow him. While endorsing his conviction of the necessity of prevenient grace, i.e. that the first aspiration of sinful men towards God must be divinely aided, and of God's foreknowledge of man's choice, the church refused assent to his abrogation of human freedom, and to the terrible doctrine that, out of a race doomed to eternal damnation, a few brands have been snatched from the burning by a *fiat* of the divine will.[1] God willed, so the church firmly main-

---

early *Confessions* should be studied in conjunction with the restatement of Augustine's position in the *Retractions*, written at the close of his life (430).

1. The Gnostics also had held to the belief that the individual's character and destiny were determined independently of his freedom of choice and action. The problem was thus a standing one from the early centuries onwards. It arose out of the consciousness of sin. The Greeks never questioned human freedom; for Plato (see the myth of Er in *Rep.*, x) it is modified by destiny and inherited conditions, while Aristotle (*Ethics*, iii. c. 1) considers it absurd to question moral responsibility. If a man is responsible for his good acts, which

tained, that all mankind should be saved. Calvinism, in its extreme form, has its roots in certain passages of Augustine. The controversy with Pelagius formed but a fragment of Augustine's theological writings. These ranged over the whole field of Christian speculation. His treatise on the Trinity remained the classical authority for western Christendom. The East had its own doctors and owed but little to Augustine. But in the West he was for centuries the fountain-head of Christian theology and metaphysics. In the 'City of God' (*de civitate Dei*, 413–26), as in the historical work undertaken by Orosius at his instigation, the history of the world was interpreted as the unfolding of the issues of man's first sin and the accomplishment of God's purpose of redemption. The aim of this great treatise was to restore the shaken faith of Christendom in divine providence.[1] The hour was dark, for the barbarians were at the gates of Rome. In 410 the city was sacked by Alaric and his Visigoths. Twenty years later, as Augustine lay dying at Hippo,

---

no one doubts, he is responsible also for his bad acts (which alone he tries to evade). A man's acts are 'in his power'. The nearest approach to determinism is in Stoicism, which bears traces of Semitic origin. It was Augustine who first explicitly raised the speculative issue.

1. The central thought of this treatise, which is unsystematic in structure and packed with lengthy digressions, is the contrast between the City of God (i.e. the invisible community of saints, symbolized imperfectly by the visible church), and the earthly City (i.e. the invisible community of the reprobate, symbolized imperfectly by the series of historic kingdoms). *Civitas* for Augustine means 'society', not 'the state'. Augustine does not unreservedly condemn the state, which is grounded, not only on the fall of man, but on the intrinsic sociality of his nature. Rather, in the true classical spirit, he recognizes its ethical function, and, particularly, the rightful authority of the Roman empire (see Vol. 1, c. vii, § 2). The state of innocence would have been a social state, but without *coercive* authority, which is justified as a means for remedying the effects of sin. Thus the earthly City of the treatise is not organized society as such, but human society organizing itself *apart from God*. The contrast is rooted in that of the two loves, love of self and love of God. Love of self is manifested in history as ambition for earthly power. The work exercised an immense influence on later thought, and gave a handle to very diverse interpretations in the Middle Ages. It is not to be regarded (as has often been alleged) as the first attempt to construct a 'philosophy of history'. It is rather a 'theodicy', i.e. an interpretation of universal history as the drama of divine operation, enacted on the stage of human history, exemplifying the principle of the Incarnation (God manifest in the flesh) as displayed in the medium of temporal occurrences. See Figgis, *The Political Aspects of St Augustine's City of God*, especially cc. iii and v.

Genseric, with his hordes of Arian Vandals, was spreading fire and slaughter throughout Africa.

§ 23. Our purpose in the foregoing sections has been to illustrate the influence of Hellenism on the process by which the primitive Christian faith was shaped into a body of theological doctrine. Before quitting this subject, we may pause to remark how Christianity, in gathering in the inheritance of Rome and Greece, achieved, in the sphere of religion, the union of two aspects, constitutive of all experience, those, namely, of historic fact and ideal value. We are wont to think of these two aspects as if they belonged to different worlds; on the one side, a world of particular occurrences, temporal events, historic situations, on the other, a world of ideal standards, absolute ends, and eternal truths. When we review the course of ancient history, we realize that the Roman mind was almost wholly immersed in the world of fact, and that the source of its remarkable achievements lay in its capacity to adjust means to practical ends. Absorbed in the emergency of the hour, it ignored or even disdained the claims of speculative theory, which lives and works in the realm of ideal values. The Greek mind, on the contrary, viewed the world of fact, of practical situations, as a spring-board whence to leap by a *salto mortale* into the realm of ends and meanings, the world of absolute and timeless truths. Phenomena were but the occasion and the stimulus; reality had its abiding home in the essence of things, in the Forms of Plato, in the intellectual actuality which is Aristotle's God, in the spiritual world of Plotinus crowned by the simple and unchanging One. The difference appears, again, as that between law and morality, between the life of the politician and that of the philosopher.[1] We have said, echoing Bacon, that, to the Greek, philosophy was a religion; or rather, that his religion was philosophy. To the Roman, religion meant rising duly to the occasion, doing the fit thing at the fit time. In the discharge of its obligations, his main concern was to ensure formal correctness; absorbed in the means, he let spiritual ideals take care of themselves. The Greek found peace in intellectual detachment, the Roman in

1. See, especially, Plato, *Theaetetus*.

security against the transitory contingencies of the actual. Now Christianity stood, as a religion, for the union of historic fact, the great concern of Rome; and of ideal value, the great concern of Greece.[1] It affirmed this union as indissoluble, refusing to gauge the truth of fact save in the light of its meaning, or to accept values that were not the inner heart of fact. The two worlds, the ideal and the actual, were for it not two, but one. We see this in the pragmatic handling of world-history, as, for example, in the 'City of God' of St Augustine, and in the constant endeavour to read the sequence of temporal occurrences as a theodicy, the revelation of a divine and eternal purpose. The early church persistently resisted the endeavour to relegate the faith to the realm of values, or to interpret it merely as a philosophic theory, an abstract speculation of the schools. It held firmly to the truth that the Divine Idea was realized in the person of the historic Jesus.[2] 'The Word was made flesh and dwelt among us.' In Him ideal and actuality, value and fact, were one. But the church was far from restricting the truth of Christ's actual existence to the series of historic incidents comprised between his birth and crucifixion. It taught that the life of the incarnate Christ is coextensive with the entire spiritual experience, as yet unfulfilled, of humanity. The Christian could not echo the Roman poet's faith in the destiny of the eternal city – 'to these I set nor bound nor period of sovereignty; I have given them an empire without an end'[3] – for he knew that all historical happenings were transitory and that here he had no continuing city, but sought one to come.

1. We have seen in the third chapter how keenly sensitive were the Hebrews, throughout their religious history, to the pressure of historic fact. But whereas historic crises served the Roman merely as a stimulus to effective action, and the Greek as a stimulus to reflective thought, their significance to the Hebrew prophets and people was primarily ethical and religious. Christianity learnt from Judaism the habit of associating moral values with historic fact, and thus was enabled to mediate between the one-sided interests of Roman statesmanship and Greek philosophy.

2. 'The religion of the Incarnation cannot be mere theology – a system of notions developed from certain metaphysical propositions – nor can it be mere ethics, a code of laws on a theistic basis' (Figgis, *op. cit.*, p. 34). This is illustrated, not only by Augustine, but earlier by Athanasius, and also by St Paul (*ibid.*, p. 35); see also Webb, *God and Personality*, pp. 81, 82, and pp. 175–80.

3. Virgil, *Aen.*, i. 282–3.

For him, this earthly life and the whole course of human history were but an episode in the unfolding, under conditions of time and space, of the divine purpose, from which they drew alike their significance and their reality. The credentials of the Christian faith cannot be measured solely in terms of particular incidents in its history. 'Make of Christ', wrote Hegel, 'what you will, exegetically, critically, historically; demonstrate as you please how the doctrines of the church were established by councils, attained currency as the result of this or that episcopal interest or passion, or originated in this or that quarter; let all such circumstances have been what they might, the only relevant question is: What is the Idea and Truth in and for itself?' [1] This does not mean that the Idea can possess truth apart from the events of history. It means that the events of history cannot possess truth apart from it. It means that there are not two orders of truth, a truth of value distinct from the truth of fact; but that the ghost of the two worlds, which haunted to the close the mind of the Greeks and still haunts that of the East, was finally laid by the declaration of the Christian faith that the divine became human in order that the human might be made divine.[2]

IV. CONCLUSION

§ 24. The fourth century was a turning-point in the history of Christianity. It witnessed the explicit acceptance of Hellenic thought by the Christian faith, and of the Christian faith by the Roman empire. The long struggle with Graeco-Roman culture and the imperial government was decided; *causa finita est: Roma locuta est* ('the case is ended: Rome has spoken'). Looking backwards, we can perceive how the conflict had been attended throughout by the presages of an eventual reconciliation. The influence of Hellenism upon Christianity was already apparent in the apostolic age. The like is true of its relations with the Roman empire. The empire from the first offered

1. *Philosophy of History*, Part III, Sect. 3, c. ii.
2. The general question referred to in this section is further discussed at the close of the concluding chapter.

facilities as well as obstacles to the propagation of the new faith. It secured throughout the Mediterranean area not only an enduring peace, but uniformity of speech and civilization, particularly in the great cities, and communication swift and sure both by land and sea.[1] Thus it furnished the material conditions for the expansion of the gospel, and brought Christianity into immediate contact with the civilization and thought of Greece. Roman jurisprudence, both in principles and in detail, was accepted, almost without question, by the Fathers of the first six centuries. The concept of a state of nature, anterior to the establishment of civil government; the doctrine that all men, as rational beings, were by nature free and equal; the distinction between natural and civil law; its application to the institutions of slavery, property, and coercive jurisdiction – these ideas were confirmed and strengthened by the Christian beliefs in man's pristine innocence, and in the changed conditions which resulted from the Fall. The visible institution of the Christian church modelled itself instinctively on the majestic structure of the imperial government. The municipalities fostered by the Roman empire formed the chief centres of ecclesiastical activity. Ecclesiastical dioceses and provinces, especially in the period following on Diocletian's reconstruction, were shaped on the lines of the political divisions of the empire. The secular capitals, such as Antioch, Alexandria, Lyon, Carthage and, later, Milan and Constantinople, became the dominant sees in their respective quarters of the Roman world. We have seen how the rise of the papacy was due, not only to the recognized need for ecclesiastical unification, still less to the personal ambition of the Roman bishops, who were individually by no means the foremost leaders of Christendom,

1. Greek was spoken in the commercial towns both in East and West. The great roads could be traversed at all seasons, piracy had been suppressed in the Mediterranean, and lines of vessels plied at regular intervals between the chief ports. There was a common coinage, common law, and common cosmopolitan culture throughout the empire. Teachers and students travelled from university to university, from Bordeaux to Tarsus. Missionaries of the Christian and other faiths did likewise. Irenaeus (adv. haer., iv. 30–3) wrote: 'The Romans have given the world peace, and we travel without fear along the roads and across the sea wherever we will.'

but, in large measure, to the compelling logic of facts, which rendered it inevitable that the bishop of the imperial metropolis should acquire a pre-eminent status in the ecclesiastical hierarchy. So it was, again, that the partition of the empire in the fourth century, of which we shall speak in the ensuing chapter, was reflected in the growing independence of the eastern and western churches. The racial differences of character, temperament, and language between the Greek and Latin peoples proved a constant obstacle to unity; though in theory both empire and church remained one and undivided, the division in secular jurisdiction was bound to accentuate the divergences of ecclesiastical policy and theological opinion. The official establishment of Christianity under Constantine and his successors was fraught with far-reaching issues upon the life of the church. Henceforward there was a close alliance between the secular government and the most powerful ecclesiastical corporation within the empire. We have remarked how conflicts within the church led to the repeated and often baneful intervention of the secular sovereign.[1] In the domain of law, the easy, simple, and equitable tribunals of the Christian bishops won increasing favour with litigants and increasing sanction from the imperial authorities.[2] But the gravest peril springing from the triumph of Christianity was that of worldliness and intolerance. The church had become rich and powerful; and the temptation to use the influence of the state to further its secular ambitions was well-nigh irresistible. Hardly had the age of persecution ceased, when that of secularization entered on its long and disastrous history. Even in the fourth century, it

1. See above, § 20, p. 371, note 2. The absence of a paramount ecclesiastical authority (for the influence of the Roman see was as yet moral rather than legal, especially in the East) necessitated imperial intervention in the affairs of the church. No Christian thought of disputing it. It was exercised chiefly in summoning councils, in sanctioning their decisions, and in choosing between rival candidates for bishoprics. The emperor, of course, claimed no power to decide doctrine or to appoint or depose a bishop; but in practice he frequently exercised a determining influence in such matters. But the clergy were not state functionaries, and the church remained a self-governing corporation.

2. It had been the rule from apostolic times for Christians to settle their disputes before the church. Now the ecclesiastical tribunals were recognized by the Roman state, not merely in cases involving religion and morals, but in all matters of law (see below, c. x, § 18).

looked as if the victory of the church over the world meant
rather the victory of the world over the church. We are apt to
ignore the other side of the picture, and to forget that the dawn
of secularization coincided with the institution of monasticism,
and that, side by side with proud and worldly prelates like the
Alexandrian bishops of the fifth century, stand the figures of
Basil and the Gregories, of Martin of Tours, of Athanasius,
Ambrose, and Augustine.[1] It was the employment of the secular
arm as an instrument of religious persecution that forms the
heaviest indictment against the church of the later empire. The
toleration promised by the first Christian emperor to his pagan
subjects soon yielded to a policy of repression, confined indeed
to the towns, and therein to the prohibition of the external
observances of the old religions. In the country districts,
paganism long survived (*paganus* = villager) with little inter-
ference from the government. In the end it died of inanition,
or was absorbed into the practices of Christian worship.[2] Very
different was the treatment meted out to heresy. Persecution of
Arian by Catholic, Catholic by Arian, became the order of the
day.[3] The reign of mutual toleration that had prevailed in pre-
Christian antiquity had passed away. The terrible consequences
of the new spirit of intolerance for the religious life of the
Christian world are obvious enough and admit of no palliation.
Yet a sober historian will reflect that, if paganism had been

1. Anchorites appear in Egypt about 270 (St Anthony); the first Egyptian
monastic settlement was fifty years later. Both practices spread rapidly in the
East, and afterwards also in the West. St Martin of Tours founded monasteries
in Gaul in the second half of the fourth century. The authorities of the church
(especially at Rome) were inclined to be suspicious of asceticism; the danger
of Manichaeism was always imminent, and the solitaries and monks often
regarded themselves as a superior type of Christians and were apt to prove a
source of disorder. Duchesne compares the danger to that of industrial strikes
at the present day. The monks and anchorites were popular with the masses and
did not hesitate to use their influence, if need be, against the ecclesiastical
authorities. '*Monachi multa scelera faciunt*' ('the monks commit many crimes'),
wrote the Emperor Theodosius to St Ambrose. The fifth-century councils
regulated monasticism and secured episcopal control of the monasteries.
2. The fourth and fifth centuries were a time of the rapid growth of devotion to local saints and of the incorporation of pagan rites and festivals into
Christian worship.
3. 'Give me the world free from heretics and I will give thee heaven', were
the words of Nestorius to Theodosius II.

tolerant, it was because its religions felt no repugnance to recognizing the existence of the gods of other peoples; and that a monotheistic faith, like the Jewish or the Christian, which refused such recognition, represented an immense spiritual advance on the polytheism that had hitherto universally prevailed. Humanity had entered on a new path, and centuries had to elapse before it could grasp the compatibility of a monotheistic worship with religious liberty. To seek for toleration among the Christians of the first centuries is like expecting to find a knowledge of the law of gravitation before Newton.[1]

§ 25. If the empire thus set its mark upon Christianity, it is no less true that Christianity set its mark upon the empire. In particular, it contributed, though unconsciously, to its imminent disintegration. The practices of asceticism and celibacy, the improvement of the status of women and slaves, an increased regard for human life, and, above all, the recognition of divine law as superior to human ordinance, and a temper of indifference towards earthly governments, sapped the groundwork on which the Roman political and social system had been based. The Christian was the member of a commonwealth that knew no distinction of Greek or barbarian, bond or free; and he looked for a city that had foundations, whose builder and maker was God. The need for a temporal embodiment of the *Civitas Dei* was met, not by the state, but by the church. He had been taught indeed to render unto Caesar the things that were Caesar's, and the recognition by Caesar of the Christian faith strengthened this secular allegiance to the empire. But it was not the crowning bulwark of his security; he could read, as Augustine read, the handwriting of God in the very catastrophe of its dismemberment. The fall of the empire was due primarily to causes other than the triumph of Christianity; but Christianity assisted rather than checked their operation. The func-

1. The way was paved for toleration by the religious controversies of the Reformation epoch and the rise of modern nation-states with national churches. The presence of dissentient minorities in many countries was of crucial importance. The free-thinkers of the eighteenth century sounded the knell of persecution: e.g. Voltaire's exposure of the Calas tragedy, which constitutes one o fthe great events in the history of civilization. See Mark Pattison, *Essays* (*The Calas Tragedy*). But now, in face of Nazi intolerance alike towards Jews and Christians, the battle has to be fought over again.

tion of the gospel was not to repair the breaches in an outworn civilization, but to infuse a new spirit into the life of the peoples and to bring peace and joy into the souls of men. The peace that the empire had conferred was an external peace and its prosperity an economic prosperity. We have seen how the majestic and all-embracing system proved an overpowering burden upon its subjects. But in the domain of the spirit they were free, and Christianity unlocked for them the secret of their freedom. In the strength of the new-won faith they went forth gladly to meet labour and suffering, and found in that very labour and suffering the inward fruition which they craved. They cared little about the issue on the institutions or the learning of the past. Their faith was unshaken by the ruin of Hellenic culture and of the stately fabric of empire to which that culture had given birth. It was the price they paid gladly for the hope of a new life, the revelation of which forms the true ground of the distinction between ancient and mediaeval history.

CHAPTER TEN

THE DECLINE AND FALL

*

I. INTRODUCTORY

§ 1. GIBBON dates the decline and fall of the Roman empire from the death of Marcus Aurelius in 180. If we look merely to the stability of the imperial system and its effective defence of the frontiers, we must accept a much later date for the beginning of the end. So securely had the foundations been laid by Augustus that the empire maintained its integrity even in the West until the great invasions of the fifth century, while in the East it presented as firm a front against its enemies under Heraclius in the seventh century as under Diocletian in the third. But if we take a wider and more imaginative view of history, the grounds for Gibbon's conclusion become apparent. Long before the barbarians burst the barriers on the Rhine and the Danube, the civilization which those barriers shielded was sinking into decay. Not enough Romans were left to carry on the work of Rome. The political liberty from which it drew life had vanished, and already in the second century the seeds of economic ruin were germinating with appalling swiftness throughout the Mediterranean lands. If we think not merely of the Roman state, but of what Rome stands for in history, we must confess that, from the moment when despotism and bureaucracy cast their blighting shadow over the world, the culture of Greece and Rome was doomed to perish. The future belonged to ideas of another order, with which that culture had little sympathy. Those who resisted the new impulse and remained loyal to the past were inspired by resignation, not by hope. A creative literature is the surest index of the vitality of a civilization, and the fountain-heads of classical poetry were dry. Claudian of Alexandria, the last Latin poet worthy of the name, wrote indeed in the fifth century, but was a belated and solitary survival. The destiny of the western world lay henceforward in the hands of alien powers, the Germanic invaders and the Christian church; and in their life-history the spirit of classical antiquity no longer played a dominant part. Yet, even thus, Gibbon's judgement requires modification. The creative energy of Graeco-Roman civilization was not yet exhausted at the close of the second century. The third century was the golden age of Roman jurisprudence. In the philosophy of Plotinus it witnessed, as we showed in the last chapter, the final blossoming of the speculative genius of Greece. The foundation of New Rome on the Bosporus by Constantine opened a fresh and memorable chapter of imperial history. Therewith the tale of original and constructive achievement is closed. Even the *Corpus juris* of Justinian was but the codification of a law, of which the principles and the content were an inheritance from the past. Thus, if we are to essay the impracticable and to fix an opening date for the decline and fall, it seems reasonable to point to the close of the third and the early years of the fourth century, to the epoch of Diocletian and of Constantine.

§ 2. In our introductory chapter, we indicated the threefold function of Rome in history. She gathered up into one world-state the civilizations of the Mediterranean, and, above all, that of ancient Greece, which she enriched through her own original contribution in the field of government and law. She kept the peace for centuries, and preserved from dissolution the inheritance thus treasured beneath her sway. And, lastly, she passed on this legacy to the younger races from the north, who, trained in the school of Rome, grew, in the ages that followed, into the civilized nations of modern history. In regard to the first of these functions, we have shown how, by the close of the third century, her work was done. As for the second, we have still to see how she availed to keep the frontiers in West and East, thereby saving the old civilization and the new Christianity from being swamped by Teutonic, Slav, and Saracen invaders. But it is the third task, that of implanting at least a fragment of ancient culture among peoples as yet uncivilized, that most concerns us in the later history of the empire. The problem was no new one. Already in Spain under the republic, and in Gaul under the early empire, the educative mission of Rome had borne rapid and surprising fruit. The alliance with Christianity, and the barbarian settlements within her borders, greatly enlarged its scope and influence. The Germanic peoples, though still uncivilized when they first came within Rome's sphere of influence, were endowed with rich potentialities of development. Their youthful energy, their poetic imagination, their love of freedom, and above all their capacity for self-government, provided the natural basis for the evolution of a new type of social order. All they needed was an example and a training such as Rome, and Rome alone, could give. That she gave it, even in the hour of her decline, was her crowning achievement in history.

§ 3. Our task in this chapter is thus mapped out. We have not to consider, even in outline, the whole story of the decline and fall, but to select those features of the period which best illustrate the transition from the ancient to the mediaeval and the modern world. We shall, first, speak briefly of the reconstruction of the imperial system, and especially of the partition of the empire under Diocletian and Constantine. We shall, next, explain the general character of the process by which the Teutonic invaders of the West from the third to the sixth century were brought into contact with Graeco-Roman civilization and with Christianity, and of the immediate impression left by that contact upon their history. Finally, we shall turn to the empire in the East, and, after a survey of its administrative system and the successive crises which confronted it from without, attempt to measure the character and influence of its culture in the long period of more than a millennium, during which the emperors at Constantinople kept the gate in the face of the Slavs, the Saracens, and the Turks.

I. THE RECONSTRUCTION OF THE EMPIRE

§ 4. A reorganization of the imperial system was called for by the changes that had come about since its establishment by Augustus. The republican institutions, which he studied to preserve, perished rapidly from sheer senility and inanition. By the close of the second century, despotism, working through a vast bureaucracy at Rome and in the provinces, was revealed in its nakedness and accepted without a murmur throughout the Roman world. A second change had resulted logically from the substitution of the empire for the republic. Though Rome still occupied a unique position, because of the greatness of her past, and as the seat of government, she had become less and less the real centre of the empire. The thought and energy of its rulers were concentrated on the armies on the frontiers. Even Italy counts only as the premier region among the surrounding provinces. The history of the empire is no longer that of Rome or Italy, but of the Mediterranean world. It was high time that these facts should be explicitly recognized in the constitution. But the most urgent motive for reorganization lay in the military situation. Since the reign of Marcus Aurelius, the onset of the Germanic tribes, checked in the last days of the republic by Marius and Julius Caesar, had threatened to break the barriers on the Rhine and the Danube; while, from the third century onwards, the rise of a powerful native Persian kingdom in place of Parthia in the Middle East provoked constant wars on the Euphrates. Moreover, the defending legions themselves proved a constant danger to internal peace. Their concentration in remote provinces left Rome at the mercy of the praetorian guards, the sole military force near the capital. In 193, for instance, the guards murdered the emperor and put the throne up to auction to the highest bidder. The frontier armies followed suit, and a struggle ensued that ended with the triumph of the Danubian legions under Severus. The phenomenon was repeated more than once in the course of the third century. A strong emperor might control the armies; but it became increasingly evident that this task, as well as that of defending the frontiers, required a reorganization of the administrative system. It was accomplished by a soldier, and in a soldier's spirit; the same motive that prompted the recognition of Mithraism and the persecution of the Christians, inspired the reconstruction of the empire by Diocletian.

§ 5. By birth an Illyrian slave, Diocletian had risen through military capacity to be governor of Moesia (the modern Serbia and Bulgaria) and chief of the palace guard, and was acclaimed emperor by the army in 284. His reforms of the system of administration, if measures which served but to enlarge the bureaucracy and impose burdens yet more crushing on the population deserve to be styled reforms, were governed by three principles. First, civil and military functions were entrusted to different hands: the praetorian prefects with their vicars, and, under these, the provincial governors, corresponding in the bureaucratic scale to the *magistri militum*, the *duces* (dukes) and *comites* (counts), who held command over the armies. In the second place, the old provinces were increased in number to about one hundred, grouped in twelve dioceses, which were, in turn, subordinated to the four great divisions of Gaul, Italy, Illyricum, and the East. Thirdly, the chiefs alike of the civil government and of the army were organized in a regularized system of grades, distinguished by their respective titles, emoluments, and privileges. Rank was still, as ever at Rome, determined by tenure of executive office. The old tradition by which public services were left to private enterprise gave way to management by State officials, whose numbers increased by leaps and bounds, and who took rank by hereditary status. Rome and Italy were henceforward governed and taxed on a par with every other province. The root-idea of the system was the centralization of all authority in the hands of the emperor, the sovereign of the official hierarchy. His unique position as autocrat of the world was asserted without disguise. His person, even his house, were proclaimed divine; throned and crowned with the royal diadem, surrounded by a court with all the pomp and ceremony of an Oriental sultan, and approachable only by the high officers of state, and by them with abject prostration, he was severed by impenetrable barriers from contact with the mass of his subjects. Continuity can be traced between the court-etiquette instituted by Diocletian and that of the Sassanid monarchs of Persia, and, less directly, of the earlier Achaemenid Persian dynasty. Thus was inaugurated the régime that prevailed for many succeeding centuries as the habit of the Byzantine empire. But Diocletian did more than remodel the bureaucracy, and institute an autocratic monarchy in place of the semi-republican principate. He recognized that the burden of government was too heavy a load to be borne by a single ruler. He desired also to provide a remedy against those disputes over the succession which had so often disturbed the peace, and weakened the efficiency, of the empire. He therefore put the empire in commission among four partners, two with superior, two with subordinate authority, associating three other Illyrian commanders with himself in the sovereign power. The two senior princes, styled *Augusti*, ruled respectively in East and West, with their capitals at Nicomedia in north-west Asia Minor, and at Milan; the two junior princes, styled *Caesares*, were entrusted, the one with Spain and the Gauls, the other with the Balkan provinces, with their capitals at Trier and Sirmium (near Belgrade). Diocletian himself reigned over the Asiatic provinces from Nicomedia. The seats of government were thus brought into convenient proximity to the frontiers. This system did not survive in the precise form instituted by Diocletian, nor did it save the empire from internal quarrels between its rulers. But the principle of partition endured. A generation after Diocletian, Constantine founded, on the site of the ancient Greek colony of Byzantium, the 'New Rome' which still perpetuates his name, to be the seat of government for the eastern half of the empire. Grounds, alike of strategy and of commerce, marked out the city on the Bosporus as a centre that commanded both the Balkan and Asiatic provinces,[1] which were menaced simultaneously by the Visigoths on the Danube and by the Persians from the East. Byzantium was a natural fortress, impregnable save by assault at once from the sea and by land. In the event, 'New Rome' was thrice saved during the fifth century at the expense of the Old. Alaric's Visigoths, Attila's Huns, and Theodoric's Ostrogoths, turned their arms westwards towards Italy at the moment when the city of Constantine seemed to lie at their mercy. We shall return to the memorable history of Constantinople in a later section of this chapter. Finally, on the death of Theodosius the Great (395), the last sole ruler of the empire, the sovereignty

1. Gibbon's description of Constantinople in his seventeenth chapter has never been surpassed.

was shared for nearly a century by two emperors, governing respectively from Italy and from Constantinople. Historians have been accustomed to speak of this change as a division of the empire into two, an eastern and a western empire. Such expressions are misleading; though its government was henceforward partitioned between two emperors, the empire itself remained indivisible and one.

§ 6. The significance of these changes was very great.[1] They contributed to prolong the life of the imperial state in the West for nearly two centuries, in the East for over a thousand years. Again, they indicate that the old Rome, the Rome of the republic, which Augustus had striven to perpetuate, was gone for ever. The change of capitals, the substitution of new offices for the historic magistracies, the installation of the pomp and splendour of an Eastern court, and the frank avowal of despotism, implied a radical breach with the traditions and sentiment of the past. The extension of Roman citizenship, and of equal rights at law, to all provincials, the enrolment of barbarian immigrants in the legions and the establishment of the Christian faith as the religion of the empire, show that Rome now stood for an order of institutions and ideas very different from those of three centuries earlier. Rome was still Rome, but whereas of old she had been an Italian city, she was now a cosmopolitan state. It was this changed Rome that confronted the wild Teutons, when, breaking across the Rhine and the Danube into the frontier provinces, they passed under the overpowering influence of Roman government and law. They found too, at least in Italy and the West, that the majestic image of empire which dazzled their vision proved to more intimate experience but the veil that shrouded the agony of a dying world. For the statesmanship of Diocletian and Constantine was impotent to heal the sore that preyed on the vitals of Graeco-Roman civilization. Their failure was not merely due to their absorption in the urgent military problem, and their consequent neglect of the economic crisis. That crisis was grave

1. Mommsen is reported to have said to Sir William Ramsay that, if he had a second lifetime, he would devote it to the period between Constantine and Justinian.

indeed, but it was a secondary symptom; the economic evils had their root in moral apathy and paralysis of human will. How could a military autocracy stir into fresh life the flagging energy of its subject-peoples? Bankruptcy, war, plague, and famine; wasted lands, decaying cities, ruined trade; a diminished population, no longer capable of furnishing an adequate quota of recruits for the legions; a listless aristocracy, a middle class impoverished by exaction and almost crushed out of being, an indolent proletariat, vast multitudes of serfs and slaves; over all, the huge machine of government, stifling local independence and individual enterprise; around all, the terrible barbarian menace, drawing nearer year by year to the gates of Italy; such was the gaunt reality that crouched in the shadow of the fourth-century empire.[1] Little wonder that the masses sought a refuge in the other-worldliness of Christianity, or that, when in the event the imperial government vanished from the western provinces, men seemed scarcely sensible of the change.[2]

III. THE ROMAN AND THE TEUTON

§ 7. The policy of the empire towards the Teutonic peoples presents the two aspects of resistance and of attraction. We have seen how war against the German hordes who pressed

1. We have summed up in this sentence a mass of economic and social phenomena, to the study of which much labour has been devoted by modern scholars. The decay of agriculture is especially important. The third and fourth centuries saw the change in the position of *coloni*, from free rent-paying cultivators to hereditary tenants tied to the soil (see Pelham, *Essays in Roman History*, 'The Imperial Domains and the Colonate'). In the fourth century arose a body of landowners with privileges and powers that foreshadowed the feudal aristocracy of the Middle Ages (see Vinogradoff in *Camb. Med. History*, vol. i, c. xix). On the history of ancient (Graeco-Roman) agriculture generally see Heitland's *Agricola*.

2. The Christianization of the empire reacted beneficially on the condition of the people, e.g. in mitigation of the hardships of slavery, encouragement of emancipation, promotion of philanthropic measures, and, above all, in the relief which episcopal jurisdiction, now recognized as an integral part of the legal system, furnished to the pressure of bureaucratic tyranny. Government and people turned more and more to the church, whose courts were speedy, cheap, and just. They enjoyed the confidence of the public, who preferred episcopal arbitration to the lay tribunals.

ceaselessly against the Rhine and Danube fortifications was a standing feature of imperial history from the days of Julius and Augustus. But the last-named emperor had already inaugurated the policy of granting lands to barbarian immigrants within the frontier provinces. Lampridius, in his life of Severus Alexander, remarks that early in the second century the Roman world was crowded with undesirable aliens.[1] This system, so perilous and yet so useful, and fraught with far-reaching consequences both for the empire and for the Teutonic settlers thus admitted within its pale, was pursued deliberately and on an extended scale in the age that followed, especially by the Illyrian emperors at the close of the third, and by the successors of Constantine in the fourth, century. The new colonists supplied a remedy for the increasing depopulation of the empire. Above all, they formed an easy recruiting-ground for the frontier legions; in the event, the defence of the frontiers fell almost entirely into the hands of these half-Romanized immigrants of Teutonic origin. Franks were enrolled in the palace guard of Constantine; Julian led Gothic troops to fight the Persians on the Euphrates. The word 'barbarian' (barbarus) came to be used as a synonym for soldier.[2] Yet this policy of assimilation tended inevitably to the breakdown of the old political and social order. The line of partition between Roman and barbarian grew less rigid. We have noted above the influence of the Christian faith, now universal throughout the empire, in weakening the consciousness of this cleavage. By the fifth century a barbarian colonist might rise to the highest posts in the imperial service. Stilicho, the general of Honorius against Alaric, was a Vandal, Rufinus and Ricimer, the viziers of the Eastern emperors, were respectively a Goth and a Suebe. On the other hand, the Germanic settlers were a source of continual unrest, and not infrequently allied themselves with their kinsmen beyond the Roman border. The grants of land which they obtained within the provinces were, more often than not, grants only in name, being in fact seized by force of arms from a reluctant but impotent government. This was, for

1. See Vinogradoff, *Roman Law in Mediaeval Europe*, p. 4.
2. Vinogradoff, p. 5.

instance, the case of Moesia with the Visigoths, who slew the
emperor Valens in battle at Adrianople (378), and with the
Burgundians a generation later (413), on the left bank of the
Rhine in the region of Worms and Speyer. The Roman territory,
beyond the Rhine and the Danube (the Black Forest and Dacia),
had long been yielded; and in the early years of the fifth century Honorius left Britain to its fate. The dykes were bursting,
and the tempest had begun to sweep over the peaceful provinces of the west and north. The invading chieftains were
already laying the foundations of Germanic kingdoms in Gaul
and Spain, owning indeed a nominal allegiance to the emperor,
but in reality ruling in independent sovereignty alike over
Roman and Teutonic subjects.

§ 8. A brief summary of the main streams of invasion will
assist to an appreciation of the catastrophe which, in overwhelming the empire in the West, at the same time initiated
the transition to the new political and social order of the
Middle Ages. The scene of the drama is western Europe, the
time the fifth and sixth centuries; and six peoples played the
leading parts in the action.

(i) Farthest towards the north, the *Franks* on the lower
Rhine occupied Holland and Flanders, expelled the Roman
garrison from Cologne early in the fifth century and pushed
westwards over the former territory of the Belgae to the
Somme.[1] For the moment Roman authority was extinguished
and Christianity barely survived in the northern parts of Gaul.
The fact of the presence of earlier Frankish colonists, who fused
easily with the invaders, facilitated the establishment of a kingdom which, a generation or two later, expanded under Clovis
(481–511) into a great power, comprising the northern half

---

1. The emperors of the later third and early fourth centuries kept the
Franks successfully at bay, punishing them heavily in campaign after campaign.
The two chief branches were (a) the Salian Franks, between the Scheldt and
the Rhine, (b) the Ripuarian Franks, between the Rhine and the Meuse. The
Salian Franks came from the shores of the North Sea; one of their early kings
was called Merovech (whence the name Merovingian), which means 'sea-born'.
Clovis was king of the Salian Franks. Both branches were enrolled as 'allies'
of Rome. The Salic law dates from the last years of Clovis, but embodies
many usages of greater antiquity.

of ancient Gaul and the western half of modern Germany.[1] Clovis was converted to the catholic faith, an event pregnant, as we shall see presently, with great issues both for the church and the Frankish empire. We find the kings of the Merovingian dynasty to which he belonged admitting a sort of dependence on the emperors at Constantinople, addressing them as 'father'; diplomatic relations were constant between the two powers, and the emperor's head was stamped on money coined in Frankish Gaul.[2]

(ii) While northern Gaul fell to the Franks, Aquitaine, in the south-west, became the seat of a Visigothic kingdom. We found the *Visigoths* (West Goths) across the Danube, fighting the emperor Valens in 378; driven westwards by Theodosius, they turned on Italy, and under their king Alaric, captured and sacked the imperial city in 410.[3] The city of the Caesars had fallen: the city of the Popes was yet to arise. It was shortly after this dramatic catastrophe that they ceased from their wanderings and settled down in Aquitaine. From their capital at Toulouse, the Visigothic princes ruled, as theoretical vice-regents of the emperor, from the Loire to the Pyrenees. Rome naturally impressed her culture more deeply on the Visigoths than on the Franks. In the middle of the fifth century they

1. Clovis conquered first the Roman Syagrius, then the Alemanni in Suabia, then (after his conversion) the Visigoths in southern Gaul. 'It irks me', he remarked, after his conversion to the orthodox faith, 'that these Arians should rule in Gaul' (see Davis, *Mediaeval Europe*, p. 41). Clovis rode into Tours clad in the purple robe of a Roman consul. His portrait and those of other Frankish kings are vividly drawn by the sixth-century historian, Gregory of Tours, whose work stands out amid the general decadence of art and literature in Gaul.

2. Bury, *Later Roman Empire*, vol. i, p. 17, points out that the Ostrogoths, Lombards, and Vandals failed to maintain their kingdoms for long, while the Franks and the Slavs (in the east) founded enduring states, and suggests that the explanation is to be found in the fact, noted in the text, of the presence of earlier settlers of the two latter races within the provinces. Such settlers gave a basis of security and permanence to the later settlements of their kinsmen.

3. The Goths migrated from their Scandinavian home, first to the district south of the Baltic, round the estuary of the Vistula, then to the northern shores of the Euxine. They fought the Romans on the Danube from c. 250 (Vol. 1, c. viii, § 13). It was the pressure of the Huns, who conquered the East Goths in the middle of the fourth century, that drove the Visigoths into the Danubian provinces. Ulfila, the Visigoth, about the same time sowed the seeds of (Arian) Christianity among his people and translated the Bible into their language.

joined with the Romans to repel the invasion of the Huns.
A generation later, under pressure from the growing power of
the Franks, they changed the seat of their kingdom to northern
Spain, which they governed, together with the relics of their
Gallic territory, till the advent of the Saracens in the eighth
century. Even after the fall of the Visigothic kingdom, a few
chieftains held out in the mountain fastnesses, preserving the
traces of Rome and Christianity throughout the Middle Ages.[1]

(iii) The *Vandals*, a Germanic tribe akin to the Goths,
crossed the Rhine in 407, and, after a wandering struggle with
Rome and their fellow-Teutons, entered Spain and conquered
the southern portion of the peninsula. About the same time the
Suebi settled in the north-west and west. Under their king,
Genseric, the Vandals crossed the straits into Africa, and overran the Roman provinces with fire and sword. They were
besieging Hippo at the moment when St Augustine lay dying
within the walls (430). By 455, Roman rule had been extinguished throughout Africa. In the same year Genseric sailed to
Italy, and Rome once again fell a victim to a Teutonic conqueror. The Vandals were Arians, and their kings set themselves with savage ferocity to extirpate the orthodox Church in
Africa. In the sixth century, Justinian crushed the Vandal power
and recovered the African provinces; but his restoration of
civilization and of catholic Christianity proved short-lived and
abortive. The Saracen conquest of the eighth century finally
obliterated every trace of Roman and of Christian influence in
the lands south of the Mediterranean sea.

(iv) In the middle years of the fifth century, the empire was
threatened by a different and a far more dangerous foe. The

1. Rome soon lost her hold of the Gallic communities that lay between the
Frankish and Visigothic kingdoms. She kept the Rhône valley longer, though
with difficulty, against the Burgundians; the temporary success of the Roman
general Aetius and the expulsion of the Burgundians to the east of the Rhine
was celebrated in the legend of the Nibelungs. Eventually the Burgundians were
conquered by the Franks. In Spain, culture was preserved under Visigothic rule,
especially at Toledo and Seville, e.g. Isidore of Seville (c. 560–636), a compiler
of encyclopaedias of science, history, theology, and the canon law, which were
important as forming part of the educational equipment of the early Middle
Ages. The fusion of Visigothic and Romano-Spanish civilization was effective
and lasting. Visigothic laws were quoted in the Spanish courts till the nineteenth century; Visigothic customs persisted in the *Fueros* of the Middle Ages.

Franks, the Goths, and the Vandals were Teutons, men of kindred Aryan stock to the Romans, and endowed, in varying measure, with the capacity for settled life and orderly government. But the *Huns* were Tartars, wild horsemen from the steppe-lands north of the Caucasus and the Aral sea. Alone of the invading races they came as mere destroyers. Swarthy, dwarf-like in stature, with long, shaggy hair and little beady eyes, living, eating, and even sleeping, on horseback, they swept under Attila their king over the West, ravaging Gaul and Spain and threatening at every moment to descend upon Italy.[1] Teuton as well as Roman realized the urgency of the common peril. In 451 the combined forces of the Roman Aetius and Theodoric the Visigoth broke their onset in a great battle near Troyes. Attila retired on Pannonia and died in the year following, while meditating an attack on Constantinople. Quarrels ensued as to the succession, and the Hunnish menace vanished

1. They had all the characteristics of the nomads of the steppe, repeated in the Mongols and the Turks, and present still in their primitive form among the Kirghiz and other Altaic tribes (see Peisker's remarkable chapter in *Camb. Med. Hist.*, vol. i). Ammianus Marcellinus (xxxi. 2) gives the following picture of the Huns (translated by Hodgkin, *Italy and her Invaders*, vol. ii, pp. 32–4): 'The nation of the Huns surpasses all other barbarians in wildness of life. In the first days of infancy, deep incisions are made in the cheeks of their boys, in order that, when the time comes for whiskers to grow there, the sprouting hairs may be kept back by the furrowed scars: and hence they grow to maturity and to old age beardless as eunuchs. They all, however, have strong and well-knit limbs and fine necks. Yet they are of portentous ugliness and so crook-backed that you would take them for some sort of two-footed beasts, or for the roughly chipped stakes which one sees used for the railings of a bridge. And though they do just bear the likeness of men, ... they are so little advanced in civilization that they make no use of fire, nor of any kind of relish, in the preparation of their food, but feed upon the roots which they find in the fields, and the half-raw flesh of any kind of animal. I say half-raw, because they give it a kind of cooking by placing it between their own thighs and the backs of their horses. [This is a misunderstanding on the part of the author. What the Huns did do was to use strips of raw meat thus to heal the sores on their horses (see Peisker in *Camb. Med. Hist.*, i).] They never seek the shelter of houses, which they look upon as little better than tombs; ... nor would one be able to find among them even a cottage of wattled rushes: but wandering at large over mountain and through forest, they are trained to bear from their infancy all the extremes of cold, of hunger, and of thirst. They are clad in linen raiment, or in the skins of fieldmice sown together, and the same suit serves them for indoors and out. ... Their heads are covered with bent caps, their hairy legs with the skins of goats; their shoes ... are so clumsy that they cannot walk comfortably. On this

as swiftly as it had come. Two issues of their devastating invasion were of permanent importance. Attila's grim figure left a
lasting impression on the creative imagination of the Germans
and the Northmen, and looms mysteriously alike in the
Teutonic and the Scandinavian sagas. The flight of the panic-
stricken populace of northern Italy from the Hunnish terror
to the safety of the islands in the Adriatic lagoons was the seed
from which sprang the city of Venice.[1]

(v) Italy itself was still unconquered; the Visigothic and
Vandal invasions were but transitory catastrophes. The Roman
emperors continued to rule, not at Rome, but at Ravenna. At
length the end came; in 476 a Danubian chieftain, Odoacer,
deposed the reigning Caesar, a boy-prince, who bore the
significant name of Romulus Augustulus. Henceforward Rome

account they are not well adapted to pedestrian encounters; but then on the
other hand they are almost welded to their horses. . . . On horseback every man
of that nation lives night and day; on horseback he buys and sells; on horseback
he takes his meat and drink, and when night comes he leans forward upon the
narrow neck of his horse, and there falls into a deep sleep. . . . More often they
fight in no regular order of battle, but being extremely swift and sudden in
their movements, they disperse and then rapidly come together again in loose
array, spread havoc over vast plains, and, flying over the rampart, they pillage
the camp of their enemy almost before he has become aware of their approach.
. . . They are the nimblest of warriors; the missile weapons which they use at a
distance being pointed with sharpened bones admirably fastened to the shaft;
when in close combat, they fight without regard to their own safety, and while
their enemy is intent upon parrying the thrusts of their swords, they throw a
net over him and so entangle his limbs that he loses all power of walking or
riding. No one among them cultivates the ground, or ever touches a plough-
handle. All wander abroad without fixed abodes, without home, or law, or
settled customs, like perpetual fugitives, with their waggons for their only
habitations. . . . If you ask them, not one can tell you what is his place of
origin. . . . They are great truce-breakers, fickle, always ready to be swayed
by the first breath of a new desire. . . . Finally, like animals devoid of
reason, they are utterly ignorant of what is seemly and what is not; they are
tricksters with words and full of dark sayings; they are never moved by either
religious or superstitious awe; they burn with unquenchable thirst for gold,
and they are so changeable and so easily moved to wrath, that many times in
the day they will quarrel with their comrades on no provocation, and be
reconciled having received no satisfaction.'

1. The settlements on the lagoons were older than the town of Venice,
which was founded in the eighth century. It was not till the thirteenth century
that the name *Venetia* was applied to the city on the Rialto as distinct from the
whole lagoon area. On the earlier seats of government and the rise of the city
on the Rialto (the Venice of to-day) to authority and independence of the
empire, see Bury, *Eastern Roman Empire*, c. x.

and Italy were governed by barbarian overlords, in nominal allegiance to the emperor at Constantinople. The deposition of Romulus Augustulus did not bring the empire to an end, for the succession fell to the eastern Caesar Zeno. But, as far as the West was concerned, the work of Diocletian was undone. From 476 to 800 there is but one emperor, who rules from Constantinople. Twelve years after Odoacer's assumption of authority, the *Ostrogoths* (East Goths) from Pannonia descended from the north-east by the Isonzo and, under their king Theodoric, mastered Rome and Italy (488–93). Theodoric, an able and intelligent sovereign, preserved as far as was possible the existing religious and social order, excluding Romans from the army, but leaving in their hands two-thirds of the land and the entire civil administration. His reign is memorable because of two men of culture and learning, who held high offices in the state, both of whom figure as important links in the transition from classical antiquity to the civilization of the Middle Ages. One of them, Cassiodorus, founded monastic settlements at his native Squillace, where he set the monks to copy manuscripts of classical authors, by which means much of ancient literature was preserved through the dark centuries that followed. The other, Boethius, a keen student of philosophy, composed a Latin version of Aristotle which proved the chief medium by which the philosopher's logic came to stimulate early mediaeval thought. He was put to death, presumably for treason, and in prison wrote his *Consolation of Philosophy*, one of the favourite works in the Middle Ages, which was translated into Anglo-Saxon by king Alfred and into English by Geoffrey Chaucer. In the middle of the ensuing century, Justinian's generals overthrew the Ostrogothic rule and united Italy, Sicily, and Africa once more under the imperial government. A part of this western reconquest was retained by the empire for several centuries. Byzantine culture influenced Sicily, Southern Italy, and, above all, the region around Ravenna; the churches of that city survive as noble examples of Byzantine art. It seemed for a brief space as though the New Rome on the Bosporus would replace the Old Rome on the Tiber as the sovereign city of the Mediterranean world.

(vi) The rule of the empire in Italy remained unchallenged only for fifteen years (553–68). Justinian was hardly in his grave when the *Lombards*, the last stream of Teutonic invaders, poured down on northern Italy.[1] A race of fighters, who cared little for agricultural pursuits, and left the old cultivators in possession of the soil, the Lombards possessed a remarkable capacity for government, and a natural instinct for making law.[2] They adopted the Latin tongue and the Christian faith, intermarried with their Italian subjects, and gave them equal rights at law. The Lombard power, from its centre at Pavia, spread, not only over Venetia and the plain that still bears their name, but also to the centre and south of Italy, where they founded the duchies of Spoletum and Beneventum. This last invasion wrecked all hopes of a reconquest of the West from Constantinople. The eastern emperors had neglected, to their cost, the defence of the Danube frontier, the way by which Alaric, Theodoric, and the Lombards passed in succession towards Italy. Henceforward the imperial authority was confined to Venice and the territories that formed the Papal states of a later day. Italy, in the seventh and eighth centuries, was partitioned between (a) the emperors, whose viceroys, styled *exarchs*, held Ravenna, Naples, a large part of the south, and Sicily; (b) the Lombards, supreme in the north, with the offshoots abovementioned in the centre and south; and (c) the Roman bishops, who had acquired, as we shall see presently, a virtual sovereignty in and around the imperial city. The Lombard invasion thus closes the story of the appropriation of the western provinces of the empire by peoples of Germanic stock.

§ 9. This brief survey of the Teutonic invasions raises the

---

1. The Lombards, whose home was on the lower Elbe, had been settled in Pannonia; in conjunction with the Avars, a Hunnish tribe, they had wiped out the Gepidae in the old province of Dacia (Hungary). By agreement the Avars occupied the lands of the Gepidae and also Pannonia, while the Lombards moved westwards to Italy. The Avars, as will be pointed out later, were a source of much trouble to the empire in the East.

2. Old Lombard law proved capable of development into a reasonable and living system. King Rotharis framed a compilation in the middle of the seventh century. The first mediaeval school of jurisprudence arose at Pavia early in the eleventh century; its teachers knew Justinian's *Institutes*, but took the Lombard law as their basis.

question: what were the effects of contact with Roman civilization upon the new masters of the western world? In the first place, we must note the deep impression which the majestic structure of the imperial system wrought on the imagination of the invaders. It would have been natural enough had the luxury, corruption, and effeminate manners of the later empire inspired contempt in its vigorous and warlike conquerors. How otherwise, we are inclined to ask, could Alaric the Visigoth have felt towards the feeble and degenerate Honorius? But it was not so; or, if contempt was felt, it was silenced by the overpowering spectacle of what Rome had achieved, and still stood for in the eyes of the world. It was the empire, not the person or the court of the emperor, that took captive the barbarian victors, as at an earlier day Greece had captivated Rome. The successor of Alaric avowed his pride at his recognition as a vassal-prince by the Roman emperor. 'It was at first', he said, 'my wish to destroy the Roman name, and erect in its place a Gothic empire, taking to myself the place and the powers of Caesar Augustus. But when experience taught me that the untamable barbarism of the Goths would not suffer them to live beneath the sway of law, and that the abolition of the institutions on which the state rested would involve the ruin of the state itself, I chose the glory of renewing and maintaining by Gothic strength the fame of Rome, desiring to go down to posterity as the restorer of that Roman power which it was beyond my power to replace. Wherefore I avoid war and strive for peace.' [1] Athanaric at Constantinople broke out with the cry, 'Without doubt the emperor is a god upon earth, and he who attacks him is guilty of his own blood.' [2]

§ 10. The establishment of the invaders within the empire was no instantaneous catastrophe, but a process spread over several successive generations. We have seen that it was part of the imperial policy to enlist earlier colonists of Teutonic stock for the defence of the frontiers against their kinsmen from without. Thus the Visigoths aided the empire to repel the Huns, as at a later date the Franks beat back the Saracens. The

1. Orosius, see Bryce, *Holy Roman Empire*, p. 19.
2. Bryce, p. 17.

naïve admiration with which they viewed the law and institutions of the empire made them eager to assimilate, within the
limits of their capacity and after their own fashion, the inheritance of civilization which persisted beneath its sway. The
historical significance of this process of Romanization cannot
easily be overestimated. It meant that the language, law, and
religion of the empire left an enduring mark on successive
groups of immigrants, who were thus educated to habits of
settled life, and trained at least in the rudiments of culture and
of Christianity, before they finally threw over their allegiance
to the Roman state. In the words of a modern historian, 'The
Roman empire was never overthrown, but took the barbarians
into itself, and so went on changing slowly till it passed
away.' [1] Of the influence of Roman jurisprudence, direct and
indirect, on the law of the Teutonic peoples, and of the transmission of such fragments of ancient learning as they were able
to absorb, we shall speak more particularly in the ensuing
chapter. The fact that a dark age supervened on the fall of the
empire, in which western Europe seemed plunged in anarchy
and ignorance, until the emergence in the eleventh century of
the political and intellectual order of the Middle Ages, must
not blind us to the value of the influences or to the real continuity between ancient and mediaeval civilization. We have to
remember that Graeco-Roman culture was in its decline when
the young races of the north first felt its contact. It was well
that it was so; had they been confronted, in the infancy of their
intellectual development, with the thought of antiquity in the
fullness of its splendour, they could hardly have profited by
its instruction. The meat would have been too strong for their
childlike minds. Above all, we must keep our eyes fixed on
the living energy with which they absorbed and utilized the
elements which they were able to digest. For nations as for
individuals, it is the fulfilment of the promise in years to come
that attests the value of the groundwork of education. The
story of the rise of the Romance languages of western and
southern Europe furnishes a simple illustration. They had their
origin, not in the literary Latin of the days of Cicero or Tacitus,

1. Creighton, *Rome*, p. 118.

but in popular Latin, the speech of the soldiers and colonists in the provinces, which developed on its own lines, and reflected the new and living experience of the common people under the later empire. Thus they assumed various distinctive yet cognate forms in different quarters of Europe, blending to a greater or less degree with the old Germanic and other native tongues, to emerge as the Rumanian, Italian, Provençal, French, Spanish, and Portuguese of mediaeval and modern use.[1] Centuries elapsed before the rude materials were shaped into instruments of expression worthy to rank beside the speech of ancient Greece and Rome; and Latin survived to the age of Dante and even beyond as the literary medium for the educated minority among the Latin races of Europe. But the fact that in the event the noblest thought and feeling of these races found utterance in the Romance languages only heightens our sense of the stimulus imparted by the speech which, in the childhood of their history, they learnt from Rome.

§ 11. The reverence felt by the Germanic tribes for Rome was strengthened by the fact of their conversion to Christianity. We have observed how the church was led to invest the empire with a peculiar sanctity as the divinely appointed instrument for the establishment of the faith. 'When Rome, the head of the world, shall have fallen,' wrote Lactantius in the third century, 'who can doubt that the end is come of human things, aye, of the earth itself? She, she alone, is the state by which all things are upheld even until now.' [2] Thus there grew up in the minds of the newly converted colonists the idea of the empire as a divinely sanctioned order, to which, in right if not in fact, all nations and governments under heaven owed allegiance. The Roman empire came to be regarded, not merely as sacred,

1. There are ten Romance languages: 1. Rumanian; 2. Dalmatian (extinct in the nineteenth century); 3. Sardinian; 4. Italian; 5. Raeto-Romanic; 6. French (*Langue d'Oil*); 7. Provençal (*Langue d'Oc*); 8. Spanish; 9. Portuguese; 10, Catalan. Sardinian is the most archaic. The first three bear little trace of German admixture (see the article 'Romance Languages' in *Encyc. Brit.*, vol. xxiii). These languages arose on a subsoil of vigorous, national life. Punic was still spoken in Africa in Augustine's time; he urges his clergy to learn it. In the Basque speech and the Breton we have survivals of the pre-Roman native languages.

2. Bryce, p. 21.

but as eternal and universal. The deposition of the emperor at Ravenna by Odoacer in no way impaired its being. The Augustus who ruled in the West had fallen, but the empire remained. Two centuries later the documents cited by Bede are dated by the regnal years of the emperors at Constantinople. The survival of the imperial tradition in the West was due, in large measure, to the church, which bore on its structure and policy the impress of the Roman mind. It kept alive, consciously and of set purpose, the memory of the Roman name. Alone of Roman institutions it had weathered intact the storms of Teutonic invasion. Thus it was that, in the hour of its unchallenged sovereignty, it reaffirmed its loyalty to the principle of the Roman empire, as the sole rightful authority in the secular government of mankind. Just as the church, in the belief of mediaeval Europe, was by right the one catholic (universal) church, despite the actual severance of the Latin Christians in the West from the Greek Christians in the East, so was it also with the empire. The outcome of this conviction was the magnificent conception of the divine scheme of government which found its loftiest expression in the works of Dante. In that conception God's government of the universe rests on the principle of unity, for government to be good must be government by one, and God is one. This principle of unity operates in relation to man's earthly discipline through two sovereign powers, vicegerents of God upon earth for man's salvation, and supreme respectively in things spiritual and in things secular, the one catholic church under the pope, and the one catholic monarchy under the emperor.[1]

§ 12. A realization of the force of this conviction, which was shaping itself gradually in the mind of western Christendom during the epoch of transition from antiquity to the Middle Ages, is essential to an understanding, not merely of the theory,

1. See Dante, *de Monarchia*, iii. 16, and *Purgatorio*, cantos 32, 33. To speak of the distinction as one between church and state is misleading; for the thought of church and state as different societies is modern, and arose first at the time of the Reformation conflict. If any mediaeval institution answers to the modern conception of the state as a self-sufficient society, it is the church, rather than the empire. The Middle Ages regarded the human race as a single society, administered by two hierarchies of rulers, the ecclesiastical and the temporal. The distinction is one of offices, functions, and jurisdiction.

but of the facts, of history. The lack of an effective imperial authority in the West was felt as a derogation from the rightful order of social government. This belief, working in close conjunction with the exigences of the practical situation, led at length to one of the most memorable events in the history of western Christendom. On Christmas Day, 800, a German king was crowned in St Peter's church at Rome by pope Leo III as emperor of the Holy Roman empire. To appreciate the significance of this act, we must resume the history of the west from the point we reached when we spoke of the last Lombard invasion of Italy in the sixth century. We saw then that the peninsula was partitioned between three powers, the eastern emperor, the Lombards, and the papacy. The temporal power of the popes had been firmly established in central Italy at the close of the sixth century by Gregory I, the Great (590–604). Trained in diplomacy and in the study of the civil law – he had been prefect of the city and papal envoy at Constantinople – he united the austerity of a monk with high gifts of statesmanship and an unbending strength of will. Personal humility, with him as so often with the great holders of the papacy, went hand in hand with pride of office. He reformed the western church, organizing monastic discipline in accordance with the rule of St Benedict, whose life he wrote, fixing authoritatively, in his manual on pastoral rule, the duties of the bishops, directing the conversion of the Anglo-Saxons in Britain through Augustine, enforcing the celibacy of the clergy and instituting a uniform type of worship and of music in the church. Gregory was a man of action rather than a thinker: we see in him an example of the Roman mind untouched by Hellenism. He took his theology from Augustine of Hippo, interpreting his teaching, e.g. on the atonement, in a narrow forensic spirit, and was frankly hostile to pagan literature and learning.[1] But in the field of public affairs, his activity was

1. See c. xi, § 3, *note* 2. Gregory is of great importance in the history of the canon law. He appropriated and defined the ecclesiastical theory of law, society, and government, under the influence of the early Fathers and of the civil law of Rome. He was the first to make fully explicit the doctrine of the divine right of the secular prince. See Carlyle, *Mediaeval Political Theory in the West*, vol. i, Parts III and IV.

untiring and brilliantly successful. The papal court was now recognized as the supreme ecclesiastical tribunal for Latin Christendom. The authority of Rome made itself felt throughout Gaul, Britain, Spain, and Africa. The pope constantly intervened at the Byzantine court. His influence with queen Brunhilda laid the foundations of the alliance between the papacy and the orthodox Franks. In Italy, he played the part which by right belonged to the imperial exarch; alike in policy and in war he figured as the defender of the Italian Catholics against the Arian Lombards. Both the secular and the ecclesiastical history of the next two centuries moved on the lines thus laid down by Gregory. Henceforward the bishop of Rome was not merely the effective spiritual head of Latin Christendom, but a secular Italian potentate, who utilized the patrimony of St Peter, i.e. the territorial possessions and the wealth of the Roman church, as the champion at once of Italian independence and of the orthodox faith. 'The independence of the popes was struck like a spark between the rival temporal powers that divided Italy.'[1] The real enemy was the Lombard, who menaced the papal provinces at once from the north and from the south. The natural protector of Italy was the emperor, but the government at Constantinople had its hands full with the wars against the Saracens, and its policy of iconoclasm (suppression of images) accentuated the religious cleavage that had long parted the East from Rome.[2] In 751 the exarchate in Italy fell before the Lombards. The popes, unable to resist without support, turned for assistance to the Franks. The Franks were orthodox, and masters of a mighty dominion north of the Alps. They had saved Christendom from the Saracens, who, after conquering Spain from the Visigoths (711–13), passed the Pyrenees and overran southern Gaul, to be crushed by the Franks under Charles Martel at Poitiers in 732. All Gaul was

1. Bury, *Later Roman Empire*, ii. 156. The power of the papacy is to be explained, not primarily as due to the individual genius of the popes, who were for the most part men of ordinary ability, but to the practical sagacity of Roman Christianity.

2. Gregory III, elected in 731, was the last pope whose appointment was referred for sanction to the emperor. The long struggle culminated in the schism of 1055. But it was continuous from the time of Gregory I. On the Iconoclast schism, which broke out in 725, see below, § 19.

now in Frankish hands. Charles Martel had indeed turned a
deaf ear to the papal appeals for help; but his son Pepin, who
had succeeded him in 740 as mayor of the palace to the
fainéant Merovingian kings, was willing enough to listen, when,
in the year after the Lombard conquest of Ravenna, the pope
anointed him king of the Franks in place of Childeric, and proclaimed him patrician of Rome (751–2).[1] Four years later,
Pepin crossed the Alps, overthrew the Lombards in northern
Italy, and conferred Ravenna and the surrounding territory on
the papacy (756). The pope was now in the position of unquestioned head of the imperial legacy in Italy. In 773 Pepin's
son, Charles the Great (Charlemagne) incorporated Lombardy
in the Frankish kingdom.[2] In 781 pope Hadrian I formally
severed the tie of allegiance to the emperor of Constantinople.
It was but the natural, though unexpected, issue, when on
Christmas Day, 800, Charles, who had once more entered Italy
to protect pope Leo III from his rivals in the church, was
crowned at Rome as the successor of Augustus. The act was
technically unconstitutional; for, despite the pretence of election by the Roman senate, which did not exist, and by the
Roman army and people, who were not consulted, the pope
had no right to institute an emperor. Such justification as he
might claim was purely practical, on the ground that for two
centuries the imperial idea in Italy had been represented and
preserved by the popes.[3] They, and not the exarchs sent from

1. Charles Martel had reformed the Frankish church on Roman lines and
had supported St Boniface (Winfrid, born at Crediton, *c.* 680) in his devoted
missionary labours in pagan Germany. It was Boniface who, with the full
assent of pope Zacharias, crowned Pepin king of the Franks. The mayor (*major*
= chief) of the palace was the chief minister; under the later Merovingians he
exercised all the authority of the king. Pepin had asked the pope whether it
were well that one man should have the name of king, while another had the
power. The office of patrician of the Romans was equivalent to a protectorate.
It was at this time, and probably to express a real compact between Pepin and
the papacy, that the Donation of Constantine was forged.

2. Charles the Great (born *c.* 742) reigned from 768 to 814. He also conquered the Saxons up to the Elbe (772–804), fought the Avars (788–96), and
in 811 incorporated the north-east of Spain in his empire, which thus stretched
from the Atlantic to the Elbe, Bohemia, and the Adriatic, and from Barcelona
to the North Sea. He was allied with the Abbasid Caliphs of Baghdad against
the Ummayyads in Spain and the Byzantine empire.

3. The act furnished a historic basis for the papalist claim, put forward in

Constantinople, had really stood for Rome. That the new emperor was a Germanic chieftain, whose forefathers of the age of Augustus had barely heard the name of Rome, was no bar to his eligibility; the empire had never rested on a hereditary basis, nor was it, either in principle or in practice, restricted by any limit of nationality. Diocletian had been an Illyrian and born a slave; as early as the second century the Spanish provincial Trajan had been called to the imperial throne. The grave fact that had to be faced was the presence of an emperor at Constantinople. Charles's coronation stood in glaring contradiction to the doctrine, universally accepted, of the unity and indivisibility of the empire. This difficulty of principle was overcome by the claim that the sovereign at Constantinople at this date, Irene, was a woman and a usurper, and that the empire was therefore vacant of a ruler.[1] In fact, Charles and his successors left no stone unturned to secure from the emperors at Constantinople the recognition of their title. This was first granted in 812, though with considerable reluctance; and from this time onwards there is a justification for speaking of two empires, an eastern and a western.[2] Latin Christendom looked henceforward upon the Frankish ruler at Aachen, not upon the emperor at Constantinople, as the secular vicegerent of God on earth. The empire, thus estab-

---

the eleventh century, that the imperial jurisdiction was subject to that of the pope. In fact, Charles had no intention of playing a subordinate part to the papacy. Even in matters of doctrine he claimed to rule the western church. In his eyes, his empire was the City of God, and he himself the divinely appointed head of Christians upon earth. The theocratic idea is dominant; Alcuin speaks of him as ruling the kingdom of eternal peace founded by the blood of Christ. See *Camb. Med. Hist.*, vol. ii, c. xix. Charles, though not a scholar, knew both Greek and Latin, was a diligent student of Augustine, and had the *de Civitate Dei* read to him at meals. The act of coronation seems to have come to Charles as a surprise, and the annoyance he felt was probably sincere; he judged the act premature.

1. On this section, see Bury, *Later Roman Empire*, vol. ii, c. xi. Charles was regarded as the successor, not of Romulus Augustulus, the last emperor in the West (deposed in 476), but of Constantine VI, who had been deposed by the empress Irene in 797. The former alternative would have implied that the popes, in recognizing the emperors in the East, had for two centuries given allegiance to usurpers.

2. Bury, *Later Roman Empire*, ii. 320 *note*, quotes the words '*orientale et occidentale imperium*' used first by Charles in a letter to the emperor Michael I.

lished in the West in the person of Charles the Great, survived, through the long period of its struggle against the rival power of the papacy in the eleventh, twelfth, and thirteenth centuries, through the storms of the Reformation conflict, and even of the French Revolution, till, long after it had ceased, in Voltaire's phrase, to be either Holy or Roman or an empire, it was finally extinguished by the strong hand of Napoleon in the first years of the nineteenth century.

IV. THE ROMAN, THE SLAV, AND THE SARACEN

§ 13. The Roman empire endured in the East with unbroken continuity until the capture of Constantinople by the Turks in 1453. From its final partition on the death of Theodosius (395) until the last decline set in during the eleventh century, it was the foremost military and naval power in the Mediterranean, the medium of commercial intercourse between East and West, and the guardian of the speech and civilization of ancient Greece. Its capital, the 'New Rome' of Constantine, was the greatest city of the world. 'As in his daily prayers,' wrote Gibbon, 'the Mussulman of Fez or Delhi still turns his face towards the temple of Mecca, the historian's eye will always be fixed on the city of Constantinople.' [1] Though its subjects belonged to many races, Hellenes and Egyptians, Syrians and Armenians, Slavs and Bulgars, parted one from the other by wide differences of speech, manners, and national sympathies, and imperilling at every crisis its political and religious unity, the imperial government preserved throughout the tradition of its Roman origin. The sovereign of the empire was the Roman *Augustus*, and its peoples were called *Romaioi*.[2] Latin remained the official language until the sixth century, when it gave way to Greek. Justinian's *Corpus juris* was the last great utterance of the Latin tongue in the East.[3] To the end, the

1. Gibbon, c. 48.

2. See Bury, *Later Roman Empire*, vol. ii, pp. 170–4. A *Hellene* came to mean a non-Christian. The Latin word *paganus* (= villager), which had this meaning in the West, was used in the East in Greek form (*paganikos*) to mean 'secular' as opposed to 'sacred', e.g. of dress.

3. The century from Justinian to Heraclius (550–650) saw the transition from a Roman to a Hellenized empire in the East.

spirit of the government was entirely faithful to the model of ancient Rome; both in its conservatism, degenerating at times into a blind adherence to tradition, at times achieving a wise adjustment to the changing requirements of the hour and place, and in its concentration on the age-long mission of Rome to defend the frontiers against enemies from without, thus preserving a civilization whose contents it was powerless to enrich. Epochs of disintegration and paralysis alternated for centuries with epochs of recovery and vigour.[1] On the shores of the Bosporus, Rome was still Rome, in its impotence as in its strength; though we look in vain for creative energy of thought or action among her peoples, she toiled unceasingly at her historic labour; and a thousand years elapsed ere the last embers of the Roman spirit were quenched in the successors of Augustus.

§ 14. It was in the defence of Christianity and Hellenism against invasion that the efficiency of the empire was most conspicuous. The border forts were repaired and extended by Justinian in the sixth century, and the ensuing epoch saw the development, in the face of the Saracen menace, of an army and navy, trained in the art of war to a pitch hitherto unequalled in history. By scientific mastery of the problem of defence the empire saved civilization. Its task was one of tremendous difficulty. If the eastern provinces were harder to conquer, and furnished a more populous and warlike recruiting-ground than those of the West, their assailants were more formidable. The struggle had to be carried on simultaneously on several fronts. We will consider briefly the historical significance, first, of the wars with the peoples of the north, who attacked the Danubian provinces, and, secondly, of those with the Persians and the Saracens in the east and the south.

(i) The sixth and seventh centuries were the era of expansion of the *Slavs*, who, at their close, were securely established over the huge tract of country east of the Elbe and the Adriatic,

---

1. Disintegration, after Justinian (in the late sixth century), after Heraclius (in the late seventh and early eighth centuries), after Leo III, the Isaurian (from the close of the eighth century). These three emperors had successively restored the efficiency of the empire.

from the southern shore of the Baltic to the Peloponnese.[1] In the Danubian region their fortunes were closely associated with the *Avars*, a nomadic people from the steppe-land, akin to the Huns, in whose wake they spread like a blighting tempest over eastern Europe, and founded an imposing, though short-lived, Tartar kingdom from Hungary to the Crimea. The Avars conquered the Slavs, and transplanted them in vast numbers to guard their western borders. These Slav colonists formed a solid bulwark, not only for their Avar lords against the Teutons, but for the Teutons against the Avars.[2] It was the doom of the Slavs to be 'slaves', to toil and fight at the bidding of Teutonic or Tartar conquerors. In temper passive and unwarlike, though excellent in defensive fighting under good leadership, they made no conquests, and formed no states on their own initiative; but lent themselves readily to organization, political and military, at the hands of alien powers. 'As a people who for immemorial ages were deprived of justice and politically broken, the Slavs longed only for an ordered legal state. ... The appeal to law and not to the sword is the basis of Old Slavonic thought and aspiration.' [3] But the Slav avenged himself nobly on his oppressors.[4] Like the Greeks, in the age of Roman domination, he gave them civilization. Two characteristics of the Slavonic peoples were already manifest, the inability to form a compact political union, save under foreign impulse, and the capacity to impress their speech and customs on the conquerors who enslaved them. They showed a genius for peaceful penetration. Avars, Bulgars, and Russians alike were

1. On the Slavs, see Peisker in *Camb. Med. Hist.*, ii, c. xiv. Their home was in the marshes of Polesie, in the middle Dnieper basin, now inhabited by the White Russians. The Slavs were a branch of the Indo-European family, blue-eyed and fair. They spread, in pre-historic times, westwards to the Carpathians and the Vistula, where they marched with the Germans. The later formation of the northern Slav states was due to German overlordship, of the southern to that of the Avars. The native Slav had little capacity for political construction.

2. 'The misery of the Slavs was the salvation of the West. The energy of the Altaians' (i.e. the Tartars) 'was exhausted in eastern Europe, and Germany and France behind the Slavic breakwater were able freely to develop their civilization' (Peisker, *loc. cit.*, p. 434).

3. Peisker, *loc. cit.*, p. 457.

4. Bury, *Later Roman Empire*, vol. ii, p. 335, compares the Slavs in this respect with the Greeks (see, generally, vol. ii, book v, cc. vii and xi).

absorbed by Slavonic culture. The Avar kingdom indeed vanished as swiftly as it arose. Weakened by the constant struggle
with the empire in the East, it received its final blow at the
hand of Charles the Great. But the Slavs remained, both within
and without the empire. During the sixth century they swept
in masses over the Balkan peninsula; then, or not long afterwards, they penetrated as far south as the Peloponnese, merging
their civilization in the Hellenic. In the ninth century these
Hellenized Slavs became Christians; and bishops, at Lacedaemon (Sparta) and other places, were appointed for their
spiritual direction. Under Heraclius (610–41), Slavs formed
the majority of the population in the Balkan provinces; two
centuries later, a solid block of Slavonic communities stretched
from the mouth of the Elbe to the shores of the Adriatic. It
looked for a moment as though central and eastern Europe lay
at their mercy.[1] The eastward advance of Charles the Great
and his successors on the one side, and, on the other, the
Magyar settlement of Hungary, and the victories of the Eastern
emperors over the Bulgars, determined the event otherwise.
But the seeds of the Slavonic states, Bohemian, Croatian,
Slovene, Serb, which loom so large in the politics of modern
Europe, were already planted.[2] An analogous process can be
traced, farther east, in the early history of Bulgaria and Russia.
The *Bulgars*, a non-Aryan Tartar tribe, akin to the Huns and the
Finns, had their home in southern Russia. A branch, pressing
south-westwards, appeared by the Danube mouth in the fifth
century, and two hundred years later had established themselves to the south of the river in the province of Moesia. There
they ruled over the earlier Slav settlers, and, as we have noted,
absorbed their manners and their language. Through the ninth
century they waged fierce wars with the eastern emperors,

1. Bury, *Eastern Roman Empire*, pp. 374, 375.
2. 'The Slav nations of to-day are therefore not original, but a gradual
crystallization since the sixth century into linguistic units, out of the peoples
transplanted by the Avars – a process already completed by the tenth century'
(Peisker, *Camb. Med. Hist.*, ii. 437). Long after the fall of the Avar kingdom,
shepherd-lords of Avar stock formed the nobility in Slav communities. They
were gradually absorbed, as were the Bulgars, in the Slav peasantry. The
Bulgarian Slavs took over the name of their former masters.

pressing up to the walls of Constantinople. Greek captives were the instrument of their conversion to Christianity; in 863–5 king Boris, despite popular opposition, renounced heathenism for the gospel. A century later, the Bulgarian kingdom fell before the imperial arms. Besides the Slavonic tribes, both within and without the frontiers, and the Bulgars, the imperial government was in constant contact, both commercial and diplomatic, with the dwellers in the lands north of the Euxine sea. Of these peoples, many in number, and often formidable – Christian *Goths* in the Crimea; 'Inner' Bulgarians on the Sea of Azov; 'Outer' Bulgarians on the Volga; the Turkish Khazars, a powerful tribe dwelling between the Caucasus and the Don, who perpetrated the strange anomaly of embracing Judaism some time about the ninth century; the Magyars, a Finnish tribe, akin to the Huns, the Avars, and the Bulgars, who moved westwards at the same epoch and settled permanently in the plain of Hungary; and the Rumanians, probably Avars and Bulgars who had become Romanized – we must content ourselves with a bare mention. But more attention is due to the people who were destined to become the leading champions of Slavonic civilization. The Rûs or Russians were not Slavs by race, but Scandinavian invaders from Sweden, who founded Novgorod, the Holmgard of the Icelandic Saga, and subjugated the surrounding Slavs. They ruled as a military aristocracy, monopolizing the trade, which they carried southwards down the Dneiper and the Volga. Already at the dawn of their history, the guiding-star of Russian policy was fixed, to secure commercial access to the sea. Prior to the ninth century, their relations with Constantinople were mainly commercial; by that date the Russian kingdom had grown into a powerful state, and counted more and more in the political system of eastern Europe. Like the Bulgarians, the Scandinavian Russians became completely Slavonized; while in the eleventh century they acquired Christianity and letters from the eastern empire. The Russian script is the old uncial (capital) script of Greece. Russian mercenaries were enlisted in the imperial guards, and the Russian sovereigns adopted the Roman style of *Caesar* (Tsar).[1]

1. The title of Tsar and the device of the double eagle were adopted by Ivan III, who married the Byzantine Sophia Palaeologus in 1472.

§ 15. (ii) The conflicts on the European frontier, prolonged until the ninth century, resulted in the implanting of Christianity and culture among peoples destined to become members of the comity of European nations. In Asia and Africa, on the other hand, the empire was faced by powers of alien religion and race, who, far from possessing either the ability or the desire to fuse with western civilization, were its bitterest and most uncompromising foes. From the third to the seventh centuries the empire had been engaged in constant warfare, broken by longer or shorter intervals of peace, with the Persians, whose kingdom had arisen in the Euphrates-Tigris valley on the ruins of that of Parthia, and who were finally crushed in a series of campaigns by the emperor Heraclius between 622 and 628. Hardly had Heraclius secured his triumph when a far more terrible antagonist appeared on the scene. The very next year saw the first brush between the Roman outposts and the Moslem Semites, by the shores of the Dead Sea. In 632 Mohammed died at Mecca, having rescued the nomadic Arabs from religious indifference and social decline, and for the first time in history secured, on the foundation of a monotheistic faith, the political unity of Arabia.[1] We are not called upon to

1. On Mohammed (*Muhammad*) see Bevan in *Camb. Med. Hist.*, vol. ii, c. x, and Margoliouth's *Life* in the *Heroes of the Nations* Series; on the expansion of Islam, see Becker in *Camb. Med. Hist.*, vol. ii, cc. xi, xii. Islam means 'surrender'; *Muslim* (Moslem), from the same verb, means 'one who surrenders himself', with reference, probably, to his acceptance of the faith. How an illiterate Arab, aided by a shrewd business head and a rich widow's fortune, was converted in mature life to the consciousness of a religious vocation, preached a faith that ethically was far in advance of the Arab code, became the political leader of Arabia, founded a world-religion, and inspired his followers with a fiery zeal that enabled them in the event to conquer half the Roman empire and many lands beyond it, is still an unsolved problem. Nöldeke, a great Oriental scholar, gave it up in despair. Circumstances, such as the prevalent unrest in Arabia and the presence of vague national aspirations, conditioned the process, forcing Mohammed to become a political ruler, outside his original purpose. In his teaching, again, he borrowed from Jewish and Christian sources, accepting the Old Testament and holding Christ to be a human prophet with a divine mission. But this hardly accounts for his ethical and religious doctrine. The personality of the man was the determining factor throughout. He had rare gifts of insight into human character and of skill in managing men; his sincerity is beyond dispute; he was without fanaticism and without fraud. It must be remembered that what with us would be literary dishonesty passed among the Arabs as a perfectly legitimate device.

dwell on the character of the religion of Islam, for it has played no part in the shaping of our western civilization.[1] Its role throughout mediaeval and modern times has been that of an alien culture, which has influenced western society only indirectly, by provoking combinations of European peoples to resist its aggression.[2] The century that followed the prophet's death was a critical epoch in the annals of civilization. Alike in West and East, the forces of Islam came within an ace of mastering the Mediterranean world. Had they triumphed, the issue would have been, not compromise or fusion, but the extermination of the Christian order of society.[3] It is the eternal merit of the empire that it bore the brunt of the onset, and, though it emerged from the struggle maimed and exhausted, saved Christian civilization from submersion. When Mohammed died, Islam was still restricted to Arabia. Ten years later, the Saracen warriors had overrun Syria, Mesopotamia, and Egypt. The Persian kingdom, weakened by Heraclius' victories, fell an easy victim to their onset. Asia Minor suffered its first invasion in 651, Constantinople its first siege from 674 to 677. The Saracens had created a navy, and fought the empire on both elements. All northern Africa had fallen to them by the end of the century, and the chequered history of Carthage (Punic, Roman, Christian, and Vandal) reached its final close (698). From Africa the conquerors crossed to Spain, overthrew the Gothic kingdom, and established the rule of the emirs at

1. On Arab learning in the Middle Ages, see below, c. xi, § 9. Philosophy was always an exotic among the Mohammedans.

2. Thus, in later days, the Austro-Hungarian monarchy of the Hapsburgs, a strange and thoroughly artificial conjunction of peoples, came into being from the common need of union for defence against the Turks.

3. It is an error to suppose that the Moslems used the sword primarily as an instrument for propagating their religion. It was rather a weapon of political sovereignty. The conversion of non-Arabian subjects was not fostered; they ceased to pay taxes on embracing Islam. Islam as a religion was not intolerant (as late as the seventeenth century we read of Quakeress preachers, expelled from the Puritan colony of Massachusetts, taking refuge at Constantinople under the very eye of the Grand Turk). Becker, *Camb. Med. Hist.*, loc. cit., writes: 'hunger and avarice, not religion, are the impelling forces, but religion supplies the essential unity and central power'. The East found in Islam the means of liberation from the yoke of western culture, dominant since the conquests of Alexander. On the other hand, the West now swung free of Oriental influence, and resumed her age-long hostility.

Cordova.¹ Pouring by the passes of the Pyrenees into Gaul, they swept northwards over the fair lands of Languedoc and Aquitaine to the valley of the Loire. Here, between Poitiers and Tours, they met their match; Charles Martel, the mayor of the palace under the Merovingian kings, and his Franks, saved the West by a decisive victory (732). But in the East the struggle raged with fury for three centuries. The Saracen power was at its zenith when Leo III (the Isaurian), the contemporary of Charles Martel, opened his reign by repelling their second onslaught on Constantinople (717–18).² Despite the Bulgarian wars in Thrace and the internal conflicts stirred by the iconoclastic policy of the crown, Islam was kept at bay during the eighth and ninth centuries. Crete and Sicily were lost to the empire; but Greece and the Balkans, the waters of the Aegean, and the greater part of Asia Minor were firmly held. The fall of the Ummayyad caliphs in 750, and their replacement at Baghdad by the Abbasids, led to a cleavage among the Saracen powers that weakened their attacks.³ The emirs of Cordova kept Spain for the Ummayyads. But it was not till the tenth century that the Saracen power ceased to be a formidable menace to the eastern empire.

§ 16. If we pause for a moment to take stock of the Mediterranean world in the course of the ninth century, the picture that it presents is at once simple and instructive.⁴ We find in existence four great powers, two in the West and two in the East. In the West were the Christian empire of the successors of Charles the Great, and the Mohammedan kingdom of the Ummayyad emirs of Cordova. The boundary line between them, in northern Spain, marks the southern limit of mediaeval

1. The Caliphs viewed the conquest of Spain with some mistrust; but the African Berbers had to be employed in war. The Arabs showed signal capacity in enlisting this wild and warlike race on their side; the Romans had never wholly succeeded in taming the Berbers.

2. This successful resistance was more decisive in world-history than the victory of Poitiers. Had Constantinople fallen, the whole future of the East would have been transformed.

3. The triumph of the Abbasids meant that of Persian over Arab, of religion over political (Arabian) nationalism: it was one more step in the recovery of the old tradition by the East.

4. See Bury, *Later Roman Empire*. Book VI, cc. iv, xii.

feudalism. In the East were the Christian empire, ruled from Constantinople, and the Abbasid caliphate of Baghdad. The force of political gravity tended to bring together in alliance the eastern empire and the Spanish Mohammedans on the one hand, the western empire and the Abbasids on the other. Beyond the confines of the two Christian powers lay two secondary and independent kingdoms, that of the Anglo-Saxons in Britain, in close contact with the western empire, and that of the Bulgarians in northern Thrace, in close contact with the empire of the East. In the centre of the Mediterranean area, southern Italy and Sicily formed, as in the old days when Greek fought Carthaginian, the scene of constant and uncertain conflict. While northern and central Italy were, in political and ecclesiastical sympathies, mainly Latin; southern Italy and Sicily were still, as in classical antiquity, mainly Greek. History was repeating itself; the eastern empire with its Greek civilization was once more contending for Sicily against the Semites. We have seen that in the ninth century the Arabs succeeded in accomplishing, what Carthage never quite achieved, the conquest of the entire island (827–902).[1] But ere long the analogy vindicated its claim; as Rome had aforetime intervened against Carthage, so in the eleventh century the Arab power was flung back from Sicily by the Normans. Meanwhile, a host of refugees from the iconoclastic persecution had come to strengthen Greek influence in southern Italy. There and in Sicily the seeds were sown of the strange blend of races – Greek, Latin, Lombard, Saracen, and Norman – which has made the dwellers in these regions so distinctive in temperament and character among the peoples of southern Europe at the present day.[2]

V. THE EMPIRE IN THE EAST

§ 17. The imperial administration in the East followed the lines laid down by Diocletian. It was a military autocracy, nor

1. They tried in vain to win a foothold in Italy: they took Bari in 841, Ostia in 846, appearing for a moment, but only for a moment, before the walls of Rome. They were driven out of Sicily by the Normans (1061–91).

2. It is interesting to note that southern Italy and Sicily have in these last

was the principle of despotism ever seriously challenged. Political liberty was an idea that had no meaning for the peoples of the eastern provinces. The conspiracies that constantly menaced the Byzantine sovereigns were directed against their persons, and not against the character of the government. The official aristocracy were often a serious danger to the emperor's life and throne. In theory he was elected by the senate, which at Constantinople included the chief administrative officers and exercised far greater power than its Roman counterpart, and afterwards acclaimed by the people, in accordance with the historic maxim of the Roman state. At the head of the huge bureaucracy were a group of prefects (praetorian, of the east, of the city, etc.), who were immediately responsible to the emperor. In the reign of Justinian (527–65), the empire comprised the Balkan Peninsula, Thrace, the islands, Asia Minor, Syria, Egypt, Italy and Sicily, Africa, and some outlying possessions in Spain. Justinian initiated a policy of reorganization which resulted, in the seventh and eighth centuries, in the division of what then remained into military districts, entitled exarchates and *strategiai*.[1] The weakness of the government lay

days given birth to a revival of metaphysics, of which the most illustrious representative is Signor Benedetto Croce.

1. Justinian (born c. 482) was a Macedonian peasant of Latin race, whose uncle, Justin, was elevated to the purple: the nephew was virtual ruler during Justin's reign (518–27), and succeeded him for thirty-eight years. He was a thorough autocrat, with astonishing energy for administrative work, a strong sense of his duty as guardian of law and order, known to his courtiers as 'the emperor who never sleeps', though prone to irresolution, jealous, and inordinately vain. The empress Theodora, who was gifted with a strong intelligence and an imperious will, had unbounded influence; after her death, Justinian's policy was vacillating and ineffective. He died leaving the empire to face the Eastern peril in a state of financial exhaustion. His interest in theology was genuine; he regarded himself as the representative alike of the empire and of the Christian faith, and strove diligently to live up to the conception. He knew that he was a symbol, and loved all symbols that were visible expressions of religion and of the imperial office; e.g. his church of Santa Sophia, and the *Corpus* of Roman law. He reconquered Africa and Italy with the aid of able generals and a mercenary army, which included Huns, Vandals, Slavs, Persians, and Arabs, controlled the papacy with a firm hand, and reorganized the civil and military administration. Devoid of genius, Justinian, like Louis XIV of France, is one of the most impressive of the second-rank rulers in history. Despite the pressing dangers from the Avars on the Danube and the Persians in the Middle East, Justinian's eyes were rather fixed upon the West, in his desire to conquer Italy and recover the sovereignty of ancient

in oppressive taxation and in the intolerable burden of bureau-cracy. Strictures on its defective economy must be modified by the reminder that the commerce and finance of the Mediter-ranean world was for centuries directed from Constantinople, the London of the time. The coinage of the eastern emperors was current over all Europe throughout the Middle Ages. The strength of the empire rested on its military efficiency, its diplomacy, and its jurisprudence. Of the first we have already spoken. In diplomacy, the art of handling the barbarians was brought to a high level of efficiency.[1] Their mutual rivalries were utilized for the advantage of the empire, a policy of sub-sidies was regularized, and the missionary activities of the church were systematically organized as an instrument of poli-tical control. Native manners and customs were studied with remarkable intelligence, and the foreign policy of the imperial government was based on admirably directed bureaux of infor-mation. The reports of the Venetian ambassadors of a later age, so valuable alike to their own government at the time and as materials for the historian of to-day, were modelled on those of the agents of the eastern empire.

§ 18. The name of Justinian is ever memorable in the annals of Roman law. By his codification he shaped it into the final form, freed in Dante's phrase 'from the excessive and the irrelevant', in which it passed to the nations of the modern world.[2] Gathering up the threads of its history from the point reached in an earlier chapter, we find that, from the time of Diocletian onwards, the right of creating new law was con-centrated exclusively in the hands of the emperor. 'Since at the present day', we read in Justinian's *Codex*, 'the power of

Rome in the Western Mediterranean, and in his projects for a religious con-cordat with the Papacy. Theodora, with surer political insight, realized the urgency of the Eastern problem and, in the interests of national unity, favoured religious toleration for the Hellenic subjects of the empire, whose theological sympathies, then as later, were strongly anti-Roman. She fully merits the proud place assigned to her in the mosaic of the apse of S. Vitale at Ravenna, where she fronts Justinian as an equal in regal majesty.

1. The system can be studied at its best under Justinian. Converted native chiefs were ruled from Constantinople through the local episcopate.

2. '*d'entro le leggi trassi il troppo e il vano*', *Par.*, vi. 12. Justinian in this canto speaks as the type of the Roman empire, whose mission, not of war, but of law and peace, was crowned by his legislation.

enacting laws is reserved to the emperor alone, his authority alone must be deemed fit to interpret the laws.'[1] All authoritative *responsa* or opinions on points of law emanated from him, in consultation with his judicial advisers, and all additions to the law took the form of imperial 'constitutions'. These were styled 'laws' (*leges*) in distinction from the older law and the works of earlier jurists, which were entitled *jus*. Under Constantine and his successors, the trend of the imperial constitutions was towards humanizing the existing law in accordance with the principles of natural right, especially in regard to the family and to testamentary successions. In certain fields, such as the law of marriage, the voice of Christianity had made itself heard.[2] We must remember, too, that the ecclesiastical courts, presided over by the bishop, exercised concurrent jurisdiction with the civil tribunals. The instrument of the *formula*, the method by which the praetors had practised what Gibbon describes as 'the art of respecting the name, and eluding the efficacy, of the laws', had now vanished, and, with it, the reference to private *judices*, and the historic distinction of the hearing *in jure* and that *in judice*. On the other hand, the opinions of the jurists of the second and third centuries received imperial recognition as an authoritative body of legal tradition. The law of Citations of Valentinian III (426) had enacted that the opinions of the five great masters, Gaius, Ulpian, Paul, Papinian, and Modestinus, and of the authorities cited by them, should, when unanimous, be unconditionally binding on the

1. *Codex* i. 14, 12, § 3, 'si enim in praesenti leges condere soli imperatori concessum est, et leges interpretari solum dignum imperio esse oportet'.
2. The influence of Christianity on Roman law, however, was not so extensive as has been supposed. An example is furnished by Constantine's repeal of the Augustan *lex Papia-Poppaea* which imposed heavy penalties on celibacy. Divorce, so easy under Roman law, was naturally restricted under Christian influence. The Christian empire prohibited the exposure of infants, and gave facilities for the manumission of slaves in church, in presence of clergy. Again, 'il n'y a à Rome que des mères naturelles, il n'y a que des pères légitimes. La paternité naturelle n'existe pas.' (Girard, *Manuel* II, 3, § 3.) Christian law altered this in both directions. Legitimatization of children became much easier. Bloody laws against heretics already appear in the fifth-century Theodosian code. The claims of the clergy to exemption from secular jurisdiction, and to certain rights or intervention in secular matters, were recognized by the later empire, and especially by Justinian.

judge; while, in cases where they were at variance, the court should decide in accordance with the majority, the voice of Papinian to prevail when the number of opinions on either side was equal. Thus Roman jurisprudence entered upon an epoch of scholasticism. The dead hand of the past blighted the living growth of the law. Its utterance was determined by counting the silent votes of the classical authorities. All that remained to the jurists of the present was to round off and codify the inheritance of antiquity.[1] From the third century onwards appeared numerous compilations of the law, initiated by private scholars or under imperial direction, especially in the East, where a famous law school flourished at Beirut; the most celebrated of these, the code of Theodosius, formed one of the chief sources for Justinian's codification.[2] The code of Justinian, prepared by two commissions of lawyers under the direction of his minister, Tribonian, appointed by the emperor, was published at intervals between the years 529 and 534. To describe its contents here is impracticable, for it would involve a survey of the whole domain of Roman law; and the task has been accomplished, where all can read it, in the famous forty-fourth chapter of Gibbon's history. Its aim was to embody, in methodical arrangement, all that was still relevant in the unwieldy mass that had accumulated during a thousand years. The spirit that informed it was, as we should expect, that of strict conservatism; the framers aspired, not to create, but to find, a system. 'Instead of a statue cast in a simple mould by the hand of an artist,' writes Gibbon, 'the works of Justinian represent a tesselated pavement of antique and costly, but too often of incoherent, fragments.' The labours of the commissioners

1. Pollock and Maitland (*History of English Law*, vol. i) remark that before 300, Roman jurisprudence, like Roman art, had been stricken with sterility, and that Justinian was as far removed in time from the jurists whose opinions he collected, as we to-day are from Coke.

2. Published by the Emperor Theodosius II in 438. The *Codex Gregorianus* (c. 300) and its supplement, the *Codex Hermogianus* (fourth century), were also used by Justinian's commissions. All these three were collections of imperial ordinances. Interesting attempts to correlate and contrast Roman and Semitic law were (a) the *Collatio legum Mosaicarum et Romanarum* (c. 400), and especially (b) the Syro-Roman law book, a manual of Roman law compiled in Greek in the East during the fifth or the sixth century, and much favoured in the ecclesiastical courts.

produced three works: (1) the *Institutes*, an introductory text-book for students of the law, (2) the *Digest* or *Pandects*, a codi-fication of jurist-made law (*jus*), including such portions of the law of the republic and the early empire as were embodied in the writings of the jurists, and (3) the *Codex*, comprising the *leges* or imperial constitutions. To these there were added (4) the *Novels*, published at a later date, containing the emperor's decisions on points found doubtful in the earlier code.[1] The *Novels* and much of the *Code* were the work of Byzantine jurists. On the other hand, the *Digest* was a collection of excerpts from the classical period, modified to some extent by Justinian. Care was taken to preserve the spirit of the classical text. It is to the *Digest* that Justinian's *Corpus Juris* owes its chief value. Jus-tinian himself introduced many reforms, e.g. to ameliorate the legal position of women, children, and slaves. The wife's status was virtually equalized with the husband's, the ancient *patria potestas*, though preserved in principle, was practically nullified in application, and the order of intestate succession determined solely on the basis of blood-relationship. It is significant of the rooted conservatism of the age, in law as in all else, that Justinian claimed finality for his code and forbade that it should ever be modified or enlarged. We have observed that he was himself forced to transgress his prohibition, and the succeeding emperors continued in like manner to issue *Novels* to meet the changing requirements of the times. Thus arose a demand for new editions of the code, such as were issued by Leo the Isaurian in the eighth, and by Basil the Macedonian in the tenth, century. The *Basilika*, or royal laws of the last-named emperor, remained the statutory authority for the empire until its fall in 1453, and were adopted anew as the law of modern Greece, when it regained its independence in 1822. Of the influence of

---

1. The distinction referred to in earlier chapters of this book between the *jus civile*, the *jus honorarium* (of the praetors), and the *jus gentium*, no longer bore any meaning, save as ancient history; the whole code of Justinian, as enacted by the emperor, was civil law. As a matter of fact, it represents the triumph of the *jus gentium* all along the line. The *Digest* compressed the substance of over 1,600 rolls, with more than three million lines, into 150,000 lines. More than 95 per cent of the material dated from the golden age of juris-prudence between Trajan and Alexander Severus. The term *Codex* implies book-form as distinct from the earlier rolls.

Justinian's code in the West, we shall say something in the ensuing chapter. When the study of Roman law was revived by the teachers of Bologna in the thirteenth century, they took Justinian as their basis. His boast of finality was therefore not wholly without justification.[1] To this day, Roman law means primarily the contents of his code. We have remarked that it was the last word uttered at Constantinople in the Latin tongue. Henceforward the empire in the East spoke Greek. Yet, though Justinian thus closed the long story of the constructive achievement of Rome, it was surely not in order to inaugurate an epoch of new life for Greece. For the Christian autocrat crushed also the dying embers of free Hellenic thought. In the very year (529) of the publication of the first edition of the *Codex*, he bade the doors be bolted on the schools of Athens, and the last pagan followers of Plato fled beyond the Euphrates, to seek a refuge – so strange are Time's revenges – at the court of the successors of Darius.

§ 19. The establishment of a separate imperial government at Constantinople reflected inevitably on the fortunes of the Christian church. In the fourth century, Alexandria had been the centre of ecclesiastical life in the East, and on great issues of theology and church statesmanship the Alexandrian bishops had worked in close accord with Rome. In the fifth century, the patriarch of Constantinople, the natural adviser of the emperor on matters of religion, became the chief ecclesiastical authority in the East. Whereas at Rome the transfer of the government to Ravenna, and the rapid downfall of the empire, strengthened the independence of the papacy and its authority over Latin Christendom, the tendency in the East lay in the reverse direction. The sovereigns were all-powerful despots, and the patriarch of Constantinople sank into a subordinate instrument of their policy. The church, in fact, if not in theory, became a department of the state, and the patriarch a state minister of religion. After the council of Chalcedon (451), constitu-

1. Yet the mediaeval lawyers added to the *Corpus juris Civilis* of Justinian; e.g. the *Liber de Feudis* was inserted in all complete copies, thus facilitating the application of Roman law to feudal conditions. See Figgis, *From Gerson to Grotius*, pp. 10, 130.

tionalism yielded place to autocracy – the judgement of councils to imperial edicts. This growth of what has been aptly termed 'Caesaropapism' reached its climax under Justinian. The machine had triumphed over the organism; and the eastern church entered upon a period of comparative stagnation. The baneful effects were visible both in the field of dogmatic theology and in that of religious practice. From the fifth century, theological debate, though raging with ever fiercer intensity, tended to degenerate into a barren strife of words. The decision of issues vital to the faith was infected by personal animosities and political opportunism. Such was the case with the Monophysite controversy which in various forms dominated the ecclesiastical arena from the fifth to the seventh century. After the doctrine of the Trinity had been defined, the mind of the church turned naturally to that of the Incarnation. That 'the Word was made flesh and dwelt among us' had been from the first a cardinal belief of the Christian faith; but how was the union of the divine and human natures in Christ to be conceived? On the one side lay the danger of so confounding his humanity in his Godhead as to negate its distinctive reality, and thus to destroy the whole significance of the Incarnation; on the other, that of stressing the difference of the two natures to the point of affirming a double personality.[1] The Monophysites, who championed a single nature, leaned towards the former, the followers of Nestorius, asserting a difference of two *hypostases*, towards the latter of these two extreme positions. The issue at stake was a grave one; but in effect, when once the implications of the problem had been explicitly realized, it was swamped in a morass of verbal disputation.[2]

1. The Monophysite controversy was an aftermath of the Arian. Arius had held that Christ united a divine soul with a human body, i.e. that his humanity was not complete humanity. The issue raised might be stated thus: Did the divine Christ really suffer on the cross, or, in the phrase round which the controversy actually raged, was the Virgin Mary the 'mother of *God*' (*theotokos*)?

2. For the justification of this statement, the reader may be referred to an authority who is not disposed to undervalue the discussion of problems essential to the Christian faith, viz. to Duchesne, especially vol. iii, c. 10, pp. 317 ff.: 'au fond', he says, 'tout le monde était d'accord': and again 'au Ve siècle, des gens qui pensaient de même tout en parlant les uns d'une nature, les autres de deux, ne parvinrent pas à s'endurer et s'entre-malmenèrent.'

This was already manifest at the council of Chalcedon, which condemned Nestorius as a heretic, while affirming his tenets, only in a different form of words. The judgement of Isidore of Pelusium, a saint of the church, that men were claiming to dispute on a matter which was divine and transcended reason, in a frenzy of personal ambition, is amply confirmed by the scandalous scenes enacted at the two councils of Ephesus in 431 and 449.[1] The issue was decided by the sane insight of pope Leo I, the Great, supported by the empress Pulcheria, at the aforementioned council of Chalcedon; but the fires of controversy continued to ravage eastern Christendom long after the mind of the church had been authoritatively declared. The Monophysite contention degenerated in the seventh century into the Monothelete, which restated the problem of the single or dual nature as that of one or two energies or wills.[2] The chief interest had come to lie in anathematizing your enemy, or rather the enemy of the ruling power at Constantinople. Rome had spoken by the mouth of pope and emperor, and it only remained to exterminate the irreconcilables. The Nestorians, excluded from the empire, went their way, and spread the doctrine of the two natures from Persia, over China and the Indies, where their adherents still survive on the coast of Malabar; the Monophysites, backed by strong sentiments of nationality, held their ground in Syria and Egypt, and, despite

1. The protagonist of the conflict in the fifth century was Cyril, archbishop of Alexandria. The student must be on his guard lest the character and actions of this prelate create a prejudice against the cause of which he was the ablest and the most unscrupulous champion. The quotation from Isidore is given by Gibbon, c. 47, note 32.

2. Monophysitism means the doctrine of a 'single *nature*'; Monotheletism that of a 'single *will*'. The former was advocated by Apollinaris, bishop of Laodicea, late in the third century; Nestorius, patriarch of Constantinople in the early fourth century, insisted on the reality of both natures. His views, though put forward in an indiscreet manner, were not substantially different from those afterwards pronounced as orthodox. There was really no serious reason for the condemnation of Nestorius. The orthodox solution is clearly formulated in the later creed which received the name of Athanasian, especially in the words; 'Who, although he be God and Man: yet he is not two, but one Christ; One, not by conversion of the Godhead into flesh: but by taking of the Manhood into God; One altogether; not by confusion of Substance: but by unity of Person. For as the reasonable soul and flesh is one man: so God and Man is one Christ.'

Saracen and Turk, the Armenian, Syrian, Coptic, and Abyssinian Christians uphold to this day the belief in a single nature. It is not surprising to find that the seventh century was also an age of spiritual decadence, marked by the baser forms of credulity and superstition. The reform instituted in the eighth century came, as in secular administration, from above. The emperor Leo III, who had saved Constantinople from the Saracens, inaugurated the religious policy of his dynasty by a vigorous attack on the use of images (*icons*), on the worship of the Virgin, on the intercession of saints, and on the monastic communities which formed the stronghold of these practices. Iconoclasm, as the policy was named, was an aftermath of Monophysitism, prompted in Leo and his successors rather by a cool rationalism than by Puritan zeal; the images and sacred pictures which they removed from the churches were replaced by landscapes and other works of secular art. The iconoclastic controversy also gave occasion for the display of the deep-rooted divergence of national temperament and aspiration within the empire. As earlier, in the Monophysite controversy, the anti-Hellenic feeling of the Syrian and Egyptian Christians rendered hopeless any reasonable compromise; so now the nerve of the iconoclast movement lay in the religious predilections of the population of central and southern Asia Minor. These abhorred, while the Greeks favoured, the presence of images in Christian worship. Leo III (the Isaurian) was a native of Commagene, and his advent to the throne meant the enforcement of Asiatic Christianity. In the event, on the fall of the Isaurian dynasty, the Greeks emerged victorious from the conflict. Finally, racial differences lay at the root of the schism between the eastern and western churches. The superior dignity of the Roman see was indeed never challenged in the East, but unofficial prestige is a very different thing from avowed authority. The intervention of pope Leo at the council of Chalcedon was swiftly followed by a breach in the relations between Rome and the eastern churches; though six centuries were yet to run before the breach became definite and final. It was natural enough that the patriarch of Constantinople should wish to be master in the East; and his aspirations were fostered by the emperors. We have seen above that after the empire was restored in the West, in the person of Charles the Frank, the two churches owed allegiance to rival powers. But the real cause of schism was the incompatibility of mind and temper that parted the Roman from the Greek. Their national self-consciousness persisted to modify the religious life of Christendom long after the fabric of ancient civilization had passed away.

§ 20. We are wont to speak of *Byzantine* art and *Byzantine* literature; the term, though a misnomer when applied to the empire, which was Roman, is less inappropriate to the culture that centred in the old Greek colony of Byzantium. That culture preserved to the end its unbroken continuity with Hellenism, though the Hellenism was coloured by the spirit of Christianity. The East offers little analogy to the passing away of the old order, and the slow birth of a new, among the Teutonic peoples of the West. It knew no Middle Ages; or, if we use the words, it must be in a very different sense from that connoted by them in the West. Of Byzantine culture we may say that the art is of higher value than the literature or the thought; and that, even in art, the period of creative vitality closes with the seventh century. The masterpieces of Byzantine architecture, the Christian basilicas such as still adorn Ravenna, Thessalonica (Salonica), and Constantinople, with their paintings and mosaics, date from the epoch before, and contemporary with, Justinian. His church of Santa Sophia (the holy wisdom), designed by Anthemius of Tralles and Isidorus of Miletus, was the noblest basilica in Christendom. Byzantine art was destined, in the fullness of time, to bear fruit in Italy, and to inspire Cimabue and his successors to inaugurate a new era in European painting. St Mark's at Venice, the city which preserved for so long a nominal fealty and a real commercial link with the eastern empire, though a building of more recent date, is a genuine offshoot of Byzantine architecture. Even after the seventh century, the art of the East had moments of revival, when much fine work was produced; but the prevalent note is that of conservatism rather than originality. In literature this conservatism was even more pronounced. Of poetry there is little that claims attention, and that little took the form of Christian hymns.[1] Theology and history were the favourite fields of authorship; but, after the sixth century, the works produced were of inferior quality.[2] The philosophical tradition of Greece was maintained by John of Damascus in the eighth, and by Michael Psellus, who revived the study of Plato and Aristotle, in the eleventh century; if those can be said to have been faithful to the tradition, who, with all their learning and acuteness of intellect, added no new thought to the inheritance of the past. The spirit of Hellenism had vanished, but the letter remained; and the letter was studied with genuine ardour by generation after generation of Byzantine scholars. A classical education was sought after, not only by clerics, as in the West, but by the laity. That archaism was the dominant note from the fifth century to the fifteenth, is evident from the sole use of classical Greek as an instrument of literary expression. The spoken idiom was banned as unworthy of the written word; and each successive revival of literature took the form of an artificial return to the masterpieces of antiquity. No poet of genius appeared to wake the popular speech into life, as Dante woke into life the vulgar tongue of Italy. How could a Dante have been born into the arid atmosphere of Byzantine culture! A language is the reflexion of a people's free thought and feeling; where these are stirring, the word must needs come, and the man. The mind and heart of the Byzantine world were impotent to generate a fresh and living stream of utterance. Yet, within the limits of their capacity, the Byzantines laboured for civilization; preserving the treasure of the past for others, who, in the fullness of time, would understand its message. They implanted the rudiments of learning in non-

1. Especially the hymns of Romanos in the seventh century. See on the whole subject of Byzantine literature the article *Greek Literature* (*Byzantine*), by Krumbacher in the *Encycl. Britannica*.

2. In the fourth century, Eusebius, bishop of Caesarea, wrote his ecclesiastical history, and theological literature was enriched by the Cappadocian Fathers (Basil and the two Gregories). Fourth-century literature had its home, not in the Hellenic provinces, but in the Asiatic. In literature, religion, and military defence, Asia is the important portion of the empire. Sacred poetry centred in Syria and Palestine. Byzantine art shows traces of Oriental influence. Procopius' history of the age of Justinian was not unworthy of its subject.

Hellenic peoples – Syrians, Armenians, Copts, Slavs, Bulgars, and Russians. They sent forth teachers to distant lands, such as Theodore of Tarsus in the seventh century, who passed from the lecture-halls of Athens to Britain, where, as archbishop of Canterbury, he organized the English church, and founded schools whence Greek learning and culture spread over western Europe. King Ina of Wessex sent to Athens for scholars, who might teach St Aldhelm Greek. 'There live even to-day,' wrote Bede in the following century, 'pupils of these men, who knew Latin and Greek as their native tongue.'[1] Seven hundred years later, we find the Byzantine teacher still busy at his task, and, in the very hour of the empire's ruin, handing on the torch of Hellenism to the peoples of the western world.[2]

VI. CONCLUSION

§ 21. There has been no attempt in this chapter to trace in detail the fortunes of the Byzantine empire during the long period that elapsed between the foundation of 'New Rome' by Constantine and its final collapse in the fifteenth century. The story is a chequered one, of repeated oscillation from triumph to disaster and from disaster to triumph; epochs of astonishing vitality alternating, as though by a periodic law, with lapses into atrophy and disintegration. Apart from the constant pressure of powerful enemies both in East and West, disruptive tendencies were actively at work beneath the surface, sapping the foundations of the imposing structure of imperial autocracy; tendencies to mutiny in the army; to strife between circus-factions in the capital; to religious dissensions that stirred popular passion to the verge of revolution; to separatist movements, ecclesiastical and political, in Syria and Egypt; to rebel-

---

1. Bury, *Later Roman Empire*, ii. 392. The church of St Nicholas at Constantinople was built by a Saxon, who fled thither for refuge from the Norman conquerors of Britain.

2. Gibbon, c. 66, 'In their lowest depths of servitude and depression, the subjects of the Byzantine throne were still possessed of a golden key that could unlock the treasures of antiquity, of a musical and prolific language that gives a soul to the objects of sense, and a body to the abstractions of philosophy.'

lion among turbulent feudal chieftains; and, above all, save
under the Macedonian princes of the eleventh century, to
economic disorders, due to oppressive taxation and exhaustion
of the resources of the exchequer. Yet what is most impressive
is the amazing recuperative power of the empire. Again and
again, in the hour of its deepest degradation, there appears,
as if by magic, a saviour, gifted with rare qualities for war and
statesmanship, by whose genius it is restored to all, or almost
all, its historic splendour. A brief chronological summary
reveals a succession of five of these periodic oscillations.

(i) When, after Justinian's death (565), the Avars and the
Persians were closing in on both fronts upon the empire he had
established, there arose within half a century a great soldier,
Heraclius (610–41) who won decisive victories over both these
enemies.

(ii) When Heraclius failed to stem the rapid onset of Islam,
and this new peril had brought the fortunes of the empire to
their lowest ebb, the ablest of his successors, Constantine IV
(668–85) stemmed the tide of invasion by his five-years'
defence of the capital and, thanks to the newly invented 'Greek
fire', by a decisive victory over the Mohammedan fleet.

(iii) The fall of Heraclius' dynasty was followed by twenty
years of anarchy (695–717), during which six emperors in
succession seized the throne by violence. The saviour presented himself in Leo the Isaurian (717–40), who – and after
him his son Constantine V (740–75) – broke the eastern
onset of Islam both by sea and by land, and by their victories
over the Bulgarians restored the imperial suzerainty over the
Balkan peninsula.

(iv) Of the Iconoclastic policy of the Isaurian emperors we
have already spoken. Once again, an epoch of brilliant success
was followed by decadence and confusion; once again, the
empire found salvation in the advent of the 'Macedonian'
dynasty, founded by an Armenian usurper, Basil I. Under Basil
(867–86) and his successors – all of them usurpers and all rulers
of exceptional capacity alike in peace and war – it enjoyed for
150 years an unexampled prosperity (867–1025). The emperors of the Macedonian line were stern military captains,

disdainful of luxury and the 'solemn plausibilities' of the court, who restored the Euphrates frontier against the Mohammedans and extended Byzantine sovereignty in the West over Southern Italy. They liberally encouraged art and Hellenic culture in the capital, and by developing industry and maintaining a monopoly of Mediterranean commerce, made the empire the wealthiest as well as the most powerful state of the age. In the North, Russia (i.e. the Kingdom of Kiev) was converted to Christianity and received the first and lasting impress of Hellenic civilization.

(v) On the death of Basil II (976–1025), perhaps the ablest prince of the Macedonian line, the glory once more departed from Constantinople, never to return in full splendour. The inevitable decline was indeed checked by the dynasty founded in 1081 by an able and powerful feudal noble, Alexius Comnenus. The recovery was partial and ephemeral; it was the last heroic effort of an exhausted empire. The peril lay, as always, in the East, in the onset of a new enemy, the Turks. Resistance might have been effectively prolonged, but for the persistent tendency of the emperors, which we have already noted in Justinian, to divert their energy and resources westwards. The memory of the world-dominion of Old Rome dazzled their vision; they nursed vain dreams of Italian conquest, of reunion with the Papacy, and, later, under the Comneni and afterwards, of salvation by aid of Venice and the Crusader.

§ 22. Thus the eastern empire preserved its integrity, in the Balkan peninsula and in Asia Minor, until the eleventh century. From that date, it entered upon a long drawn-out and irrecoverable decline. It fell stricken by mortal blows, alike from the East and from the West. In Asia, the Seljuk Turks wrested away the provinces that had furnished the backbone of the army, and formed a kingdom, whose name, *Rûm*, echoed the memory of its former masters. In Europe, the eastward movement of peoples, which began with the Norman migrations, received a twofold impetus, from the religious zeal of the Crusaders and the commercial ambitions of Venice and other western states. Sicily had been long lost to the Saracens; in the eleventh century the Normans occupied southern Italy; and now, in 1204, the Franks and the Venetians attacked and took Constantinople. Their rule was transitory; but the empire never rallied from the shock. Its death-agony was prolonged, not by any inherent vitality, but by the force of circumstance. The devastating onset of Timur stayed the hand of the Seljuks, already outstretched to grasp the prize. By the fourteenth century, the empire of Justinian had dwindled into a petty Greek state, clinging round the walls of the capital. The final stab came from the Ottoman Turks. In 1453 Mohammed II stormed Constantinople, the last of Constantine's successors, Constantine Palaeologus, being slain while defending the last breach with a courage that showed him not unworthy of the name he bore, and the Roman empire in the East vanished from the scene of history.

§ 23. There is a sombre justice in the fate that overtook the empire, to fall enslaved beneath the blighting tyranny of the Turk. The leaden weights of autocracy and of conservatism had crushed the life out of Christian Hellenism. In things of the spirit, it had staked its all upon the past, and the past proved powerless to save it. Yet the doom, though merited, was not final. The darkness that fell upon the Hellenic world persisted for nearly four hundred years. The Ottoman empire became one of the great military powers, whose fleets were the terror of the Mediterranean, and whose armies swept the plain of Hungary and thundered at the gates of Vienna. The veil has hardly lifted at the present day. The nineteenth century has witnessed the long-deferred liberation of the Hellenic and Slavonic peoples, who, through ages of bondage, held faithfully to the religion and the culture which they had inherited from the Roman empire. It lies beyond our purpose to forecast the fruits that may sprout in the future, from the seed thus sown in the forerunners of the Greeks, the Serbs, the Bulgars, the Rumanians, and the Russians of to-day. Our uncertain vision serves but to show how impracticable is the attempt to circumscribe the influence wielded by the Roman empire upon after-time. We have spoken of the structure of the empire, and of the value of its work within the bounds of its duration. It grappled effectively for centuries with the herculean labour of defending the frontiers of civilization against barbarism. We have learnt also to appreciate, with a juster criticism than was current fifty years ago, both the merits and the limitations of its culture. Up to and indeed for long after the age of Justinian, that culture was not unworthy of its great traditions. Thenceforward it displayed at best a negative force of self-preservation. Yet there is something pathetic, and even magnificent, in the tenacity with which the Byzantines of the later empire guarded loyally, through a vigil of a thousand years, the legacy of their Hellenic forefathers.

CHAPTER ELEVEN

THE LEGACY IN THE MIDDLE AGES

*

I. INTRODUCTORY

§ 1. Thus far our discussion has proceeded within the bounds of what is commonly known as ancient history. Those bounds cannot be fixed with rigorous precision, and we have been led more than once in the last two chapters to carry forward our survey into the epoch of transition that parts antiquity from the Middle Ages. It now remains to confirm and illustrate our judgement on the significance of ancient civilization by a reference to its reception into mediaeval life and thought. We shall choose our examples from the legacy of Greece and Rome. We have touched already on the manner in which the spiritual inheritance of Israel was absorbed by the church of the first centuries.[1] To trace out its subsequent effects within the Christian pale would involve a review of the entire history not only of mediaeval Christianity, but of the sixteenth-century Reformation. Even the story of the Graeco-Roman tradition covers too wide a field. We must leave unnoticed much that is of importance, and content ourselves with showing how Greek philosophy and Roman law contributed to mould the mediaeval view of life. In conclusion, we shall speak briefly of the changes wrought by the final revival of classical learning in the age of the Renaissance.

§ 2. While scholars are in substantial agreement as to the essential features of ancient and modern civilization, those of the Middle Ages are harder to define. The name merely serves to indicate the chronological relation to what goes before and after, and throws no light on its positive character. Yet the period saw the birth of a new type of culture, none the less distinctive, because it is hard to characterize, and has often

1. See Vol. I, c. iii, § 11; and above, c. ix. § 2.

been misunderstood.[1] The Middle Ages were a scene of turmoil and conflict, the soil in which ideas and institutions germinated into maturity, silently shaping men's thoughts and wills, long before their implications and consequences were consciously apprehended. Its peculiar interest lies in the spectacle of a civilization struggling to its birth amidst a welter of barbarism; of the gradual conquest of brute force by right, anarchy by law, instinct and passion by reflective intelligence and reasoned purpose; above all, of an ardour of aspiration which, in face of facts that seemed at every point to give the lie to the ideal, kept its gaze firmly fixed on the spiritual goal of human life. There is, indeed, much in the Middle Ages that recalls, as we read its story, Hobbes' picture of the state of nature before the institution of civil society by the social contract. 'In such condition there is no place for industry, because the fruit thereof is uncertain, and consequently no culture of the earth; no navigation, nor use of the commodities that may be imported by sea; no commodious building; no instruments of moving and removing such things as require much force; no knowledge of the face of the earth; no account of time; no arts; no letters; no society; and, which is worst of all, continual fear and danger of violent death; and the life of man, solitary, poor, nasty, brutish and short.'[2] The seventh century might well have seemed such to the eyes of the seventeenth. The modern reader is often tempted to echo the sweeping verdict of rationalism, and to see in the Middle Ages only ignorance and credulity, crime and witchcraft, tyranny ecclesiastical and secular, anarchy, war, rapine, and persecution. These things are there, but there is much else. The barbarism of the early Middle Ages was in reality but the raw material from which were moulded, by strength of human mind and will, new forms of civilization, eminent alike for originality and grandeur. The

1. We refer here to the views on the Middle Ages which prevailed in Europe from the sixteenth to the nineteenth century, not from any desire to flog a dead horse, but because one-sided prejudice, bred of an inevitable reaction against the mediaeval view of life, still obscures the thought of many outside the ranks of historical students. Gibbon did more than anyone to fix this prejudice in the mind of the public, Carlyle more than anyone to correct it.

2. *Leviathan*, Part I, c. 13.

Middle Ages stand for an order of society and for an order of thought. As an order of society, it means a specific group of processes in the history of western Europe; processes creative of political and ecclesiastical institutions, law, language, social custom, and personal character, which are ceaselessly changing, and reveal at any given moment a rich diversity of features, yet are continuous, alike with the culture of the Roman empire, and with that of the modern world. We think of the feudal system, the papacy and the Holy Roman empire, monasticism, the Crusades, the structure of the village, the growth of the borough, the trade-gild, the Romance languages, Norman castles, Gothic cathedrals, the rise of the university, and the emergence of the nation-state. But the Middle Ages mean also – and it is with this aspect that we are particularly concerned – a specific group of processes in the history of the human mind; processes of reasoned thought as to the meaning and conduct of life, the right government of society, and the relations of man and the world to God. These processes, too, were, as living acts of man's spirit, in constant change, varied in content, and continuous both with the thought of antiquity and with that of modern times. We think here of the *Divina Commedia* of Dante and the *Summae* of Aquinas, of the speculations of philosophers and jurists on the law of nature and on the ideal relations of church and empire, of the *Fioretti* of Saint Francis, and of the visions of Christian mystics. In point of time, as was natural, the mediaeval order of society achieved stability earlier than did the order of reflective thought. But both stand from the first – we are often tempted to forget it – in organic connexion with each other. Mediaeval philosophy was, in no small measure, an induction from the facts of experience. Nor must the inconsistency between the theory and the practice of the Middle Ages blind us to the real potency of its ideal aspirations over the conduct of mankind. Dante's poem alone suffices as a reminder, how every detail, alike of his personal experience and of the story of political faction in the republics of Italy, was illumined by his vision of the divine scheme for the government of the world.

§ 3. The mediaeval view of life, like the order of society

from which it sprang, was the product of three factors, which came into fusion in western Europe in the centuries following the break-up of the Roman empire. There was the stream of Germanic and Scandinavian immigrants, who founded lordships and kingdoms in Britain, Gaul, Spain, and Italy, between the fifth and the eleventh centuries. Though these people brought with them no inheritance of learning or reflective thought, they had evolved a type of custom and belief, an unconscious 'way of life', which left an enduring impress on the ideas of the Middle Ages. The convictions that monarchy was the rightful form of human government, and that law or right (*recht*) was not derived from, but superior to, the state, whose function was to realize and maintain law, were deeply rooted in the Germanic and Scandinavian mind; and found expression, at a later day, among the cardinal principles of political and legal theory. Above all, these races leavened mediaeval thought with their strong sense of the worth of individual liberty. In this point their view of life harmonized with the teaching of Christianity, which had insisted on personal responsibility, and on the infinite value of the individual in the sight of God. But it conflicted with the tendency of Hellenic thought to deny independence to the individual, and to regard him as a fragment of the universe, as a part, rather than as a whole. The mediaeval mind strove earnestly to reconcile the two positions, by defining the status of the individual as at once a self-contained whole, and a part of the larger orders of the human species and of the world. It never entirely succeeded in effecting the desired harmony; and, in the event, the individualism, which had always coloured its outlook, triumphed decisively over the Graeco-Roman tradition. The second formative factor was the Christian church, with its ideal of other-worldliness, and its equipment of theology, law, and ecclesiastical institutions. We have seen how, prior to the dissolution of the empire in the West, the church had absorbed much of the ancient tradition, and had developed with its aid an ordered system of thought and discipline. Hence it was enabled to act as the chief instrument in mediating between Rome and her barbarian conquerors, and in transmitting to them Graeco-Roman civilization, though in a form radically modified by Christian faith and practice. This deposit of Graeco-Roman culture was the third agency which co-operated in the fashioning of the mediaeval mind. The first Teutonic invaders came into immediate contact with the language, law, and government of Rome, and passed on what they were able to assimilate to the generations that came after them.[1] The western church also, in its ecclesiastical system, in the canon law, and in its use of the Latin tongue as the medium of literature and public worship, maintained unbroken the continuity of the Roman tradition. Not all the avowed hostility of pope Gregory the Great towards ancient culture could hinder the church from disseminating fragments of pagan learning.[2] Nor must we forget that the culture of antiquity was kept alive in the empire of the East, and that there was constant intercourse between the West and Constantinople throughout the Middle Ages. It will be clear from this review of the channels of communication that the thought and culture of antiquity reached the mediaeval world neither in its purity, nor as a whole. Only fragments were preserved, and the residue had to be harvested by a long and arduous labour of rediscovery. Nor were the surviving fragments the choicest fruits of the classical genius. They were the relics cast up from its wrecks. Porphyry, not Plato, Boethius, not Aristotle, unnamed codifiers of the later empire, not Ulpian or Papinian, nourished the infant mind of the West during the eighth and the succeeding century.[3] Per-

1. It is easy to explain why the Middle Ages regarded the legacy of Rome with even greater reverence than that of Greece. Greek culture was transmitted through Rome, and the Greek and Roman contributions were not clearly distinguished. Above all, Rome was closely associated with Christianity as being divinely ordained for a religious mission.

2. When Gregory learnt that a certain bishop taught grammar and read the Latin poets, he admonished him in the following words (quoted by Poole, *Illustrations*, p. 8): 'A report has reached us which we cannot mention without a blush, that thou expoundest grammar to certain friends; whereat we are so offended and filled with scorn that our former opinion of thee is turned to mourning and sorrow. The same mouth singeth not the praises of Jove and the praises of Christ.' Tertullian and St Jerome had expressed similar sentiments. 'Grammar' was practically equivalent to 'pagan literature'.

3. See, further, below, § 8. The Irish monks of the seventh and eighth centuries form a notable exception by their knowledge of Greek. An Irishman of the seventh century edited the Psalms from the Hebrew text. The Irish were

haps even this was as it should be. Had the students in the
Frankish schools of the ninth century been confronted with the
entire *Corpus* of Aristotle or of Justinian, they would have been
paralysed, not stimulated, by the wealth of thought that lay
before them. A time would surely come when they would be
ripe to enter upon the full heritage of Greece and Rome. In the
meantime, we must do justice to the impulse furnished by the
mangled and meagre relics of that heritage, as also to the stern
disciplinary authorities that piloted the first thinkers of the
Middle Ages on their search for reasoned truth.[1]

§ 4. A word must be added as to the chronological limits of
the Middle Ages. To a comprehensive survey, it spreads over a
thousand years, from the fifth century to the sixteenth; while,
if we confine its range to the epoch when the mediaeval order
was dominant and stable, the term is particularly appropriate
to the period from 1100 to 1400.[2] In any case, it is a grave error
to restrict the rediscovery of ancient learning to the fifteenth-
and sixteenth-century Renaissance, when mediaeval society and
thought were crumbling into decay. To apply the name the
'dark ages' to the five preceding centuries was possible only for
men blinded to their true character by prejudices, inherited

great missionaries; a seventh-century writer observes that to them travel was
a second nature. St Columban (born in 543) converted Burgundy and founded
there, and at Bobbio in northern Italy, monasteries which became famous seats
of learning. His companion, St Gallus, founded the monastery of St Gallen on
the lake of Constance. The libraries both at Bobbio and at St Gallen were
enriched with MSS. of the chief Latin classical authors. Later, Irish teachers
were welcomed at the court of Charles the Great; on John the Scot, in the
ninth century, see § 8. Learning in Ireland received a deathblow with the
coming of the Northmen at the end of the eighth century.

1. It must be remembered that the names of famous authors were assigned
freely in mediaeval times to work which later criticism would not assign to
them. Roger Bacon's chief authority throughout his life was the *Secretum
Secretorum*, supposed to represent Aristotle's teaching to his most intimate
disciples. See the edition of the *Secretum* with Bacon's own notes, brought out
by R. Steele. Aristotle, according to this book, was half a saint, and quoted
the Vulgate.

2. If we seek to date the Middle Ages from the time when their dominant
beliefs had their origin, we must go back beyond the first century, and include
the whole view of Christianity and Neo-Platonism within the scope of mediaeval
history. So M. Picavet (*Esquisse*, c. 2) makes the Middle Ages extend from
Philo of Alexandria to Galileo and Descartes. This merely shows the imprac-
ticability of fixing a hard and fast limit of time to historical periods.

from those who knew the Middle Ages in the hour of their decline. The ninth and the twelfth and thirteenth centuries witnessed a genuine revival of classical knowledge, anticipating in vitality and fruitfulness the Renaissance of a later day. The daring speculations of John the Scot, the learning of John of Salisbury, the critical energy of Abelard, the genius of Aquinas for systematic construction, were worthy of the most notable epochs in the history of civilization.[1] The age which these men adorned saw also the institution of the universities of Paris, Oxford, and Bologna, the building of noble churches and their enrichment with sculptures and glass of unequalled beauty, and, as we shall see presently, the moulding of the law of western Europe on the principles of the code of Justinian. To sum up, we may say that, from the time of the barbarian invasions and the dissolution of the Roman empire in the West in the fifth century, Europe entered upon a transitional period of anarchy and confusion, amidst which the mediaeval order wakened slowly into life; that, somewhere about the year 1100, this order emerged into view, endowed with definitely recognizable organs and relatively stable functions; and that, after flourishing for more than three centuries, it yielded place, again by slow gradations, to new forces, political, religious, and intellectual, the appearance of which marks the dawn of modern history. The close of the eleventh and the early years of the twelfth century are critical moments in the Middle Ages; and the thirteenth century, for reasons which we shall make clear in the sequel, forms the high-water mark of their development.

II. THE RECEPTION OF GREEK PHILOSOPHY

§ 5. 'It cannot be expected of anyone', wrote Hegel, 'to know at first hand the philosophy of the Middle Ages, for it is as comprehensive and voluminous as it is barren and ill-expressed.'[2] The sting of this verdict, and its falsity, lies in the charge of barrenness; we can only conclude that Hegel had absolved him-

---

1. John the Scot, c. 810 to c. 875; John of Salisbury, 1110–80; Abelard, d. 1142; Aquinas, 1227–74.
2. *History of Philosophy*, E. Tr., iii. 38.

self as well as his readers from the labour of studying mediaeval philosophy at first hand. The days are past when a serious historian can treat the thought of the Middle Ages *de haut en bas*. Yet it is not so long ago that teachers were wont to pilot their classes through Greek philosophy as far as Aristotle, and then, after a cursory reference to the Stoics and Epicureans, stride with seven-league boots over some two thousand years of the life of the human spirit, to plunge with Descartes into the problems of modern metaphysics. The Neo-Platonists and the mediaeval doctors alike were dismissed with a few contemptuous generalities about mysticism, credulity, and superstition. The student left the university, itself a creation of the mediaeval genius,[1] hardly aware of the bare names of Plotinus or Aquinas. Abelard was known only as the hero of Pope's version of the letters of Eloisa. The schoolmen were branded as sciolists who travestied Aristotle's logic and wrangled in futile syllogisms over the problem of universals.[2] Even in Roman Catholic academies the mediaeval tradition had passed almost out of mind. When Newman visited Rome after his conversion, he was amazed to find that no one cared about St Thomas. That was in the half-century prior to the restoration of the Thomistic philosophy by the most illustrious of modern popes, assisted

---

1. On the mediaeval universities, see Rashdall, *Universities of Europe in the Middle Ages*. Over seventy were founded between 1150 and 1500. Salerno, the great medical school, dates from the middle of the eleventh century; Paris (theology and philosophy) and Bologna (law) from the beginning of the twelfth; Oxford (arts) and Montpellier (medicine) from the middle of the twelfth. Cambridge, Padua, Salamanca, and Toulouse arose in the thirteenth century. We note how learning migrated from the monasteries to the universities; Anselm was the last of the great monastic, Abelard the first of the great university, teachers. The mediaeval universities were not the result of definite foundation; they grew naturally out of colonies of students, who gathered to learn from famous masters.

2. The controversy on universals was as to whether general concepts, such as man, horse, etc. (*genera* and *species*), were mere notions of the mind without any real counterpart in things (Nominalism and Conceptualism), or existed also in things (*in rebus*) as constituents of their real being (Realism). Realists also held that universals existed prior to individual things (*ante res*) as eternal thoughts of God. This latter doctrine had its source in Neo-Platonism and was transmitted to the Middle Ages through Augustine. The main stream of mediaeval thought is realist. There were many subordinate varieties of Nominalism and Realism.

by his chosen allies in the university of Louvain.[1] Ten years later, in 1888, the *École pratique des hautes études* at Paris embarked on a series of researches into the relations between religion and philosophy in the Middle Ages. Their labours and those of a host of scholars of all nations who have followed in their train have enabled students to gauge in its true proportions the value of Neo-Platonic and of mediaeval speculation. We know now, for instance, that the line of thinkers, from John the Scot in the ninth century to William of Ockham in the fourteenth, drew inspiration, not merely or even primarily from Aristotle, but from many other sources, and especially from Neo-Platonism; that the logical controversy as to universals was but a subordinate and transitory episode in an epoch of far-reaching metaphysical ferment; and that, far from uncritically accommodating a garbled and jaded Aristotelianism to the dogmas of the church, mediaeval thinkers essayed a reasoned synthesis of theology and metaphysics, which can claim to stand among the most impressive yet achieved in the history of thought.

§ 6. The problem was common both to Hellenic and mediaeval philosophy, though each approached it from a different angle. The distinction is that between the religion of science and the science of religion. The thinkers of Greece, starting from metaphysical assumptions and working on a metaphysical method, found in philosophy the satisfaction of spiritual desire and the secret of the religious life. Aristotle applied the term 'theology', i.e. the reasoned doctrine of God, to what we should now call metaphysical science. In consequence, religion was rationalized, and became the monopoly of the philosopher, a tendency which we have observed even in Plotinus, in whose system the religious factor came into its own more fully than in any earlier Greek philosophy. The thinkers of the Middle Ages, on the other hand, started from the pre-

---

1. Leo XIII in the encyclical *Aeterni Patris* (1878). 'Of all my encyclicals,' he wrote in 1900, 'that which is nearest my heart and has given me most comfort, is the encyclical *Aeterni Patris* on the restoration of the Scholastic and Thomist philosophy.' The centre of the revival was the university of Louvain under the direction of Mgr Mercier, later a cardinal and archbishop of Malines.

suppositions of theology, and worked their way to metaphysics.[1]
They aimed at a reconciliation of reason and revelation,
science, and faith, in a coherent theory of the relations of man
and the world to God. From the days of the Apologists and of
Origen in the second and third centuries, Christian thinkers
had felt that the two interests could not be divorced. Religion
and philosophy alike claim to give knowledge, and knowledge
of a common truth; neither is restricted to a special field of
human experience, but both, as 'spectators of all time and all
existence', take the universe as their province. Religion, again,
falls short of its ideal as religion, unless it embraces within its
scope the whole nature of man, and satisfies, not merely his
practical and emotional aspirations, but those also of his intelligence. In other words, religion must come to an understanding
with philosophy. For the mediaeval philosophers, as for the
earlier Christian theologians, this was possible only by use of
the Hellenic method, the logical instrument that had been
forged by the genius of Plato and Aristotle. They built, indeed,
with originality and freedom, for, as we have said, their orientation was new. '*Aliud tempus fuit tunc et aliud nunc est*', said
Roger Bacon, 'it was one time then, and now it is another'.
The school of Chartres was as distinctive in its teaching from
that of the Academy as was the architecture of its cathedral
from that of the Doric Parthenon.[2] But they built in the
strength of the legacy of Hellenic thought. Nor was this inheritance restricted to the mind of Christendom. It was the
common source of inspiration to the efforts after a synthesis of
theology and metaphysics put forth by each of the three great
world-religions of the Middle Ages. For Islam and Judaism were

1. This difference of orientation was intensified by the fact that throughout
the Middle Ages learning, at least in western Christendom, was a monopoly
of monks and clerics. But we must not forget that among the Arabs and the
Jews, lay thinkers also approached the problem from the point of view of
theology.
2. On the school of Chartres; see Poole, *Illustrations*, c. iv. It became
famous under Fulbert early in the eleventh century. John of Salisbury (middle
of the twelfth century), the best-known of its members, the most learned
writer of his age, was acquainted with Cicero and the chief Latin poets: see
also Sandys, *History of Classical Scholarship*, pp. 537–42, and Poole, c. vii. He
was secretary to archbishops Theobald and Becket of Canterbury.

confronted by the same problem as Christianity. Despite their diversity and mutual antipathies, these three religions had much in common. All three were monotheistic, and taught the doctrines of a divine creation and providential government of the world, of a supernatural sphere peopled by supernatural powers, of heaven and hell, of the immortality of the soul, and the hope of personal salvation. All three appealed to a revelation embodied in sacred writings and to the authority of prophetic teachers – Moses, Jesus, Mohammed – who had delivered an inspired message to mankind. All three found themselves obliged to explain and defend their faith in the face of heretics and unbelievers, and had recourse to the allegorical method, first utilized by the Stoics, as the instrument of theological exegesis. In other words, all alike felt, though in varying measure, the need of a rational theology, which should harmonize science and revelation. We shall see presently how these currents of religious thought among Christians, Arabs, and Jews arose independently, at the close of the eighth century, and converged in the speculative systems of the Christian doctors of the thirteenth. It is the community of aim and method among the three streams of thought that gives the philosophy of the Middle Ages its characteristic unity. For Christian, Arab, and Jew, philosophy meant the rational interpretation of religious experience, a *praeparatio evangelica* for their respective gospels. The solutions proffered were divergent, but the interest was the same. Mediaeval metaphysics centred in the problems of the being and operations of God, the freedom of the will, and the immortality of the human soul. Its story is that of the fusion of a common deposit of Greek philosophy with the theological tradition of three different, though analogous, religions.

§ 7. We must guard here against a natural and familiar misconception. The mediaeval synthesis was no frigid republication of ancient theories, in artificial conjunction with a revelation that belied their truth. That the mediaeval thinkers felt a profound respect for authority in thought and action, in things spiritual and things secular, is beyond question, and has exposed them to the charges of servility and obscurantism. The tradition of scripture and the Fathers, the injunctions of the canon and the civil law, and the judgements of Aristotle and his interpreters, assuredly wielded at times an almost overwhelming influence. It was inevitable, in an age when individual self-assertion and the unbridled thirst for liberty of action threatened at every point to dissolve into anarchy the new-born structures of social order and stable conviction, that the need of authoritative control should be urgently felt both by thinkers and by statesmen. For Anselm and Aquinas, as for Hildebrand and William the Norman, authority was the rock on which alone the fabric of truth and justice could be reared. The Middle Ages were deeply conscious of instability and ignorance; of how insecure were the foundations of its society, and how much of the inheritance of the past was yet unknown. Little wonder that it clutched eagerly, and often uncritically, at the fragmentary relics of ancient wisdom that lay beneath its hand. But the appeal to authority was no bar to intellectual independence. From the time when Abelard wrote his *Sic et non* in the twelfth century to the publication of Aquinas' *Summae* in the thirteenth, we note a continuous energy of critical selection and comparison among the divergent voices of the recognized authorities. When Aristotle clashed with scripture, the mediaeval mind was forced to think for itself. Above all, men were ready and able to offer rational grounds for allegiance to the authorities of their choice. The dominant note of the mediaeval spirit was not reverence for authority, but other-worldliness. To call the Middle Ages an age of faith is a truism; all ages are ages of faith, and the only pertinent enquiry is into the nature and quality of the conviction. To its thinkers and men of action the supersensible world possessed a reality denied to the scene of man's temporal pilgrimage. This does not mean that they were indifferent to motives of gain and glory, to the claims of military or political ambition, or even to those of knowledge of physical nature.[1] But those who were most absorbed in mun-

1. It must not be rashly supposed that the mediaeval thinkers were heedless of the interest of physical science. Albertus Magnus, following in the steps of Michael Scot, revived biological science in his commentaries on Aristotle, esp. the *de Animalibus*. Roger Bacon's experiments in chemistry were neither unimportant nor unique. Dante furnishes abundant illustrations of interest in

dane concerns never questioned, when they paused to think, that these were of secondary moment, that 'this earth, our habitation' was but a transitory stage of discipline, or that the only knowledge of intrinsic worth was that of man's spiritual goal and of the instruments that led to its attainment. The mind of the Middle Ages held unswervingly to the convictions that society ought to be controlled by the moral law, that above all differences of status and nationality men were linked in human fellowship as members of an ideal commonwealth, and that reason and revelation alike pointed to the knowledge of an end which was the absolute and perfect good for man and for the universe. It sought a reasoned basis for these convictions. The conception which it framed of the divine order of the world was one of unique speculative grandeur. Let any who feel disposed to cavil at its reverence for theological authority as involving the imprisonment of the human spirit, set, we will not say the *Summae* of Aquinas, but the *Divina Commedia*, inspired in almost every canto by Aquinas' teaching, beside Milton's *Paradise Lost* and Goethe's *Faust*, and ask dispassionately which of these great poets, the child of the Middle Ages or the inheritors of modern humanism, have most effectively achieved an imaginative synthesis of man's relation to the world and God. The answer to this question will serve as a measure of the claim of the mediaeval mind to originality and freedom, and of its response to the inspiration that it drew from the legacy of the ancient world.

§ 8. It was in the thirteenth century that the effort of mediaeval thought after a synthesis of theology and metaphysics culminated in a relatively stable solution. This achievement was chiefly due to St Thomas Aquinas (1227–74). Aquinas stood at the meeting-point of the three currents of thought that had flowed in separate channels for some four hundred years. These

astronomy and cosmology. Aristotle's authority exercised a baneful influence in physics, especially through his distinction of the sublunary and the super-lunary worlds. Yet even here the best minds of the Middle Ages were opened to new ideas; e.g. Aquinas' words (*de caelo et mundo*, Book II, Lect. 17) on the theory of planetary motions: 'Though the phenomena can be saved on these hypotheses, we do not assert that they are true, since perchance the phenomena of the heavenly bodies may be saved in some other way not yet grasped by men.'

were, first, the philosophy of western Christendom, that took its rise in the Carolingian schools of the ninth century; secondly, the Arab philosophy, which had its birth under the Baghdad caliphs of the eighth century, and reached its zenith under the emirs of Cordova in the twelfth; and, thirdly, the unbroken speculative tradition of the scholars and *literati* of the Byzantine empire. (i) The Christian schools had been founded, by Charles the Great and his Frankish successors, in Gaul and on the Rhine, at the close of the eighth and the opening of the ninth century. The first teachers, many of whom, like Alcuin of York, were drawn from the British Isles, built as best they could out of the rubble of the shattered edifice of Graeco-Roman culture.[1] The materials to their hand were unpromising. The Latin versions of certain of Aristotle's logical treatises compiled by Boethius, the philosophic minister of Theodoric the Ostrogoth, in the sixth century, the same writer's *Consolation of Philosophy*, a few late and imperfect commentaries, and some inferior manuals of the same period, furnished garbled hints of the great tradition, and an introduction to the more formal rules of logic. Augustine and other Fathers of the church helped to an acquaintance with Neo-Platonism. Plato himself was known only through a Latin translation of the *Timaeus*.[2] On this fragmentary basis they founded the teaching of dialectic, comprising a discipline in logical method with a tincture of Neo-Platonic rather than Aristotelian metaphysics, and forming, with grammar and rhetoric, the *Trivium* of the mediaeval schools.[3] The marvel is

---

1. See R. L. Poole, *Illustrations*, Introduction.
2. The treatises of Aristotle referred to did not include the most important, which were not discovered till the eleventh century in the Christian west. For Boethius, see c. x, § 8, and for Augustine, see c. ix, § 22. The works attributed to Dionysius the Areopagite, on the *Divine Names* and the *Celestial Hierarchy*, and composed late in the sixth century, were also very influential throughout the Middle Ages (e.g. upon John the Scot, who translated them into Latin, and upon Dante, Par. x. 115-17, xxviii. 97 to end). The translation of the *Timaeus* was that of Chalcidius. This dialogue appealed to the mediaeval mind as natural science set in a theological context.
3. The *Trivium* was followed by the *Quadrivium*, consisting of arithmetic, geometry, astronomy, and music. The whole curriculum was subordinate to the study of Christian theology. The origin of the *Trivium* and the *Quadrivium*, like that of the university, is to be traced to Plato's Academy and to the pro-

that they made such use of what they had. A century had not
elapsed before there appeared, at the court of Charles the Bald,
a thinker whose writings are perhaps the most astonishing
phenomenon in the history of philosophy. John the Scot
(Johannes Scotus Erigena, *flor. c.* 850), working with rare
originality and freedom on the basis of the Neo-Platonic tradition handed down by Augustine and the pseudo-Dionysius, produced in his treatise *On the Division of Nature* a system of philosophy which, alike in logical coherence and in speculative content, anticipates that of Spinoza. He asserted boldly that true
religion is identical with philosophy. All that is, in so far as it
has being, is God, the beginning and the end, the Alpha and
the Omega, of the universe, which is, therefore, immortal and
wholly good. Nature, i.e. reality (we seem to hear the *Deus
sive Natura* of Spinoza), is interpreted in the light of a four-
fold division: (1) That which is uncreated and creative (God
as universal cause); (2) that which is created and creative (the
world of archetypal ideas); (3) that which is created and uncreative (the sensible image of the ideas); and (4) that which is
uncreated and uncreative (the final rest of restored creation in
God's undivided unity). Thus evil has no real existence, but is
mere privation of good; and, having no being, cannot be
caused or foreknown by God. It is small wonder that John's
response, in his tract on *Predestination*, to the appeal of archbishop Hincmar of Rheims, to defend human freedom against
the assertion of predestination to damnation, fluttered the
ecclesiastical dovecote and seemed more perilous even than the
heresy of his antagonist. John the Scot was an isolated figure,
and founded no enduring school; though here and there in the
ages that followed, we find a few daring minds who, quarrying
in his mine of treasure, braved the wrath of the orthodox
authorities and the terrible charge of pantheism.[1] But the

gramme of studies outlined in the seventh book of the *Republic*. It is not a mere
accident of history that logic is taught to-day in the French *lycées*. English
public schoolboys are less fortunate.
    1. On John the Scot, see R. L. Poole, *Illustrations*, c. ii. 'Scot' means that
he came from Ireland; 'Erigena' is a later substitute for 'Ierugena', which
probably means 'of Irish birth'. A good edition of his works is sorely needed.
How near John came to pantheism is evident from the following passages:

Platonic tradition continued to dominate the thought of the early Middle Ages. After two centuries of speculative poverty, it woke to fresh life with Anselm of Aosta (1033–1109, abbot of Bec and archbishop of Canterbury), and Peter Abelard (1079–1142); the latter of whom entitled Plato the greatest of philosophers, and endeavoured, by his identification of the Holy Spirit with the world-soul, to accommodate Platonic teaching to the Christian doctrine of the Trinity. It was Abelard, too, who, marshalling one against the other the judgements of divergent authorities, Christian and pagan, forged the characteristic instrument of expression for the succeeding age. His fame as a master of dialectic was largely due to the fact that the rediscovery of the chief logical works of Aristotle inspired him to breathe fresh life into that branch of knowledge. Abelard was the pioneer of the second phase in the mediaeval revival of learning, which was marked by the recognition of Aristotle, side by side with Plato, as a regulative authority in western Christendom. The opening years of the thirteenth century saw the rediscovery of the *Physics*, *Metaphysics*, and *de Animâ*. At the same time the doctors of the West gathered in the fruits of Arab, Jewish, and Byzantine speculation.

§ 9. (ii) The Arab philosophy, which arose under the caliphs of Baghdad in the eighth century, differed in two respects from that of the Christian schools of the West. From the first it reaped a richer harvest from the legacy of Hellenic thought. The Arabs had access to the entire Aristotelian *Corpus* and to a large mass of both Platonic and Neo-Platonic writings, through Syriac translations from the Greek. Hence the rapid advance and the comparative maturity of their meta-

'When we hear that God does everything, we should understand that God is in everything, i.e. that he subsists as the essence of everything' (i. 72).

'He (God) is the beginning, middle and end: the beginning, because from him are all things that have essence; the middle, because in and through him all things subsist; the end, because they move to him, seeking rest from their motion and fixity of their perfection' (i. 12).

But John can hardly be charged with pantheism, for he combines this doctrine with the assertion, on Neo-Platonic lines, of God's transcendence. The belief in a purely immanent God was branded as atheism in the Middle Ages, as later in the case of Spinoza.

physics. But philosophy failed to acclimatize itself to the religious atmosphere of Islam. As Renan has remarked, the Arab genius, fertile in poetry and art, has never taken kindly to metaphysics. Their philosophy was always an exotic, which enjoyed a transitory efflorescence, thanks to the patronage of enlightened princes, first in Mesopotamia, and afterwards in Spain. On the fall of the Ummayyad emirs of Cordova, it was crushed out of existence by the hostility of orthodox Mohammedanism. The last great name was that of Averroes of Cordova (Ibn Roshd: 1127–98). But before its brief and brilliant splendour faded, it had handed on the torch to the adherents of another faith. The Arabs taught the Jews to think, and the lesson, once learnt, was not forgotten. The most illustrious of Jewish mediaeval thinkers, Maimonides (Moses ben Maimon: 1135–1204) was the forerunner of a long line of philosophers, culminating in the seventeenth century with Baruch de Spinoza, whose system on its religious side – and no philosophy is more profoundly religious – reflects the conception of union with God through intellectual love, which his Jewish predecessors had inherited through the Arabs from Plotinus and Plato. Not only in finance and trade, but in things of the mind, the mediaeval Jew played the part of a middleman of civilization. But, both among the Arabs and the Jews, the Platonic tradition was more evenly balanced by the Aristotelian than it was in the Christian West, until the twelfth and thirteenth centuries.[1] Lastly, (iii) a third speculative current flowed into western Europe in the early years of the thirteenth century from the Christian East. The Byzantine scholars had preserved the genuine classical tradition, and knew Plato, Aristotle, and the Neo-Platonists at first hand. The ties of intellectual contact between West and East were drawn closer by the Crusades, and especially by the Latin occupation of Constantinople in 1204.[2] The study of ancient thought had been revived there in the

1. The student who is interested should consult Renan, *Averroës et l'Averroisme*, and the English translation of Maimonides' *Moreh Nebuchim* or 'Guide of the Perplexed'.

2. It had never been entirely broken, e.g. the writings of the Pseudo-Dionysius had come from the East to the West through Rome in the eighth century.

eleventh century by the Comnenian dynasty.[1] In 1205, pope
Innocent III despatched western missionaries to the East, while
king Philip Augustus of France opened at Paris a college for
Byzantine students. Theological discussions were actively
carried on between the Latin and Greek churches. Amongst
other results of this association, the works of Aristotle,
hitherto studied in Latin translations of Arabic translations of
Syriac translations from the Greek, were read henceforward
by western scholars in the original.[2]

§ 10. The convergence of these three currents in the thirteenth century had momentous results on the thought of
western Christendom. The influence of Aristotle, whose works
could now for the first time be studied in their entirety, became
increasingly predominant over the earlier Platonic tradition.
In making this distinction, we must bear in mind that Aristotle's
philosophy was grounded on that of Plato, and that it reached
the Middle Ages overlaid with Neo-Platonic commentaries and
accretions.[3] Plato, again, was known chiefly through a Neo-
Platonic medium, in which a large measure of Aristotelian
doctrine had been already fused with the Platonic. Thus it was
possible for Arab and later Christian thinkers, in possession of
the Aristotelian *Corpus*, to embody the results of both traditions in a single speculative system. Broadly speaking, we may
say that Aristotle's contribution to mediaeval thought was twofold, in that (*a*) his logic, and especially his theory of the
syllogism, set the type of scientific method; while (*b*) the
contents of his physical, psychological, political and metaphysical treatises were accepted, with reservations as to the
eternity of the world and the mortality of the soul, as a basis

1. Michael Psellus was the chief thinker in this revival, which had its precursors in the late seventh century (John of Damascus), and in the ninth
(Photius). The Syriac Christians, through whom the Arabs came to know
Greek philosophy, had learnt in their turn from the Byzantine Greeks.
2. Aquinas, for instance, though himself ignorant of Greek, employed a
Greek scholar, William of Moerbeke, as his collaborator on Aristotle.
3. Among these accretions were two treatises assigned in the Middle Ages
to Aristotle, that '*On causes*' (*De causis*) and the so-called '*Theology*'. Both were
translations from the Neo-Platonist Proclus. The *Fons vitae* of the Jew
Avicebron (Ibn-Gebirol), hailed also from the same source, and was probably
influenced by John the Scot.

for construction in the natural and moral sciences.[1] Aristotle, in effect, supplied the theory of nature, which was needed to supplement the church's theory of grace. When, on the other hand, mediaeval thought was turned to the nature of God and the destiny of the human soul, it followed mainly in the tracks of Christian Neo-Platonism. The principles that grades of perfection within our experience imply the reality of an absolute standard; that the higher the grade of being the more pervasive is its causal efficacy; that the effect is inferior to, yet mirrors the likeness of, its cause; that evil is nothing positive but privation of good; that the rational soul is a substantial entity independent of the body and immortal; that the human intellect in this life can know God only by analogy, and by denying of Him all that we are able to conceive; that universals (the Platonic Forms) exist timelessly as thoughts in the divine mind, and that, in God, essence and existence, intellect and will, thought and reality, are one and the same; these and many other tenets common to the main body of mediaeval speculation are all of them, though blended in their presentation with the teaching of revealed religion, in their origin 'fragments of the great banquet' of Plotinus. We may go further and say that in the spirit, if hardly in the letter, they carry the mind back beyond Plotinus to their fountain-head in Plato. There is, however, a remarkable exception to this general tendency to draw on the Platonic tradition for the theory of supersensible reality. In their endeavours to base the belief in the fact of God's existence on rational grounds, the great majority of mediaeval thinkers refused to accept as valid the famous *a priori* argument of Anselm (the 'ontological' argument), viz. that our thought of God involves his necessary being. They preferred to appeal to the Aristotelian proof (the 'cosmological') from the experienced fact of motion to the existence of an unmoved mover as its first casue.[2] Despite their

1. The church hesitated long before sanctioning the study of the newly-discovered Aristotle. It was the labours of Albert of Cologne and, especially, of Aquinas that secured eventual recognition for the Aristotelian tradition as harmonized by them with the doctrine of the catholic church, especially as regards the points mentioned above.

2. For the ontological proof see Anselm's *Proslogium*, Gaunilo's criticism

sense of the worth of human personality, they shrank from exalting the mind of the finite individual into the basis of so ambitious a construction. Their instinct told them that the ontological argument was hard to reconcile with their firm conviction of God's transcendence. For more than five hundred years, Anselm's bold flight found no following, until, in an age that looked to human reason as the key to all the secrets of the universe, his proof was revived, as a chief cornerstone of metaphysics, by Descartes.

§ 11. But the reception of Aristotle was not the sole or the greatest intellectual achievement of the thirteenth century. The touch of the Greek spirit stirred the thinkers of the age to energy of creative thought. They would have learnt their lesson ill had it been otherwise. The mediaeval mind had long laboured to effect a synthesis of reason and revelation, in the conviction that both alike had their source in God, and as such could not stand in mutual contradiction. The advocates of a double truth, i.e. that what is valid in philosophy is false in religion and *vice versâ*, won few adherents.[1] On the other hand, there were not many to echo the frank avowal of John the Scot, that 'true philosophy is true religion, and conversely true religion is true philosophy'.[2] The great majority steered a course between these two extremes. Anselm thanks God that 'what by thy gift I first believed, I now by thy illumination understand, so that even though I refused to believe in thy existence, I could not fail to grasp it with my intelligence'.[3] 'God alone', wrote Abelard, 'is the plenitude of all the sciences, whose gift all science is.' And of revealed truth he said: 'It is not to be believed because God spake it, but it is accepted because we are convinced that

(analogous to Kant's) and Anselm's reply; also Aquinas' criticism, *S. Th.*, I. q. 2. art. 1, and *S.c.G.*, I. 10. For the cosmological proof, see Aquinas, *S. Th.*, I. q. 2. art. 3, and *S.c.G.*, I. 13. The ontological argument is a development of hints in Augustine and the Neo-Platonists.

1. This was maintained by Siger of Brabant, an Averroist contemporary and opponent of Aquinas at Paris. See Mandonnet, *Siger de Brabant*, on this, and on the whole matter of §§ 9–11.

2. *De predestinatione*, i. 1.

3. *Proslogium*, c. 4; cf. *Monologium*, c. 1. Anselm's 'I do not seek to understand in order to believe, but I believe in order that I may understand' (*credo ut intelligam, Proslog.*, c. 1) is a far cry from Tertullian's 'it is certain because it is impossible' (*certum est quia impossibile est*).

it is true.' [1] But Aquinas (1227–74) was the first to define with the requisite lucidity and precision the nature at once of the relationship and of the distinction.[2] To do so was an urgent necessity; for the organized system of Christian theology was now at last confronted with an equally organized system of metaphysics in the Aristotelian *Corpus*, and there were points where the latter appeared to clash directly with the faith. Averroes, the 'Commentator' *par excellence*, had interpreted Aristotle rightly as holding that the world was eternal and that the human soul perished with the body of which it was the form. Either it must be shown that the master taught otherwise – and this was no easy task – or an endeavour must be made to reason out the truth where his authority proved defective. Aquinas set himself to meet the situation thus created. He set his course midway between the Augustinian Neo-Platonism which held the field in the orthodox schools and the literal Aristotelianism of the disciples of Averroes. As against the former, who had dallied dangerously with the principle that pagan philosophy and Christian dogma were both immediately inspired by God, he drew with a firm hand, perhaps, as some would object, with too firm a hand, the line of demarcation between reason and revelation, nature and grace. His native genius for grasping the distinctions between things had been fortified by the study of Aristotle and of Roman law. That 'every thing is what it is and is not another thing' was implanted as deeply in the typically Italian mind of Thomas of Aquino as

1. *Introd. ad Theologiam*, ii. 2, 3.
2. Aquinas wrote, besides a multitude of other works, two *Summae*, i.e. encyclopaedic treatises, covering the whole fields of theology and metaphysics. They were entitled the *Summa Theologica* and the *Summa contra Gentiles* (against the heathen); the latter was designed for the use of missionaries to the Mohammedans and the Jews, who required a justification of the Christian faith on grounds of reason. The two *Summae* form the most systematic expression of thirteenth-century thought. They comprise also much discussion of psychological, ethical, and political questions. References to the *S. Th.* are by parts (e.g. II. 1 = 1st division of Part II, II. 2 = 2nd division of Part II, etc.), questions and articles (into which each question is subdivided). Thus *S. Th.*, II. 1. q.17. art. 1 = the 1st article of the 17th question of the 1st division of Part II. Only the Second Part (II) is further subdivided into parts (1 and 2). References to the *S.c.G.* are by parts and chapters. The *S. Th.* has been translated by the English Dominicans.

in the typically English mind of bishop Butler. As against the Averroists, on the other hand, he stood for independence of tradition and freedom of enquiry. 'The argument from authority', he declared, 'is of all arguments the weakest.' 'What was well said by the ancients we will accept for our profit; what they said wrongly, we will discard.' 'The aim of philosophy is not to know what men have thought, but how the truth of the matter stands.'[1] It would carry us beyond our purpose to discuss the detail of Aquinas' solution, or to dwell on the other speculative problems which witness to the originality of thirteenth-century thought. We have already indicated that the mediaeval philosophers devoted themselves to an analytic study of human personality – a field in which ancient thought afforded them no sure guidance. It is noteworthy that the three problems, of God, freedom, and immortality, first came by their own at the hands of Aquinas and the other great thinkers of the thirteenth century.[2] Greek philosophy had treated these questions with scant justice. They kept their place in the forefront of modern thought, long after the Middle Ages had passed away; constituting the central issue of metaphysics, at the close of the eighteenth century, for Immanuel Kant. The creative impulse to reasoned thought, which awoke at the first reception of the Hellenic legacy in the dawn of the Middle Ages, has operated with unbroken continuity from the ninth century to the present day.

§ 12. Aquinas' greatness as a philosopher rests chiefly on his achievement as a mediator, not only (as we have just seen) between the Platonic and Aristotelian traditions, but, more generally, between the Judaic-Christian religious legacy and that of Hellenic metaphysics. In this lies his originality as a thinker, that he thus provoked new speculative problems of which Plato

1. *S. Th.*, I. q. 32. art. 1; cf. q. 1. art. 1–8, *sup. Boeth. de Trin.*, q. 11. art. 3, and *de unitate intellectus contra Averroistas*, c. 27. In Dante's poem, the vision in Paradise of the union of the divine and human natures in Christ is declared by Justinian to be clear with the intuitive self-evidence that attaches to the metaphysical principle of Contradiction (viz. that A cannot both be and not be B in the same sense and at the same time), *Par.*, vi. 19–21.

2. 'Genuine theology is thus at the same time a real philosophy of religion, as it was, we may add, in the Middle Ages.' – Hegel, *Logic*, § 36 (E. Tr. by Wallace, p. 73).

and Aristotle had hardly dreamed and which went far to determine the subsequent course of philosophical enquiry. Three examples will serve to make this clear. (1) His distinction between faith and reason was endorsed in principle by the leading thinkers of the next six centuries, and still persists in the minds of philosophers at the present day. They are different and mutually exclusive modes of apprehending truth, for faith is *de absentibus* and implies defective insight, while reason, proceeding from self-evident principles by way of vigorous demonstration, attains to full comprehension of its objects. *Impossibile est quod de eodem sit fides et scientia.*[1] Impossible, that is to say, for a given mind at a given moment; for Aquinas is far from suggesting that a truth revealed to faith may not also be demonstrable by reason, so that it can be apprehended now in the one way, now in the other. This is the case with what he calls the 'preambles of faith', e.g. God's existence and unity, which, though falling within the content of revelation, admit also of proof by natural reason. On the other hand, many revealed truths (e.g. the Trinity and the Incarnation) altogether transcend the grasp of reason and are accessible only by the way of faith.[2] Not that any contradiction is conceivable between faith and reason, both alike having their source in God; faith is *praeter naturam*, not *contra naturam*. Its objects are intrinsically intelligible; for the redeemed in Paradise who enjoy the direct vision of God, they will be (as Dante says) as self-evident to the intellect as is for us the basic principle of Contradiction. Faith is relative to man's present state *in viâ*. Reason therefore, as giving full insight, is the superior mode of apprehension, though faith, as resting on divine revelation, speaks with a higher authority and achieves a higher grade of certitude.[3] On this distinction between faith and reason is grounded that between theology on the one hand and, on the other,

1. *de Ver.* xiv. g. *ad resp.*
2. Though even here there is scope for the exercise of reason, in the refutation of sophism and error and in adducing probable arguments in support of truths that lie beyond its grasp.
3. See *S.c.G.*, I, 3–7 and my *Towards a Religious Philosophy*, Additional Note to c. XI, pp. 215 ff., for Aquinas' argument to the need, in view of man's function and appointed goal, of a revelation transcending the scope of natural reason.

metaphysics and the sciences. The theologian, taking his start from principles of revelation, known by the light of grace infused by the Holy Spirit, works downwards from God to the world of His creation; the philosopher (and the scientist) starts from the creaturely, which is the proper object of human reason, and works upwards to God by principles of rational demonstration. From the distinctions thus drawn, two results follow, of cardinal importance for the thought of the succeeding age. The door is thrown open for the advance of the physical sciences, whose autonomy is secured against any intrusion from the theologian in the supposed interest of truths revealed to faith. Reason is established in all, and more than all, its ancient rights, so far, that is, as the interpretation of sensible phenomena is the subject of enquiry. As, in political theory, Aquinas heralds the advent of constitutional government, so, in theory of knowledge, he heralds that of modern science. The second noteworthy consequence concerns the status of religious faith. With the gradual restriction of reason, in the hands of Descartes and those who followed him, to the methods of mathematics and the sciences, and the realization (e.g. by David Hume) of the narrow bounds of demonstrative reasoning, more and more of the (so-called) knowledge, religious, ethical, aesthetic and other, to which man attaches value and significance, was relegated away from the sphere of 'cognitive' faculties to that of irrational belief and referred to the 'sensitive' faculties of feeling and imagination.[1] The paradoxical result was that, in the heyday of the 'Age of Rationalism', reason fell into general discredit. Not only poets, like Wordsworth and Shelley, but philosophers also, whose horizon stretched beyond the data and methods of the positive sciences, have turned to other activities than those of intellect in their search for truth, appealing, as did Bergson, to non-inferential intuition, or, as did William James, to a pragmatist criterion. For this trend towards anti-rationalism, Aquinas cannot be wholly acquitted of responsibility. He had drawn too rigid a line of demarcation

1. See Hume, *Treatise* (Bk. III, Pt. I, Sec. I). Hume's use of the term 'judgement' in this connexion is ambiguous and instructive. We may compare the views of the Logical Positivists to-day.

between faith and reason. Though he allowed a restricted place to reason within the domain of faith, his analysis of the procedure of reason was defective. It never occurred to him to ask, whether faith (and other non-logical operations) was not integral to all rational processes, whether any exercise of rational activity was possible, even in metaphysics and the sciences, without an act of reasonable faith.

§ 13. Secondly (2), Aquinas conceived God, in accordance with the Jewish-Christian religious tradition and in a manner alien to that of Greek philosophy, as the supreme and sole existent, whose nature or essence is to be. In Him, essence and existence, which in all other beings fall asunder, are one and the same. He Himself is self-existent, the sole ground of His own being; 'I am that I am' is the final answer to all further questioning. How then, if God is infinite and total being, can we ascribe real existence (as we needs must) to the finite world of our experience? Are we not impaled on the dilemma of Kant's fourth antinomy? [1] If God is, there can be no universe; if there be a universe, there is something outside God. Aquinas answers this problem by his doctrine of Creation. Being for him is no abstract concept, else it would indeed be what Hegel called it, 'the poorest of all predicates'; it is pure activity, the power to be and to impart being. As Plotinus had said, 'it is of the nature of being to beget', i.e. to go forth from itself in creative energy.[2] It is because of God's infinite wealth of being that he displays infinite power to create and conserve in being what owes all its being to Him and yet is other than Himself. The problem thus set by the Christian revelation, and the solution offered, alike constitute a new departure in the history of thought. Neither Plato, whose demiurge was but an architect, fashioning the sense-world in a given 'receptacle' after the likeness of timeless Forms, nor Aristotle, the activity of whose God was confined within the bounds of His self-consciousness, had ever entertained the idea of creation. For them the problem which has eluded enquiry all down the ages, Why is there an existent world at all?, simply did not arise.

1. *Critique of Pure Reason*, A. 452–460 = B. 480–489.
2. On Plotinus, see c. ix, pp. 319–87.

The categorical assertion of God's being marks the difference between the theistic faith of Christianity and the conclusion of any inferential process. Whereas Greek philosophy and modern science alike concentrate attention on the general characters of things, which, being expressible in concepted formulas, are intelligible to human reason; Christianity grapples with the problem of their existence which, since it allows of no such formulation, presents a final inexplicability to the intellect. This is the *raison d'être* of the age-long controversies between religion and science, theology, and metaphysics. Except for a Christian philosophy, like that of Aquinas, these controversies are without a remedy. For such a philosophy they are quarrels over unsubstantial shadows, which vanish in presence of an existential faith and 'leave not a wrack behind'.[1]

§ 14. My last illustration (3) shows how Aquinas utilized the Aristotelian legacy in the service of a purely Christian theology. I refer to the principle known as *analogia entis*. It is obvious from what we have just said that the being of the Creator and that of His creatures are very different modes of being, parted one from the other by an infinite gulf. The one is total being, self-existent, necessary, and infinite; the other is partial being, dependent, contingent, and finite. The one is wholly in act, exclusive of all potentiality, becoming, and not-being; the other is through and through permeated by unrealized possibilities, change, and not-being. How can man's finite mind, riddled by these deficiencies, bridge the gulf even in conception, so as to attain knowledge of the Creator? Man seems to be faced by an ineluctable dilemma, tossed helplessly between Scylla and Charybdis. Either the term 'being' is applicable univocally (i.e. in the same meaning) to the Creator and the creatures, in which case 'being' is a generic character common to the two specific modes, and the door is open to all the wild vagaries of anthropomorphism, i.e. the interpretation

1. Those contemporary theologians, especially on the Continent, who, paying scant heed to the main Catholic tradition, follow Kierkegaard, Karl Barth, and other champions of an 'existential' Christianity, would find in Aquinas all, and more than all, they claim to have garnered from the Reformers of the sixteenth century.

of God's being in terms of the creaturely being of our human experience. Or the term 'being' is equivocal (i.e. different in meaning); so that we have no warrant for regarding God's goodness, power, or wisdom as having any affinity to our own. For all we can tell, God's goodness may be our badness. Our only resource is to follow the *via remotionis* and to refuse to ascribe to God any positive predicate drawn from the finite world of our experience. Any such determination of His character is to impress a limit on the unlimited. Everything that can be affirmed of God is, strictly, affirmed falsely; at best it has an ambiguous value as symbolism or metaphor. We escape from the Scylla of anthropomorphism only to be wrecked in the Charybdis of agnosticism. Aquinas evaded this dilemma by borrowing from Aristotle's doctrine of the Categories the theory of analogous predication. Being is asserted of God and of the creature neither univocally nor equivocally, but analogously. That is what Aristotle had asserted of being in the ten Categories (substance, quality, relation, and the rest); they were not ten species of a common genus, 'being', nor were they wholly different from one another in their 'being'; there was identity amid the difference and differences amid the identity. You could not single out or specify with clear precision the identical factor from that of difference, so inseparably were they integrated in the unity of each mode of being. In adapting to his purpose this logical doctrine, Aquinas gave it a new and far more profound application, alike in metaphysics and in theology. It was possible henceforward to predicate positively of God by transferring to Him such perfections as were discernible in human experience, in accordance with the following scheme of proportion. As the 'being' of the Creator is to that of the creature; so are the Creator's goodness, intelligence, power, etc., to the goodness, intelligence, power, etc., of the creature. Thus the gulf was bridged; and theology was freed from the dangers both of anthropomorphism and of agnosticism. Another dilemma, which is a besetting menace to philosophy, was likewise shorn of its terrors. Neither the extremes of Monism nor Pluralism can hold their ground against the doctrine of *analogia entis*.

In light of that doctrine, it is no longer possible to say: 'Whatever it is, it is all one', or 'If you analyse far enough, you will be faced with an absolute diversity.' Pantheism was thus warned off the theological premises and a Christian philosophy saved, and Christianity saved, from one of the chief pitfalls of modern Idealist metaphysics. No more convincing refutation of pure immanentism (Spinoza's, Hegel's, or, in more recent times, Gentile's) can be found than in Aquinas' masterly tractate, *de unitate intellectus contra Averroistas*. It stands, side by side with the first part of Plato's *Theaetetus*, as one of the final achievements in the history of philosophy.

III. THE RECEPTION OF ROMAN LAW [1]

§ 15. Roman law, like Greek philosophy, reached the Middle Ages in a debased and fragmentary form.[2] The code of Justinian was virtually unknown in the West until the eleventh century, save in those parts of Italy where the eastern emperors retained their jurisdiction. Elsewhere the chief source of legal tradition was the code of Theodosius II (438), a compilation framed by eastern lawyers, but promulgated coincidently in the West by Valentinian III. In the five succeeding centuries, the epoch of the barbarian invasions and the dark age that followed them, we can trace the influence of Roman law on the new kingdoms in four directions. (i) Barbarian chieftains began to write down, in imitation of the Roman practice, their native Germanic law. Thus did Euric the Visigoth (c. 470), Clovis the Salian Frank (486–511), the kings of the Burgundians and of the Ripuarian Franks (sixth century). Bede tells how Aethelberht of Kent (c. 600), after the coming of Augustine to Britain, collected the laws of his people 'according to the pattern of

1. The term 'Reception', generally used of the introduction of Roman law into Germany at the close of the fifteenth century, and later into the common law of Scotland, is used here to mean the influence of the Roman legal tradition on the law and thought of western Europe throughout the Middle Ages.
2. On the matter of the following sections, the author is largely indebted to the early chapters in vol. i. of Pollock and Maitland's *History of the Laws of England*, Vinogradoff's *Roman Law in Mediaeval Europe*, and Gierke's *Political Theories of the Middle Age* (tr. Maitland).

the Romans'.[1] Of these Germanic codes the most remarkable were those of the Lombard kings of northern Italy in the seventh and eighth centuries, whose work served as a basis for a scientific jurisprudence, and persisted in force long after the conquest of Lombardy by the Franks in 744. (ii) The Teutonic kings also compiled codes of Roman law for their Roman subjects, who retained their legal status as Romans under barbarian overlords. Under the Goths, Franks, and Lombards, law was personal rather than territorial. Bishop Agobard of Lyon (c. 850) tells how five men might meet together in a single room, each with a claim to be judged in accordance with his own racial law.[2] To borrow Maitland's analogy, it was as with the peoples of British India to-day; though we must suppose one of them to be possessed of an old law-book, too good for them and for us, which becomes in course of time a subject of scientific study and the basis of a revival of jurisprudence.[3] Of these later Roman codes the most important was the *lex Romana Visigothorum*, drawn up by Alaric II, the son of Euric, in 506 for the use of his Roman subjects in Gaul and Spain, and known commonly as the *Breviarium Alaricianum*. Written in very tolerable Latin, it comprised a clear statement of those portions of Roman law which were intelligible to the degenerate lawyers of that age and relevant to the practical requirements of the Visigothic courts. In its formal arrangement into institutes, common law (*jus*), and statute law (*leges*), it anticipated the threefold division adopted in the East a generation later by Justinian. Despite the comparative poverty of its contents, it kept alive the law of Rome, and remained for over five hundred years the chief authority in the countries north of the Alps. In its train there appeared in western Europe a customary version of Roman law, standing to the old law in much the same relation as the Romance languages to the pure classical Latin. (iii) During the same period Roman elements crept into native Germanic law, and conversely, the inheritance of Roman

1. Bede, *Eccl. Hist.*, ii. 5, '*juxta exempla Romanorum*'. The example of Roman law acted as a stimulus not only to the written compilation of existing native law, but to its enrichment by means of royal statutes.
2. Vinogradoff, p. 16.
3. Pollock and Maitland, i. p. 15.

law was gradually coloured by elements of Germanic origin. The laws of Euric derived from a Roman source such provisions as the prohibition of legal actions after a lapse of thirty years, and the admission of women to inheritance on equal terms with men. Among Franks and Lombards, formulas for contracts were adapted from Roman models. The converse tendency may be illustrated by the incorporation of Germanic customs in the *lex Romana Curiensis*, an eighth-century code compiled for the Romance population of eastern Switzerland. (iv) Finally, the tradition of Roman law was preserved by the western church. We have seen how problems of internal discipline had from early times engaged the attention of synods and councils, and how, when the empire became Christian, episcopal jurisdiction received official recognition. Thus, from the fourth century onwards, came into being the canon law. Its main sources were the scriptures, the writings of the Fathers, the decrees of general councils, certain letters of the Roman bishops, and the custom of the church. From these materials were formed collections of canons, which were enlarged by extracts from Roman law-books, and by a mass of spurious papal letters, produced in France during the ninth century, and known as the *pseudo-Isidore*. In 774, the collection framed early in the sixth century by a Scythian monk, Dionysius the Small (*Exiguus*), was presented by pope Hadrian I to Charles the Great, and adopted as a standard canonical authority throughout the Frankish kingdom. In language, in form, and in many of its maxims, the canon law reflected the influence of the civil law of Rome. Pope Gregory the Great (590-604) had known and utilized Justinian's *Digest*. When the Frankish monarchy began to decay in the ninth century, the canon law alone continued to show signs of life. By preserving something of the tradition and spirit of Roman law, it contributed materially to the eleventh-century revival of jurisprudence in the schools of Pavia and Bologna.

§ 16. 'The study of Roman law never dies. When it seems to be dying it always returns to the texts and is born anew.' [1] So it was in Provence and in northern Italy in the eleventh cen-

1. Pollock and Maitland, i. p. 24.

tury, as at a later day in France and Germany. In that century
the mediaeval order was shaping itself into definite outline on
every side. Hildebrand (pope Gregory VII) thundered the
claims of papal supremacy into the ears of all Christendom;
Norman rulers, gifted with a rare capacity for law and government, reared with a strong hand the fabric of political order in
their dominions; Bernard at Clairvaux disciplined the pious,
for the service of God and his church, under the austere rule of
Benedict; Anselm and Abelard woke the slumbering intellect
of the schools to new vitality. The time was ripe for lawyers, in
south-eastern France, at Pavia in Lombardy, at Ravenna, once
the seat of Justinian's viceroys, and, above all, at Bologna, in
the school founded by Hildebrand's champion, Matilda of Tuscany, to turn away from the *Breviary* of Alaric and the mangled
sources that had sufficed a more ignorant generation, and to
study the *Digest* at first hand. In 1038, the emperor Conrad II
had restored Roman law as the territorial law of the Roman
city. In 1076, the *Digest*, which had been a dead letter for
more than four centuries, was cited in a Tuscan court. A line
of great juristic teachers, from Irnerius (*c.* 1100) to Azo and
Accursius (*c.* 1250), made the university of Bologna the legal
training ground for all Europe.[1] They set themselves first to
recover the text of Justinian's *Corpus*, then to unfold its interpretation. The fruits of their labour and teaching are manifest
in many treatises of the twelfth and thirteenth centuries, such
as the Provençal *Codi* (*c.* 1150), summary of Justinian's code
for the use of judges, and the *Coutume de Beauvaisis* of Philippe
de Beaumanoir (*c.* 1280), which shows how legal ideas of
Roman origin had been already blended with the local custom
of northern France. In England, Roman doctrines were introduced from Bologna towards the close of the twelfth century
by Vacarius, who founded a school of law at Oxford. But the
most striking example, both of the extent and of the limits of
the Roman influence in this country, is furnished by Bracton's

1. Accursius' *glossa ordinaria* summed up the work of the glossators (from
Irnerius onward), who as theoretic jurists studied the *Corpus* as a system. Later,
the post-glossators set themselves to apply the principles to practical needs:
see de Zulueta in *Legacy of Rome*, pp. 378 f.

famous treatise on the laws of England (*de legibus Angliae*, *c.* 1250), where the teaching of Azo of Bologna is applied with a thoroughly characteristic independence. The legislation of Norman and early Plantagenet sovereigns had evolved a large measure of order and stability out of the chaos of local custom, and Englishmen, justly proud of their established tradition, viewed with natural suspicion any attempt to impose a cosmopolitan jurisprudence on the developed structure of native law. Hence the resistance offered alike by king and nobles to the importation of Roman ideas from the schools of Italy. The church also, in England and elsewhere, was inclined to be jealous of the civil law. The same age that saw the rise of the university of Bologna gave birth also to the codification of ecclesiastical law. Gratian's *Decretum* (1139–42) became the legal text-book of the church courts. A century later (1234), pope Gregory IX embodied subsequent enactments in a complete and authoritative code of canon law.[1] Inferior in legal quality as was the canon law to the civil, these efforts in codification are proof, both of the impulse towards a scientific jurisprudence that was stirring in the papal courts, and of the growing claims of the papacy to extend its legal jurisdiction. It was the epoch of the struggle over investitures, and the rivalry of church and empire. The story of this specially mediaeval conflict lies beyond our province. It is enough to indicate that it was fought out, not only in the political area, but also on the ground of legal argument, and that both parties to the controversy appealed for support to the inheritance of Roman law.

§ 17. Great as was the influence of the law of Rome on that of the mediaeval peoples, it left a yet deeper mark on their moral and political ideals. Morality and law alike claim to regulate man's action as a social being; and the line of distinction between them is by no means easy to define. For the Greeks,

1. Gratian's *Decretum* was the first attempt to present a *Corpus* of church law. Its title was *Concordia discordantium Canonum*. Canonists commented on its text, just as the civilians of Bologna commented on the *Corpus Juris Civilis*. The collection of Gregory IX was known as the *Decretals*; it became henceforward the chief law-book of the Church. Boniface VIII and Clement V added further decretals, known respectively as the *Sext* and the *Clementines*.

both in their theory and in their practice, the obligations to conform to the law of the *Polis* were also moral duties. That they were not unconscious of the distinction is evident from the question raised by their philosophers, whether the dictates of morality were founded on nature (*physis*) or on mutable convention (*nomos*).[1] But the whole tendency of Hellenic thought, as we see it in Plato and Aristotle, was rather to moralize law than to reduce morality to legal terms. The standard of conduct was conceived as good rather than as duty; the *Polis* was looked upon as the fitting sphere for a life of civic virtue, and law as the means to its achievement. In the Middle Ages, on the other hand, the governing ethical concept was that of moral law. Several grounds combined to bring about this change of orientation. For one thing, Christianity took over the Old Testament scriptures, where the Mosaic legislation is presented as covering the whole field of moral and religious obligation. The terms 'law', 'commandments', 'statutes', as interpreted by the developed spiritual consciousness of prophets and psalmists, refer, not merely or mainly to external actions, but to the inner disposition of the heart. They are sanctioned by the authority, not of a secular sovereign, but of God himself. Such precepts, claiming divine origin and absolute validity, while retaining the title and form of law, could hardly be compared, in view of their richer spiritual import, with the laws of the Hellenic *Polis* or the *jus civile* of Rome. Again, to the Christian, with his vivid consciousness of sin and his doctrine of man's fall, the moral life inevitably assumed the form of a discipline under the stern control of law, rather than of a harmonious realization of natural human aspirations. Thus far, perhaps, there was little risk of falling into the confusion, which has constantly obscured ethical thinking, of resolving morality into legalism and its science into jurisprudence. It was otherwise when the influence of Roman law came into play. For the Roman, moral and religious practice had always been coloured by legal formalism. If the Latin word *virtus* (manliness) suggested the excellence of the citizen-soldier, the term for 'duties' (*officia*) pointed to the life

1. See Vol. I, c. iv, §§ 14-16; c. v, § 15.

of the punctilious bureaucrat, spent in a ceaseless round of official functions. If the Greek strove to moralize law, the Roman legalized morality. We have seen how the great jurists of the early empire accommodated Stoic doctrine to their science. They taught that behind the civil law of Rome, behind even the common law of nations, lay the law of nature, rooted in man's constitution as a rational and, therefore, a moral being. The acceptance of this juristic tradition went far to strengthen the mediaeval tendency to interpret morality under the form of law.[1] The groundwork was laid for a reconciliation between the enacted law of the land and the principles of morality, as being two different but mutually consistent expressions of reason, which was the image of the divine original stamped at the creation upon the soul of man.[2] This *rapprochement* was facilitated by the obvious facts, that the discharge of legal obligations fell within the scope of moral duty, and that justice was recognized by mediaeval thinkers as one of the cardinal moral virtues. Side by side with the triad of the theological virtues, faith, hope, and charity, revealed under the Christian dispensation, and attainable only by its believers, they set prudence, fortitude, temperance, and justice, which, as pagan philosophy had witnessed, were the fruit of man's rational nature, independent of special revelation.[3] The distinction is familiar to all students of Dante and of the allegorical creations

1. The Fathers of the church appropriated these ideas of the jurists. We find them, e.g. in Augustine. An example of the influence of Roman legalism in religious thought is afforded by the history of the doctrine of the atonement. Christ's sacrifice is presented as the payment of legal satisfaction, either to the devil (Augustine's theory that God buys man from the devil by Christ's death on the cross), or to God (Anselm's view, based on Tertullian, Cyprian, and other western teachers), who has been defrauded and must be repaid; since the debt is too great for man to repay, Christ offers himself and thereby satisfies the claim, receiving forgiveness from God, and (since he needs it not himself) bestowing it on man.

2. Law of nature is, however, sometimes understood to mean the principles (e.g. to nourish and rear their offspring) implicit in the nature of *all* animals. But the view stated in the text predominates in mediaeval thought (see Aquinas, *S. Th.*, II. 1. q. 95. art. 4. ad. 1 ᵃᵐ; II. 2. q. 57. art. 3).

3. The statement in the text needs amplification, in that the theological virtues, when infused by grace into the soul of the Christian, raise the natural (Aristotelian) virtues to a higher plane, so that, thus enriched, they merit the title of 'infused' virtues (see Wicksteed, *Reactions*, pp. 492–3, 516–22).

of mediaeval art. It is in the interpretation of justice that the relationship of morality and law is most apparent. Aristotle, in treating of this virtue as a form of moral excellence, had chiefly in mind its application to the legal practice of the Greek city-state. The Roman jurists, approaching the question from the point of view of the law, recognized that justice rested on a moral basis. They defined *jus* as 'the art of the good and the equitable' (*ars boni et aequi*); and justice as 'the constant and perpetual volition to assign to each man his *jus*'. The Christian Fathers accepted these definitions, which were adopted both in the civil and in the canon law. Aquinas followed closely on their path. No one can stir a step in the field of mediaeval thought without realizing how ethical and political problems were debated on the *terrain* of jurisprudence, and solved by the aid of concepts that had their source in Roman law.[1]

§ 18. It was Aquinas, who, in the light of the reception of Aristotle and of the *Digest*, fixed the main outlines of the theory of law for the later Middle Ages. He devoted to the subject a special section of the first division of the second part of his *Summa Theologica*.[2] A summary of his doctrine will show how

1. Aristotle, on justice; *Eth. Nic.*, v. The jurists' definitions; *jus, Dig.*, i. 1, 1, *justice, Dig.*, i. 1. 6. Aquinas discusses justice in *S. Th.*, II. 2. qq. 57 ff.; his definition of justice is given in q. 58. art. 1, of *jus* in q. 57. art. 1 and 2, of *lex* in q. 90. art. 4. By *justitia* mediaeval thinkers meant both 'justice' and 'righteousness'. Law (*lex*) is a species of right (*jus*), viz. its written and promulgated expression. The English language, with its one word 'law', enhances the difficulty, already felt by mediaeval writers, of distinguishing between *jus* and *lex*.

2. The section referred to is *S. Th.*, II. 1. qq. 90–108, forming a treatise *de legibus*. The scheme is as follows:

A. Introductory (qq. 90–2).
B. The several kinds of law:

lex aeterna (q. 93)
|
```
        lex divina                          lex naturalis
   (q. 91. art. 4, qq. 98–108)           (q. 91. art. 2, q. 94)
           |                                       |
    ┌──────┴──────┐                                |
lex vetus (O.T.)   lex nova (N.T.)            lex humana
  (qq. 98–105)      (qq. 106–8)         = (i) jus commune gentium (q. 95)
                                         (ii) jus civile (lex positiva)
                                                 (q. 91. art. 3)
                                                 (qq. 95–7)
```

deeply the conception of a law of nature had set its mark on the mediaeval mind. It will show how reflexion on the principles of law opened the door to larger problems of political government. For Aquinas, the ultimate source of all law is the eternal ordinance of God (*lex aeterna*), 'the very principle (*ratio*) of the government of things, existing in God as the ruler of the universe', and, as such, not other than God himself. This eternal law is the timeless judgement of the divine reason, made binding by the divine will, known as it is by the blessed in paradise, and by us, through the reflexions that flow from it.[1] These reflexions are (i) God's revealed law as declared in the Old and the New Testaments (*lex divina*), and (ii) the law of nature (*lex naturalis*), 'the participation of the rational creature in the eternal law', consisting of principles of action self-evident, infallible, universal, and unalterable, promulgated by God, for 'God instilled it into man's mind so as to be known by him naturally'.[2] From natural law in turn is derived positive man-made law (*lex humana*), enacted by human will and resting for its basis on a social compact. 'A thing is made just in two ways; in one way by the very nature of the thing, and this is called *jus naturale*; in another, by a certain compact (*condictum*) among men, and this is called *jus positivum*.'[3] Human or positive law comprises (*a*) the *jus gentium*, closely akin to natural law and deriving therefrom a portion of its cogency, e.g. the prohibition of murder, which is deducible from the precept of nature to do no evil to any; and (*b*) the *jus civile*, which,

1. *S. Th.*, II. 1. q. 91. art. 1, q. 93. art.2.
2. On the precepts, see q. 94. art. 2. In addition, Aquinas mentions secondary and variable dictates of natural law, such as observance of contracts and the institution of private property, added by human reason in conformity with the immutable primary precepts. The problem of property had been urgent since the days of the Roman jurists, and pressed heavily on the Christian Fathers. In the state of nature, all things were common; yet private property was a fact, and seemed essential to social order. The jurists generally referred it to the *jus gentium* as distinct from *jus naturae*: the Fathers (e.g. Augustine) explained it as due to man's sin, but as a necessary remedy for the consequences of the Fall. But the doctrine of natural law, that all men had a right to the necessaries of life, was unimpaired; Aquinas even held that it was lawful, in certain cases, to take a rich man's goods and give them to the poor. The canonists taught that a man possessed wealth only subject to the condition of right use.
3. *Positivum*, i.e. posited, enacted by human will.

though derived also from natural law, involves local and temporal determinations, and draws its cogency from human enactment, e.g. that a given crime should be punished in a particular way. The end of this positive law is 'the temporal tranquillity of the state', and its validity depends on four conditions: It must trace its derivation to natural law, must be ordained for the common good of the state, must be framed by the person in whose hand is the government of the community, and must serve as a directive rule for human acts of justice, whereas divine and natural law are regulative of all human actions whatsoever.

§ 19. This distinction of natural and positive law carried with it corollaries of the utmost importance for political theory. The maxim of Augustine, that an unjust law was no law at all, was universally accepted in the Middle Ages. Positive law, though promulgated by pope or emperor, had no validity, if it were inconsistent with the law of nature. A tyrant's laws are no true laws; according to Aquinas, obedience to them is not obligatory 'in the court of conscience', save in so far as transgression would give rise to scandal or disorder.[1] Obviously such views offered wide latitude for interpretation. *A fortiori*, a law that contradicts *lex divina* had no claim upon the subject under any circumstances. No one in the Middle Ages dreamed of questioning the doctrine that God must be obeyed rather than man. In the second place it followed that positive law was a mutable instrument of government, dependent for its original enactment, and for its interpretation, on the ruling authority.[2] The prince in a monarchical state was, like Aristotle's ideal ruler, a *lex animata*, a living fount of positive law; where, as in a republic, the people exercise sovereignty, the executive magistrate was subject to the popularly enacted law. Thus the texts of the Roman *Digest*: 'the will of the prince has the force of law'; 'the prince holds all law (*jura*) in his heart'; 'the

1. See q. 93. art. 3, ad 2ᵃᵐ, q. 95. art. 1, 2, 4; II. 2. q. 57. art. 2. ad 2ᵃᵐ; *de regimine principum*, I. cc. 3–11; Dante, *de Monarchia*, ii. 5. It was open to reformers to appeal against the actual state to the ideal state in which these requirements would be satisfied; and the appeal was sanctioned, not only by morality, but by law.

2. II. 2. q. 60. art. 6; II. 1. q. 90. art. 3.

prince is free from the bonds of the laws', could be reconciled with the mediaeval system of society, though always subject to the reservation that the laws in question were positive human law. Here, again, there was room for diversity of interpretation. Aquinas himself favoured a form of constitution which, like Aristotle's 'polity', united the characteristics of monarchy, aristocracy, and democracy. The prince should be elected by the people, and assisted by a nobility based on the possession of eminent virtue.[1] We can thus trace the lines on which the political thinkers of the Middle Ages solved the problem of the relation between law and the state. The conviction that the state derived its rightful authority from law, and that its mission was to realize the reign of law, was implanted deep in the Germanic mind. The doctrine diametrically opposed to this, and known both to Hellenic and to modern thought, that might is right, and that the state is wholly independent of ethical restraint, found no adherents, even among the most ardent champions of monarchical power throughout the Middle Ages. The ever-present danger of anarchy and private war invested law with a halo of ideal attributes. It was reverenced as the immediate utterance of God, speaking to the princes and peoples of the earth. When the theory that the state was above all controls of morality or natural law was asserted by Machiavelli in the sixteenth century, it seemed a monstrous subversion of ethical and religious principle. But a difficulty of another kind had arisen, three centuries earlier, when mediaeval theory was first confronted with the political doctrines of the Greek philosophers. We have seen how Plato and Aristotle taught that the state, as existing by nature, was superior to law, which served as the instrument of its ethical function. Here lay the problem: how was the Germanic conviction that the state was subordinate to law, to be reconciled with the classical tradition that law was subordinate to the state? A solution was reached by aid of the distinction between law of nature and

---

1. II. 1. q. 105. art. 1. The prince should be subject to the *vis directiva* (guiding force) and be entrusted with the *vis coactiva* (coercive force) of human law (q. 96. art. 5. ad 2^{am}). That the executive ruler should take counsel, was a principle as firmly rooted in Teutonic, as in Roman republican, custom.

positive law. While the state and its ruler derived their right from the higher authority of natural or, *a fortiori*, of divine, law and were consequently subject to ethical obligations; positive law, representing the variable applications of natural law to particular circumstances of time and place, was the creation of, and dependent upon, the state. Thus the outcome of mediaeval theory was to broaden the concept of law so as to include within its scope the moral foundations and ideal purpose of political society.

§ 20. The fusion of native Germanic ideas with the legacy of Greece and Rome is further exemplified in the mediaeval doctrines of monarchy, and of the derivation of sovereignty from the public will.[1] The Teutonic peoples showed an instinctive preference for monarchical government. Their belief in its inherent rightfulness was strengthened, not merely by the fact that, throughout the Middle Ages, a strong ruler was the only effective safeguard against anarchy and injustice, but also by political and legal theories. The character of these may best be studied in the first book of Dante's treatise on Monarchy (*de Monarchia*). He marshals both speculative and practical arguments in support of the claims of monarchical government, and, particularly, of the Holy Roman empire as a universal monarchy, embracing by right the entire human race.[2] The nerve of his metaphysical argument was the conception of the created universe as a whole composed of parts, such as the human species, subordinate forms of association (kingdoms, provinces, civic communities, and households), and individual men; each of which parts was in its turn a whole, possessing a relative independence, and a specific end or good, in definite subordination to the end or good of the whole universe. Thus

1. The principles (*a*) that law, rooted in the custom of the community, is supreme, and (*b*) that recognition by the community was requisite for each successor to the kingship, were imbedded in the Teutonic tradition. Roman jurists had laid down that the *original source* of all political authority lay with the Roman people; Teutonic societies regarded the consent of the people as an *actually existing* condition of all rightful rule. So, again, the law in Teutonic societies was regarded as that of the community, not as that of the king; whereas, on the Roman doctrine, the emperor was the supreme legislative authority. See Carlyle, *Mediaeval Political Theory in the West*, vol. iii. Introduction.

2. See, especially, *de Mon.*, i. cc. 5–8, 15.

he reflected the effort of mediaeval thought to do full justice, alike to the claims of the universal whole, emphasized by the Hellenic tradition, and to those of the individual, recognized as of intrinsic value both by the Germanic spirit and by the teaching of Christianity. The created universe in its entirety formed a commonwealth, ruled by God as king; and human society should, by right, mirror the constitution of the macro-cosm of which it was a member. Aristotle, too, had taught that unity of end carried with it unity of direction (*ordinatio ad unum*). Again, scripture declared that man was created in God's image; and the human race could only realize this divine inten-tion if it possessed unity, which it does most perfectly when united under the rule of one. That unity was the root of good, while evil consisted in forsaking unity for multiplicity, was a cardinal tenet of mediaeval (as of Neo-Platonic) metaphysics; a concordant unity of human wills is, therefore, essential to a good disposition of human society, and this concord is best secured under a single governing will.[1] To these arguments Dante added others of an ethical character, e.g. that justice and liberty are best secured under a monarchical government, and that a universal monarchy alone can serve as an effective super-national tribunal.[2] Finally, he supports his conclusion by adducing the fact of history, that God sent his Son into the world at a moment when, for the first time since man's fall, it reposed in peace under the universal sovereignty of Augustus.[3] Thus we see how, for Dante, the political theory of Aristotle,

1. It is noteworthy that neither Dante, the originator of this last argument, nor any other thinker attained to the conception of a real unification of the wills of individual members in a group-will, and that when the doctrine of corporate personality was introduced into juristic theory by the great master of canon law, pope Innocent IV (Sinibald Fieschi, pope 1243–54), it was regarded as a legal fiction (*persona ficta*). The mediaeval conviction of the exclu-sive reality of individual personality was so deep-rooted that it proved an insuperable obstacle to the growth of an adequate legal theory of groups and corporations. The influence of Roman law, which furnished the concept of *societas*, i.e. an artificial partnership of individuals, tended in the same direction. It was not till well on in the eighteenth century that Rousseau, in his doctrine of the general will (*volonté générale*), lighted on the thought which was needed to overcome the individualist tradition of man's relation to society (see Maitland's *Introduction* to Gierke).

2. *de Mon.*, i. cc. 10–14.

3. *Ibid.*, i. c. 16.

the tradition of Roman history and law, and the world-outlook of the Christian religion, converged to strengthen and expand the native Germanic partiality for monarchical rule. It follows that all monarchy, whether ecclesiastical or temporal, is of divine right; for all lordship is from God (*omne dominium est a Deo*).[1] It follows also, and here reflective theory is in close harmony with Germanic tradition, that all monarchy, as a *ministerium a Deo commissum*, is 'office', i.e. it involves duties as well as rights.[2] The monarch, says Aquinas, is 'a public person' ruling 'for the common good'. His function is threefold: to establish the good life in the community, to preserve it in being when established, and to promote its progress to a still higher plane.[3] Hence the monarch's power is necessarily limited by the duties of his office. Neither pope nor kaiser can for a moment claim that *l'église*, or *l'état*, *c'est moi*. His private and his public personalities are manifestly distinct. Commands issued *ultra vires* are null and void. He is the representative of his people, bearing their person, as John of Salisbury puts it; his dignity is inalienable, for he did not confer it on himself, and therefore cannot of himself dispose of it.[4] 'The authority of the prince is his only for use, for no prince can create his own authority.' [5] We are here confronted by the second of the afore-mentioned convictions of mediaeval political theory, that of the derivation of sovereignty from the popular will.

§ 21. Despite this bias towards monarchical government,

1. The doctrine that secular princes ruled by divine right commended itself to the early church, as supported both by the New Testament and by the Jewish tradition of the king as the Lord's anointed. See Luke xx. 25, John xix. 11, Rom. xiii. 1–7, 1 Pet. ii. 13–17; and also 2 Sam. i. 16 and v. 3. In the later Middle Ages, it became the watchword of the imperialists, who maintained that the secular ruler held his authority directly from God, not indirectly through the pope (see *de Mon.*, iii).

2. The phrase quoted is as old as the ninth century. Thus the doctrine of divine right implied that the monarch's power was conditional on its proper exercise.

3. *de Mon.*, i. c. 15. See also the quotations from mediaeval writers in Poole, *Illustrations*, pp. 232, 234–5.

4. *Universitatis subiectorum personam gerit.* Cf. Aquinas, *S. Th.*, II. 1. q. 90. art. 3. ad 2^{am} and Dante, *Par.* xii. 89–90 for the distinction between the pope's private personality and his papal office. Dante does not hesitate to place popes in hell.

5. *de Mon.*, iii. c. 7.

the theory of the sovereignty of the people was germinating in the mediaeval mind. It was also part of the tradition of the Germanic races. Moreover, the Christian church had accepted from Augustine that in man's pristine state of nature there prevailed freedom from coercive authority, and that lordship and servitude were reciprocal consequences of the Fall. 'God willed not that the rational creature made in his image should have lordship save over irrational creatures. . . . The condition of servitude is rightly understood as imposed on man as sinner.' [1] With the rediscovery of Aristotle, a new and a very different theory was disclosed to the thinkers of the thirteenth century. Political society, with its forms of organization and government, was rooted, not in sin, but in the original sociality of human nature. Aquinas had no hesitation in accepting the Hellenic tradition. Had man continued in the state of innocence, he would have developed, not indeed *dominium servile*, but *dominium politicum*. The garden of Eden, in short, would have been administered by a constitutional monarchy. Men would not have been equal, for there would have been grades of virtue and of knowledge.[2] Lordship and social preference are creations of the law of nations (*jus gentium*), and rest on reason; though the state, like the visible church, is relative to a scene of probation, and has no significance in the life beyond the grave. How then did the state come into being? The answer to this question, dating from the time of the quarrel over investitures in the eleventh century, was, that it originated in a contract, by which the people, the ultimate sovereign, handed over their rights and powers to a ruler, and thereby instituted a civil society (*societas*).[3] This term, whose individualist implication we have already noted, had been applied to the organized

1. Aug., *de Civ. Dei*, xix. c. 15. See Gierke, *note* 16. Gregory VII (eleventh century) and John of Salisbury (twelfth century) voice this view. It finds expression later in Milton's lines on Nimrod, *Paradise Lost*, xii., init. Servitude and coercive jurisdiction were, however, justified, like private property, as remedial instruments, incidental to man's altered circumstances after the Fall. As such, they were regarded as sanctioned by the divine will. Thus a door was left open for the reception of the Aristotelian tradition.

2. *S. Th.*, I. q. 96. art. 3 and 4.

3. So John of Salisbury and Aquinas. Appeal was made to Augustine and to 2 Sam. v. 3.

community by Cicero. Roman law taught that by the *jus gentium* a free people could institute a superior, and that in actual fact the powers of the Roman emperor had been thus conferred by a single statute.[1] It is obvious that this doctrine of a social contract, like others that we have mentioned, lent itself to a wide diversity of interpretation. The champions of autocracy could stretch the terms of the surrender in the interest of the monarch, while the advocates of popular rights could insist on the inherent sovereignty of the people, and erect a theory of republicanism on the maxim that 'the people is greater than the prince' (*populus major principe*). This last was the direction followed by two notable political thinkers of the later Middle Ages, Marsilius of Padua (*Defensor Pacis*, 1324–26), and Cardinal Nicolas of Cues (1401–64).[2] Aquinas, as we have seen, preferred to steer a middle course. Here, as elsewhere, he displayed the rare sobriety of his judgement, and his consummate skill in blending the Graeco-Roman legacy with the spirit of mediaeval life. It is easy, but scarcely profitable, to criticize the theory of the social contract as abstract and unhistorical. It would, indeed, be difficult to find a more fitting formula to express the facts of feudal society. That society was characterized by the assimilation of public to private law. The king ruled over the 'estates' of the realm, with a title analogous to that of any feudal proprietor. The feudal tie, as illustrated, for example, by the coronation oath, was contractual in its

1. The *lex regia*, of which we hear in the third century and in Justinian's *Corpus*. It was erroneously believed that Augustus had received his power in this way.
2. Marsilius taught the absorption of church in state. A striking anticipation of his position, however, is found in the *Tractatus Eboracensis*, written by a canon of York under Henry II. Marsilius is a republican: the right of legislation is vested inalienably in the people, acting as a primary assembly, or through elected representatives. The ruler is appointed, and can be deposed, by the people, and his authority is always subordinate to the popular will. Nicolas of Cues, in his *de Concordantiâ Catholicâ*, written during the Conciliar movement, gave noble expression to the mediaeval ideal of a perfect harmony between the order of the universe and that of human society; temporal and ecclesiastical authorities are independent, but harmonious, instruments; government rests on popular sovereignty, and the elective and representative principles are championed, both in church and in state. The new spirit of nationalism is clearly recognized. This great work best illustrates the attempt to unite old and new ideas, at the close of the mediaeval period.

nature, and bound ruler and ruled by reciprocal obligations of protection and obedience.[1] Above all, the contract theory, resting, as it did, on that of natural law, kept alive, through the Middle Ages, the faith that government was founded on right, and not on violence, and that above and beyond the ruler lay the binding dictates of ideal justice. If the doctrine of divine right served to justify the secular state in its struggle against ecclesiastical domination, that of the social contract became the watchword of popular resistance to the growth of arbitrary despotism.

§ 22. Mediaeval theory, as we have indicated, developed in close conjunction with mediaeval practice; and its bearings can hardly be appreciated without a study of the historical movements of the time, such as the rivalry of papacy and empire, the effort to substitute conciliar government in the church for papal absolutism, and the rise, as the fruit of a growing national consciousness, of the independent kingdoms of modern Europe. But the work of the mediaeval thinkers possessed significance not only for contemporaries, but for after-time. They achieved a synthesis, and on a grand scale; in theoretical science, between metaphysics and theology; in practical science, between the claims of human personality and those of the larger systems within which man's life is lived. The solutions that they offered were not final; but they held their ground for generations, and when they fell, the theories that replaced them were their own offspring. The structure of modern ethical and political thought, from the seventeenth to the nineteenth century, was built, in the main, of stones hewn in the mediaeval quarries. The doctrines of a state of nature, of natural law, of the social contract, and of the rights of man, are still alive in political theory.[2] They loom large not merely in the philosophy of the eighteenth-century enlightenment, but in the manifestos of

1. See Figgis, *From Gerson to Grotius*, pp. 10 ff., 129 ff. The idea of civil society as based upon contract was distinctively mediaeval, and originated probably out of the promises to obey the law and govern justly, made by the king on his accession.

2. As is evidenced by R. G. Collingwood's *New Leviathan*. On the application of the conception of law of nature by the founders of international law in the seventeenth century, and on their obligations to Roman law generally, see Maine, *Ancient Law*, c. iv.

political reformers, in the American Declaration of Independence, and in the debates of the French revolutionary assemblies. If Bentham and his disciples scorned these ideas as abstract jargon, and substituted the standard of utility for that of right, they still inherited the individualist implications of the rejected doctrine.[1] Lord Acton knew what he meant when he said, that not the devil, but St Thomas Aquinas, was 'the first Whig'. Modern constitutionalism is the child of the Middle Ages. Its origin lies farther back than the times of Hobbes and Locke, in the days when Aquinas and his successors strove, with a broader speculative outlook, to base the institution of civil society on natural law, and to harmonize the ingrained individualism of the Teutonic peoples with the metaphysical legacy of Greece and the juristic legacy of Rome.

IV. THE RENAISSANCE

§ 23. The power of ancient culture to leaven and shape civilization is seen vividly in the effects of the rediscovery of Greek learning in the age of the Renaissance.

If we pass in thought from the fourteenth century to the seventeenth, from the Europe of the Hundred Years War to the Europe of Richelieu, and from the speculations of the later schoolmen to those of Galileo, Bacon, and Descartes, we seem to be moving in a different world. The difference is that between mediaeval and modern civilization. The velocity with which one phase of history succeeds another is not uniform, and, in these intervening centuries, change had followed change with astonishing swiftness. A new order was brought to birth, both of society and of thought. By 1600, the institutions – economic, political, and religious – which symbolized the hard-won stability of mediaeval society, were everywhere falling into decay. Feudalism lingered as an effete survival, or as a grotesque, or romantic, memory; the Catholic church was

1. These implications still harass our political thinking, even when we are striving our hardest to be quit of them, thwarting the recognition of a true theory of group-personality in our reflections on government and law. They were fortified by the illegitimate intrusion, in the seventeenth century, of the concepts of mechanical physics into the domain of political and moral science.

viewed with hatred and horror by millions in northern
Christendom; while the Catholic empire had lost all relics of
supernational sovereignty, and scarcely commanded even a
titular respect. In their stead were arising commercial and
industrial communities, with hands outstretched to grasp the
prize of a world-trade; Protestant churches with diverse creeds
and forms of government; national states, powerful, mutually
suspicious, and jealous of their independence.

The nation-state, the type of political organization characteristic of modern Europe, arose in the sixteenth century in
Spain, France, and Tudor England, contemporaneously with
the gradual break-down of mediaeval universalism. Its watchword was 'sovereignty', with its twofold implication of complete independence as against all states outside its borders, and
internally of the institution of a clearly recognizable authority,
normally an individual prince supreme alike over subordinate
corporations and individual citizens, in whose hands lay the sole
right of making and enforcing law. It arose as the original
expression in the field of political government of the natural
growth of self-consciousness in European peoples which was
also reflected in the rise, heralded, e.g. by Dante, of national
languages and literature in place of Latin, and in the revolt
against the papal jurisdiction in the countries which embraced
the Reformation. This new-born national consciousness could
not rest satisfied with political structures that were at best
imitations of historic models. Mediaeval ideas of world-unity
(e.g. the conception of the Holy Roman Empire) took shape,
consciously or unconsciously, under the influence of the tradition of the world-empire of ancient Rome. So the city-states
that arose in Italy and Flanders in the interest of economic
freedom were but tame republications of the old Hellenic
Polis. To-day, after more than three centuries, when we are
reaping a hundred-fold this baneful harvest of national separa-
tism, the glory has departed from the nation-states. The present
generation is witnessing the evolution, under pressure of
political, economic, and moral forces, of a new type of social
structure. By an impulse as natural as that which in the sixteenth century led to the establishment of nation-states, the

peoples of the civilized world are groping their way towards the formation, on the one hand, of federal states (the British Commonwealth, the American Union, the union of Soviet republics, as well as smaller confederations like Switzerland), and, on the other, of a regulative super-national authority, such as would be represented by a fully effective league of nations.[1]

In the field of thought, the change was yet more startling. Moral and political obligations were grounded no longer on a universal scheme of divine providence, but on the needs and mutual relationships of human individuals. The authority of Aristotle and of the doctors of the church had yielded place to the claim of private judgement. Above all, intellectual interest was centred on the study of physical fact, and the discovery of laws of nature. The scientific spirit, dormant since the fall of Hellenism, had awoken to life in the mind of western Europe, which had grown to intellectual manhood during the long minority of the Middle Ages. Men were asking themselves new questions, to which the mediaeval tradition gave no answer. Its ideals and methods of knowledge were as alien to the intellectual temper of the sixteenth century as the ardour of knight-errantry to the readers of *Don Quixote*. The children mocked at the aspirations which had stirred their fathers to heroic ventures. The contrast between the mediaeval spirit and that of the Renaissance lay in this, that the one was absorbed in the scheme of divine providence and man's eternal destiny, the other, in his life on an earth recognized as a scene of intrinsic value, and pronounced, as by God on the creation morning, a thing that was very good. The other-worldliness of the Middle Ages had yielded place to the desire to know man in his relation to nature, and nature in its relation to man. It was a sign of the times that, whereas mediaeval learning had been the monopoly of monks and clergy, and the voice of the layman found expression only in poetry and art, the laity now claimed the right to think.[2] Equally significant is the contrast in the subject-matter of literature. We have only to turn from Dante to the great humanists of the sixteenth century, Rabelais,

1. See below, Appendix I, p. 528.
2. See C. S. Lewis, *The Allegory of Love*.

Montaigne, Cervantes, and Shakespeare, to appreciate the magnitude of the revolution. Shakespeare's interest is almost wholly absorbed in human life, as enacted amid its actual surroundings; and, in portraying men's intellectual perplexities and moral crises, he gives scarcely a thought to God or to the life to come.[1] By the sixteenth century, humanism was in the ascendant; and the spirit of secularism was dominant, explicitly in men's thought, and instinctively in their practice. The age of Reason had begun.

§ 24. It is customary to speak of this epoch as the Renaissance, marking thereby, as its distinctive feature, the rebirth of classical culture in western Europe. We are told in all the history books how, in the dark hour when the Turks were closing round Constantinople, the exodus of Greek teachers from the East disclosed the secrets of the Hellenic genius to the wondering gaze of the western world. Broadly, indeed, this is the truth; the fifteenth century saw a wide extension of men's knowledge of antiquity, and the rediscovery of treasures that had lain buried for a thousand years. But we must not forget that classical culture had been already active and fruitful far back in the Middle Ages. From the late eighth century onwards, the story of Western civilization is a progressive anticipation of the Renaissance. Michelet, in a famous passage of his history, recalls how the Sibyl thrice offered her treasures to the Etruscan lord of early Rome.[2] The analogy is in one point misleading; for Tarquin twice rejected the proffered gift, whereas the mediaeval thinkers from the first clutched eagerly at all they could get, and strained their youthful energy to the full in the use of it. The few mediaeval scholars who knew Greek had before them but scattered fragments of the literature. They were neither able nor curious to determine the text; they were concerned exclusively with the interpretation,

1. Such references, e.g. as are to be found in *Hamlet*, in his famous soliloquy, or in the words

> 'There's a divinity that shapes our ends,
> Rough-hew them how we will,'

might in this respect at least have been uttered by a poet of antiquity. See also Webb, *History of Philosophy* (Home University Library), p. 76, for references to *Measure for Measure* and *Much Ado about Nothing*.

2. *Histoire de France*, Introduction to the volume on *The Renaissance* (1855).

with what Aristotle's writings meant to them, rather than with what they meant to Aristotle.[1] The fifteenth and following centuries saw the rediscovery of manuscripts long consigned to oblivion, and the restoration on this basis of the original text of the Greek masters. Above all, there was a rapid spread of the study of the Greek language in the universities and schools. Thus the Renaissance drew its inspiration direct from classical antiquity.[2] Had this been all, however, it would hardly have figured as an epoch in the history of civilization. The rediscovery of Hellenic culture evoked a deeper response in the mind of western Europe. Its significance lay, not so much in the realization of the positive achievement in science and philosophy, embodied in Greek literature, far as this achievement stretched beyond the horizon envisaged by the Middle Ages. Nor did it lie merely in the revelation of beauty in art and poetry, that fixed the gaze of painters and poets on the deathless masterpieces of the Hellenic genius. The source of inspiration was rather the spirit that informed the life and thought of ancient Greece, the habit of free enquiry, the confidence in reason, the untiring energy of thought and action, and the delight in the actual world, present before man's eye as a field for practical experiment, aesthetic creation and reasoned knowledge. This was the key that unlocked to the peoples of the modern world the gate of their earthly paradise.

§ 25. They were swift to reap the fruits of their discovery. Familiar as we are at the present day with the advance of science, we read with amazement of the marvellous achievements that mark the golden age of the Renaissance. If we take the brief period of little more than seventy years, the span of a

1. This statement must be read with reservations. Aquinas, for instance, had laboured, with the aid of William of Moerbeke, to get at the true text of Aristotle. But the obstacles were insuperable. Even if a sufficient number of manuscripts had been available, the critical faculty was lacking; and, in the days before printing, the permanence of a scholar's labours rested on the fate of a single copy of his work. There was not much inducement to spend time and energy on the production of a sound text.

2. The home of the Renaissance was Italy, where the new spirit was alive in the first half of the fifteenth century. It spread north of the Alps after 1450, encountering more active resistance in the northern universities, the strongholds of mediaeval philosophy in its great days.

single human life, between the fall of Constantinople in 1453 and the sack of Rome by the Germans in 1527, we find that within it were laid the foundations of scientific knowledge for the five succeeding centuries. (*a*) The physical surface of the globe was first explored. Daring seamen, guided by scientific research and trained in the new learning at the school founded by Prince Henry of Portugal ('the Navigator': 1394–1460), sailed along the Atlantic coast of Africa, rounded the Cape (1486–9) and laid open to the Portuguese the wealth of the Indies. As the fruit of the same scientific impulse, united with the desire of the Spanish sovereigns for commercial expansion, Columbus in 1492 reached the New World.[1] Thirty years later Magellan's expedition (1519–22) circumnavigated the globe. The issues of these great voyages and of numberless others in the same age were evident in the revolution that rapidly came about in the fields of commerce and of empire.[2] In a word, civilization, hitherto centred in the Mediterranean, became, in an ever-increasing degree, oceanic. (*b*) A vaster transformation of men's outlook upon nature was effected when the place of the earth in the solar system was determined by Copernicus in 1543. For more than a thousand years the learned as well as the vulgar had accepted the Ptolemaic hypothesis, with the earth as the centre of the universe. We still speak, in terms of that hypothesis, of the rising and setting of the sun. The Copernican theory of the daily rotation of the earth, and of its revolution and that of the other planets round the sun, was

1. The chief instrument of these discoveries was, of course, the mariner's compass, which had been in use in the Mediterranean since the thirteenth century. The art of cartography, which was rapidly perfected in this age, was an invaluable requisite.

2. The influx of precious metals altered the value of money and the scale of prices; the imported products of the East led to changes in dress, food and the style of life among the well-to-do classes. It has been remarked (by Mr. C. S. Lewis) that the interest of the *Merchant of Venice* is focused on the precious metals. The leading maritime nations eagerly competed for access to and control of the Asiatic markets; and the nothern states, France, Holland, and England, contended for sea-power, first against Portugal and Spain, then amongst themselves. The struggle lasted till the close of the Napoleonic war in 1815. The foundations both of British commerce with India and the Far East, and of British colonies in the New World, were laid within a century of the voyages of da Gama and Columbus.

decisively confirmed by Galileo (1564–1642), with the aid of the new invention of the telescope. It was no longer possible to accept the Aristotelian distinction between the unchanging heavens and a mutable sublunary world. Galileo and Descartes (1596–1650) together called mathematical physics into being, swinging free from the mediaeval doctrine of spiritual forces, and interpreting physical nature, organic and inorganic, animate and inanimate, exclusively in terms of matter and motion. We cannot wonder that conservative authority suffered a rude shock, and fought stubbornly against the new ideas. In 1600, Giordano Bruno, a fervent admirer of Copernicus, was burnt at Rome; in 1633 Galileo was forced by the Inquisition to retract his views on the motion of the earth.[1] The expansion of man's view of the universe to include worlds beyond worlds in unbounded space, the relegation of the earth, his habitation, to an insignificant and transitory position within one of these numberless systems, and the explanation of nature in terms that seemed to exclude any reference to purpose or freedom, struck at the roots of long-cherished convictions as to his spiritual worth and destiny. So indeed it must have appeared; though the thinker who of all others in that age most vigorously vindicated physical science from metaphysical or theological intrusion, and who saw even in living organisms nothing but the mechanism of matter in motion, was also the first of modern philosophers to proclaim the independent sovereignty of mind, and to base all knowledge of the external world on man's immediate consciousness of his existence as a thinking being.[2] (c) The sixteenth century witnessed the rebirth, not only of astronomy and physics, but also of the biological sciences. The Renaissance, in Michelet's phrase, bore fruit alike in the rediscovery of the world, and in the rediscovery of man. The

1. The tale that he muttered the words 'e pur si muove' ('all the same it does move') as he rose from his knees is legendary; yet the thought was doubtless in his mind. In 1624 the Parlement of Paris decreed the death penalty for anyone who advanced opinions contrary to those of Aristotle.

2. Descartes, for whom cogito, ergo sum (I think, therefore I am) was the most certain of all truths. The dethronement of man's planet from its central seat in the physical universe by the heliocentric theory was accompanied by an extreme anthropocentric doctrine in metaphysics (see the closing sentences of this section).

anatomical researches of Vesalius (1514–64) formed the groundwork that led, in the succeeding century, to Harvey's discovery of the circulation of the blood.[1] Descartes built on Harvey's work, when he strove to explain the facts of psychical life in terms of physiological process, and to trace the links that connect the physical stimulus, through the sense organs and the nervous system, with the brain, and thus give rise to mental feelings and sensations. For the first time the problem of the relation of mind and body was formulated in scientific terms. The revolution thus effected in men's view of physical nature and organic life extended also (d) to the field of their moral, intellectual and social interests. The new spirit was active in reshaping the structure of religious belief, of philosophy, and of political government. The study of the ancient languages and literature, the unfettered exercise of criticism on authorities and documents, struck at the credentials of the existing ecclesiastical order. The scriptures were examined in the original Hebrew and Greek. We have noted that, whereas in the Middle Ages the study of the text had been subordinated to symbolic and allegorical interpretation, interpretation was now grounded upon knowledge of the text. The invention of printing (c. 1455) was here of decisive importance. Early in the sixteenth century the Spanish cardinal Ximenes directed the preparation of a polyglot edition of the Bible in Hebrew, Greek, and Latin (published 1522).[2] Above all, a reading public came into being outside the bounds of the university, the monastery, and the church. The appeal to the judgement of the individual layman substituted a new criterion for the disciplinary authorities which had guided the thought of the Middle Ages. Everywhere,

1. Vesalius was a Fleming, who studied at Paris and migrated to Italy, where anatomical researches were most freely practised. He was condemned, later, by the Spanish Inquisition for dissecting the body of a grandee, and, despite Philip II's patronage, forced on a pilgrimage to Jerusalem; he died on the return journey. Fabricius ab Aquapendente (1537–1619) had founded modern embryology under inspiration from Aristotle. Harvey (1578–1657), building on Fabricius' work, commented on Aristotle's treatise on *The Generation of Animals* (1651). He rested his enquiries on Herophilus (c. 300 B.C.), as did Vesalius on Galen and Sydenham on Hippocrates. In 1532, Rabelais edited the first Greek text of Hippocrates' *Aphorisms*. See Singer in *The Legacy of Greece*.
2. See Allen, *Age of Erasmus*, pp. 259 ff.

in the closing years of the fifteenth and early years of the sixteenth century, there arose a humanistic revival, resting on the classics of Israel, Greece, and Rome; and an individualist revolt, which found utterance first in religion and later in philosophy. These movements co-operated with the spirit of German nationalism to bring about the Reformation. Moreover, political loyalties were still, as in the Middle Ages, inextricably interwoven with those of religion; cleavage and reconstruction in the one involved cleavage and reconstruction in the other. The cosmopolitan ideal that had hovered before the mind of mediaeval Europe had broken down under the pressure of national aspirations. We have only to read the history of the Tudor monarchy to see how the ambition of strong sovereigns evoked a popular response. This new spirit of nationalism found expression in the demand for national churches, in the rise of national literatures and in political speculations, such as those of Machiavelli in Italy, and of Hobbes in the England of the Puritan revolution. 'Reason of state', to the exclusion of ethical control, was frankly proclaimed as the criterion of policy and government. German Lutheranism pinned itself to the maxim that the religion of the prince determined the religion of the people.[1] Finally, the appeal to private judgement, that had been the watchword of the Reformation, became in the following century the foundation-stone of metaphysics. Within the narrow circle of Protestant theology, the principle of rationalism found but negative and restricted expression.[2] It came by its own for the first time

---

1. The Lutherans subordinated church to state; and the Tudor monarchs secured the same result in England. Henry VIII, in Stubbs' phrase, was determined to be 'the pope, the whole pope, and something more than the pope'; Elizabeth, by Act of Parliament, was recognized as 'over all causes, as well ecclesiastical as temporal, throughout her dominions supreme'. The Calvinist churches, on the other hand, stood for the distinction of church and state as two societies, of which the former was wholly independent of the latter (save, of course, where the absorption of the state in the church, as a single theocratic society, was possible, as at Geneva and in certain New England colonies).

2. The Reformation churches were by no means partial to intellectual liberty. Calvinism, the least tolerant form of Protestantism, gave rise to political freedom (as is illustrated by the history of Geneva, Scotland, New England), but indirectly; for within the congregation, social distinctions had no place. All alike were sinners in the sight of God, and those who were predestined

in the 'I think, therefore I am' of Descartes. It reigned over the thought of western Europe till the close of the eighteenth century.[1]

§ 26. Such was the potency of thought to transform man's outlook upon life, and, by generating knowledge, to inaugurate a new era of civilization. The Renaissance was the rebirth of science, and, in naming science, we name the modern world.[2] We need not wonder, then, that the champions of the new movement were keenly conscious of the breach with the past. or that they condemned, over-hastily and often without a hearing, the entire structure of mediaeval learning. These bold fighters came to destroy as well as to create. John Wessel, one of the pioneers of educational reform in the latter half of the fifteenth century, having learnt in Greece itself to read Aristotle in the original, stung the Dominicans into fury by his abuse of Aquinas. 'Was Thomas a doctor?' he asked; 'so am I'. 'Thomas scarcely knew Latin, and that was his only tongue; I have a fair knowledge of the three languages. Thomas saw Aristotle only as a phantom; I have read him in Greece in his own words.'[3] They were on stronger ground who demanded a new discipline of method to replace the formal logic of the schools. That instrument had indeed sunk into decrepitude; the life had well-nigh vanished from the great Aristotelian tradition, and the rattle of dry bones echoed throughout the land. Even had it preserved its vigour, the scholastic logic could hardly have sufficed. The new science called for a new method.

to salvation owed it to God's free grace, and to no human merit. Democratic equality in religion was bound, sooner or later, to find application in politics.

1. The appeal of Descartes and his successors was to the *reason* in the individual thinker. For reason, though part of the nature of the individual, is not his private monopoly, but the source of a knowledge valid for all rational minds. Truth implies a common standard, independent of particular tastes or wants. 'Private judgement' is strictly a contradiction in terms; if it be 'judgement', it is not merely mine, but claims universal validity as truth.

2. 'Science' is, of course, used here in its proper and comprehensive meaning, viz. methodical investigation by human reason of the facts of human experience. Science thus comprises history, ethics, and metaphysics, as well as psychology and the natural sciences. The essence of scientific as distinct from unscientific thinking lies, not in the object thought about, but in thinking about it on rational method. Here, too, as elsewhere, 'God cares a great deal more for adverbs than he does for verbs.'

3. Allen, *Age of Erasmus*, p. 12.

Galileo and his compeers walked in untrodden paths wherein the syllogism furnished little guidance. Bacon, in his *Novum Organum* (1620), and, with a firmer hand and deeper insight, Descartes, in his *Discours sur la Méthode* (1637), endeavoured to construct a logic that aimed, not at the attainment of formal consistency, but at the discovery of scientific truth. The triumphs of science were, in fact, won by the method of experiment, and by the application of mathematics to the study of physical nature. The former was a new-forged weapon; the latter rested on the work of the mathematicians of ancient Greece. Herein lies the chief significance of the Renaissance for modern civilization. It was not merely the classical scholars who drew inspiration from antiquity. Science also owed its awakening to the legacy of Greece and Rome. The great discoverers, with all their contempt for the Aristotle of mediaeval tradition, were eager to recognize the obligation. Copernicus told the pope that his hypothesis of the earth's rotation had been suggested to him by the records of Pythagorean astronomy. Columbus sailed on his western voyage believing not merely in the sphericity of the earth, but that eastern Asia was comparatively near to the coasts of Europe; and the source of both convictions, the true and the erroneous, lay in the tradition of Hellenic science.[1] If Aristotle suffered unmerited obloquy through the sins of his degenerate disciples, this was an added motive for a return to Plato, the mathematician *par excellence* among Greek philosophers. Mediaeval thought, when it swung loose from orthodox bearings, had invariably drawn freely on Neo-Platonic sources. Now for the first time Plato's complete works could be read, and in the original. This revival of Platonism had its home towards the close of the fifteenth century in the Florentine Academy, established under the patronage of Lorenzo de Medici. Ficino (1433–99), one of the chief among its members, translated not only Plato, but Plotinus and Proclus into Latin. The Swiss reformer, Zwingli, carried Florentine Platonism into the field of Protestant theology.

1. See Payne, *History of the New World called America*, i. 102–5, for Toscanelli's letter formulating these arguments. M. Picavet (*Esquisse*, p. 193) points out that both beliefs are to be found in Albertus Magnus and Aquinas.

Meanwhile at Padua Aristotelian freethinkers defended Averroës' denial of divine providence and of human freedom against the orthodox scholastics. That even these last felt the humanist impulse is evident from the reaction towards a simpler method and a more critical interpretation in the Spanish university of Salamanca. The Jesuit Suarez (1548–1617) united a return to Aquinas with liberal views on politics, hardly to be looked for in a Spanish ecclesiastic, such as the sovereignty of the people and their right to depose princes.[1] The revival of learning thus coloured the speculation alike of philosophers and theologians, of scholars and men of science. In literature and art its influence was all-pervading. We need not pause to insist how the Elizabethan drama or Jacobean architecture were stamped with the classical tradition. It set its mark on all the arts in all civilized countries of Europe. But it is interesting to note that the earliest opera, the *Eurydice* of Jacopo Peri, performed at Florence in 1600, on the occasion of the marriage of Marie de Medici to Henry IV of France, claimed to be 'founded on the declamation of the ancient Greeks'.[2]

§ 27. The revival of learning had two widely divergent effects on European culture. On the one hand, it stimulated to original creation. We have seen above how magnificently true this was in the domain of science. It was the same in the arts. The architecture of the Italian Renaissance was no tame imitation of the ancient styles. If Shakespeare drew on antiquity for

1. Scholasticism spread even in the Protestant ranks; Melanchthon, who did the thinking for the Lutheran Reformation, worked with mediaeval methods and on an Aristotelian basis.

2. We have spoken in the text exclusively of the influence of the Graeco-Roman legacy. Israel, too, came by more than her own in the Reformation epoch. See Vol. I, c. iii, p. 76, *note*. The Old Testament tradition deepened its mark, at all events in Protestant countries, on language, theology, law (e.g. New England), political ideas (theocracy), literature and art, as is evidenced by its influence on Milton's *Paradise Lost* and *Samson Agonistes*, on Racine's *Esther* and *Athalie* (Racine was Jansenist in sympathies, i.e. a Catholic Calvinist), on Bunyan and Dryden (who could use an Old Testament story for the purpose of political satire in *Absalom and Achitophel*: and a satire must be intelligible to the general public), and also of the oratorio as a new form of musical art, in which Old Testament subjects replaced the Catholic mass as the theme of sacred music (Handel).

the plots of his drama, it was but to portray living Elizabethans in Greek and Roman guise. On the other hand, archaism was in the air, and archaism stifles originality; the glamour of the historic past blinds men's vision to the possibilities of the future. It had been thus in the latter days of Hellenism, when scholars were content, from sheer lack of constructive energy, to gild the shrines of their great progenitors. Thus was it also, in a certain measure, in the age of the Renaissance. This tendency to archaism was most apparent in theology, and in pure scholarship. Orthodox Catholicism and orthodox Protestantism alike recked little of the march of science or of the claim of the human intellect for liberty of thought. If the Inquisition burnt Bruno and forced Galileo to recant, Calvin sent Servetus to the stake in the market-place of Geneva. It was in the Protestant churches that the Christian religion was faced, for the first time in its history, with the temptation to degenerate into the religion of a book. The invention of printing, with all its inestimable advantages, had opened the door to the domination of the letter over the spirit. The new learning had its dangerous side. Humanist scholars, intent upon the text, were led often to stress the form rather than the substance, the manner of expression rather than the living thought. Too frequently logic was banished to make room for grammar. The passion for verbal correctness was but scholasticism masquerading in a less honourable dress. The learning of the Middle Ages was contemptuously dismissed because its Latin was not Ciceronian. The ideal of 'formal' education reigned in the reformed universities and schools. Ascham (1570) taught that to write Latin like Cicero was the high-water mark of scholarly ambition.[1] Book-learning, especially in the lore of classical antiquity, became not seldom the test of academic eminence. The light of Hellenism was obscured by an excessive veneration for Latin literature.[2] Erudition reaped the honours that were due by right to discovery. This, it must be understood, was

1. Though Erasmus and Bacon knew better. '*La Renaissance, qui compte un si grand nombre d'érudits, a produit beaucoup moins de penseurs*' (Hauréau, *Hist. de la phil. scolastique*, iii. 429).

2. Scaliger compared Virgil with Homer, almost wholly to the disparagement of the latter.

but one aspect of the humanist revival, but its presence, fraught with baneful issues in the story of education, must not be ignored. Yet, even in the domain of classical learning, the gain more than compensated for the loss. The foremost minds of the new learning soared high above the clouds that dulled the vision of their disciples.

§ 28. The spirit of free enquiry that inspired the revival of classical learning found brilliant expression in the person of Erasmus of Rotterdam. Erasmus was, if not the greatest scholar, at all events the greatest man of letters, of the Renaissance. Born about the year 1466, thrust at an early age into the uncongenial atmosphere of a Flemish monastery, he discovered his vocation as a scholar by the aid of the monastic library. In Paris, he learnt and taught the Greek language, and laid the foundation of his fame as the leading humanist in Europe. From Italy the new learning had already spread northwards beyond the Alps, borne to Paris by the French invaders of Italy, and to Germany and Flanders along the commercial highway of the Rhine. It struck root in Britain, and when, in 1499, Erasmus's English friends brought him on his visit to this country, he was welcomed by a distinguished circle of kindred minds. In the reign of Henry VII, Grocyn, Linacre, and Colet had journeyed to Italy to drink at the head-waters of humanism. The new spirit had taken root among the traders of London, the home of Colet and More, where Grocyn held a living, and classical studies were a fashionable pastime at the court. Movements of thought in England have generally been associated with the larger world of affairs rather than with the cloistered life of the universities, and Erasmus noted how there was more Greek learning in the busy metropolis than in the academic seclusion of Oxford.[1] Favoured by Henry VIII and

1. British philosophy, for example, has rarely been academic and its appeal has been directly to the cultured public outside the universities. This is true of Hobbes, Locke, Berkeley, Hume, Butler, and the Utilitarians. On the other hand, German philosophy has been the work of professors writing for professors. Such exceptions to the rule as Schopenhauer and Nietzsche were voices crying in the wilderness, in revolt against the academic tradition. The result is that, while British philosophy has often lacked precision and depth, it has wielded considerable influence on the public mind and provided men of affairs with a training in the handling of ideas.

archbishop Warham, he renewed his visits to England, lectured at Cambridge, advised Dean Colet in his foundation of St Paul's school, and wrote his brilliant satire on the ignorance and superstititon of princes and clerics, the 'Praise of Folly' (*Encomium Moriae*), at More's house in Chelsea. But Erasmus belonged strictly to no nation; his culture was cosmopolitan, and he made his home indifferently, wherever in that troubled age he could find a haven of refuge, in Paris or in London or in Basel. His editions of the New Testament and of the Greek Fathers show his enthusiasm for the Greek language. It had been so in the early days of poverty: 'First I will buy some Greek books, and after that some clothes.' His 'Proverbs' (*Adagia*), 'Colloquia', and 'Letters' are rich in the learning of the ancient world.[1] Both in his thought and in his style we can see that the classical tongues were to him no dead languages, but a living source of inspiration. His humanism was ever free from formalism. He had caught the free spirit of Greece; by nature a knight-errant of intellect, he displayed in his life and writings a power of wit and irony rivalled among the ancients by Lucian alone. In *Julius exclusus* (1517), he poured the vials of his satire on the most militarist and secular of the Renaissance popes. Julius II approaches the door of Paradise, and to his amazement is confronted by St Peter with the catalogue of his crimes. The anonymous pamphlet roused Europe to wrath and laughter; Erasmus, with natural timidity, disclaimed the authorship. A fighter in things of the mind, he shrank from the conflicts that were darkening the field of action. The outbreak of the Reformation brought him only sorrow and anxiety. He had lavished his wealth of wit and learning on the abuses and ignorance of the monks and clergy, but he trembled before the prospect of confusion and anarchy opened out by Luther's breach with Rome. 'If Luther stands by the Catholic church', he wrote in 1521, 'I will gladly join him.' Religious strife and civil wars were little to the taste of the scholar, whose *Complaint of Peace thrust forth from all lands* (1517) had but just issued from the press. He viewed the Reformation conflict with the

1. They have been used with admirable skill by Charles Reade in his novel, *The Cloister and the Hearth.*

natural conservatism of an intellectual. Yet his keen intelligence had served, no less than the ruder weapons of Luther, to sap the authority of the church. He, too, as well as Luther, had 'hit the pope on the crown, the monks on the belly'; 'by his irony', wrote a contemporary, 'he had injured the Roman pontiff more severely than had Luther by his wrath'. In truth, Erasmus was a champion of liberty, and his mistrust of the Reformers was based not a little on his fear of their intellectual obscurantism. Thus amid the storms of religious and social revolution he went down to the grave at Basel in 1536, distrusted alike by Catholic and by Protestant. His fame for all ages is that of an apostle of light and liberty. He was the fore-runner of Montaigne and Voltaire, one who, impregnated with the true Hellenic spirit, looked to reason and knowledge to guide and renovate the world.

V. CONCLUSION

§ 29. We have traced in this chapter, briefly and through representative selection, the story of the Graeco-Roman legacy, during the thousand years between the disruption of the Roman empire, and the coming of age of the European peoples in the sixteenth and seventeenth centuries. We have seen the fruits of the reception in the impulse of classicism, and the impulse to liberty of thought. In the event, these two currents ran in divergent channels. The one sought models for imitation, either in erudition and scholarship, within academic precincts, or, beyond them, in literature, politics and the arts. Two of the chief facts of modern civilization, the plays of Shakespeare and the French Revolution, were influenced, in no small measure, by the examples of Greek and Roman character depicted in the pages of Plutarch's *Lives*. The Parliamentary debates in England during the seventeenth and eighteenth centuries are packed with classical allusion, as when Sir John Eliot branded Bucking-ham as a Sejanus, and Pitt cited Virgil in his appeal for the abolition of the slave trade. Oratory was consciously modelled on Demosthenes and Cicero. Artists were trained in the study of the antique; architects turned aside from the Gothic style of the later Middle Ages to the classic monuments of the south; and there is scarcely a page of English poetry that does not bear the impress of the literature or the mythology of Greece and Rome. On the other hand, the spirit of Hellenism woke the impulse to creative thought. It inspired new philosophy, new science. The controversy, now of long standing, between the claims of a classical and a scientific education, was but one symptom of the divergence. We have shown how the very knowledge of nature, that has striven to displace a formal classicism, was fostered into life by the spirit of Hellenic thought. It is to modern philosophy and modern science, rather than to the archaism of the humanist revival, that we must look for the true measure of the enduring worth of Hellenism. Not Casaubon, nor Scaliger, nor Bentley, for all the wealth and purity of their scholarship, but Galileo, Descartes, and Newton, were the true inheritors of the kingdom. Theirs was the faith in reason, to set and to solve the riddles of an experience which is ever changing and therefore ever new. Theirs was the desire, not to copy, but to create; to win fresh realms for knowledge, to discover fresh fields of truth. Above all, it was by their labours that humanity was enabled to recover, hardly and after the travail of generations, the title-deeds of its birth-right of free thought. The modern world needs, at times, a salutary reminder, that its enjoyment of this liberty is due to those who had learnt their secret from the first champions of reason, and had lit their torches at the ever-burning hearth-fires of ancient Greece.[1]

1. For further reference to the subsequent course of the humanist movement, see below, Appendix III.

CHAPTER TWELVE

CONCLUSION: ON PROGRESS; AND ON THE LIVING INTEREST OF ANCIENT CIVILIZATION

*

I. ON PROGRESS

§ 1. THE civilizations of Israel, Greece, and Rome are the basis of our world; and, since it is in relation to our world that we think and act, they are also the basis of ourselves. To justify and illustrate this claim has been the object of this book. But, over and above the historical appeal, the genius of these peoples still lives as an inspiration and an example. We shall speak presently of the living interest of ancient culture for the modern world, but reference must first be made to a yet more general problem, that arises out of the theme of the preceding chapters.

We have taken a wide sweep, from the early civilizations of Egypt, Babylonia, and Crete, stretching back to the fourth millennium before Christ and even beyond, to the birth of modern science in the fifteenth to the seventeenth centuries of our era. It is natural and reasonable to ask: How far do the known facts support a belief in progress? Is the march of human history a forward movement, if not uniformly, at least on the whole? Or is it, as it seemed to Hesiod of old, a process of retrogression? Or are the currents intermingled, and the record one of advance chequered by failure, of victory by defeat? To some minds, history unfolds a series of cyclical revolutions; civilizations appear, flourish, and decay, in obedience to a periodic law. To others, the whole sequence has seemed capricious and unmeaning, a medley of upward and downward motions, a madness without a method, yielding no sign of rational principle or informing purpose.

These are large questions, ranging over the whole fields of philosophy and history; and we must content ourselves with a few general reflexions. The last-mentioned alternative, at all events, can be excluded at the outset. The very search for a solution implies a faith in the possibility of a rational interpretation. To hold that historical facts can be recorded, but not explained, is a confession of intellectual bankruptcy, a negation of the claim of history to be a branch of scientific knowledge. Man is, above all things, a metaphysical, that is, an ideal-forming, animal; he seeks for reason everywhere, in history as in nature, and his thirst will not be quenched until he find it.

§ 2. A little reflexion will limit still further the range of alternatives. Neither an uncritical optimism nor an uncritical pessimism can stand for a moment in the light of the facts. History shows no unbroken advance or retrogression. The scene disclosed is a vast battlefield, where the forces that make for civilization contend with varying fortunes against those that make for anarchy and barbarism. In one quarter, they press forward with a persistent sweep, despite resistance and transitory repulse; in another, the line sways to and fro, hardly holding the ground; in yet another, it is broken and over-whelmed by the destroyers. Whole civilizations, as in Egypt or China, seem to have vanished, save only as their buried fragments are unearthed by the spade of the archaeologist, to be enshrined, as data for the expert and a spectacle for the curious, in the galleries of our museums. Where progress is discernible, it is already pregnant with the seeds of dissolution, and yields, slowly but surely, to inward stagnation or the pressure of forces from without. The religion of Israel, at the very hour when the prophetic vision had pierced to the goal, congealed into a rigid formalism; the swift growth of Hellenism was followed by lingering decay; the might of the Eternal City fell before the barbarian invaders. Facts like these have suggested to reflective minds in all ages, from Empedocles to Nietzsche, the idea of a cyclical revolution.[1] But a closer survey reveals a distinction

1. The Orphic brotherhoods and the Stoics taught this doctrine. It is familiar to Indian thought. In Nietzsche, it takes an extreme form, as that of cyclical *recurrence*, the past being repeated in the future in precise detail. Faith in progress is distinctive of Christian thought. The Greeks, generally, regarded the course of history as a retrogression from a golden age in the remote past: so Hesiod, and Plato in the *Republic* (esp. Books VIII and IX, which illustrate the periodic law of deterioration in all earthly societies). Lucretius furnishes an exception, in his conception of evolutionary progress:

fatal to this hypothesis. In the records of the East, indeed, phase seems to follow phase in interminable cycles, without discernible connexion or ordered sequence; as 'Amurath an Amurath succeeds', each conquering race develops its own culture in comparative indifference to that which it supersedes, and gives way in turn to a successor equally heedless of its achievements.[1] This is the monotony, often remarked in the story of the East, of cycles of civilization that rise and fall, but are bound together by no organic tie of progress. When, however, we turn our eyes westwards to the Mediterranean world, we behold a very different picture. Western civilization, from its beginnings in the city-states of Greece and Italy, to the time when the modern nations emerge slowly from the wreckage of the Roman empire, displays throughout the signs of an ordered evolution. This was due mainly to the intellectual quality of the Greek genius, which stamped on its creations the hall-mark of individuality and life. In the fields of political action, artistic production, and speculative thought, the diversity is that of variations on a common theme. The inner thread of continuity is never cut. Even the revolutions that appear to engulf the past are but the prelude to its restitution. The backward eddies serve rather to strengthen than to retard the current. We strike here on a law of human progress. Great ideas, it has been said, must die to live. So Judaism died to be reborn in the western mind as Christianity, Hellas to be reborn as Hellenism.[2] Epochs of so-called decadence are in truth epochs of transition from an old life to a new. It may even have been thus far back in the obscure period of northern immigration that intervened between the Minoan civilizations and the dawn of historic Greece. It was so, certainly, in the dark age of Teutonic invasion, which issued, as we know, in the birth of

see Book V, lines 771 to end, especially lines 1454–7: 'Thus time by degrees brings each several thing forth before men's eyes and reason raises it up into the borders of light; for things must be brought to light one after the other and in due order in the different arts, until these have reached their highest point of development.' (tr. Munro).

1. Of course, this statement is only true with reservations. The point is that an *inner* connexion, the growth of the later phase *out of* the earlier, seems to be lacking.

2. Inge, *Outspoken Essays*, p. 223.

an intellectual and social order, the product of a new impulse in fusion with the legacy of the past.[1] In the introductory chapter we pointed out how Israel, Greece, and Rome severally stood for one of the essential factors in a complete civilization. The vision of a spiritual kingdom, comprising all peoples as its members under God as king; the claim of reason to think, create, and act with untrammelled freedom; the recognition of authority and law as necessary instruments to man's conquest over barbarism; these three conceptions, blended in the course of ages with one another and with ideas derived from the races of northern Europe, are acknowledged in their union as the ideal of the modern world. It would be idle to deny that much has perished in the process, or that the advance, even in western lands, has been restricted to certain lines of development. We may question whether men's practice has kept pace with the progressive enlargement of their horizon. We know but too well that the profession of a religion of universal peace is compatible with the enactment of a world war. The naïve optimism of the middle and later years of the last century has been rudely shattered. There is all the more reason to insist that a survey of western civilization reveals, in its broad outlines, a picture of relatively coherent evolution.[2]

§ 3. The error of the Victorians may be ascribed, in part, to their lack of critical discernment; in part, to their failure amid an enthusiasm for construction to recognize the ugly facts that stared them in the face; in part, to the complacency that blinded them to the chasm between ideal aspiration and attainment.[3] Above all, it lay in their defective criterion of

1. Thus the title of *The Decline and Fall of the Roman Empire*, established by the authority of Gibbon, is, if taken absolutely, a misnomer; an equally just view, directed upon the future, would mark the period as that of *The Rise of Teuton, Saracen, and Slav*.

2. We are surely justified in treating western civilization, throughout the last three thousand years of its history, as a relatively closed system. The occasional incursions of the East into the West, such as the Hunnish, Saracen, and Tartar invasions, contributed little that was constructive to its development. The single exception of moment was the permeation of the West by Jewish religion through Christianity, and the Jews dwelt within the Mediterranean area. Western culture preserved, and still preserves, a comparative homogeneity, for which intermarriage serves as a rough criterion.

3. We must not fail to give due credit to the constructive energy of the

progress. They construed progress in terms of human happiness, and happiness in terms of economic welfare. They never dreamed that men could be comfortable and yet not happy, happy and yet not comfortable. We have seen how the paternal despotism of the Roman empire, while furnishing the Mediterranean peoples with security and material provision to a degree previously unknown, failed to give them the one thing necessary to their happiness, inward peace. They scorned the proffered comforts, and took refuge in a faith that hourly exposed them to penury, contempt, and martyrdom. We may question whether all our mastery over physical nature and all the improvements that are the harvest of modern science have increased the sum of human happiness.[1] When we contemplate the conditions of life in modern cities, the hustle in which men spend their days, the blighting uniformity that has sprung from the growing specialization of labour, the ugliness with which the industrial revolution has defiled the land, we realize that all the efforts of bureaucracy and benevolence to make life tolerable for the masses are but the palliative of a disease that is gnawing at the vitals of modern society.[2] The measure of happiness is not, as the Utilitarians fancied, material prosperity,

Victorians, manifested not only in technical invention and in the expansion of industry and commerce, but in pure science, literature, and political action. It was the age of Faraday and Darwin, of Thackeray and Dickens, of Carlyle, Tennyson, and Browning, of the organization of British India, the growth of the overseas Dominions, the extension of the franchise, and the institution of national education. The present generation is keenly critical of its immediate progenitors; this is always the case, and signifies that it has absorbed their achievement and, fortified by that inheritance, is turning to fresh efforts of its own.

1. Of course, if *we* were transplanted back to the days prior to these discoveries, we should regret their absence; but the question is whether those who lived then were more unhappy than those who live now. We may remember, too, the words of the old French *marquis* in the play: 'en mon temps on avait Dieu'.

2. Let the reader journey with his eyes open from Fenchurch Street to Barking, or take his stand for half an hour on the platform at Stratford, or at Landore Junction in South Wales. It has been observed that the faces of the men and the women in East London contrast favourably, in point of happiness, with those to be seen in the West. Idleness has more to do with unhappiness than poverty; the cure, in the majority of cases, is to eat less and work more. The cry of the crowd, in Lewis Carroll's tale, for 'less bread, more taxes' is not so irrational as it sounds.

but fullness of life. The old doctrine of Aristotle is still valid, that the end of man is not to live, but to live well; that felicity lies in the realization of the highest promise of his nature; and that pleasure is not an external commodity, but the sense of living, the glow of consciousness, inherent in the free exercise of faculty.[1] Christianity, in endorsing this conception of felicity, transferred its realization to another sphere. It assumed that the fruition, if confined within the compass of the present life, was attainable only by a select few, and very imperfectly even by these. It had no illusions about earthly progress, and it read in the pages of history a lesson of warning rather than of hope. But it was at one with Hellenism in gauging happiness by a spiritual, not an economic, standard. The moral, intellectual and aesthetic interests, satisfaction of which alone makes life worth living, find little justification on the economic level. Moral excellence is not, within our experience, proportioned to prosperity; if it were, the term 'duty' would be shorn of all its meaning.[2] The joy that attends the creative effort of the lover, the discoverer, or the artist, is something different in kind from pleasure.[3] The manifest fact that, every day and all day long, men and women sacrifice comfort, health, and economic gain in the pursuit of truth, goodness, and beauty, welcoming any burden so long as it affords scope for high activity, shows the irrelevance of material welfare as a criterion of progress.

§ 4. It is when we pass to details, and endeavour to unravel the various threads of progress and to estimate their value, that the enquiry is beset with difficulties. The task lies beyond our scope, and we must be content with one obvious illustration, drawn from the history of knowledge. If signs of progress are to be found anywhere, we expect to find them here. The issue is not complicated, as it is in the records of moral and religious

1. *Eth. Nic.*, x, cc. 4, 5; and cf. above, c. vi, § 14.
2. See Kant, *Critique of Practical Reason* (tr. Abbott, Bk. I, c. i). Moral experience implies the contrast between duty and inclination; if moral action were necessarily the most pleasurable, the motive of duty would disappear, and the action would lose its moral quality.
3. See Bergson, 'Life and Consciousness', in the volume entitled *Mind Energy*.

experience, by the severance of theory from practice.[1] The speculative advance of knowledge is at the same time its realized achievement. We have traced in the foregoing chapters the continuity of Hellenic thought from its birth in the sixth century B.C. to the logical fulfilment of its earlier efforts in the systems of Plato and Aristotle, and thence to its differentiation into the special sciences, and its diffusion among various philosophic schools. We have seen the revival of Greek metaphysic in close alliance with religion in Neo-Platonism, its absorption into Christian theology, its recovery after centuries of comparative oblivion by the thinkers of the Middle Ages, and its crowning triumph as the motive that inspired the creation of modern science in the sixteenth and seventeenth centuries. At each stage there was loss as well as gain; but even when the stream of intellectual energy ran thinnest, the event proved that the gain more than compensated for the loss. Hellenism was decaying from within, when the Teuton and the Saracen swept over the Mediterranean lands; and the Christian church, with its contempt for pagan learning, abetted rather than stemmed the tide of barbarism. Yet the inheritance survived the storm, maimed, indeed, but potent to nourish the growing minds of Christian Franks and Moslem Arabs. We have seen, too, how the Middle Ages, despite their ignorance of the physical sciences, won a knowledge of their own. The three problems, of God, freedom, and immortality, which had received but stepmotherly treatment at the hands of Greek philosophers, came by their own in the philosophy of the Middle Ages. In the

1. We must remember, (a) that, even in morals and religion, this distinction is not absolute: ideals are the outcome of conduct, and react upon conduct; (b) that, the higher the aim, the wider the gulf that separates profession from performance; and (c) that the practice of an age is to be judged by its highest expressions. We do not measure the intellectual plane of the late seventeenth century by the scientific attainments of Nell Gwynne or Titus Oates, but by those of Locke and Newton. Similarly, the spiritual achievement of the Middle Ages is to be judged in the light of men like Anselm, St Bernard, St Francis of Assisi. Finally (d) the problems of conduct have been complicated by the recognition, distinctive of Christian ethics, of obligation towards all mankind. Our duty to our neighbour is tolerably clear, when (as was the case in the Hellenic Polis) our neighbour is, intellectually and morally, our equal; it is anything but obvious when we are called upon to practise it towards the criminal, the lunatic, and the savage.

hour of the rebirth of science they were not consigned to oblivion, but were borne onwards, in close contact with the new interest in physical nature, into the heart of modern thought. The effort after their solution, pursued by widely divergent methods and issuing in very different conclusions, as we pass from Descartes to Kant, from Kant to Hegel, from Hegel to the thinkers of to-day, bears witness to their dominant and enduring interest for metaphysics.[1] A like growth is traceable in the history of the positive sciences. The Middle Age, with its mind fixed on the spiritual purpose of the universe, found a key to every riddle in the teleology of Aristotle, construed in the light of the Christian revelation. The scientific thinkers of the Renaissance sought an explanation on wholly different lines. Rejecting final causes as irrelevant and beyond human ken, they set themselves to interpret physical nature as the product of mechanical laws, which could be formulated with perfect simplicity and precision in mathematical terms. The discoveries of science during the last three centuries have been mainly due to the instruments and methods of mathematical measurement. In the hands of Galileo and Descartes, Leibniz and Newton, mathematical physics forged ahead with lightning rapidity, setting its stamp on the metaphysics, psychology, ethics, and theology of the seventeenth and eighteenth centuries, and wielding, for the time, an almost unquestioned sovereignty over the realm of thought. Chemistry followed in its train, resting for its foundations on the mathematical measurement of weights and volumes.[2] The biological sciences, though of contemporary origin,[3] hardly entered upon their inheritance till the nineteenth century was under way. Their

1. We have here an illustration of a law that governs intellectual progress. The enrichment of knowledge is never by mere accretion of new to old; the process is one of interpenetration, in which new and old alike are modified.

2. Yet chemistry owes much to the mediaeval alchemists. They had not, however, our simple and easy system of mathematical calculation. The adoption of the 'zero' from the East, enabling *ten* to be written as 10, was a great advance. See *The Earliest Arithmetics in English*, ed. R. Steele, who points out that 'in the thirteenth-century scientific treatises addressed to advanced students, contemplated the likelihood of their not being able to do simple division'.

3. Vesalius (1514–64) and Harvey (1578–1657) were respectively the contemporaries of Copernicus and of Descartes.

exponents, too, have sought to bring the phenomena of organic life under the laws of chemistry and physics. The same aspiration has haunted even those who, following out the natural order in the development of the sciences, turned, as psychologists and as historians, to study the nature and operations of the human mind. The endeavour to apply mechanical principles to the facts of life, of consciousness, and of human society, has led inevitably to the recognition of their limits. Science finds itself here in the presence of individuality, which defies quantitative measurement and is incapable of expression in mathematical formulas. Hence, we can observe in the scientific thought of the present day an effort towards a new line of interpretation, which gives their due to the concepts of meaning and value, and affords a basis for a common understanding between science and philosophy. It seems as though the hour has come for a reconstitution of the broken unity of knowledge. This endeavour, visible in the attempts to reconcile once more the long severed claims of philosophy and religion, and to effect a *rapprochement* between metaphysics and the physical sciences, is not merely a deeply interesting feature of modern thought, but an evidence of the coherent development exhibited in the intellectual life of the western world.[1] To this mark of intellectual progress must be added another, relative, not to the content of knowledge, but to its diffusion. The last two generations have set their hands to a task without precedent, that of opening the gates of knowledge to the whole of civilized mankind. The intellectual inheritance is to be no longer, as in antiquity and the Middle Ages, the monopoly of a favoured few. The democratic spirit has invaded the realms

1. The *rapprochement* between philosophy and mathematical physics is evident in the writings of Mr Bertrand Russell, Professor Alexander, Professor Whitehead, Lord Haldane, and, recently, of Sir Arthur Eddington and Sir James Jeans. M. Bergson works in the same direction from biological, physiological, and psychological data. Psychology, which has one foot in the domain of the physiologist, the other in that of the philosopher, furnishes an obvious meeting-point between philosophy and science. Even Signor Croce, who insists uncompromisingly on the severance between these two, affirms the identity of philosophy and history (i.e. of ideal value and temporal happenings). Yet the ghost of the distinction between the 'eternal truths' of mathematics and 'matters of fact' (i.e. between values and events) still haunts the sanctuaries (or, shall we say, the graveyards?) of metaphysics.

of art and learning. The nations that have shouldered the burden of universal education have hardly yet awoken to a sense of their audacity. Knowledge has its perils; as Plato saw, when he put the searching question, how could the state study philosophy without being ruined?[1] Ideas are forces, terrible in their power to sway multitudes for weal or bane. The speculations of a recluse, spread abroad by the press, may furnish leverage for a revolution. Rousseau's *Contrat Social* heralded the guillotine. Out of the mouth of science has come forth blessing and cursing, the cures for foul disease and the ghastly implements of human slaughter. But these dangers, and that of the degradation of literature and the arts through their prostitution to a meretricious popular demand, must not blind us to the magnitude or to the promise of the adventure. That the modern world has dared to face the risks is a fresh instance of the unconquerable faith in reason, that was born, five and twenty centuries ago, in ancient Greece.[2]

§ 5. The foregoing illustration carries us but a little way towards a solution of the general problem of human progress. It is confined to one aspect of western civilization during some five and twenty centuries. Even were it supported by a survey of other fields of experience, it would at best serve as fragmentary confirmation to those whose conviction that the world is purposive rests on evidence other than that of historical fact. History of itself offers no revelation of a theodicy.[3] For such an enterprise we should require to broaden our survey so as to include not merely the whole story of human development, but the process of cosmic evolution. In a celebrated address Huxley maintained that the cosmic process stood in direct

---

1. *Rep.*, vi. 497. See Appendix III, below.
2. Nothing has been said in the text on the all-important question of progress in literature and the arts. For reasons stated in the preface, the author has refrained as far as possible from drawing illustrations from this field. The discerning reader will apply the suggestions offered above with the needed reserves and modifications. Further, the question would arise whether one art can be ranked higher in the scale than any other. The development of music, side by side with the other arts, in forms that show obvious advance on ancient and mediaeval models, is perhaps the most striking sign of progress in modern art.
3. See Appendix I, below.

antagonism to man's effort to realize his ethical ideals.[1] Man, as a moral agent, is engaged in a life-and-death struggle with physical nature, ever on the alert to reconquer the ground he has arduously won. Such a dualism belies the truth that man is part of the cosmos, and his moral endeavour itself a phase in the evolutionary process. The study of infra-human species and of inorganic nature rather indicates that this process is one from less to greater individuality, and that, to this extent at least, it bears the mark of progress. We may question, indeed, whether anything discoverable in the universe is wholly bereft of individuality. Even the atom may have a will of its own. But we are clearly justified in saying that, below the level of organic life, within the preserves of the physicist and the chemist, uniformity among individuals of a given type is not the exception, but the rule. They can be treated, for purposes of scientific study and its practical applications, as if they were all alike. It is otherwise in the case of biological species. Classification here becomes increasingly difficult and artificial. In the animal world, capacity for variation and for learning by experience is manifested in a multitude of different grades. 'The ox knoweth his owner and the ass his master's crib'; dogs and horses respond to the touch of human love; the poet and the gardener tell us that the like is true of plants.[2] When we turn to humankind, the field of anthropology and history, the record is through and through personal. Whereas the physicist revels in the uniform, resolving the most unique occurrences into the interplay of general laws, the historian knows that his material cannot be handled in the lump, and labours to pierce behind the broad features of a social order to the concrete thoughts and acts of its individual members. He explains events

    1. See the Romanes Lecture on *Evolution and Ethics*, reprinted in the volume with that title in Huxley's collected works.
    2. Cf. Shelley, *The Sensitive Plant*; and Wordsworth's
            'For 'tis my faith that every flower
                Enjoys the air it breathes.'
'All life', said Plotinus, 'is a kind of spiritual vision'; *Enn.*, III. 8. 8 (see Inge, i. 161). The psychology and sociology of plants is a relatively unexplored field; there are sympathies in nature that call for study, as well as mechanism. Plants form associations and secure their ground against rivals. On the whole question, see Bergson's *Creative Evolution*.

by deciphering a plan, not by subsuming particulars under uniformities. The higher the plane of civilization, the less scope there is for generalization. Personality figures less in the story of the Basuto or the Mongol than in that of Periclean Athens or Dante's Florence. Thus far, the cosmic process, and that of human history, reveal a consistent picture. Both have their dark shadows; there is infinite waste in nature, and, like history, she 'paints her grey in grey'. But a graver difficulty awaits us, if we are moved by these analogies to draw an inference to universal progress. Empirical science cannot guarantee the future, any more than empirical history. Its predictions are conditioned by the assumption, which no amount of experience can justify, that the unknown is governed by the same laws as the known. It can give no assurance even of the permanence of organic life on our planet. For all that science can tell us, it may well be, as Cyprian thought in the third century, *senuisse jam mundum*, that our world is ageing to its death.[1] Yet man's belief in the purpose of the universe is undimmed by those forebodings. For it is grounded, not on historical experience, but on faith. There is no absolute antithesis between faith and reason. The mediaeval thinkers rendered lasting service to philosophy by their insistence on the inability of unaided reason to satisfy its inherent claims.[2] We may not assent to their interpretation of the content of the faith that

1. It is at this point that I fail to follow Professor Alexander (*Space, Time and Deity*) in his view that the present stage of the evolutionary process is bound to be succeeded by one marked by the emergence of a new and higher quality than mind. His faith in 'deity', as he calls this next higher, and yet unknown, quality, rests, I gather, on the law that each new quality is conditioned by a new and more complex configuration, arising within an older and simpler configuration, of spatio-temporal elements. But what empirical warrant (and his philosophy claims to be empirical) is there for supposing that the process in the future will be to a higher complexity? May not the process be reversed, and the qualities of mind, life, etc., successively disappear? Professor Alexander appears to me to make heavy drafts upon the future.

2. While, on the one hand, the fact that we want a thing (e.g., personal immortality, or to understand the universe) is no guarantee that we shall get it, and the exercise of reason is throughout a discipline in repressing personal inclination in the service of truth; there is, on the other hand, justice in the claim of mediaeval (and modern) thinkers that a desire, which is not personal to the individual, but deep-rooted in human nature, must, if the universe be not unmeaning, find somewhere and somehow its satisfaction. This assumption underlies all religion, all morality, and all science.

reason requires as its complement. But the principle that underlay their argument still holds the field. It was reaffirmed in the later eighteenth century by Immanuel Kant, when he declared that the ultimate problems arising out of man's experience, the being of God, the freedom of the will, and the ethical order of the universe, indemonstrable for scientific knowledge, find their solution, not indeed in religious experience, but in moral faith. Practical reason thus gives the assurance which reason in its speculative exercise is impotent to confirm or to deny. We cannot here discuss the difficulties attendant on the doctrine of religious and moral faith. It is enough to indicate that the belief in a rational purpose governing the course of history must be justified, if at all, on this basis and on this alone. Intellectual research and moral action alike rest on the conviction that the universe, the object of our knowledge and volition, is an intelligible system. We cannot, with our finite capacity and finite experience, formulate its purpose, still less can we construe it in detail; we can but conjecture, here and there, the fragmentary signs of its operation. In face of the easy optimism, which brushes aside the palpable suffering and evil of life as accidental ingredients in the best possible of worlds, and of the warped temper of the pessimist, who measures the infinite whole in the light of his own experience of disillusionment, we do well to remind ourselves of Butler's *dictum*, that 'we are not competent judges of this scheme from the small parts of it that come within our view in this present life'.[1] It is well also to remember that the effort to understand the most trivial fragment of the universe is implicitly conditioned by a belief in the coherent order of the whole, and that not only religion and morality, but also science and history, rest on the foundations of a reasonable faith.[2]

1. Cf. *Analogy*, Introduction; and *Sermon* XV. On optimism, cf. Voltaire, in *Candide*, c. iv: '*Les malheurs particuliers font le bien général; de sorte que plus il y a de malheurs particuliers, et plus tout est bien.*'
2. This is the true 'free man's worship'. Mr Bertrand Russell's well-known essay with this title (reprinted in his *Mysticism and Logic*) errs, it seems to me, in that he builds on the distinction of fact from value. The world of fact revealed by science is for Mr Russell purposeless, and man is driven for consolation to a world of values, that exists only in his imagination.

II. ON THE LIVING INTEREST OF ANCIENT CIVILIZATION

§ 6. If the past were no more than the historic groundwork of the present, its appeal would be less insistent. It is interesting to learn our origins; but, after all, they belong to a bygone age, and it is in the present that we are called upon to live. We have to create the future; and there is peril, as well as profit, in the study of the past as past. The richness of the inheritance may serve but to paralyse the energy and enslave the mind. History itself points a warning, when it tells how the Jews of the dispersion and the Greeks in the last days of Hellenism were stifled by the hot air of archaism. They had not the strength to let the dead bury their dead, but squandered their declining energies in building the sepulchres of their forefathers. We can read the same lesson in the lives of individuals. No one who has passed his youth under the shadow of buildings enriched by the learning and piety of many generations, would deny their power to refine and ennoble the growing mind. Yet those whose years are spent amid such associations are too often crushed beneath their burden. We do not look instinctively to the cathedral cloister for the signal that heralds the coming day. We turn rather to the wharves and factories, the creations of yesterday, where thronging crowds are forging a new world, heedless of the traditions of the past. All down the ages, knowledge and the arts have arisen and fructified in close contact with industry and trade. Athens and Alexandria, Florence and Venice, Antwerp and Rotterdam were great commercial cities, where artists and thinkers drew life and gave it back, by just exchange, amid the seething tide of human energy.[1] If this be so, the study of antiquity must needs seem an irrelevant luxury, divorced, for the vast majority of mankind, from the serious business of life. The question arises, therefore: has it not a

1. The same is true in our own land. Erasmus found London a headquarters of Greek studies; Shakespeare and Milton came to London from the fields of Stratford and Buckinghamshire. Our hopes for the art and science of the future rest on cities like London, Manchester, and Glasgow. It is no unreasoning caprice that has planted our new universities in centres of industry and commerce.

value for the present, quite apart from the light it throws on the background of our history? We answer that it has; that it is still a living source of inspiration, with power to stimulate and direct the thought and action of the modern world.

§ 7. The creations of Israel, Greece, and Rome cannot be measured by their antiquity, or even by their influence on after-time. Their worth is independent of chronology, and endures untouched by the lapse of centuries. The prophecies of Isaiah, the tragedies of Aeschylus, the Parthenon marbles, Plato's dialogues, the *Aeneid* of Virgil, exist in their imperishable grandeur and beauty, now as in the hour of their first production. They have even gained in meaning, through the larger experience which is ours to-day. They are not ancient or modern, not merely Hebrew or Greek or Roman, but great visions, great thought, great poetry, with a meaning for all peoples and for all time. They reveal what is most permanent and universal in the life of the spirit. Man's nature, his relations to God and to the world, and the problems arising out of these relations, were interpreted with unequalled insight and power of expression by the great minds of antiquity; and their creations have the lasting value of the ideas they represent. They have the value also of the spirit that informed them. We have learnt something of the nature of that spirit. It was the spirit, in the hearts of the prophets and psalmists of Israel, of longing for the vision of the living God. It was the spirit of freedom, in the artists and thinkers of Greece, the desire of their reason to know themselves and the world, and, in the power of that knowledge, to realize their ideal of human excellence. In the Roman, it was the spirit of reverence for public law, inspiring the citizen to willing sacrifice for the community, the statesman, the soldier and the jurist to erect a firm bulwark of authority against the tide of disorder, and the poet to sing with patriotic ardour the glory of the Latin race. Hence it is that not only the works, but the men who wrought them, are an abiding possession for all ages. 'Their names are held in everlasting remembrance.' Isaiah and St Paul, Pericles and Alexander, Socrates and Augustine, were more than makers of history; they live, not merely as themes for the historian, but as ideal types of personality.

The philosopher of to-day, wrestling with speculative problems of which the ancients hardly dreamed, can gather strength for his endeavour by seeing with the eyes and thinking with the mind of Plato or of Aristotle. Men of action can find, in the deeds of bygone leaders, inspiration to guide them in their task of shaping the future of the world. Alexander nourished his imagination on the *Iliad*, that his own acts might be informed by the temper of the heroic age. It was in a like spirit that Napoleon studied Caesar. The secret of Plutarch's influence over later generations lay in the unique charm and moral insight with which he portrayed the characters of the famous men of old, for an example to those of after-time.

§ 8. We will consider, briefly, this living interest, first of Hebrew, and then of Graeco-Roman civilization.

(i) Israel dwells in our midst; little skill is needed to discern its presence in our science, our art, our finance, our revolutions. The marvellous persistence of the Jewish type, both of physiognomy and of character, blinds us to the changes wrought by time and persecution. King Saul himself might have sat as a model for Rembrandt's great picture at The Hague.[1] Driven from his native land by the Roman conqueror, the Jew of the dispersion henceforth made the world his home. Sheltered now for a brief season by his Semitic kinsmen at Baghdad and Cordova, now branded as a pariah for long centuries throughout Catholic Christendom, he set himself, in prosperity and in tribulation, to master the instruments of western culture. Banned from political office and social intercourse, he sought release from bondage by the path of philosophy, which none could close to him, and by that of finance, which Christian scorn left open to the unbeliever. The Jew of the Old Testament showed little desire or capacity for metaphysics; it was at Alexandria under the Ptolemies, and, above all, from the Arabs of the Middle Ages, that he learnt the lesson of Greece, to think. The fruits of Jewish Hellenism are visible in a long line of philosophers from Philo to Maimonides, from Maimonides to Spinoza, and from Spinoza to Bergson and Einstein

---

1. *David playing before Saul*, in the Mauritshuis.

in our own day.[1] For the rest, the modern Jew is the old Jew writ large. His portrait reveals the same arresting contrasts. Now as then, intense pride of race goes hand in hand with an easy cosmopolitanism, a readiness to assimilate foreign culture, and an extraordinary plasticity in adjusting his life and habits to those of alien lands. Himself of no country, he belongs to all; the unity he cherishes rests, not on civic loyalties, but on a spiritual faith.[2] He despises place and title and all 'the solemn plausibilities' of life; the seed of Abraham can afford to smile with pity on others' puny claims to Norman ancestry.[3] He has probed the secret sources both of ethical and of economic power, and his grasp on the gold of the spirit and on that of the currency is firm and unrelenting. He combines a reverence for spiritual values with an almost uncanny sense of the bearings of historical situations; like Elijah on mount Carmel, he will descry the coming tempest in the cloud that is yet 'small as a man's hand'. Again, the craving for riches and material possessions is, as of old, blended with a deep conviction that the poor and the lowly are the chosen children of Jehovah. The benevolence of the wealthy Jew, especially to his own people, is proverbial. Hence the Jew comes forward, now as the bulwark of capitalism, now as the champion of the proletariat; Rothschild and Karl Marx are but the modern representatives of an age-long cleavage within the ranks of Judaism.[4] The faith

1. The Jew has, in these latter days, shown his power also in the arts, especially in that of music; Mendelssohn was a Jew. The ancient Hebrews had little gift for art. What the Jew has never succeeded in acquiring is the nicety of critical discernment, for which western culture is indebted to Hellenism. This defect is apparent even in works of a high order of imaginative genius, such as Disraeli's novels.

2. The Jews of the Old Testament were always merging with their neighbours. The statement in the text must not be taken as suggesting that the Jews of to-day lack loyalty towards the land of their adoption; such an assertion would be manifestly false.

3. It is not merely because of legal disabilities that Jews have rarely been found in high public office. Disraeli is, of course, an obvious exception. But Jews seem naturally to prefer other avenues to power. It is worth remarking that no Jew is eminent in the annals of modern war, yet the ancient Jews were great fighters. The ideals and temper of modern Judaism are unsympathetic towards any form of militarism.

4. Karl Marx, though a baptized Christian, was the son of a converted Jew; one of his first writings was an attack on Jewish capitalism in the interest of

professed by Jews in all lands remains, in essence, the same ethical monotheism that inspired the prophets in the time of the captivity. Their daily life is still regulated in minute detail by the law, delivered by Ezra to the restored community twenty-five centuries ago.[1] Only the language of their fathers is dead, save to the expert in the university and in the synagogue. The very fact is suggestive of the living influence of the religion of Israel among men. The Bible, alone of the masterworks of antiquity, has preserved its vitality in the distorting medium of translation.[2] We have seen how the faith and worship of the Hebrew set an enduring mark on Christianity, and how the Old Testament scriptures were incorporated by the early church in the canon of inspired writings. Their translation into the vulgar tongues by the Reformation scholars gave fresh stimulus to their influence. The temper of Protestant enthusiasm found congenial nourishment in the ideals, and also in the practice, of ancient Israel. The sword of the Lord was unsheathed against his foes in the religious wars of the seventeenth century with a vindictiveness as merciless as in the days of Joshua and Gideon.[3] Cromwell heartened his cavalry at Dunbar with the old Hebrew war-cry, 'Arise, O Lord, and let thine enemies be scattered.' Frederick's Prussians marched to victory at Leuthen to the chant of Hebrew Psalms. Fathers named their children after the worthies, and even after the

the Jewish proletariat. It is often said that the Bolshevist leaders are mostly Jews; but this is true also of leaders of other parties in the Russian revolution. The Russian *intelligentsia* is largely Jewish.

1. The domestic life of the poorest and most ignorant Jews can furnish a model of moral purity to the most cultured Christian societies (see the sympathetic study in George Eliot's *Daniel Deronda*). The popular travesty of the Jewish character, in so far as it has any foundation in fact, is an exaggeration of defects which are the outcome of centuries of Christian persecution. Even in these defects we can trace the amazing persistency of the race, driven to pursue its ends along devious paths.

2. This is true both of the English Authorized Version and of Luther's German translation. Of course, no modern rendering can perfectly reproduce the meaning and spirit of the original. But that meaning has been deepened, and its value enriched, by the spiritual experience that is embodied in the languages of modern peoples. We translate *Elohim* by 'God', *nephesh* by 'soul'; but 'God' and 'soul' mean far more to us than the Hebrew equivalents to those who used them.

3. Cf. the types of Scottish Covenanters in Scott's *Old Mortality*, especially Ephraim Macbriar and Habakkuk Mucklewrath.

texts, of the Old Testament. Milton's *Paradise Lost* and *Samson Agonistes*, Racine's *Athalie* and *Esther*, and the vogue of the Scriptural oratorio in eighteenth-century music, show how the influence pervaded poetry and the arts. Its echo is audible even in Dryden's satire and in Byron's lyrics. The works of John Bunyan carried it into every homestead throughout the land. Recent years have witnessed a reaction. Theologians no longer seek with confidence for the evidences of Christianity in the miracles and prophecies of the Old Testament. The ten commandments are no longer interpreted as an epitome of Christian ethics. The young grow up to manhood unfamiliar with the narratives of Hebrew history.[1] It is the inevitable revolt against an age of bibliolatry, with its narrow conception of revelation, its strained interpretation of the text, its bondage to the letter, rather than to the spirit, of the scriptures. We may regret that, at the moment when critical enquiry has, for the first time, thrown clear light on the ordered evolution of spiritual life in ancient Israel, and rendered possible, as never before, an understanding of God's education of his chosen people, the records of this process should be losing their hold upon the world. Yet the sacrifice is worth making, if men's apprehension of Christ's teaching is liberated from its long association with a code in which the precepts of justice and mercy were obscured by traditions of ferocity and barbarism. The Psalms can never lose their power to express the spiritual aspirations common to every race and time; and there are surely many who, in these last years, have turned for relief from the tragic spectacle of a world at war to the prophetic vision of a day when 'they shall not hurt nor destroy in all my holy mountain: for the earth shall be full of the knowledge of the Lord, as the waters cover the sea'.[2]

1. There is matter here for regret, not only because of the religious and literary value of the Old Testament, but because many boys and girls miss what is perhaps the only opportunity in their lives of reading first-hand historical documents.

2. Is. xi. 9 = Hab. ii. 14. The truth of the statement that the Psalms possess an ever-living spiritual value is not disproved by the reservations that must be made in regard to certain Psalms, such as the 58th, 69th, and 109th, which contain passages in a vein directly contradictory to the express teaching of Christ.

§ 9. (ii) The place held by classical studies in our schools and universities bears witness to the living potency of Greece and Rome in modern life.[1] It is true that their inheritance has been subjected to misuse from its advocates and malignity from its foes. Popular opinion ranks Greek and Latin with Hebrew and Sanskrit as 'dead' languages.[2] It opposes classical to modern studies, and a scientific to a humanistic ideal of education. This prejudice is mainly due to the facts that in the generations following on the Renaissance a training in Greek and Latin came to mean the study of philology rather than of literature, history, and thought, and that the ideal set by the great humanists was tarnished with pedantry and antiquarianism. The efforts of teachers were frequently confined to making their pupils compose slavish imitations of classical models. Thus arose a breach between a discipline that taught the pupil to fix his eyes exclusively on the past, and that which trained his mind to analyse the phenomena of the present, and predict those of the future. Yet, as we have seen, the modern sciences themselves had their roots in the impulse that sprang from Greece. It would be indeed strange if the spirit that could touch the mind to such fine issues should have lost its magic in the few centuries that have since elapsed. A classical education, again, in contrast with that in the applied sciences, is commonly

1. The term 'classical', as applied to the languages and literatures of Greece and Rome, is apt to carry misleading associations. It suggests opposition between the classical and the romantic. We think of the rigid and prosaic standards of the eighteenth century, when the *Poetics* of Aristotle had become a storehouse of dogmas for dramatic criticism, and the 'unities' were all in all. The results of this doctrinal pedantry were laughable enough, and provoked the revolt of the 'Romantics' in Germany against the 'classicism' of France. Voltaire had written a *Philoctetes*, in which the plot of Sophocles' masterpiece was adapted to the taste of Parisian society by the insertion of a heroine and her chaperon. It was high time that Goethe led the revolt in the name of Shakespeare and of the living spirit of Greece herself. The great poets of Greece and Rome stand on a height far above the antithesis of classical and romantic; their works are 'classics' in the sense in which all great art is 'classical', as enrolled among the master-creations of the human mind. On the confusions implied in the antithesis, see Professor W. P. Ker on *The Humanist Ideal* (*Essays and Studies* by members of the English Association, vol. vi).

2. Latin has remained to this day a spoken language in Roman Catholic colleges; and in recent years, on the initiative of Dr Rouse, of the Perse school, Cambridge, the 'direct' method has been applied with success to its teaching in many English schools.

disparaged as unpractical. The word 'practical', in everyday thought and speech, is almost synonymous with 'vocational'. Men mean by it something that contributes directly to professional efficiency, to earning a material livelihood; they forget that without friendship, morality, religion, and art, life would not for a moment be worth living.[1] The Greeks of ancient days were wiser. They saw clearly that education, to be practical, must take account of these higher humanistic interests. Since man's end is not merely to live, but to live well, they distinguished between the knowledge that is a means to livelihood and that which is an integral factor in a good life. The one was 'necessary', as a training for vocations which no man would follow of his own will, but are forced on him by the pressure of material wants; the other, as the satisfaction of spontaneous human desire, was 'liberal' or free. Thus they escaped the confusion of thought that opposes theory to practice. They grasped what we are just beginning to understand, that even the economic life can only be conducted with efficiency, if it rests on a foundation of scientific knowledge. This conception of a liberal education, embracing in its scope literature and the arts, science and philosophy, morals and religion, is as valid now as it was then. The teacher of to-day has more to learn from the pages of the *Republic* than from all our modern text-books of pedagogy, English, German, American, put together.[2]

§ 10. But Greek culture means something more for the world to-day than an instrument of youthful education. The

1. Mr G. Sampson, in his *English for the English*, p. 10, remarks: 'I am prepared to maintain, and, indeed, do maintain, without any reservations or perhapses, that it is the purpose of education, not to prepare children *for* their occupations, but to prepare them *against* their occupations.' It should furnish a relief for the monotony, which, in this age of specialization, weighs with a crushing burden on the spirits of millions, especially clerks and manual labourers in large towns.

2. The literature of pedagogy, extending over more than 2,000 years, and multiplying to an appalling degree at the present day, contains some half-dozen or so of works that are worth reading. Of these, the *Republic* is by far the greatest. In recent times, Newman's *Idea of a University* also forms an honourable exception. The array of educational manuals on the shelves of a college library affords as dismal a consolation to the misanthrope as the prospect from the platform at Landore Junction, referred to in an earlier note.

people who created science, who first grasped the meaning and worth of freedom in thought and action, and displayed in their activities such independence of character, energy of will, and clearness of intellectual vision, cannot fail to stir a like response in all who study their works with understanding. The Greeks are, now as ever, the surest guides to lead mankind along the path of self-expression. They were the greatest masters of experiment in life that the world has known.[1] In life, as in science, the fruitfulness of the experimental method is not to be gauged by the success or failure of isolated adventures, but by the daring and skill with which men work out an idea to its issue, probing every avenue that experience offers in the effort to bring theory to the test of fact. We find this energy of self-expression, not only in artists and philosophers, but in the ordinary Hellenic citizen, who was never weary, on his own lower plane, of seeing new sights, hearing new tidings, making new things. The Greek was a born craftsman, alike in special arts, such as pottery or shoe-making, and in the wider art of life. We may imagine what would rouse his interest, were he to appear in the England of to-day. Not our politics, for the cumbrous machinery of the modern state would bewilder his intelligence; not our warfare, which would strike him as horrible and barbaric; not our art, which would simply leave him cold.[2] The things that would stir him to enthusiasm would be our inventions, our aeroplanes and microscopes, our use of steam and electricity, the applications of scientific knowledge to the exploration of the ways of life. These would excite in him the wonder, not of a savage, but of a wise child, who recognizes by unerring instinct the impress of the human mind forging the instruments of human life. The phrases 'humanism', 'humane learning', 'the humanities', point to the distinctive quality that gives to Hellenism its abiding value. The theme of Greek thought and literature was humanity; man as he is amid his actual environment. But the Greek thinker never forgot,

1. Even in physical science, Greek thinkers used the experimental method, as far as their slender resources allowed. Their thought and action was always, in the wider and perfectly legitimate sense, experimental.

2. We can perhaps imagine the Athenian visitor touched to a thrill of recognition by Synge's *Deirdre of the Sorrows*.

as the modern world is prone to forget, that man, with all his potency of thought and will, is part of a whole, a member of an ordered universe. Our passion, in the economic field, for production, heedless of leisure and the fitting enjoyment of the produce of our toil; our rejection, in the field of politics, of any institution or form of government that is not the creation of the popular will; the efforts of science, to remould nature after our heart's desire, and of philosophy, to interpret reality as relative, through and through, to human mind; would appear to his astonished vision as the wild audacity of *hubris*. Where, he would ask, in this seething whirlpool of motion, is there place for rest? Where lies the spiritual goal of all this striving, the unity of purpose that gives direction and meaning to man's hustling enterprise? He would point in answer, with calm assurance and a deep pity for our confusion, beyond the realm of becoming to that of being, beyond the temporal to the eternal, beyond the many to the one.[1] *Theoria*, as well as *praxis*, knowing as well as doing and making, is essential to enduring satisfaction. Human nature is two-sided; man's effort is both to know things as they are and to discharge his moral obligations. He cannot do the one without the other. If he is to keep clear of fantasy and illusion, his knowledge must be closely related to practical activity. If his practical achievement is to be fruitful, it must rest on knowledge of what is. Man cannot act blindfold or in the dark. He needs light, and light is what the Greeks valued above all else. Further, if he is to know the world and share its future, he must first know and shape himself. In the power of self-knowledge he must be the architect of his own character. Personality is an ideal rather than a *fait accompli*; it is the finished form to be realized in the raw material of human nature. So taught Socrates, Plato, and Aristotle; and the lesson is one that mankind, after more than two thousand years, has still to learn from Greece.

§ 11. And what of Rome? Can the world still profit by her example also? Or is the depreciatory judgement that we have

1. The contrast between the Greek and the modern view of life, here indicated, is admirably presented in Professor G. P. Adams' book, *Idealism and the Modern Age*.

passed more than once in the course of the preceding pages, our last word on Rome's work in history? It is true that, in the higher things of the mind, the Roman lived on a lower plane than the Greek, or even than the Jew. His world was one of temporal events and historic situations, not one of enduring values. Even within that world, he lacked imaginative vision. He contributed little that was original to the art, the knowledge, the religion of after-times. Therefore the living interest of Rome for the present day is proportionately less than that of Israel or of Greece. The study of the Latin tongue and of Latin literature cannot claim an equal place in a liberal education with that of the Greek. But this does not mean that the work of Rome was negligible, or its interest merely historical. The masterpieces of Latin literature are worthy of their Hellenic models. The study of Roman law is an integral part of a modern juristic training. Moreover, the maxims and methods of Roman public policy are still discernible in those of the Roman church. We have seen how the influence of the empire was already stamped upon its early history, notably in the growth of papal prerogatives and in the severance of Greek from Latin Christendom. In the Middle Ages, the papacy, fashioned after the likeness of the empire, claimed to inherit its authority and its mission. Thomas Hobbes of Malmesbury, writing in the days of the Puritan revolution, spoke of the papacy as 'no other than the ghost of the deceased Roman empire sitting crowned upon the grave thereof'.[1] So at least it seemed to the Protestant philosopher and arch-enemy of ecclesiastical dominion. In an essay on von Ranke's *History of the Popes*, Macaulay insisted with his wonted energy of style on the historic significance of the Roman church. 'The history of that church', he wrote, 'joins together the two great ages of human civilization. No other institution is left standing which carries the mind back to the times when the smoke of sacrifice rose from the Pantheon, and when camelopards and tigers bounded in the Flavian amphitheatre.' In its claims to temporal power, in the canon law, in its organization, in its policy towards subordinate associations,

1. *Leviathan*, c. 47. Sir Christopher Wren, thinking of Roman architecture, wrote that: 'Modern Rome subsists still by the ruins and imitation of the old.'

as well as in its traditions and its seat of government, the papacy stands to-day as the inheritor of imperial Rome. It was while listening to the bare-footed friars chanting the office among the ruins of the Capitol, that Gibbon conceived the idea of narrating the 'Decline and Fall'. Now if Rome thus lives still in the literature, the law, and the religious life of the present day, it must be through some quality of lasting interest in the character of her people. We must do justice to her capacities as well as to her limitations. We find the clue if we think of the habit of mind that is stamped on the most characteristic achievements of the Romans, on their public policy and their jurisprudence, as also, at a later day, on the philosophy and the theology of the Roman church.[1] We see an intellect that revels in general rules, in clear-cut definitions and rigid distinctions, in subsuming cases under principles and in discerning the means appropriate to a given end. It is the legal cast of mind, with its formalism, its respect for precedent and the established order, its narrow horizon, its stereotyped doctrines, its abhorrence of vague conceptions and suspicion of all that savours of the visionary and the mystical.[2] Such an intelligence could not avail to unlock the secrets of the higher realms of knowledge. But its logic and precision furnished a discipline, which was, and still is, indispensable to intellectual progress. This quality of mind was the counterpart in the field of thought to the Roman instinct for government in the field of action. Rome realized more fully than any other race the value of authority. Authority is regarded with much suspicion by the present age. There is reason in the mistrust; for authority rests on force and fear, imposes an external discipline, and looks to the means, not to the end, of the moral life. But our suspicion is also fraught with danger; in their rebellion against external regulation, formal observances, and the casuistry of the law, men may

1. This Roman habit of mind is specially evident in Aquinas, for all his indebtedness to Aristotle and Neo-Platonism.

2. The following quotation from Inge's *Outspoken Essays* (p. 246) affords an excellent example of the formalism of the Roman mind: 'When the Romans repudiate their "scrap of paper" with the Samnites, they deliver up to the enemy the officers who signed it, though (with characteristic "slimness") not the army which the mountaineers had captured and liberated under the agreement.'

fall victims to antinomianism and anarchy. It is the spirit that giveth life, but the spirit can only win expression through the letter. Rome is there to put us in mind of the disabilities of our present state, that preclude man's attainment of his goal solely in his own strength, and necessitate the provision of outward controls as the conditions of inward progress. In the second book of the *de Monarchia*, Dante tells how he had once thought that the Roman race had won its sovereignty, not by right, but by force of arms alone; and how clearer insight had dispelled his error. The arguments by which he justifies its title to world-empire will hardly be convincing to the reader of to-day. But at the close of the treatise, he bases this theory of the functions of the empire and the church under the scheme of divine providence on grounds which, in principle, go to the root of the problem of authority and law. Man, as sharing alike in corruptibility and in incorruptibility, holds a middle place in the created universe. His twofold nature marks him as destined for the two ends of temporal and eternal felicity. The fitting means to these ends are the teachings of philosophy and of revelation. But, by reason of their sinful greed, men are unable to enjoy these fruits, and must 'like horses going astray in their brutishness, be held in the way by bit and rein', i.e. by the twofold directive power of the catholic empire and the catholic church. Thus alone, 'upon this threshing-floor of mortality', can human life be lived in peace.[1] The enduring element of truth in Dante's theory of government is the recognition that, where there is no restraint of law, war and tyranny, the off-spring of man's evil passions, must abound. If we owe to Israel and to Greece the essential constituents of a good life, we owe to Rome its regulative instruments. She fell in the event because she confounded the scaffolding with the structure, the means with the end. The *pax Romana* imposed upon her sub-jects was no positive peace; it meant only repression of dis-

---

1. *De Mon.*, iii. 16; cf. *Purg.*, xxvii. 140–2, where Dante, having passed through Purgatory, enters the earthly Paradise (the garden of Eden), the scene of pristine innocence, and is declared by Virgil free to follow his own pleasure, and is crowned and mitred by him as henceforth his own emperor and pope. He has passed beyond the stage of discipline, where external authority is needed, and is now a law to himself.

order. She knew not that behind Rome lay Jerusalem, behind the empire of this world the kingdom of God and Christ. One thing alone she saw clearly, that civilization must perish apart from government. Her history teaches, for all who have ears to hear, that, if liberty is to be more than an empty name, it must be founded on reverence for authority and law.[1]

§ 12. Thus it is that the civilized world can still learn its lesson at the feet of ancient Greece and Rome. In each succeeding age, artists, poets, and thinkers have turned to this perennial spring of inspiration, to gather strength for their own efforts. History never repeats itself; and what the Greeks and the Romans did in their generation needs not to be done again. The art and the philosophy of the present and of the future will express the present and the future, not the past. They must be as original, in their form and in their content, as the life which they interpret. The creations of Greece and Rome mean little to the pedant and the dilettante, who are moved to study them by no impulse save that of idle curiosity. They mean much to those who labour with strength and courage to build the future, whether in art or science, thought or action; for such share most fully in the spirit that inspired them. When artists cease to draw life from the Phidian sculptures, when thinkers fail to find in Plato the living movement of the human spirit in its unwearied search for truth, when poets no longer turn, as Dante and Milton turned, to Homer and to Virgil as to the well-springs of poetic inspiration – then, and then only, will the Greek and Roman tongues be dead.

III. CONCLUDING REMARKS

§ 13. The speculative problems that we have touched upon in this closing chapter are not peculiar to the study of ancient

1. The problem whether in an ideal society there is any room for authority, lies beyond our scope. The conception of the kingdom of heaven implies the sovereignty of God, 'whose service is perfect freedom'. Thus interpreted, authority is no longer an instrument, but an essential factor in the ideal life. Dante, of course, recognized such authority in Paradise. But this takes us far from the external authority of which Rome is the embodiment in history. On the question here indicated, see Webb's *Gifford Lectures, Second Course*, Lect. v.

civilization. They are common to all history, though presented by each succeeding age in a new and different form. They may be difficult to answer, but they must not be shelved. For they mark the points where history and philosophy meet on common ground.

The function of the historian is not merely to describe facts, but to explain them. In other words, he cannot cut off the ideal from the actual, and, reserving the actual for his own province, relegate the ideal to the philosopher. He must himself philosophize, or be unfaithful to his vocation as a historian. For ideals, though transcending the bounds of men's achievement, belong to the same world of reality; and the facts are not the facts without them.[1]

There is no such thing as a fact without a meaning. The meaning of a fact is not added to it from the outside, as if the fact could be complete without it. It is constitutive of the fact itself.[2] On the side of knowledge, it follows that the description of the fact includes the explanation of its meaning. Even in his initial selection of relevant data, the historian is guided by a hypothesis as to their significance; he is, from the outset, an interpreter, a judge. To assign a meaning is to value in the light of an ideal standard. Plato is more important than Aristippus, Cicero than Roscius, St Paul than Silas, because, in the judgement of the historian, they contributed something of higher quality, of more enduring value, to the course of human

1. This implies criticism of the conception of a 'philosophy of history', which means that history is one thing, philosophy another; that, after the historian has determined the facts, he hands them over to the philosopher for effective valuation. It is no wonder that such a conception is anathema to the historian. He knows that he, too, has a mind and can judge. What he does not always see is that when he does so, he is *ipso facto* a philosopher. Herein lies the justification of Croce's doctrine of the identity of philosophy and history. Both alike, as implying the integration of values with facts, must, in ideal completion, form a single science. But, in the existing state of human knowledge, their methods and achievements are necessarily divergent.

2. Doubtless, the meaning is unfolded by the context of other facts. This is but to say that the initial fact, and the other facts, are only so called by courtesy, that they are each a fragment of the total fact under investigation, as Picton's charge and Lord Anglesey's loss of a leg were partial factors in the fact of the battle of Waterloo. The same is true of the battle, which gets its meaning in the context of the Napoleonic struggle; and so on, until our search for a genuine fact expands into a philosophy of experience.

civilization. In the long run, this judgement on what counts implies a philosophy – that is, a reasoned doctrine of the ideal ends of life. A given historian may not be conscious of this implication, but it is none the less involved in every step of his enquiry. Ideals cannot be dissevered from historic fact. They are the creations of actual minds in actual situations, and have their life and being in the acts and lives of actual men. Philosophy has often been tempted to dissociate the two realms, and to point men away from historical events to a timeless world of values. So did the Neo-Platonists; so, emphatically, did not Christianity, which, with a faith grounded in the historic personality of its founder, declared in one breath that the kingdom of God was life eternal, and that this kingdom existed here and now. The issue is even graver in the field of religion than in those of philosophy and history. Thinkers who, like Plotinus of old and certain Christian theologians, Protestants of the school of Ritschl, and Catholic modernists, in our own day, stress the reality of ideals to the point of scorning temporal facts, will always evoke a response from minds that revolt from bondage to historic events as from an irrelevant encumbrance to the spiritual life. They achieve by this means an easy escape from the difficulties raised in the path of religion by the advance of the historical and physical sciences; but it is at the cost of the very religion they desire to save. A Christianity cut adrift from the course of history is no longer a gospel of salvation to all mankind; it has become the preserve of an enlightened few. The world cannot be redeemed by an abstraction. The sternly practical Roman mind rejected the attempt to reduce religion to philosophy, bearing witness, by its instinctive sense that a living faith must find expression in the facts of history, to the truth of one of Christ's most pregnant sayings, that 'the children of this world are in their generation wiser than the children of light'.[1]

1. In modern thought, the distinction of the two worlds of fact and of value has its source in Kant, whose tenets were applied to theology by Ritschl. It implies a dualism, which, if taken as ultimate, runs counter to the impulse of reason to find unity and system in experience. On Catholic modernism, see Giovanni Gentile's volume of essays, entitled *Il Modernismo*, and (from the Christian standpoint) Figgis, *The Gospel and Human Needs*, Lect. iii. 'Complete

This conviction, that the events of history are not unmeaning but informed and sustained by an ideal purpose, is the basis of man's endeavour both in thought and action.[1] It is the motive force that inspires, not only the leaders among men, but the humblest worker who labours faithfully to lead a worthy life, and, so far as in him lies, to leave the world better than he found it. It has proved an unfailing strength in troubled times, as to Augustine and his fellow-Christians in the fourth century, amid the wreckage of a historic civilization, and to ourselves at the present day. For it gives assurance that time, in the great words of Plato, is but 'a moving image of eternity', and that the changes and chances of temporal history are a revelation of the eternal gospel, bearing its age-long message: 'Behold, I make all things new'.

severance', writes the latter (p. 124), 'between the Christ of fact and the Christ of faith would, in the long run, be destructive of belief in either.'

1. This is obviously true of moral action, but the same faith lies at the root of all social intercourse. Commerce and industry rest upon credit, which is the analogue, in the economic sphere, of that which is 'the substance of things hoped for, the evidence of things not seen'. Faith is no idiosyncrasy of the religious consciousness, but a primary condition of all reasonable life.

CIVILIZATION AND HISTORY

*

§ 1. In the opening chapter of this book (Chap. I, § 1), we defined the field of history provisionally as identical with that of civilization. This definition provokes certain questions of a speculative character, the discussion of which would have been premature at the outset of our inquiry. Among these there are two, which concern respectively the philosopher and the historian. On both questions definite convictions have been repeatedly expressed in the course of the preceding survey, and particularly in the concluding chapter (XII). A fuller consideration of the grounds for these convictions can now no longer be deferred.

(1) The philosopher will ask, what is the status in reality of ideal value and how is it related to fact? Clearly in some sense the two realms fall apart; the pursuit of ideals implies that men are moved by desire for something that lies beyond their actual attainment. Even the drunkard at the door of the tavern displays this much of reason in his nature that he can want a thing before he gets it. The goods that men desire are infinitely various and of varying grades of perfection, but, however closely integrated they may be with what is present to the senses, they one and all as 'goods' surpass the range of what is actually possessed. Moreover, ideals, when viewed in abstraction from their embodiment in facts, are seen to be, not temporal occurrences, but timeless entities; whereas the realm of actuality is constituted by events that occur in time. I cannot give a date in the time-series to my ideal of justice any more than to my conception of triangularity, as I can to the battle of Hastings or my own birth. If we try to think out the speculative problem thus presented, we find ourselves confronted by two alternatives. On the one hand, there are those, who, like the Platonists, ascribe to values a supersensible existence, whether in their own right, or as thoughts in the mind of God.[1] On the other hand, there are those who, like the advocates of

---

1. The alternatives are here stated in their extreme form. No mention is made of such intermediate theories as (e.g.) the Phenomenologist position that values (and universals) are 'subsistent' entities, real though non-existent. See my Gifford lectures (*From Morality to Religion*, pp. 183–6). On the Plato-

scientific naturalism, deny the claim to objectivity, holding that values (and universals generally) are products of human thinking, 'logical constructions' fashioned by actual individuals in the natural course of their mental development, and existing only in the minds of those who frame them. The nature of our answer to this metaphysical problem will already have become clear from the preceding chapters (esp. IX, XI and XII). A naturalist explanation of values is manifestly incompatible with faith in a theistic interpretation of the universe. Suffice it to say here that in naturalism there is at least this measure of truth, that ideals, whatever may be their ultimate status in reality, are closely integrated with facts. Actual institutions, laws, and ways of conduct are what they are because individuals and societies have approved certain ends and devoted energy of thought and action to effect their realization. Moreover, these ends have been shaped in men's minds under provocation from the facts of their inner and outer experience. Thus, as Christianity affirms, the two worlds, though widely different, are not, in the phase of an early Greek philosopher, 'cut off one from the other by a hatchet'.[1]

§ 2. (2) Our second question is for the historian, since it concerns the scope of history, and therefore calls for more detailed consideration here. Were we right in treating history as though its field were coterminous with civilization? For, if we take the term 'history' in its widest sense, it seems to include much more. It can be stretched to cover the whole process of nature. Not merely human societies, but all living organisms, as well as the earth and the solar system, have a history; and the business of the physical sciences lies largely in recording it. Some recent philosophers, following in the wake of evolutionary science, have posited 'the historicity of things' as the basis of all that happens in the universe.[2] But before we commit ourselves to this wider view of history, a distinction must be borne in mind between mere *events* that occur without conscious agency and *actions* that have their source in man's purposive volition. To talk, as we habitually do, of the 'action' of a bicycle or a chemical substance is to close our eyes to this distinction. Now the proper

nist doctrine, see above, c. v, § 20, and c. ix, § 13, and for mediaeval views on universals, c. xi, p. 444, *note* 2.

1. Anaxagoras (*fr.* 8). The point has been made with special reference to Christianity, in cc. x and xii, above.

2. I have here in mind the philosophical doctrines of Alexander and Dr Whitehead. See especially Alexander's essay on *The Historicity of Things* in the volume presented to Dr E. Cassirer, and reprinted in the posthumous collection of Alexander's writings, *Philosophical and Literary Pieces*, edited by Prof. Laird.

field of history is the past acts of human beings. With events as such the historian is concerned only in so far as they condition men's purposive actions. This distinction between actions and events is grounded on the far-reaching assumption that man is free both to choose the end towards which his action is directed and to act in accordance with his preference. Otherwise man's so-called actions are mere events. This assumption is not the conclusion of an inferential process; rather it is 'taken for granted' universally in the moment of action. It never enters into a man's mind, when acting, to questoin whether he is free to act or not. The question arises only for subsequent reflection, under provocation from scientific theories of mechanical causation. Man's freedom, as thus assumed, is not absolute, but relative, alike to his capacities of insight and strength of will, and to opportunity and circumstance, the former conditioning his act of volition, the latter his ability to achieve what he sets himself to do. The rejection of scientific determinism, i.e. the doctrine that all so-called 'acts' are rigorously necessitated by their psychical and/or physical antecedents, does not mean that actions are wholly undetermined, or products of blind chance.[1] It simply implies that man is, in Aristotle's language, an $\dot{a}\rho\chi\dot{\eta}$, a causal agent capable of initiating a course of action. In reality there is no such an entity as ' chance'; the use of the word is merely a disguise for our inability to give a rational explanation of an action or an event. When the historian, as is often the case, speaks of an event as fortuitous or accidental, he simply means that its occurrence falls outside of the particular causal sequence that at the moment engages his attention. The web of history is woven of multitudinous strands, each of which constitutes a distinguishable causal series. When one such series x cuts across another v, we have an effect, the cause of which must be sought, not in prior events in series y, but in an alien series x; whose intrusion into y strikes the mind as a coincidence. Thus Alexander's death in 323 by infection from a bacillus seems fortuitous, though an expert in tropical medicine, had he been on the spot, might easily have diagnosed the malady and prevented death by scientific treatment. Again the causal factor, though alien to series x, may well be due to purposive volition, just as Caesar's murder, though an accident as regards Caesar's own actions, was due to deliberate purpose on the part of his republican

1. On this question of the extension of the deterministic hypothesis to cover human actions, science speaks to-day less dogmatically than even half a century ago. But the reader should be on his guard against construing its recent provisional hesitations as implying a decisive verdict in favour of the libertarian alternative.

enemies. In the case of Socrates' death, on the other hand, there is nothing that can be regarded as fortuitous; Socrates himself deliberately chose the course of action that led to the fatal issue. Further, just as there is no such thing as blind Chance, so there is no such thing as blind Necessity (ἀνάγκη) or Fate. History, which lives and moves in the world of concrete actuality, has no place for such hypostasized abstractions. They merely veil the obvious truth, that there are causes beyond the grasp of man's intelligence and the range of his control. 'There's a divinity that shapes our ends, rough-hew them how we will.' So is it, again, with the modern invocation of the *Zeitgeist*. No individual, however endowed with genius, is impervious to the ideas that dominate his world. Ideas are *ideés-forces*, which tend to realization; but they affect history solely through the medium of the characters and actions of individuals. The same is true also of the alleged dialectical laws of economics and politics.[1] These carry no mysterious prerogative of compulsion; in so far as they hold, it is as formulas descriptive of the ways in which individuals and groups have been found to act. I make special reference to groups, not with any intention of affirming a doctrine of 'corporate personality' or of ascribing to organized societies a real individuality of a higher order than that of their members,[2] but because the historian is directly concerned with the life of such societies – their growth, maturity, and decay – as conditioning the lives of individuals. Realizing that man is by nature a social being, he fixes his attention not on individuals in isolation (for none such can either be or be conceived), but on their acts as members of more or less civilized groups, exhibiting a relatively complex type of social structure. Below this somewhat arbitrarily selected level lies the province of pre-history, the special preserve of the anthropologist. I have here in mind not only states, but churches and confraternities, gilds and municipal corporations, universities and trade unions, as well as larger political federations, such as the United States of America, the Union of Soviet Socialist Republics, and the British Commonwealth of Nations at the present day. We must be on our guard against the natural tendency to think of political organization exclusively in terms of the nation-state. The nation-state is a modern growth, which saw its rise in the fifteenth and sixteenth centuries, and it already shows signs of yielding place to a different

---

1. I have specially in mind Hegel's metaphysical dialectic, as expressed in the process of history, and that of Karl Marx in the special field of economic development.

2. As for example does Bosanquet, following Hegel, in his *Theory of the State* and his Gifford lectures on *Individuality and Value*.

form of supra-national organization. Looking ahead for a moment, we can envisage new types of political unification, embracing not only a plurality of nation-states, but even whole continents and hemispheres.[1] And there is another and even more consoling prospect. A graver menace to civilization even than international wars is that, the larger the political community, the more the individual citizen is swamped in the mass, and finds himself deprived of opportunity for the expression and development of his personality. He counts for little or nothing, even when in a democratic state he is registering his vote at an election. Against this peril, the smaller communities within the state offer a remedy. In his church, his university, his professional organization or his trade union, he can not only exercise personal influence, and acquire training in affairs and skill in the handling of personal relationship with his fellows, but can play an effective part, if indirectly, in shaping the policy of the government. No government, if legislating, say, on public health, can afford to neglect the corporate opinion of the medical profession, or, on matters of education, that of universities and teachers, or, on labour questions, that of employers' federations and trade unions. Thus even to-day democracy functions in *concreto* less through direct constitutional machinery than through the active expression of the general thought of the community in the medium of non-political confraternities. To foster their vigour and independence is thus increasingly a main interest of the national or supra-national Commonwealth.[2]

§ 3. But our original question presses itself upon us from another angle. History is the record of the past acts of civilized mankind; but we can say that all civilization falls within its purview? With regard to the facts, there can be no question; the historian is concerned with them all, in their varying measure of importance. No fact is intrinsically too trivial for his notice; a broken potsherd or a memorandum of personal expenditure may at any moment throw a flood of light on his researches. History has become democratic, like the rest of us; it is a crude fallacy to suppose that the historian is solely interested in outstanding personalities rather than in the sentiments and behaviour of ordinary human beings. So much for his concern with the facts of civilization; but what about its ideals, which, as we have seen, are

1. See above, c. xi.
2. See Miss Ruth Follett's well-known book, *The New State*, with special application to the training furnished to American citizens in the New England township. The 'corporative' principle advocated above has been recognized alike by Soviet Russia and in Fascist states. See Mr Christopher Dawson on the Turkey reformed by Mustapha Kemal as the earliest and most instructive type of Fascist state.

integral to man's civilized life? With these also the historian is concerned, not, however, in their timeless being, but in their influence as motives determining human actions and in their effects on man's cultural history. He will note, for instance, how the Calvinistic conviction that all men are equally sinful in the sight of God had its repercussion on secular politics in fostering the principle of democratic equality at Geneva, in the Scottish Lowlands, and in the Puritan settlements in New England. So, again, St Paul's missionary journeys and the adoption, under Constantine, of Christianity as the official religion of the Roman Empire, will hold in his eyes a greater historical significance than the writing of the Fourth Gospel or the martyrdom of Saints Felicitas and Perpetua. It is therefore untrue to say that ideals lie altogether outside his province. No one will question the legitimacy of extending the range of history to include the history of art and literature, of philosophy and religion, or of any of the innumerable specialized branches that, with the ever-increasing accumulation of materials, have come to be discriminated within the area of human civilization. But what the historian takes note of is not the intrinsic worth of aesthetic, ethical, religious, or speculative ideals, so much as their temporal effects on the cultural life of individuals and societies.[1] He accounts for these effects by tracing them to their causal antecedents, thus constructing an intelligible pattern, say, of the rise of Christianity or of the Renaissance. With any causal agency from beyond the scene of temporal events such as divine intervention in the lives of individuals or communities or with any other-worldly purpose implied in such intervention, the historian, *qua* historian, is not concerned. As a man and a Christian he may acknowledge such agency, but to explain its existence and its manner of operation falls outside his competence. For the historian as such, the supernatural is equivalent to the non-existent. In Bacon's phrase, *Deum semper excipimus*. In the traditional language of the schools, he confines his attention to secondary causes.[2] Where these fail to account for the phenomena, his only recourse is frankly to admit his inability to offer

1. See Appendix II, pp. 538–53, for the historian's criterion of 'importance'.
2. See Aq. *S.c.G.*, iii. 71 (*ad fin.*). A difficult theological problem here arises. God's causality extends to everything, and therefore is operative concomitantly with instrumental and secondary causes. Moreover, it is immanent in such secondary causes, not added to them *ab extra*. It is no more possible to refer the effect partly to God, partly to natural causality than to distinguish within the unitary Person of the Incarnate Christ those features which exemplify His divinity from those which exemplify His human nature. All is alike at once human and divine. The same applies to God's immanence in the created universe as creating it and conserving it in being.

a reasonable explanation. To have recourse to the miraculous is to quit the ground of scientific history. Only in so far as actual men have been inspired to act in certain ways by their (real or supposed) vision of an other-worldly order do such ideals come within his province.

§ 4. This is the reason why (as I have stated in the Preface to Vol. I, and at the opening of the chapter on Christianity) I have contented myself with indicating the personality of Jesus of Nazareth as the source from which the first disciples and the Church as a corporate body drew the living energy that enabled them to preach the Gospel and, in the course of four centuries, to Christianize the civilized world. So it has been all down the ages and so it still is to-day. All that has been achieved in accordance with the divine purpose has its sole spring in the abiding presence of Christ among men, inspiring individual Christians and the Christian church by the indwelling in their hearts of His Holy Spirit. The visible effects of this inspiration are legitimate matter for the labours of the historian. But to analyse the nature and activity of the divine Person who inspired them lies beyond his scope. That is why, in writing a work on history, I have purposely refrained from any such enquiry.

This must be my answer to the complaint of a fair-minded, and even generous, reviewer in a notice of the first edition of the present book, in the *British Weekly*. 'It is unpardonable', he writes, 'in a work conceived on this scale that, although the writer is convinced "that the history of Christianity can only be accounted for by the unique personality of its Founder", he applies infinitely more psychological insight in his estimate of the personalities of Amos and Jeremiah than in the single page [he might have said with truth, "the single sentence"] devoted to the personality of Jesus of Nazareth. Our Lord's conception of religious authority is assumed rather than defined.' Was it not assumed rather than defined by our Lord Himself? He claimed unique authority as the Son of God, leaving the task of defining that doctrine to His followers, to whom He delegated that authority. As for a psychological estimate of His personality, this depends for its possibility on the answer we give to a simple question. Was Christ a mere man or was He God incarnate? in the former case, his personality, like that of Amos, Jeremiah, or any other man, allows of psychological analysis. But if He was no mere man, but very God incarnate, how can we dare, how can we claim the competence, to enter upon such an undertaking? As a recent living Christian writer has put it, 'We are in no position to draw up maps of God's psychology.' [1] We know indeed that on certain occasions Christ was moved

1. Mr C. S. Lewis, in an address in Southwark Cathedral, March 16, 1943.

to pity or to anger and we can draw rough generalizations from such cases; we know that His presence excited curiosity, devotion, love, hatred and, most frequently, awe and astonishment, in His disciples; but what inference can we draw from these broken lights as to what He was Himself? He was, on occasion, such as this or that; but He was infinitely more than this or that, and the 'infinitely more' lies beyond our comprehension. We cannot, for instance, draw any clear line of demarcation between those of Christ's actions which are due to His divine and those which are due to His human nature. It was the vain attempt to discriminate in this matter that entangled Christendom in the Monophysite and Monothelete controversies of the sixth century. Cyril of Alexandria, who, though not in all respects an estimable character, was a supremely able theologian, rightly insisted on the presence of both natures in every detail of Christ's life and character. It is the same with the attempt to account for His acts in the light of their historical antecedents. Much may be learnt by enquiry into Jewish thought and practice before and at the time of His earthly sojourn; and we know that His life and teaching were designed so as to bring His revelation of the Gospel within the comprehension of His hearers. But, again, our historical researches carry us only a few steps towards the knowledge of God's infinite purpose in the Incarnation and of the grounds for Christ's fulfilment of it in His life and death. Nor is the significance of Christ's life and the evidence for His divinity to be sought in the historical consequences or in its influence on civilization, however widespread and persistent in after times. Were that so, the absurd conclusion would have to be drawn, that the value of His Incarnation increased with each successive generation, in proportion to its historical effects on human culture. If Christ be truly God, His acts, though occurring in the time-process, transcend that process in their originating principle and, as proceeding from a supertemporal $\dot{a}\rho\chi\dot{\eta}$, defy explanation by the methods of the scientific historian.

§ 5. The futility of the attempt to prove Christ's divinity or to measure the significance of His life by appeal to historical consequences has been impressively exposed by Søren Kierkegaard in his *Training in Christianity*.[1] He contends that Christ's life was in and for itself infinitely noteworthy and that, even if it had had no historical consequences, its intrinsic value as the life of God on earth would have been unaltered. 'From history', he says, 'one can learn nothing about Christ'; faith alone, implying contemporaneousness on the part of the believer with Christ's supertemporal presence, can reveal the truth.

1. English translation by Lowrie, pp. 28 ff.

Kierkegaard presses over-hard the rigid distinction of faith from reason, and his view that the history ruled out as irrelevant is secular, not sacred, history is not free from ambiguity. The following passage from a Catholic theologian [1] puts the main point with less obscurity and one-sidedness. Writing of the mystery of the *Parousia*, of Christ's coming in all ages to each individual, as a judgement (*krisis*), he insists that the decisive act of acceptance or rejection is not a temporal process but is complete in the moment of its occurrence. 'It is the privilege of personal beings not to come to be, but to be themselves at any moment they will. ... It is for this reason that, according to the traditional teaching, at any moment of our rational life (even *in articulo mortis*) we can sin grievously or win eternity by an act of love, be for God or against Him. So to think of ourselves is not to deny that we can grow and become more perfect. The truth for us lies in the special character of our development which is by means of a series of complete acts, of what Aristotle, in writing of acts of knowledge, called τελείαι, because they do not end a process.' I suggest that it is in some such way as this that we should conceive the integration of God's eternal causal agency with temporal events in the course of human history.

§ 6. Leaving this difficult, yet all-important problem of the relation of the two worlds, the eternal and the temporal, to one another, there is one further point to be noted strictly relevant to a discussion of the historian's technical procedure. We remarked above that any fact, however trivial, is of potential interest for history. But this is not to suggest that all facts are equally important. The historian has to select from a vast mass of material the specific problems for his investigation, and for a given enquiry certain data will be more relevant than others and therefore, for his immediate purpose, more important. But, apart from this pragmatic and largely subjective criterion, can we not ascribe to certain events, say, Caesar's murder or the outbreak of the Russian revolution, an objective significance, which others (say, the composition of this paragraph) do not possess? What, then, is the criterion by which the objective importance of historical personalities and events is to be gauged? The only standard available for the historian is the cultural achievement of his own race and age, including its acknowledged values, and enlarged by a generous recognition of achievements alien to his experience. Thus the Western European will be ready to ascribe value to the civilizations of India or

1. Father M. C. D'Arcy, S.J., Master of Campion Hall, Oxford, in his Presidential address to the Oxford Society of Historical Theology (1938–9) on *The Christian View of History*.

China, however remote their outlook upon life may be from his own. But the standard remains this-worldly and humanistic. Judgement on other-worldly ideals will be strictly determined by their fruits as displayed within the framework of a historical civilization. For him, as for Protagoras of Abdera in the fifth century B.C., 'man is the measure of all things'. This is why the scales of historical greatness and of religious or moral excellence present such a disconcerting discrepancy. But this raises a large and difficult problem, requiring consideration in a separate Appendix.

ON HISTORICAL GREATNESS AND
MORAL GOODNESS

*

I

§ 1. THE problem referred to at the close of the preceding Appendix, of the distinction between the historian's valuations and those of the moralist, is one which most writers on the theory of value seem to have ignored. The usual practice is to treat of values under the threefold rubric of truth, beauty, and moral goodness. This threefold classification, grounded on the misleading eighteenth-century distinction of cognition, feeling, and will as mutually exclusive modes of consciousness, is not exhaustive. For one thing, it limits value to the sphere of rational consciousness, whereas we discern valuation, in some measure, at infra-human levels; indeed, if Spinoza and Dr Whitehead are in the right, it is present even below the plane of consciousness in every 'actual entity'. Among ideal values, again, there are other claimants to recognition; the religious life, for instance, though practical, is not, like morality, merely practical, but is inspired by theoretical vision, nor is its characteristic value, holiness, the *virtus infusa* of the saint, identifiable with moral virtue. Once more, within the domain of ethics, there is the distinction between the standards of right and of good, about which much has been written of late, especially by Oxford philosophers. In what follows I shall use the terms 'moral' and 'ethical' indiscriminately to cover both types of value, without prejudice to my convictions, which have been expressed elsewhere,[1] that rightness cannot be interpreted as due to intrinsic or consequential goodness, that an action is moral only when done for its intrinsic rightness, that action *sub ratione boni* is a type of action distinct from moral action, and that both types, the moral and the optimific, have ethical value. Further, in the field of aesthetic valuation, we discern a manifest qualitative difference between the sublime and the beautiful. All this shows the error of over-hasty simplification. Value itself is a highly abstract term, which is bereft of significance when divorced from concrete experience. It implies compresence with a valuing subject, whose individuality is reflected

---

1. *From Morality to Religion*, c. I, pp. 4–5, cc. II and III.

in his acts of valuation. Moreover, standards of value are no bare
formal unities, universals standing aloof from embodiment in particular instances and awaiting a content to be externally supplied from
the realm of empirical fact. The values are found in the facts, which
would not be the facts without them, though it takes a living mind to
find them; and when found they are pregnant with anticipatory
inspiration of the novel response to the practical situation.[1] The
ethical ideal of goodness, for example, is no empty rule or form, but a
form *of life*, a synthetic principle of unification, which, however
vaguely apprehended, is capable of generating, in relation to the
changing current of events, schemes and purposes that are ever
individual and new. So it is also with truth, beauty, or holiness. When
held apart from the concrete truths of the special sciences, from the
artist's manifold intuitions, from the personal revelations of the
religious life, these values degenerate into barren formulas, as impotent as they are unmeaning.

§ 2. I come now to the problem. Everyone will agree that ethical
valuation – whether the judgement be that of rightness or of goodness
– is concerned with human character and conduct. Few, again, would
question that in this practical sphere the ethical valuation is ultimate,
even in regard to the pursuit of truth or beauty.[2] It is a moral duty
for the philosopher to seek truth for truth's sake, and for the artist to
seek beauty for the sake of beauty. Moral obligations control not only
the choice of a vocation, but also its exercise in detail, as when a man
is called upon to forgo the practice of his art or his science in order
to serve his country, or, again, to be single-minded in his devotion,
in the face of temptation to do inferior work for the sake of gain or
popularity. Herein lies the primacy of the Practical Reason. Yet the
historian habitually employs, in judgements upon human achievements, another and apparently a very different standard, that of
eminence or greatness.[3] The two measures of value are not merely

1. As has repeatedly been pointed out in the course of this book (see esp.
c. ix, xii, and Appendix I).

2. I do not here discriminate between ethical and religious valuation. Where
these fall apart, the religious valuation is final.

3. The view that it is the philosopher's prerogative to value the facts
recorded by the historian has already been rejected (see c. xii, p. 525, note 1).
Hegel himself would have repudiated any such severance of fact from value;
indeed, in the *Introduction* to the *Philosophy of History*, he poured contempt on
the suggestion that the philosopher, 'so far from leaving history as it is, should
force it into conformity with an idea and construe it *a priori*'. But Hegel's pro-
fessions were not infrequently belied by his performance, as when he relegates
to romance all that, in his judgement, is irrelevant to the manifestation of
Spirit, declaring that 'the essential characteristic of the Spirit ... is always

different; they can, and frequently do, conflict with one another. It is evident that great men are not necessarily good, or at any rate that their goodness is not proportioned to their greatness; also, happily for most of us, that it is possible to be good without being great. We recall the closing words of *Middlemarch*: 'The growing good of the world is partly dependent on unhistoric acts; and that things are not so ill with you and me as they might have been, is half owing to the number who lived faithfully a hidden life, and rest in unvisited tombs.' The day-labourer who gives his life to save a drowning child merits ethical approval, though his deed finds no place in history. The peoples of the civilized world showed a fine sense of this distinction when, at the close of World War I, they paid their tribute of honour, not only to famous generals and statesmen, but also to the 'unknown warrior', recognizing thereby the moral value of a thousand unrecorded acts of sacrifice. On the other side, both imaginative literature and history afford numberless examples of great characters, whose ethical goodness or badness has little relevance for our estimate of their greatness. '*Il y a des héros en mal comme en bien*'; we admire Aeschylus' Clytaemnestra, Dante's Farinata, Milton's Satan, as we admire Caesar or Napoleon, by a valuation of a very different order from that of moral approval or disapprobation. Greatness, again, is ascribed on grounds that in the main are non-ethical, to societies and institutions, such as the Roman Senate or the English Parliament. Dante, following Augustine, saw in Pagan Rome a supreme example of imperial greatness, which went far to justify her selection by Divine providence as the secular instrument for the foundation of Christianity. Hers was not indeed the excellence of the *civitas Dei*, but that of the *civitas terrena*, the city of the world; yet she held, among reprobate principalities, an unquestioned primacy, on a valuation parted by an abyss from that of moral goodness.[1]

II

§ 3. Surely there is here a serious problem, alike for the philosopher and for the historian. But, before addressing ourselves to its solution, we must show that it cannot be eluded by subordinating either of the two standards to the other, either (1) by interpreting historical greatness in terms of goodness, or (2) by restricting judgements of moral contained in great events' and that 'all the particular facts which remain are a superfluous mass, which, when faithfully collected, only oppress and obscure the objects worthy of history'. Such a doctrine as this is, as we have said, anathema to the historian.

1. See above, c. xi, p. 476, and c. xii, pp. 520-4.

approbation to acts and persons whom the historian accounts 'great'.

(1) First, we may call in question the autonomy of the historian's valuation. The so-called great who are not good are, it may be said, not really great; and the sooner the historian recognizes this and renounces his own standard for that of morality, the better will it be for history. Alexander and Napoleon were, like 'Tamburlaine the Great', mere organizers of slaughter; historians, like the public, have simply been deluded by the glamour of successful ἀδικία on a grand scale. We may reply that the villainy, if villainy it be, is yet on a grand scale, and as such commands admiration by its sheer magnificence and splendour. Yet, even if we throw conquerors and tyrants to the lions, what are we to say of those morally bad men, like Henry II of England, whose claim to greatness rests on their achievements in the fields of government and law? More deserving of consideration is the variant on this view which seeks the criterion of a man's greatness in the good effects of his work upon the world.[1] Socrates or St Francis, it will be said, were great in themselves, for they were also good; but the Caesars and Napoleons owe their greatness to the fact that what they achieved enabled good people to promote the moral welfare of mankind. I do not, however, think that this doctrine is satisfactory. In the first place, it makes greatness, at least in the case of bad men, solely dependent on consequences for good, and in no wise intrinsic to its possessor. Secondly, the criterion proposed is beyond the historian's or anyone else's power of application. Who can gauge the moral issues of an act through a long course of history? Even if moral goodness were determinable by causal laws, the laws are manifestly incalculable; while the knowledge of the effects has to be gathered from their overt expression, and is restricted to the rare instances where goodness emerges from its normal obscurity and is proclaimed upon the house-tops. Moreover, if by goodness we mean 'moral goodness' – and this is certainly what is intended by the view in question – we throw the historian's estimate overboard and deny all value to achievement that cannot justify itself at the bar of ethics. The moralist may acquiesce – indeed, if I understand him aright, Dr Ross has defended this position[2] – but is it seriously proposed that history should be rewritten on such a principle? Ethics cannot claim a right to question the canons of the historian within the bounds of his own enquiry. This admission, however, does not imply that his valuation is final beyond its own limits, or that his estimate of greatness and the ethical estimate of goodness stand on the same plane.

1. T. H. Green seems at times to approximate to this variant.
2. *The Right and the Good*, pp. 152 f.

§ 4. (2) If greatness cannot be explained in terms of goodness, intrinsic or consequential, can moral goodness be explained in terms of greatness? This alternative method of evading the issue lands us in even wilder paradox. It would mean that a man's title to be called good rested solely on his own greatness or on his capacity to produce the conditions of greatness for others. It is true that moral excellence enters into the ideal of civilized life which, as we shall see, is the historian's criterion of greatness, but only as one cultural factor among many. Virtue can hardly be identified with the specific excellences of the artist or the philosopher. The two most serious objections, however, are the following. (a) If goodness is to be measured in terms of greatness, it will be limited by its possessor's ability to display it overtly in the public life of his generation, by shaping the thought and practice of society to ethical ends. Of the inward springs of moral action, as distinct from its expression in notable achievements, the historian takes no account. Whether Scott wrote his novels to get money for building Abbotsford or to pay Ballantyne's debts; whether Rembrandt painted in order to provide Saskia with a necklace or from pure joy in creative work; whether Caesar conquered Ariovistus to win power for himself or to protect Roman territory from Teutonic invasion is irrelevant to the estimate of his greatness. What matters is that Ariovistus was conquered, and that by Caesar's genius and his strong right arm. The estimate is based on the thing done, not upon the disposition of the man who does it; and the thing done must be on a memorable scale. But in judging goodness of character – whatever may be the case with the rightness of the action – motive is all-important. So, again, the problem of freedom, which the moral thinker is bound to take in earnest, simply does not exist for the historian. For him determinism has no terrors. 'Ought implies can'; but the estimate of greatness rests on the thing done, not on the disposition of the man who does it. Greatness depends both on gifts of natural endowment and the presence of opportunity favourable to its display. With moral goodness it is otherwise. (b) Morality is very independent of circumstance; in every practical situation there is a duty to be done or a good to be realized, and the value hinges on the effort that the agent makes in willing it. If few achieve goodness, the possibility is there for all, and those who fail fail on their own responsibility. Herein lies the democratic appeal of morality, which impressed Kant so deeply, accounting for his admiration for Rousseau's writings, where it found eloquent expression. A man's goodness is never, like greatness, 'thrust upon him'; he is master of his moral personality, whatever be his station or his talent. Greatness, on the other hand – and this holds also of *moral* greatness – is dependent both on rare gifts of natural endowment and on an exceptionally favourable environment. This is why genius so often strikes us as accidental, so that we can understand Napoleon's question in regard to candidates for high command: 'Is he lucky?' What from an other-worldly standpoint is the 'cunning of reason' or the decree of divine providence, appears to the historian as the gift of Fortune. We have noted how the great man of action is often blind to the ends for which he is working and to the real significance of his achievements. Greatness, like pleasure, comes to him by the way. If he has flashes of clear vision at crucial moments in his career, his thought is for the most part concentrated on the solution of particular problems, each of which, taken in isolation, is trivial and monotonous. Great men lay themselves open at every turn to the charge of opportunism; for they know better than others that to act effectively they must wait on the ever-shifting movement of events. 'There are sudden providences in things', said Cromwell; and a Caesar or a Napoleon or a Bismarck, though they might discard the religious implication, wait with a like patience the signal from an agency not their own.

§ 5. Thus it is that great men seem conscious, when face to face with the critical opportunity, of being in the presence of an alien and overwhelming power. The situation, which calls their whole personality into action, is not of their own choosing. They see in it, according to their varying temperament, the hand of destiny or chance or God. Their response is felt by them as a response to something greater than themselves; they create, but with a sense of restricted freedom. This consciousness of the numinous – to use a hard-worked term – in history cannot be accounted for by any wiles of psychological analysis. The objective order of things – to employ the secular language proper to the historian – has in some mysterious and unfathomable manner given birth to a richly pregnant crisis, which breaks as a unique intrusion into the normal process of historical development. You may trace out in detail the genesis of the French or the Russian revolutions; but when all has been said and done, the issue defies resolution into its antecedents. The historian, like the actor in the drama, is confronted by what, from the standpoint of scientific method, he must confess to be irrational. It is the same with greatness in art or science, with the experiences that inspired Dante to compose the *Divina Commedia*, or Faraday to discover the hidden secrets of electro-magnetism. Now for the historian, as such, the presence of this disturbing factor in history furnishes no speculative problem. He probes into the story of its origin, notes the emergence of a new phenomenon and, if the action that ensues tallies with his criterion of human culture, pronounces the action or the agent 'great'. But the philosopher must go farther and ask questions that may well carry him beyond the bounds of human history. Is the mysterious power that of the spatio-temporal universe, sweeping onward in its totality towards a higher level of evolutionary development? Or is it, as for Hegel, the 'cunning of reason', overruling the petty interests and designs of mortals at the behest of the Absolute Idea? Or, once more, is it that Power to which religion does obeisance, a supernatural Providence whose designs lie beyond the scope even of metaphysics, save in so far as metaphysics furnishes justification for religious faith? It is noteworthy that in all ages greatness has been the form of value most commonly ascribed to the object of religious worship. 'Allah alone is great.' 'Great is the Holy One of Israel in the midst of thee.' Has not the philosopher defined God, when arguing to his existence, as *id quo maius cogitari nequit*?[1] Something of this numinous quality seems to attach to all forms of greatness. This is why some have been led to rank greatness above goodness and have striven to emancipate 'world-historical individuals' from allegiance to the moral law.

These considerations seem to be conclusive against any attempt to evade the problem of the dualism of valuation by reducing moral goodness to historical greatness. Yet I cannot help suspecting that a good many writers on ethics, including all those who adopt a Naturalistic theory, are committed to this view by implication. I do not see how, if we identify the good with a form of civilization immanent in the temporal process, we can differentiate the moral ideal from the historian's criterion of greatness. For that criterion, as we shall see presently, is nothing other than just such a form of social life, in which cultural values find scope for actualization. Are not the advocates of humanism in ethics logically bound to renounce the claim of ethics to autonomy, and to accept the historian's standard of greatness as the measure of the moral life?

III

§ 6. Since, then, the difficulty cannot be side-tracked by reducing either greatness to terms of goodness, or goodness to terms of greatness, we must frankly recognize a divergence of standards of value. Let us first ask what the historian means when he calls a personality or an achievement 'great'. The following considerations will serve as an approach to an answer.

    1. Anselm: *Proslogion*, c. ii. 'Than which nothing greater can be conceived.'

(i) Greatness, like goodness, has a variety of meanings, not all of which are relevant to our purpose. Its use, in popular speech, to signify mere quantitative magnitude, as when we talk of a great river or a great fortune, may be ruled out of account. It is as a qualitative factor that magnitude enters into the estimate of historical greatness. A university may be of smaller size than a big business corporation like Imperial Chemical Industries, but it is a greater thing. We recall Coleridge's saying about Milton: 'If there be one character of genius, predominant in Milton, it is this, that he never passes off bigness for greatness.' The late Professor Alexander, writing on 'Beauty and Greatness in Art', points out that an analogous distinction arises also in science and morality. It is idle, he says, to ask, e.g. among works of art, whether one is more beautiful than another; for all alike are beautiful, as all truths alike are true, and all ethically good actions alike are virtuous. Whether this be so or not is another story; what is relevant to our purpose is his recognition that though there are no degrees of beauty, truth, or goodness, there are degrees of greatness. Scott's novels, he holds, rank higher in the scale of greatness than Jane Austen's, the truth of the law of gravitation than that of a property of a botanical species. So with morals; 'there is a double standard by which conduct is measured or judged. ... Within virtuous action there is an order of greatness or smallness, an order of perfection.' Now the greatness in each kind depends, according to Professor Alexander, on the subject-matter, the beauty, truth, or goodness on the form. That which is great, he says, is great by virtue of the 'magnitude or splendour' of its theme – including under or along with these its 'complexity'; or, again – though here surely form comes into play as well as subject-matter – by virtue of the subject being handled 'more extensively, more profoundly and more subtly', with 'deeper insight and penetration'. Greatness thus indicates a differentiation within the wider areas of the beautiful, the true, and the good, great art being always also beautiful, great science true, great virtue good; the differentiation being determined by the magnitude or splendour of the subject. This doctrine, that greatness lies in the splendour of the theme of art, science, or conduct, is, I am sure, sound; with the addition, perhaps, of the mark of completeness. Great works of art, like the *Divina Commedia* or the *Fifth Symphony*, great philosophical constructions, like the *Republic* or Spinoza's *Ethics*, feats of action like the battles of Blenheim or Trafalgar, strike upon the mind with a finality which no criticism, however conscious we may be of its validity, can utterly destroy. In the moment of appreciation, they are self-contained and satisfying; within the limits of the aesthetic, intellectual, or practical situation – and, in the moment of appreciation, we do not look beyond – there is no more to be said or done.[1]

§ 7. But, while thus indicating a generic property of greatness, Professor Alexander does not consider in his paper the relation to goodness of the specific type of greatness that we have called historical. He discusses the relation of *moral* greatness to goodness, explaining that it is goodness *plus* the characters of magnitude and splendour, which add to the goodness a distinctive value. But, as he points out, between *morally* great action and action that is just good there can be no opposition, any more than between great art and art that is just beautiful, or between great philosophy and philosophy that is just true. Hence his conclusions, acceptable as they are, scarcely touch the root of our problem. Historically great action is not good action, enriched by the distinctive value of greatness. It is not necessarily good at all. It may be good, bad, or morally indifferent. The question: How is it that within the field of human action there have come to be two rival orders of valuation, which are frequently found to conflict, and each of which claims independence of the other? remains unanswered. Unlike 'good', which is often employed as a predicate, 'great' is rarely used except as a qualifying epithet, and never properly of abstracts; we say that pleasure is good and talk of good pleasures, but the phrase 'a great sincerity', though admissible, carries a suggestion of metaphor. The natural use of the term is (a) of persons, and (b) of things or events as expressive of personal agency, as when we speak

1. The difference in the case of these other forms of greatness, e.g. in art and science, lies in this, that here the historian accepts the estimate of experts in other fields, the musicians' estimate of Beethoven's greatness, the scientists' of Darwin's, the philosophers' of Aristotle's or Spinoza's. I admit that the line is hard to draw; for the historian of art or philosophy must understand his subject, as we say, from within. Conversely, an adequate understanding needs some knowledge of the historical context. Yet the activities are distinguishable; a given individual's capacity for *Kunstgeschichte* is not proportionate to his capacity as an artist. Even in philosophy, where the moments are least separable, the difference is discernible; Kant was but poorly instructed in the thought of the past, and Zeller was a more erudite historian of philosophy than Hegel. The historian's verdict in these matters is not autonomous; but he judges Caesar or Napoleon great on his own authority, in the light of his own standard of civilization. That standard embraces all cultural values, while assigning primacy to the establishment and maintenance of social organization and law. That Richelieu composed a tragedy and founded the French Academy, that Frederick of Prussia enjoyed intellectual companionship with Voltaire, will condition the judgement as to their historical greatness. So too with ethical values; it is equally obvious that moral goodness enters as a factor into the historian's judgement, and that it is not his sole or dominant criterion (see § 10, 549).

of a great poem or discovery or, again, of a great city, meaning one that has unique significance in human history. Rome is a great city, not for its size – Athens too is great, while Peking and Chicago are not – but because it is the outcome and embodiment of significant human activity and has profoundly influenced the course of human activity both within and beyond its bounds. But greatness cannot be measured simply by its effects. While 'good' is also applicable to what is not good in itself, but merely conducive to a good result, greatness is a quality intrinsic to its possessor. To judge an individual or an institution great on the strength of its causal efficacy, and of that alone, is to confound a property of greatness with its essence. If offered as a definition, it lands us in a circle. For every action, how-ever trivial, has innumerable effects; what is characteristic of great action is that its effects also are great. 'Spirits are not finely touched but to fine issues.' True; but this brings us no nearer to an under-standing of what greatness means.

§ 8. (ii) The view that the key to a man's greatness is to be found in the fact that he is typical or representative of his age has a certain *prima facie* plausibility. Great historical personages do seem, as Emerson noted in the case of Napoleon, to sum up and embody, in their thought and actions, the dominant pattern of their time. So is it with great works of art and literature and with great philosophy; Dante's *Divina Commedia* and the *Summae* of St Thomas, in their several ways, express in encyclopaedic form the spirit of mediaeval culture. But here again we are in danger of falling into a circle. Great men and their works represent what is of high significance, patterns of thought and life which are judged to be dominant, on the score not merely of their prevalence, but of their greatness. Some ages are moulded to patterns which are trivial and insignificant; in these, greatness, if it appears at all, is revolutionary rather than representa-tive. There is a sense, again, in which every individual represents his age, representing it indeed in inverse proportion to his individuality. The great man stands rather for the forward *nisus*, implicit, it may be, but not explicit, in the life of his generation, for the pattern that is not yet, but thanks to his creative genius is to be. Great men of action are as a rule unaware of the full significance of their under-takings, which becomes clear to the historian of a later generation only after long lapse of time. They are aware only that the time is ripe for new development, and are driven onwards by a dim but compelling sense of vast possibilities, to reshape their world to ends that lie beyond their vision. Thus, so far from being typical of the life and sentiment of their age, they are, as we say, 'ahead of their time', and

liable to misrepresentation, obloquy, or persecution from their contemporaries. To quote Hegel again, so far from great men enjoying
happiness, 'their whole life is labour and trouble. ... When their
object is attained, they fall off like empty husks from the kernel.' That
this is so they are themselves aware. Cromwell's words to his Parliament, 'I would have been glad to have lived under my woodside, to
have kept a flock of sheep rather than undertaken such a government
as this', can be paralleled in the case of many famous men in history.
For this reason the appeal to the social sentiment, the 'standardized
mind', on which Professor Alexander lays so much stress in his treatment of ethical value, fails alike in the case of goodness and in that of
greatness.

§ 9. (iii) Continuing this process of elimination, we must rule out
of account all attempts to make greatness dependent, solely or mainly,
on the formal character of the agent's will. It does not consist in
mere efficiency or in successful adaptation to the practical situation.
Efficiency, sheer force of will, is, as Croce has shown, a condition
sine quâ non of every action; if it be not willed effectively, there is no
action, but failure to act. What is willed – the matter of the action
rather than its form – is the factor decisive of the greatness. So with
successful adjustment, appropriateness, fitness; these are characteristics which may be exhibited in quite unhistoric situations, as
when I 'do the right thing' in guiding my car skilfully in a sudden and
perilous emergency. Appropriateness for what? is the relevant question, and the answer must be in terms not of mere efficiency or fitness
but of specific ends. Nor does greatness lie in mere talent, however
brilliantly displayed. Lord Brougham was called 'prodigious' by his
generation just on this account; but no historian would judge him
great, for great purpose was lacking to his life and actions. Nor will
the test of coherence of wills, for all its array of philosophic champions, avail us better. Every action demands a measure of coherence,
as of efficiency, both inwardly among the agent's dispositions and out-
wardly in co-operation with his fellows. At the other extreme, perfect coherence of wills is an ideal assured only to moral and religious
faith, and belongs to a realm of vision of which the historian at all
events takes no account. Within his purview, conflict and incoherence
are as evident as harmony and coherence; men and societies cohere
for evil purposes as well as good, as when three of the leading states
of Europe cohered to effect the partition of Poland. The lives of
historically great men have been lives of ceaseless conflict, both
within and without, and history goes far to justify religion in its
relegation of ideal harmony to another world and in its characteriza-

tion of man's secular condition as a *militia*. At each stage in our search for the meaning of greatness we are led away from the formal characters of action to the consideration of its subject-matter and its purpose.

§ 10. (iv) Once more: The distinction between greatness and goodness is complicated by the fact of moral greatness, greatness, i.e. that is grounded upon goodness. A morally great character or action is also good, just as a great work of art is also beautiful; but the converse does not hold, though, given a practical situation which calls for a heroic solution, the action cannot be called good unless it solves the problem and is therefore, in this instance, great. Now, great goodness is also great historically, as are great art and science; for these have their histories, integral with that of man's action in society and recognized by the historian as legitimate branches of his science. There is thus a wider sense of historical greatness, in which it covers the whole field of greatness, in addition to its more specific application to social and political action. Hence it is untrue to say that the historian in estimating greatness takes no account of ethical values. Even where the greatness is not greatness in goodness, moral qualities enter as factors into the life or action, which are judged great as unitary wholes. But the historian's judgement on these qualities differs from the ethical, in that he looks not to the agent's inward disposition, but to its overt expression. The achievement is largely dependent for its greatness on conditions that lie beyond the scope of the moral judgement. If, thanks to uncovenanted graces and opportunity, a man is enabled to display his goodness conspicuously in the public life of his generation, by shaping its thought and practice to his ethical ideal, he is entitled to be called not only good, but great. The same is true of religion. In so far as a St Paul or a St Augustine sets the stamp of his spiritual faith on the institutional life of secular or ecclesiastical societies, either by direct participation in their affairs or by influencing the beliefs and practice of those who govern them, he becomes significant in human history. But the inward springs of religious devotion the ὁμοίωσις τῷ θεῷ, which is the be-all and end-all of the religious life, lie outside the historian's province. They win for their possessor the salvation of his soul and the enjoyment of the celestial kingdom; but they do not make him historically great. Thus it is with the mystics, save when, as in the case of St Bernard, their vision prompts to effective action in public affairs, or when, as in the case of St Francis, it finds expression in the establishment of an order that leavens the social life of their age. Thomas à Kempis, like the vast majority of morally good men, calls for scant notice from the historian.

§ 11. (v) It is at this point that Croce comes to our aid, with his distinction, within the field of the practical, of economic and moral activity. He is, I think, the one philosopher of our time who has clearly grasped the problem, though, for a reason to which I shall refer presently, I am unable to accept his answer. Economic volition or action – these are for Croce identical – is volition of the particular; moral volition or action is volition of the universal. The former embraces all material ends, the latter is, as moral, purely formal. Since the universal can only be effectively willed in willing particular ends, all action, including moral, is economic, i.e. the economic moment, though distinct, is present in every moral act of will. But not all economic action is moral; for the particular may be willed for its own sake, and not as an embodiment of the universal. Such purely economic action is neither moral nor immoral, but amoral. Moreover, each form of action has its own standard of value; we approve moral action for its goodness, or – in logical, Kantian, terms – for its universality; but we approve also economic action for its efficiency, quite apart from its moral worth. The two forms are not co-ordinate, nor is economic action a lower grade of moral action; they are distinct types of practical activity, the economic being capable of standing alone, while the moral necessarily presupposes the economic.

§ 12. We seem here to have found the clue to the nature of the distinction between historical greatness and goodness. For Croce not only recognizes two distinct types of practical valuation, but grounds the distinction on that between two sorts of activity, each directed to a different end. The one is wholly immersed in the finite and temporal, the other, while immanent in the finite and temporal, works therein in the light of the infinite and the eternal. 'The volitional act,' he writes,[1] '*quâ* economic, satisfies us as individuals in a determinate point of time and space', but 'unless it satisfies us at the same time as beings transcending time and space, our satisfaction will prove ephemeral and will be changed swiftly into dissatisfaction.' And he goes on to show how purely economic volition, since it fails to satisfy, misses the mark that volition of the universal can alone attain. How this is consistent with his doctrine of the rationality and independent value of economic action, it is a little difficult to understand.[2] But in so far as Croce is faithful to the dualism of activities and ends, and to the distinction between the temporal and eternal on which it rests, his theory of economic action gives the clue to what the historian

1. *Filosofia della Pratica*, p. 221.
2. See my essay in *From Morality to Religion*, pp. 311–28, on *Croce's Theory of Economic Action.*

means by greatness. The historian's outlook is limited to an ideal construction, reached by an enlargement of the ascertained course of history. He recks nothing of timeless or absolute values, save in so far as such values – let us say, truth, beauty, and goodness – find concrete exemplification within the temporal process.[1] He abstracts rigorously from any other-worldly reference. His estimate of historic achievement is made in the light of an ideal form of human civilization, which, while it transcends the *fait accompli*, lies strictly within the range of possible future attainment, and is filled out with detail drawn from man's actual attainment in the past. He is profoundly distrustful of visionary Utopias, knowing that all such, even the *Republic* of Plato, would, if realized, prove hells upon earth. Moreover, in judging the characters and actions of historic personalities, he keeps his eye fixed on the type of civilization realizable in a given age, e.g. on what was practicable for Alexander or Caesar or Napoleon under the actual conditions in which they worked. His standard of judgement is no clear and distinct concept, cut to the measure of Cartesian Rationalism, but a form of desirable social life, shadowily envisaged and incapable of precise definition. Such an ideal is not a final or perfect state, but a phase, vaguely conjecturable on the basis of what has been realized in past experience, and itself a temporal process and a becoming. This is not to affirm uniform progress; epochs long past may exemplify details in the ideal type more perfectly than the present or recent times. It implies, certainly, an immanent *nisus* in human development, towards a goal that, however dimly apprehended, transcends actual attainment. But the transcendence falls wholly within the bounds of the spatio-temporal process. The ideal is purely secular and humanistic. From the mass of persons and events within this temporal process, all in their degree possessing historical interest and significance, those that bear the further qualities, in Professor Alexander's phrase, of 'magnitude and splendour' are selected by the historian as 'great'.

§ 13. A further difference between the standards of greatness and goodness leads directly to our conclusion. The historian's valuation is relative, in that his measures of greatness have no finality, but grow with the growth of his knowledge and experience. The ideal, were it actualized, would cease to be an ideal and would yield place to a new ideal, as provisional as the former, and so on *ad indefinitum*. Moreover, it is a purely ideal standard, devoid of actuality save in the thought of the mind that thinks it. It is a light of man's own projection, that witnesses indeed to his unconquerable thirst for self-transcendence,

1. See above, p. 539.

yet, being temporal, ever recedes into the future, as he moves forward, he knows not whither, on its track.

With morality it is otherwise; the standard of valuation is both absolute and actual. Morality is a cheat, if moral obligation be not unconditional; and how can a standard that is dependent on the vague and ever-shifting apprehension of it by the human mind possess unconditional validity? Many philosophers will, I know, question these assertions, and even among those who recognize the absoluteness of obligation many again will deny its actuality. Goodness, they will say, is real and has objective being; but its being is that not of existence, but of subsistence. I have no desire to quarrel over words, but the term 'subsistence' seems to me to state a problem without answering it, and I fall back on the unambiguous doctrine of Dr Whitehead, that universals and values – his 'eternal objects' – are devoid of being save as ingredient in an actual entity.[1] This is not the place for a detailed discussion of this argument, familiar from Kant's time onwards. The point I wish to make is that, if we are prepared, as I am certainly prepared, to accept it, moral experience, when thought out, implies the belief in an other-worldly reality, transcendent of the world of spatio-temporal events; and that this implication furnishes a firm basis for the distinction between historical greatness and moral goodness. Human action is judged great by a standard relative to the temporal process; it is judged good by a standard that as absolute is super-temporal and super-human. This affirmation of transcendence is not a denial of immanence; indeed, immanence seems unmeaning unless that which is immanent transcends that which it informs. It is Croce's uncompromising refusal to admit any reality beyond possible historical experience, any reality save '*l'umana e il terrena*', that vitiates his solution of the problem of greatness and goodness. No answer to that problem is possible on purely humanistic grounds.

§ 14. Our discussion has led us from a special difficulty in the theory of conduct into deep waters of metaphysics and the philosophy of religion. In speaking of the various meanings of greatness, I made no reference to its application to the object of religious worship. The being or beings which, in Dr Otto's phrase, are charged with numinosity, excite in a supreme degree those impressions of magnitude and splendour and, above all, of finality, which we have seen to be the properties of greatness. We have here an exception to the rule that the term 'great' is used only as an attribute, not predicatively; we do not say 'the great God', but rather that 'God is great'. Such super-human greatness obviously implies transcendence and is very far

1. See my *From Morality to Religion*, pp. 182–6.

removed from the greatness displayed in human history. Nor does it give rise to any problem of rival valuations. For in God, as revealed in religious experience, all values meet in unbroken unity. Moreover, for religious faith the temporal process, which the historian values on a purely immanent standard, appears as the scene for the manifestation of a transcendent purpose. Human history is transfigured into a theodicy; in events, which the historian finds fortuitous and irrational, religion sees the hand of Providence, overruling the unchancy and the evil for other-worldly ends.

This recognition of other-worldly value in no way abrogates the claim of history to form its independent valuation. Man is a creature of two worlds, the temporal and the eternal, the one a derivative, the other an original reality, the one the object of rational enquiry, the other of moral or religious faith.[1] Each world has its proper measure of value. The historian is fully justified in refusing to trespass beyond his own domain or to embark on the vain endeavour to decipher a pattern that lies beyond the scope of the methods of his science. But when, as in the problem I have been considering in this Appendix, we attempt to relate his valuations to those of morality or religion, it is only by reference to other-worldly value that a solution can be found. In no other way can we escape the *impasse* which gave the initial impulse to our enquiry. Either history must be rewritten in the light of ethics, or the historian's verdict of greatness must be accepted as the criterion of what is morally good. And, on either alternative, it is evident that – to quote the words of Browning's *Cleon* –

'The doctrine could be held by no sane man.'

1. I have not attempted in this Appendix to bridge the gulf between the consciousness of moral obligation as implying a super-historical reality and the identification of that reality with God. I know that any reference to other-worldliness and transcendence suggests a two-world metaphysic; and that no one who is serious about philosophy can rest satisfied in a final dualism. But such a dualism is very far from my thoughts. If it be urged that the 'other world' is but 'this world' fully understood, I readily assent; but on two conditions. Within 'this world' must be found a place, not only for the ever incomplete stream of historical occurrences, but also for the abiding presence of a super-human and super-temporal power, whence the course of history derives its origin and its value; and the 'right understanding' must not be restricted to what is clearly and distinctly known by inference and analysis, but must include therewith the assurances of a reasonable faith.

HUMANISM AND THE WORLD CRISIS

*

I

§ 1. In the concluding chapter (XII) we quitted the proper terrain of the historian, viz. the record and interpretation of what has happened in the past, to consider how the legacy of antiquity has contributed to shape our contemporary world. This enlargement of our horizon brought into view speculative problems, which fall within the province of the philosopher as well as that of the historian. We were led to ask what light the study of past history casts on the meaning of human experience and, in particular, to what extent it supports the belief in the progress of civilization. Leaving on one side the pessimistic theories, widely prevalent in antiquity but alien to modern thought, of progressive deterioration and cyclical recurrence, we reached the conclusion that, while the last four centuries have witnessed a steady advance, in accord with a logical order of development, in the fields of pure, and even more markedly of applied, science, any wider generalization as to the onward march of civilization can hardly be sustained. In particular, it remains highly questionable whether man's intellectual progress has been attended by any corresponding growth in his moral and other spiritual achievement.[1] This doubt has inevitably been intensified by the catastrophic events that have menaced the very foundations of our culture within our own life-time. Some reflections on the nature and import of these phenomena, written amid the stress of world-war, will form a fitting close to our survey of historic civilizations.

§ 2. Let us revert for a moment to the outline of historical movement, known as the Renaissance, traced in the concluding sections of the eleventh chapter. There we were primarily concerned with pointing the contrast between the life and thought of the Middle Ages and that of the new Humanism that followed their gradual disintegration. Here our attention will be fixed rather upon the characteristics of that new outlook and upon its issues from the epoch of the Renaissance up to the present day. The profound change that then revolutionized men's view of life was marked, first, (*a*) by the assertion of individuality, illustrated or exemplified; in religion, by

1. See c. xii, p. 507.

the appeal to private judgement against the authority of the Church; in politics, by the rise (as already noted) [1] of nation-states swayed by separatist ambitions and rivalries; and in philosophy, by Descartes' insistence on the consciousness of the individual thinker as the basis for metaphysical construction. [2] Secondly, (b) it was marked by a vigorous rationalism, reason being construed, in accordance with mathematical and scientific procedure, as the faculty of logical ratio-cination, which recognizes only 'clear and distinct' concepts and proportions, relegating all thinking that is vague, shadowy, and mys-sterious to the limbo of irrational feeling and imagination. That was the 'short way' taken with religion by the philosophers of the En-lightenment, save with such 'natural theology' as could be held to fall within the domain of reason as thus defined; all else, i.e. 'revealed religion' generally, being regarded as matter for unreasoning faith. Thirdly, (c) as we have already seen, a this-worldliness of outlook, and the restriction of intellectual interest to spatio-temporal phenomena and their laws replaced the other-worldliness that had dominated medieval thought. Hence the new Humanism, unlike that of the Middle Ages, was frankly secularist and anthropocentric. Man was the measure of all things. The God of Judaism and Christianity survived for a season, shorn of His revelational accretions, as the 'Author of Nature', posited to account for the inexplicable fact of the existence of a universe, governed by 'immutable laws' of Nature, which had been indeed imposed by the Creator, but which allowed of no further supernatural intervention. The faith that inspired the leading minds of Europe in the epoch of the so-called 'Enlightenment', that reached its climax at the time of the French Revolution and persisted in the intelligentsia of the nineteenth century, especially in France (from Condorcet to Auguste Comte), and in England (William Godwin and the Utilitarian school of Bentham), and is still influential (witness the writings of Bertrand Russell and H. G. Wells), was centred in man, and in his power, thanks to the methods and achievements of the positive sciences, to control his own nature and the world in the service of human purposes. Its articles may be summarized as follows. First, its disciples had a touching confidence in the inborn excellence of human nature, in the perfectibility of man, and in the possibility of unlimited progress. The evils that block the way are due, not, as Christianity taught, to original sin, but to the bad organization of society, and are curable by remedial legislation. Secondly, they cham-

1. See c. xi, § 23.
2. He proceeded from the individual thinker to God (*viâ* the idea of God in the thinker's mind) and to the world (*viâ* God).

pioned individual liberty, dreaming of a millennium when each will achieve salvation by his own effort, and therewith the happiness of all other members of the community. Thirdly, this happiness, the goal of all endeavour, was interpreted as economic welfare, the possession by each individual of a sufficiency, and something more, of this world's goods. Lastly, the way to this Utopia lay in rational enlightenment, dispelling the mists of superstition, above all in education in the sciences, which already gave promise to man of boundless mastery over nature.[1] If few serious thinkers to-day would endorse this creed without reserve, this is due rather to its practical failure to cope with the evils that beset the world than to a conviction of its theoretical deficiencies. But in truth the latter presents as serious an obstacle to its acceptance as the former. Both lines of criticism will be discussed in the ensuing pages, with the view of deciding the question whether the secularist Gospel or its rival, Christianity, offers the more reasonable alternative, and one better adapted to man's nature and to his situation in the universe.

II. THE ABUSE OF KNOWLEDGE

§ 3. Readers of Plato's *Republic* must often have been startled by a question, put by Socrates at a critical turn of the argument: 'How can the State handle philosophy without being ruined?'[2] He was thinking of the use or abuse of knowledge and of the power that knowledge gives. The issue depends on the moral character of the rulers, on the end or good to which they dedicate their lives. By philosophy, he meant the reasoned enquiry into the intelligible realities that lie behind the show of sensible appearances; an enquiry culminating in the vision of the sovereign reality, the source of all being and of all value, the Idea or Form of the Good. Plato was convinced that only those whose intellectual efforts were grounded on a firm foundation of moral principle were privileged to achieve this vision.[3] In his view it was one of the most difficult problems to secure in the same individual both intellectual acuteness and moral stability – clever men are so rarely good, and good people are so often stupid. That is why he insisted on moral discipline as the initial stage in the training of anyone who aspired to the knowledge of the absolute Good. Unless philosophic studies were based on this foundation the State would be

1. See, for more detail, my book *Towards a Religious Philosophy*, c. xi and Conclusion.
2. *Rep.*, vi. 497D.
3. See Vol. I, c. v, §§ 19–24.

ruined. Men of intellectual power and force of will, lacking the vision of the true Good, would be dazzled and enchanted by finite, this-worldly, goods and would throw all their energies into the pursuit of them. They would be the victims of that ignorance of the true principle of goodness that Plato elsewhere calls 'the lie in the soul', and would become the bane of society instead of its salvation. For knowledge is power, and the use or abuse of power determines the fate, for good or evil, of the entire community.

What Plato said more than two thousand years ago is as true now as it was then. The advance of modern science has outstripped man's competence to make right use of it. In their blindness to the vision of the true Good, men have set their affections on this-worldly ends, forgetful of the things that are above. Their ambition has been centred on the transitory and mundane goods that science has placed within their grasp. In the language of Christianity they have chosen to live for the glory of man and not for the glory of God. I propose to trace the issues of this failure in modern civilization, and, particu-larly, to consider the severance that has come about between men's progress in knowledge and the development of their moral character.

§ 4. The term 'progress' is in constant use, but few take thought as to its meaning. 'Words', said Hobbes, 'are wise men's counters, but the money of fools.' We are apt to forget – though Hogarth's *Rake's Progress* is there to remind us – that advance may be towards evil as well as towards good; and that, even when we have in mind the process from a lower to a higher level of value, any significant asser-tion on the matter must be made under qualification. It is difficult to say anything with truth about the general progress of civilization. The question has to be considered under limitations of time and place, and with reference to specific fields of cultural activity. We have traced, for instance, among the Hebrew people from the ninth to the fifth century B.C., the advance under prophetic influence from a relatively primitive monolatry to a pure form of ethical monotheism. But this religious progress went hand in hand with the disruption of the Jewish state, and culminated in the hour of its political annihilation. We must be equally guarded in our characterization of the intellectual progress of modern Europe in the centuries since the Revival of Learning and the Renaissance. The progress has been within a deter-minate field of knowledge, that of the sciences of man and nature. It may well be that the thinkers and poets and saints of the Middle Ages – Bernard and Anselm, Dante and Aquinas – possessed a deeper know-ledge of God and of the things pertaining to God's service than any save a few of the philosophers and theologians of the last four hundred years. The knowledge distinctive of the modern period is of another order; being centred on nature, and on man as part of nature, the speculative outlook that it has brought to birth is essentially humanistic and this-worldly. But within these limitations it offers as fine an illustration of intellectual progress as can be found in history. In the first place, the process throughout is luminously intelligible to the mind of the observer. Science follows upon science in the natural order of development: at the outset the reasoned study of matter and motion (mechanical physics) in the century between Galileo and Newton, followed (especially in the nineteenth century) by the development of chemistry and of the biological sciences, and finally, in quite recent times, by the application of scientific method to mental processes and behaviour in psychology. At each stage, the new discoveries give occasion for efforts after philosophic synthesis, in the speculative systems of Descartes, Leibniz, Kant, and, in our own day, in those of Alexander and Whitehead. Moreover, the sciences which were first developed, far from yielding place in man's interest to those of later appearance, rather continued to progress with increased vigour; Faraday and Clerk Maxwell were in physics the contemporaries of Lamarck and Darwin, as in our own generation Einstein is the contemporary of the psychologists Freud and Jung. In the second place, we may note how this advance in scientific knowledge has enlarged beyond belief the range of man's control over his environment. All knowledge gives power; as the knowledge of God gave power in things of the spirit to the saints of the Middle Ages, so has science given power over physical nature to the peoples of the modern world. The practical applications of science to the conditions of human life have, in the last few generations, revolutionized the face of nature and the whole order of social intercourse. Were an Englishman of the early sixteenth century wafted back four centuries into the past, he would still be able to thread his way in the England of the Plantagenets. After the first shock of surprise was over he could make himself comparatively at home. But if we imagine him transported over an equal stretch of time into the England of to-day, he would feel a hopeless alien. Here and there, at the sight of a cathedral or village church (until he entered them), in the procedure of Parliament and of the Law Courts, and in the rites of the Roman church, he might, if gifted with exceptional intelligence, catch the echoes of the England he had known. But the more obtrusive sights and sounds of the factory, the railroad, the aeroplane, the wireless, and the newspaper, would soon blot from his mind these scanty relics of antiquity. Now the knowledge that has thus enabled man to transform his physical and social surroundings and to adjust his behaviour and modes of life to the changed world is primarily, though not exclusively, a knowledge that gives power over things perceived by sense. All human knowledge and all human desire take their origin perforce from objects of sense-perception; prolonged effort of thought and will is needed, if man is to rise above what is obviously on a level with his capacities, so as to know and desire the spiritual world that lies beyond. To be beguiled by the lure of material things, and by pride in his mastery of nature into a this-worldly philosophy of life, is the temptation that besets the most gifted in the modern age, and, most of all, those who are marked out to be leaders in their community. We are brought back to Socrates' searching question: whether such a philosophy, if it gains ascendancy, must not be ruinous to the state.

§ 5. That there has been progress in knowledge, and in the power that knowledge gives, is beyond dispute, but has there been a corresponding progress in morality? Are men the better, or the worse, for their intellectual achievements? We have only to put the question to see that it admits of no cut and dried answer in terms of Yes or No. Let us consider only a single aspect of the problem, what we may call the ethics of public policy and public practice. Of course the public life of the community is inextricably interwoven with the private life of the individual members; no man lives to himself, nor has the state any being apart from the citizens who compose it. Yet a distinction may surely be drawn between the use of the wireless by Smith in his drawing-room and by the government for purposes of propaganda, or between Jones's use of an aeroplane for a business visit to Amsterdam or Paris, and its employment as an engine of destruction in war. But even if we follow Plato's precedent and limit our discussion to morality as exhibited 'in large letters' in the state, the verdict must still be a mixed one. On the one hand, there is undeniably less corruption and far more public spirit to-day in corporate bodies, such as parliaments, churches, trades unions, and universities than at any period in the past. Above all, the troubles that have recently beset us have aroused in civilized peoples a widespread desire, not merely for security, but for a constructive peace, i.e. for effective co-operation in the establishment and maintenance of a stable and just international order. The League of Nations may have failed to realize the hopes of its founders, but the aims formulated in the Preamble to the Covenant are more alive in men's minds and hearts to-day than at any previous moment in its history. But it is to the other side of the picture that we must turn in our search for the sources of world-trouble. Over against the evidence for moral betterment we must set the evils that have spread in these last years with startling rapidity through the abuse by governments, both in peace and war, of the weapons that science has placed within their reach. I will give three examples.

§ 6. (1) Recent inventions have vastly increased the resources at the disposal of governments for sustaining and strengthening their power. Love of power is, as Plato remarked, one of the most potent forces in human nature; and its gratification acts as a stimulus to yet wider ambitions. Even in democratic countries the danger from the tyranny of public opinion, dreaded by so strong an advocate of representative government as John Stuart Mill, is far greater to-day than when he wrote his book on *Liberty*. In the totalitarian states, be they Fascist or National Socialist, tyranny stalks naked and unashamed. Such constitutional checks as have been suffered to survive seem impotent to curb the power of the dictators. *Plébiscites* have always lent themselves easily to manipulation from headquarters. It would be an error to suppose that the power thus concentrated in the rulers' hands is used to gratify purely personal ambitions; the personal aims of Mussolini and Hitler were identified with public causes, such as Italian imperialism, the dominance of the Aryan race, or the overthrow of capitalism. They pursued these ideals with a zeal religious in its intensity, and by the traditional methods of religious propaganda – giving and demanding from others a single-minded loyalty that is rightfully due to God alone. Whole peoples have been forced, under penalties of incarceration or even of death, to bow down in worship before these temporal and finite idols. The potent weapons of mass-suggestion by the controlled press and wireless have been utilized to stifle freedom of thought in the citizen from childhood onwards, and to bar the doors of his mind from a disinterested regard for truth. Napoleon threatened to dominate Europe a century and more ago; he, too, rose to greatness as the champion of a new order called into being by the French Revolution; but he lacked the scientific means of mastery – the telegraph, the telephone, the railroad, the aeroplane, and the mechanized army – that are at the disposal of our modern autocrats. The peril to-day is graver than it was then. Moreover, the likelihood of a successful revolution is greatly lessened by the government's monopoly of the instruments for its suppression. The rulers can strike at a distance and with a swiftness that allow to a popular rising little chance of victory.

§ 7. (2) My second example is of an evil that directly touches ourselves, viz. the increase of mechanization, not only in industry but over the whole of life, menacing human personality with atrophy or asphyxiation. Think of the fate of a factory hand, doomed to pass eight hours of each day mechanically tapping eggs with the same gesture on the same spot! What chance has he for the expansion or development of individual character?[1] This is one of the issues of man's application of science and the machines he has invented. I am not blaming the scientists or the employers who make use of their discoveries. I am pointing out a case of cause and effect. The effect is monotony and standardization, in every walk in life, the clerk's, the teacher's, even that of a professor in a university. The worker on the land, whom hourly contact with Nature in her infinite variety has hitherto preserved from contamination, is now threatened by the tyranny of the machine. In each succeeding decade there is less scope in men's lives for originality, independence, freedom. We all desire workers in a mine or mill to have shorter hours and higher wages, that they may enjoy leisure for their soul's good; but what a confession of failure lies behind the desire! We are at best tinkering – if you will, generously and nobly – with the evil; like the doctor whose high calling would have no occasion for exercise were there no diseased bodies to be healed. In our modern industrial system the work is perforce so monotonous that the worker can find no joy in it. Fancy suggesting to St Paul that he should preach the gospel for only eight hours a day, and seek his joy and peace at leisure in the time left over from his vocation: or to Beethoven that he would be branded as a blackleg if he spent more than eight hours a day at the keyboard. Ideally work should be a delight; yet it is becoming every year more of a drudgery. True, we educate the workers; but the very immensity of the task forces us to mechanize the education. There are millions of children to be taught, and heaven-born teachers are very few; teachers must therefore be manufactured, on standardized methods, as in a machine. You cannot help this, any more than you can help using machinery in the manufactory; it is better that all children should be taught, even at the cost of sacrificing quality to quantity in the teaching. But let us at least discern the evil, and be on our guard against its consequences. The young workers have been educated to self-consciousness; they are asking questions and pressing for a full share in determining their own and their country's future. The new gospels that have spread like wildfire over many European peoples, Communism, Fascism, and National Socialism, draw their main strength from their appeal to youth. They have given to the youth of Russia, Italy, and Germany an opportunity to play their part in remoulding the world after their heart's desire.

1. See D. H. Lawrence's *Letters*, edited by Aldous Huxley (p. 771), for a passionate protest against asphyxiation of personality.

Let us be under no illusion. The war now smouldering to its close was not a war against Germany and the German people, but neither was it solely against Hitler and Hitler's government. The real enemy was and still is the Nazi youth. They can be counted by millions. Hitler could never have risen to power save for their enthusiastic response to his leadership. The Germans are a people of high intelligence though of a mentality different from our own, and they would never have been beguiled into loyalty towards a cause that had no grip on their personality. In Germany, as in Russia, youth saw its chance and took it; a chance – be it noted – that is denied to youth under the more monotonous, leisurely, conservative *régime* of our own land.

§ 8. (3) My third illustration is the most important, for it touches the source of our failure to use rightly the power placed in our hands by the applied sciences. The source, though not the responsibility, lies in large measure in science itself. As all know, physical research during the last century has resolved the Newtonian conception of a universe of moving bodies into something that is scarcely distinguishable from pure motion. Atoms and particles of matter have gone by the board as physical ultimates; in their place we have centres of energy – electrons, protons, and the like – eddying with incredible velocity and diffusing, each of them, its activity over all space. Under the influence of the new physics, philosophers, like M. Bergson and the late Professor Alexander, have rejected the traditional dogma that only the permanent can change, and have posited motion, without a *mobile*, at the very heart of reality. The same influence has set its stamp on the mind of the public. Just as all science has its roots in pre-scientific popular thinking, in the rough-and-ready generalizations of the plain man in presence of natural phenomena, so, at the other extreme, its conclusions, the fruit of mysterious processes of calculation and experiment that are 'caviare to the general', are appropriated by the intelligent public and pass into the structure of ordinary thought. It has happened thus with the apotheosis of motion; only that, in this instance, the public has gone out to meet the new deity with willing worship. Speed records, moving pictures, swift transport, ceaseless change of occupation and amusement are the idols of the modern generation. The passion for movement has even invaded their religion; churches would be crowded if the preacher taught belief in a suffering and striving God, who looked to men for help in His effort for victory over evil. The older views of God as without variability or shadow of turning, and of man's heart as restless until it find rest in Him, are no longer congenial to the taste of the modern world. The effects of this changed outlook on morality are not far to seek. Not only has the traditional belief that the distinction between good and evil, right and wrong, rests on an immutable foundation – the will of God or the principles of natural reason – been relegated to the museum of speculative antiquities; even the mention of absolute and eternal values is apt to be greeted by serious thinkers with a smile of sceptical forbearance. Relativity holds the field, in ethics as in physics.

If secular moralists to-day still claim objective validity for moral ideals and are inspired, as is frequently the case, to acts of sacrifice and unselfish devotion in the cause of humanity and justice, this is not so much on account of any reasoned faith in an other-worldly absolute, a Platonic Form of Good or Kantian Moral Law, as because an aroma of sanctity still clings around those principles, long after their detachment from their original source in Christianity. My point is that if ethical standards express merely changing adaptations to the this-worldly requirements of a particular society in a particular epoch of its history, their pretensions to universal validity are null and void. Unless we are convinced of the reality of an other-worldly order, and of eternal and absolute principles of right and wrong, our criticism, for instance, of Hitler for saying one thing one day at Munich and contradicting it by his action a few days later, is devoid of any ethical justification. We may contend that he acted ill-advisedly – that is a matter of prudential calculation; but, save in the name of an other-worldly ideal, we have no right to pass moral condemnation on his conduct. A thorough-going ethical relativism, as Plato saw clearly, can find no place for morality; it knows only interests.

§ 9. Where, then, lies the remedy? How can the gulf be bridged between men's knowledge, with the power it has brought, and their halting moral endeavour in matters of public policy and conduct?

Obviously the remedy does not lie in barring the way to intellectual progress. Such a counsel of despair is neither possible nor desirable. The example of the very men who have most abused the instruments of public power is there to warn us. Intellectual progress is possible only where thought is free, and what freedom have men had, even to think, in present-day Germany? It is not the scientists who are to blame for the misuse of their inventions; the responsibility falls wholly on those who, from lack of moral vision, have perverted the knowledge that could have saved society into an engine for its ruin.

Nor can we look to the further promotion of knowledge for a remedy, tempting as is the suggestion, and one that in time past has had many advocates. It is a faith of long standing, dating back to

Condorcet and the French revolutionary idealists, that universal education, especially in the sciences and their applications, would prove a panacea for all human maladies, and would banish all sin, sorrow, and suffering from the earth. Bitter experience has taught us that this is not the case. Knowledge, as we learn from Plato, is a two-edged sword, that has power to make or mar the lives of those possessed of it, according as they use or abuse it, for weal or woe. The cure for our present ills can only lie in raising the level of moral character and conduct. The familiar *cliché*, 'moral rearmament', is evidence that the need is widely felt. The phrase is a metaphor, and not a very happy one. It suggests that morality itself can furnish the means of moral regeneration. Those who use it will perhaps appeal in defence to a famous passage in St Paul's *Epistle to the Philippians*. But the weapons of which St Paul spoke were forged in the armoury, not of morality, but of religion. The armour he bade the Christian put on was the armour of God.

§ 10. Mere morality is not enough. I contend that progress in morality can only become possible if inspired by religious faith. What the world needs is to recover the conviction that moral distinctions are not relative, but absolute, independent of what you or I, or even the entire community, like to think. Men's changing moral valuations have never been mere adaptations to a historical environment; all down the ages, they have expressed his groping effort to grasp the vision of an other-worldly reality, of an abiding moral order that is at once transcendent of, and immanent in, the world in which we live. Secular morality, apart from religion, can hardly avail to inspire this saving faith. Yet without this faith we are plunged ever deeper into the maelstrom of relativity. There are two reasons why morality is unequal to this task of self-preservation. In the first place, its scope is limited to the field of human actions. There are other values beside the practical; the knowledge of the truth, for instance, that is the goal of the scientist, the historian, and the philosopher, or, again, the expression of truth and beauty in the arts. There is a plurality of values, each with an absolute claim on our allegiance; when the claims conflict, no single claimant, not even morality, has the right to decide the issue. Religion alone can give a final judgement, for religion knows no departmental limits. It embraces the whole personality of the worshipper, his mind and heart and will; and God, the object of worship, is the Alpha and the Omega, the source of all being and of all value, compassing with His presence the whole universe of reality. There is a further reason why morality is incapable of healing its own sickness. It is true that reflexion upon the nature of moral obligation lifts us, as Kant impressively showed, beyond the spatio-temporal processes of nature and history to the recognition of an other-worldly and eternal Moral Law. It is true also, as Plato showed, that reflexion on finite goods lifts us to the vision of an other-worldly principle of goodness, in which alone the soul of man, with its restless aspiration for the infinite, can find rest and final satisfaction. But both these objects of moral faith, the eternal Moral Law and the eternal Form of Good, remain, for moral vision, abstract and impersonal. I fully admit, what is in the light of human history indisputable, that wise and strong natures, such as are endowed with a wide culture and a lofty pride in their own rectitude, are able to direct their lives aright by reliance on such impersonal ideals. Stoicism is still a living power among such men to-day. But it offers no solution to our main problem. For one thing, I am convinced that reason cannot rest satisfied with an other-world of self-supporting values. Absolute goodness, absolute beauty and the rest are intelligible only if integrated with the consciousness of an existing individual as their bearer (*Träger*), in other words, with God. I have discussed the philosophical approach from ethics to theism elsewhere,[1] and must content myself here with this bare statement of conviction. Moreover, even were the Stoic doctrine proved adequate in philosophy, it could never be a gospel of salvation for the multitude. Its appeal is to a moral aristocracy, to the cultured few who are able by strength of will to stand four-square against all winds that blow.[2] The rank and file – and it is these who, in this democratic age most need moral rearmament – will never be stirred to sacrifice by an abstraction, not even though it be Kant's transcendent Moral Law or Plato's transcendent Form of Good. They must have an object of worship that can evoke response, not only from the intellect and will, but from the imagination and the heart. Of this the leaders of National Socialism were well aware, when, in their contempt for rational justification, they set in its place a battle-cry for victory.[3] These false creeds with their false promises of a terrestrial millennium must be combated by a living theistic faith. *In hoc signo vinces.* The religion that sets its trust in man can only be conquered by a religion that sets its trust in God.

1. See my Gifford Lectures, *From Morality to Religion.*
2. I have in mind the teaching of Nietzsche, which many (erroneously) hold responsible for the ideology of National Socialism. For the error, see Father Copleston's discerning study, entitled *The Philosophy of Friedrich Nietzsche.*
3. It is matter of common knowledge that the adherents of such doctrines habitually decline to engage in speculative discussion of their validity. They regard argument as irrelevant. Embrace the creed and you will be assured by faith of its credibility. On the whole subject, Georges Sorel's *Réflexions sur la*

III. THE IDOL OF HUMANISM

§ 11. In the preceding sections of this Appendix, I have tried to show that the only hope for the world lies in the revival of faith in Christianity. I now proceed to reinforce the conviction from a different, though allied, standpoint.

The distinctive note of European thought in the last four centuries is the growth of Humanism. I am using the term in the sense hallowed by the Oxford English Dictionary, where humanism is defined as 'any system of thought or action which is concerned with merely human interests (as distinguished from divine), or with those of the human race in general'. Thus understood, it implies an essentially this-worldly outlook, in contrast to that of the Middle Ages, when not only scientists and thinkers, but ordinary men in their rare moments of reflexion never questioned that this earthly life was a transitory state of probation, the ante-room of heaven and hell. Not that such an other-worldly outlook is incompatible with the claims of humanism within the larger scheme. Indeed we shall see presently that it is only in subordination to a theocentric world-view that those claims can be realized without contradiction and disaster. But modern humanism is absolute, not relative, an end to be sought for its own sake, regardless of any other-worldly sanctions. That this should be so is at once strange and inevitable. It is strange that the scientific revolution which dethroned man and 'this earth his habitation' from their central position in the universe should have led to the exaltation of human interests and welfare as the final aim of both thought and conduct. Yet it could not have been otherwise. The new science owed its triumphs to the exercise of man's natural powers of reason, independently of religious faith or supernatural illumination. Mathematical deduction and inductive generalization from data of observation and experiment call for no intrusion on the part of divine grace. That Dr Whitehead is a theist, Earl Russell an agnostic, is quite irrelevant to the value of their work in mathematics. Moreover, the objects on which the activity of reason was directed were events in space and time, to be explained solely in terms of their spatio-temporal antecedents. Reference to divine agency or, indeed, to any grounds outside the process of nature lies beyond the province of the scientist. Can we wonder, then, that men's thought should have been diverted

violence, one of the most significant books of the last half-century, should be consulted (see especially, in the Introduction to the volume, on the application of Bergson's doctrine of the 'myth', the references to Pascal, and the analogy with early Christianity).

more and more from the mediaeval tradition, to be concentrated more and more on the promise of a humanistic millennium, to be achieved in the strength of their own powers of thought and will? The uniform progress of civilization, the perfectibility of human nature, the eventual banishment, through rational enlightenment, of vice and suffering, the advent of an age when all men equally should enjoy material prosperity and social concord; such was the faith that inspired the reformers of the French Revolution, and that won classic expression in Condorcet's *Esquisse d'un tableau historique du progrès de l'esprit humain*, written in prison under the shadow of the guillotine. Half a century later Comte openly proclaimed the religion of humanity. The 'idol of humanism' was set up for worship, the image of a Man-god in place of the God-man of Christianity.

§ 12. Comte, it is true, found few disciples; the apotheosis of man was too extravagant a demand to secure acknowledgement even from an age bewitched by the spell of humanism. Yet he did but draw the logical conclusion from the premises implicit in the dominant thought of his generation. That they still dominate the minds of multitudes to-day is evident from a moment's glance at the warring creeds which threaten our civilization. Mr Michael Oakeshott, in his book entitled *The Social and Political Doctrines of Contemporary Europe*, has collected documents illustrative of the five main types of political and social theory, each of which commands the passionate loyalty of millions of our fellow human beings. Of these five, only one, the Catholic doctrine as embodied in the *Encyclicals* of Popes Leo XIII and Pius XI, is grounded on faith in an other-worldly order, within which the claims of human nature to temporal satisfaction are accorded their full measure of recognition.[1] All the other four types are, in their several ways, secularist and humanistic. Communism, as exemplified in the Marx–Engels–Lenin doctrines, is avowedly atheistic; its programme, the achievement of a classless society by means of a class war, is, if not wholly materialistic, at any rate wholly this-worldly. National Socialism, as the event has made tragically manifest, subjects religion, morality, and all other activities of the spirit, to the interests of the state, in its effort to secure an earthly hegemony for the peoples of Aryan race. Italian Fascism, despite its opportunist compromise with the papacy, is equally insistent in principle on the absolute claim of the state to unquestioning obedience from the citizens. 'Mussolini', so ran the authoritative decalogue, 'is always right.' 'The Fascist state,' wrote the Duce in his article on the doctrine of Fascism, 'the

1. The preamble to the constitution of Eire, included among Mr Oakeshott's documents, is instructive in this connexion.

highest and most powerful form of personality, is a force, but a spiritual force, which takes over all the forms of the moral and intellectual life of man.' When we pass to what Mr Oakeshott calls Representative Democracy, i.e. to the conception of society fostered, if not with religious zeal, at least with resolute conviction, by the peoples of the British Commonwealth, France, the United States, and many other of the smaller states of Europe, it is more difficult to pronounce judgement. The view in question has a long history, during which it has shown remarkable elasticity, nor have its principles ever received precise formulation as have those of the other four types. Many of them, such as the promotion of human welfare, the maintenance of liberty for each individual and nation to work out its own salvation in its own way, the furtherance of social and international justice – the aims, in fact, for which we now contend – are consistent with loyalty to the Christian faith. It is otherwise with the materialist interpretation of human happiness, and the baneful economic and industrial doctrines that have so often been held integral to it. But the link between representative democracy and Christianity is, on the side of the former, not essential but contingent. It is true, as we shall see later, that Liberalism – I use the word in its broadest sense – is impregnated with ideas of Christian origin. But how many of its supporters would admit that their advocacy was inspired by any but purely secularist motives? When I read in the *Church Times* that it is 'matter of common consent that the only hope of civilization is a return to the religion on which it is based', I open my eyes in amazement. The truth is rather, as we read in the same issue, that 'nations will only be Christian when the majority of their citizens are Christians'. In fact they are not; nor, I fear, are the majority of statesmen in the self-governing democracies of to-day. They regard their political principles as ends in themselves, not as attempts to realize the Kingdom of God among men. They live and move and have their being under the spell of secularist humanism.

§ 13. Is it not strange that this faith in man's ability to achieve the aims of humanism by his own strength should have persisted despite the tragic experiences of the last thirty years? One would have thought that if man had been endowed by nature with the faculties requisite for the mastery of his environment, his progress in knowledge and in the power that knowledge brings would have proved more successful in effecting the desired result. One would have thought, for instance, that the resources now at his disposal for securing social unity – the steamship, the telegraph, the telephone, the aeroplane, the wireless – would have furthered, instead of hindered, inter-racial and international harmony. In the nineteenth century, when material prosperity was on the upward grade, the humanistic creed could offer a certain plausibility; but to-day in the light of the widespread disintegration of the bonds of human fellowship and social order, it is surely a paradox that it should retain its power to inspire thinking men. We are confronted with a practical *reductio ad absurdum* of the secularist faith. If this be so, is it not high time that we should set ourselves to question its foundations, and consider whether man's final goal can be found in a state where there is no finality, and not rather in an other-worldly reality, that embraces the temporal and human in integration with the eternal and the divine? I use the word 'integration' designedly, with reference to M. Jacques Maritain's book, entitled *L'Humanisme intégrale*. It means that the two realms, the kingdoms of nature and of grace, are not severed one from the other, or arbitrarily conjoined, but that the latter is 'integral' to the former, in that apart from God, nature can neither be, nor be conceived. I do not here raise the difficult question whether the world is as necessary to God as God is to the world, but content myself with the Christian answer, that the facts of experience level with our capacities reveal the necessary dependence of man and the world upon God. I want to show that to assert man's self-sufficiency is to imagine him to be other than he is, and that the recognition of his dependence, so far from belying the claims of humanism, is the primary condition of their realization. To this end, I offer the following considerations.

§ 14. (1) If we analyse man's nature, as it unfolds itself in the course of his brief history, we find in it potentialities and desires that can never be satisfied under the conditions of earthly life. The contrast between these claims of his nature and the narrow limits that thwart their attainment gives rise, as consciousness develops, to an inward tension that serves at once to stimulate activity and to baffle it. In richly-endowed personalities, the tension may even be felt as intense agony; 'As the hart longeth for the waterbrooks, so longeth my soul for the living God'. All men, at some times and in some degree, experience a sense of shortcoming, an awareness that their reach exceeds their grasp. So in a pre-Christian age Socrates measured his advance towards wisdom by his growing consciousness of ignorance; so, again, the saints of the Church, realizing more than ordinary men the gulf that parts their imperfect achievement from the infinite holiness of God, confess themselves with truth to be miserable sinners. Let me give two illustrations. In the *Summa contra Gentiles*, Aquinas grounds his argument to a future life on the fact that man's intellect, with its infinite desire for knowledge, a desire that defies fulfilment under this-worldly conditions, marks him out as designed by the very constitution of his nature for an other-worldly consummation. For 'nature does nothing in vain'. Implicit in man's finite intellectual capacity is an unrest which spurs him onwards from partial truth to partial truth, but which cannot be quieted by any knowledge short of a truth that is absolute and complete. The same holds of man's natural desire of good. In the magnificent passage with which Spinoza prefaces the *Tractatus de Intellectus Emendatione*, he tells how in youth and early manhood he vainly sought felicity in this-worldly goods, till he learnt how in the love of a *res infinita et aeterna* alone could he attain fruition. 'A mere case of wish-fulfilment', as many in these latter days will protest; to draw from which an inference to an other-worldly reality is simply to offer men an opiate. Georges Sorel saw deeper in this matter than Marx and Lenin. He rejected, it is true, the Christian conclusion, but he recognized how deep-rooted in man's nature is the '*tourment de l'infini*', and how urgent is its claim for satisfaction. He sought to quench it in ardour for the 'general strike' and the class-war against capitalism. Rather, as the event has proved, it is such temporal remedies that are the opiates. Butler's argument still holds its ground. If earthly happiness were man's proper end, the constitution of nature is very ill-adapted to its attainment. Whereas the world is admirably fitted to be the scene of his moral probation and discipline. There is no half-way house between passive acquiescence in a meaningless universe and faith in the sovereignty of an other-worldly order.

§ 15. (2) Let us, secondly, approach the question from the opposite pole, and, assuming the truth of the theocentric world-view, ask whether it allows full scope for man's this-worldly interests and aspirations. Here we find ourselves in presence of an apparent paradox. On the one hand, the claim of religion is all-embracing. There is nothing in the universe that does not draw its life and being from God. He demands the consecration of our whole personality to his service. 'Whether ye eat or drink, or whatsoever ye do, do all to the glory of God.' Ultimately, then, all human activities and all human knowledge fall within the province of religion. Yet, within this larger view of the religious life, there exists a real distinction between the religious and the secular. St Paul's motive in tent-making was doubtless to earn the wherewithal to enable him to preach the gospel without being a burden on his converts. But when actually engaged on his craft, his attention must have been wholly concentrated on its exercise. Otherwise he would have made bad tents. A man's activity, in private prayer or in the reception of the Sacrament, is manifestly of an order different from his activity in solving a mathematical problem or

playing a round of golf. The paradox, however, is but apparent; for --
and this is the point of interest -- the distinction between the religious
and the secular has its roots in religion itself.[1] A God who is the object
of religious worship must be transcendent of the world of his creation.
Now between the being of the Creator and that of the creature there
is a difference of kind, that can only be bridged *ex parte Dei* by God's
revelation of Himself to man. For only God can truly create; man is
never more than an architect working on given materials. If we talk
loosely of the creative activity of the artist, it is to signify that, as the
late Professor Alexander put it, the artist's mind is blended with the
material in the product, which is therefore something genuinely new.
It follows from this that the distinction between man's activities and
knowledge, in so far as they are directed immediately upon God, and
man's activities and knowledge, in so far as they are directed upon the
world of God's creation, is not only sanctioned by religious experience, but is its necessary consequence. Thus the *Deum semper excipimus*
of the scientist and the historian finds its secular justification. I do not
know how science first had its birth from amid the rough and tumble
of man's sense perceptions; but in any case it must sooner or later
have arisen in obedience to the demands of the religious consciousness.

Thus we find (1) that not only do the facts of man's nature in his
present state point on examination to his other-worldly destiny, but
also (2) that the theocentric world-view -- and, we may add, it alone --
allows full scope and satisfaction for his humanistic aspirations.

§ 16. (3) If we consider the concepts most distinctive of modern
humanism, we shall find that they not only have their source in Christianity, but that, when severed from their religious context, they are
robbed of all intelligible meaning. The concepts I have chiefly in mind
are those of *Fraternity* and *Personality*. Liberty and Equality, for the
French Revolutionists, were terms of negative import, calling on
men to sweep away the abuses of tyranny and privilege that marked
the *Ancien Régime*. Their positive implications are ambiguous so long
as our outlook is confined within this-worldly limits. What we want
to be freed *from* is clear; but what we want freedom *for* is greatly dark.
Men are not, and never can be, equal; 'one to count as one and as one
only' is a formula that has no relevance beyond the ballot-box; and
'equality of opportunity' means merely that all alike should start at
scratch in the race to achieve superiority. The only positive liberty
is to be found in the service of God which is perfect freedom; the
only positive equality in the status of all mankind as children of their

1. See Bowman, *Studies in The Philosophy of Religion* (c. xvi), and above,
c. xi, § 15 (on Aquinas).

heavenly Father. But in the concept of *Fraternity* we strike the nerve of the appeal of humanism to the modern world. The brotherhood of mankind is the clarion-note heralding the goal towards which the workers of all nations march as 'comrades'. That this conception had its birth in Christianity is beyond question. It was reached, not by progressive enlargement from love of kinsmen or fellow-citizens, but as the direct corollary of God's all-embracing love of man. 'Beloved, if God so loved us, we ought also to love one another.' 'This commandment have we from him, that he who loveth God love his brother also.' It was for their love, one for another, that the early followers of Christ were remarkable in the eyes of the pagan world. How far has the concept retained its force in the theory or the practice of modern secularism? The word survives with its glamour scarcely dimmed; but in unnatural union with the gospels of class-war and racial antagonism. The contradiction thus avowed in theory is yet more evident in action. I am thinking not merely of the hatred *à l'outrance* displayed by Communists towards adherents of capitalism or heretics who question any detail in the authoritative doctrine, but rather the temper of suspicion that has spread within the fold, and threatens even the ranks of the orthodox with disintegration. What most appals me in the gospels of class-war and racial antagonism is the poisoning of the sources of personal friendship among the young, of that free intercourse that is the salt and savour, for instance, of life at a university between the youth of either sex – a thing to which we may surely apply Aristotle's great saying about justice, that it is 'fairer than the morning or the evening star'. 'See how these comrades hate one another' – such surely will be the epitaph to be inscribed on the graves of the victims of the illusion of a terrestrial millennium. The concept of *Personality* – and we may add, the allied concept of humanity – tells the same tale. The 'infinite worth of the individual' is a catch-word on everyone's lips; but as signifying a truth of human nature it draws its meaning from the religion in which it had its origin. It has won its hold on modern thought chiefly through Kant's well-known formula: 'Treat humanity, whether in thine own person or that of any other, always as an end withal, never merely as a means.' But by 'person' Kant meant not the empirical human self, as a phenomenon in space and time, but the noumenal ego, the purely rational selfhood by virtue of which every man is a member of the supersensible 'kingdom of ends', the other-worldly community of which God is sovereign. What claim to infinite worth can be ascribed to any man, regarded purely as a denizen of the world of nature? Even the greatest, when so regarded, has only relative and finite value; of the rest, there are many whose value is rather a minus quantity or disvalue, of whom it might be truly said that from the standpoint of this-worldly interests 'it were better if this man had never been born'. It is questionable whether, for instance, of men now living there is any that is of equal worth, as a creature in time, to a masterpiece by Rembrandt. Can we then be surprised when we turn to the actual behaviour of those whose pretension it is to free men from 'self-alienation' in bondage to religion to realize their true inherent personality, to find such an utter disregard for life as has led Nazi Germany to doom hordes of Jews, Czechs, and Poles to wholesale torture and execution? What again are we to think of the more subtle but equally disastrous wastage of individuality, in our own as well as in foreign lands, due to the growing mechanization of industry?[1] 'By their fruits ye shall know them.' The bane of secularist humanism, and its *reductio ad absurdum*, is the appalling inhumanity of its performance. Nor can the advocates of Totalitarianism ride off triumphant by pointing to the dark record of animosity and persecution in the history of the Christian church. For by their own admission the crimes enacted are the logical outcome of the precepts of their respective gospels. These prescribe war as the necessary means to peace, hatred as the chosen instrument of love. Thus even the fair-sounding claims of fraternity and personality have been bereft of all concrete significance. In the mouth of the this-worldly humanist, they are no longer *verba*, words fraught with meaning, but mere *voces*, i.e. meaningless sounds.

The term *Humanity* itself, which in this last century and a half has stirred men to so much sacrifice and to so much crime; what significance does it retain apart from an other-worldly reference? Does it mean our common human nature? Man's spirit will hardly be touched to fine, or even to baser, issues by a conceptual abstraction. What is clearly intended by those who proclaim the service of humanity as our final goal is mankind as a collective whole of individuals, the totality of the human race. But where is such a totality to be found? Can it even be conceived in imagination within the bounds of temporal history? And what of the generations that are past? How can they have part or lot in the love and service that claim to be offered to all mankind? It is otherwise indeed if we lift our eyes above this earthly scene to the vision of the other-worldly community, where all men, past, present, and future, are fellow-citizens in the kingdom of which God is King.

§ 17. There is but one remedy for this two-fold canker which for three centuries has been menacing the heart of European civilization

1. See Appendix II, pp. 538–53.

– the lack of moral principle in the exercise of the power that knowledge brings, and the progressive secularization of men's outlook – to wit, the restoration of faith in Christianity. That alone can effect moral regeneration; that alone can establish humanistic culture on a sure foundation. For a world-view centred in sense there must be substituted a world-view centred in God. This in no way implies a sterile return to the tradition of mediaevalism. History never repeats itself; least of all, the history of a great religion. The task that has been laid upon the Christian in each succeeding age is to prepare the world for the coming of God's kingdom. But that kingdom is no mere temporal phenomenon, past, present, or future. Though manifested temporally alike in the past, the present and the future, it is an eternal reality, above the vicissitudes of time and change.

Thus there remains for Christian men the further problem, that of the application of the theocentric world-view to the ever changing situations of public life, and particularly to the present crisis in international history. The problem is one of special difficulty, in that Christ laid down no programmes or rules of policy; he laid down principles, leaving it to men's free judgement, to their enlightened consciences to apply them to the variable circumstances of this present life. To embark in any detail on a discussion of this further question is, of course, impossible here. But there are two points where our consideration of the general principles has already touched upon the manner of their application. Whenever a state pursues a policy directly contrary to Christ's religion, it is the Christian's duty to resist it. I do not see, for instance, how whole-hearted co-operation can be possible even within a Federated Europe, if any major power should persist in uncompromising hostility to the Christian faith. On the other hand, the question of the merits of Communism as an economic doctrine, or of the totalitarian form of government, is one that is largely independent of considerations of religion. This brings me to my second point of contrast, the real, though relative, distinction between the religious and the secular. To prepare the way for God's kingdom does not mean to subordinate state to church or to set up in Europe the rule of the saints. The state has its legitimate autonomy, recognized by Christ himself. 'Render unto Caesar the things that are Caesar's, and unto God the things that are God's.' But the recognition of this relative distinction must never blind men to the ultimate universality of the divine sovereignty. In this sense we may say that the future of civilization lies in the hands of the conscientious objector.

Returning at the close to Plato's question with which we started, How can the state study philosophy without being ruined?, we are now able to give the answer. The state can only survive and flourish if finite and temporal goods be acknowledged as dependent on the one good that is absolute and eternal, that is, on God.

IV. CONCLUSION

§ 18. I wish in conclusion to guard against a possible misunderstanding of the views on Humanism expressed in the foregoing pages. We have seen how both philosophical reflexion and a survey of the recent history of civilization point to the conclusion that a purely secularist humanism, such as is advocated in many quarters at the present time, is incompatible alike with the facts of human nature and the structure of the universe in which we are placed. Man is an animal, but not merely an animal; there are potencies in his nature, intellectual, moral, and religious, which cannot achieve satisfaction within the bounds of temporal existence. Nor is the world, as it appears in time, intelligible without remainder as the historical fulfilment of the principle of order in the light of which science and philosophy seek to understand it. But it is an error to regard these two types of humanism, the anthropocentric and the theocentric, as co-ordinate species of a common genus. The position I am maintaining is rather that a secularist humanism, since it is grounded on a mutilation of our nature and experience, is not to be regarded as humanism, but as a travesty of humanism; and that integration with a theocentric world-view, as in a Christian philosophy, is requisite even for the satisfaction of man's cultural aspirations. The Provost of King's, when addressing a meeting of the Classical Association at Cambridge, rightly deprecated the introduction of controversial *clichés* and party battle-cries. 'The challenge to the validity of ancient standards must', he allowed, 'be answered.' But he added: 'Let there be, however, no "I am for the Classics", "I am for Religion", "I am for Science, sacred Science".' [1] That the classics and the sciences both fall within humanistic culture, no serious thinker will now dispute; but what about religion? The pitting of religious and secularist humanism one against the other is a yet graver menace; for it does violence alike to humanism and to religion. We can learn better from a study of the Christian philosophy which was the crowning glory of the Middle Ages, with its ever-memorable watch-word; *gratia perficit naturam, non tollit*. Human nature, apart from supernatural grace, is doomed to imperfection and, being foiled of its connatural end, to disillusionment and eventual despair; religion, unless grounded on man's nature,

1. Quoted from *The Times* report, April 16, 1943.

is, together with the entire supernatural economy, relegated to the
limbo of irrationality. The worship of the Creator is bereft of its due
homage. Nor, again, can there be any rivalry of 'I am for Hebraism',
and 'I am for Hellenism'. Here too, as we have seen,[1] the Christian
philosophy of Aquinas offers a corrective, with its impressive synthesis of the Hebrew, Greek, and Roman legacies. True, the Hebraic–
Christian legacy is revelational, the Hellenic rational. Yet, for all the
difference in their credentials, they present noteworthy affinities.
Both affirm a cosmic teleology, grounded on an other-worldly reality,
apprehended by an act, in the one case, of religion, in the other, of
metaphysical faith. To neither was it granted to transcend the bounds
of human reason, so as to comprehend in full detail how the rational
purpose of the Creator is fulfilled in the temporal processes of nature
and history, in the life whether of the individual or of the race. When
we seek, as we needs must, to know the nature of this principle of
cosmic order and its manner of working, there is a further affinity
in the answers given by both traditions. The order, whether its
source be in the nature of metaphysical reality or in the will of the
Creator, is a moral order, so that, in ways that to men's finite
intellect are greatly dark, the chequered course of history is at every
point overruled for good.

> All shall be well and
> All manner of things shall be well
> When the tongues of flame are in-folded
> Into the crowned knot of fire,
> And the fire and the rose (the purificatory suffering and its
> reward) are one.[2]

Once more – and here lies the relevance of this faith for man's life and
destiny – both the Hebraic and the Hellenic traditions assert the
paramount obligation binding men to rule their conduct in conformity
to the order of the universe, and define sin as *hubris*, the temper of
pride of self that prompts him to rebellion against the moral law.
Both are at one in teaching that for sin, as thus defined, the law exacts
inevitable retribution. He who, like Agamemnon, treads the purple,
subjects himself to an inexorable doom. He sows the wind and reaps
the whirlwind. Where the traditions part company is in their respective doctrines of salvation. Whereas the Platonist taught salvation by
philosophical wisdom and the Stoic salvation by self-sufficiency rooted
in strength of will, the Christian preached the gospel of redemption
through the Incarnate Christ. 'God so loved the world.' The gulf here

1. C. xi, above.
2. T. S. Eliot, *Little Gidding*.

is immeasurable. Of the love of God for His creation, and of the consequent obligations upon man to love God with his whole heart and his neighbour as himself, Greek philosophy knew nothing. These are revealed truths inaccessible to unaided reason; but if we bear firmly in mind that the grace which perfects is *praeter*, not *contra*, *naturam*, we can understand how a Christian philosophy, and it alone, enables man to realize his human capacities in full measure as a freeman of an otherworldly commonwealth.

BIBLIOGRAPHICAL APPENDIX

The list given below represents merely a selection of trustworthy English works, admittedly incomplete, but sufficient to start the reader on a closer study of the main topics handled in this volume. All the books should be accessible in a good public library. Excellent bibliographies will be found at the close of the principal articles in the Encyclopaedia Britannica *and in the* Cambridge Ancient *and* Medieval Histories, *to which the student is referred for fuller information throughout.*

I. HISTORICAL ATLASES

Kiepert's *Atlas Antiquus* (Williams and Norgate), W. R. Sheppard's *Historical Atlas* (Henry Holt), and the *Atlas of Ancient and Classical Geography* in the *Everyman* Series (the last less expensive).

II. CHAPTER I

J. L. Myres: *The Dawn of History* (Home University Library).

III. CHAPTER II

The articles on *Egypt, Babylonia and Assyria, Hittites, Aegean Civilization, Crete,* and *Persia* in the 11th edition of the *Encyclopaedia Britannica*; and the *Cambridge Ancient History*, vols. i (Egypt and Babylonia to 1580 B.C.) and ii.

Breasted: *History of Egypt.*
Budge: *Egypt* (Home University Library).
Rogers: *History of Babylonia and Assyria.*
Maspero: *The Dawn of Civilization, Egypt and Chaldaea* (ed. Sayce).
Maspero: *The Struggle of the Nations* (ed. Sayce).
Maspero: *The Passing of the Empires* (ed. Sayce).
Woolley: *The Sumerians.*

The original documents are translated with introductions and comments in the series of volumes entitled *Ancient Records of Egypt* (ed. Breasted), *Ancient Records of Assyria and Babylonia* (ed. Harper), *Ancient Records of Palestine, Phoenicia and Syria* (ed. Harper), published by the University of Chicago.

On the religions, consult

Sayce: *Religions of Ancient Egypt and Babylonia* (Gifford Lectures, 1902).
Jastrow: *Religion of Assyria and Babylonia.*
King: *Babylonian Religion and Mythology.*
Pinches: *Religion of Babylonia and Assyria.*

On the laws of Khammurabi,

Johns: *The Oldest Code in the World.*
Handcock: *The Code of Hammurabi* (S.P.C.K. Texts for Students, cheap).
Cowley: *The Hittites* (Schweich Lectures, 1918).
Burrows: *The Discoveries in Crete.*
Hawes: *Crete, the Forerunner of Greece* (inexpensive).
Schuchhardt: *Schliemann's Excavations.*

Above all, the monuments in the British Museum should be visited, with the aid of the cheap and well-illustrated guide-books to the various collections. Parties are shown round by an admirable official guide.

IV. CHAPTER III

Consult the article *Bible* (*A. Old Testament*) in the *Encyclopaedia Britannica*; also those on *Hebrew literature, Hebrew religion, Jews*, etc. Hastings' *Dictionary of the Bible* and the *Encyclopaedia Biblica* may be referred to; the latter represents the extreme of radical criticism. The several Books of the Old Testament should be studied with the aid of the volumes in the *International Critical Commentary*. Peake: *Commentary*; and the volumes of the *Cambridge Bible for Schools and Colleges* are also recommended. Driver's *Introduction to the Literature of the Old Testament* (9th edition, revised, 1913) is an invaluable guide to Old Testament study and contains full bibliographies. See also the brief survey in Moore: *Literature of the Old Testament* (Home University Library).

> F. C. Burkitt: *Jewish and Christian Apocalypses.*
> R. H. Charles: *Eschatology.*
> R. H. Charles: *Apocrypha and Pseudepigrapha.*
> Klausner: *Jesus of Nazareth.*
> Manson: *A Companion to the Bible* (with bibliographies).
> G. F. Moore: *Judaism.*
> Oesterley and Robinson: *History of Israel.*
> Schürer: *History of the Jewish People in the Time of Jesus Christ.*
> W. Robertson Smith: *The Religion of the Semites.*
> W. Robertson Smith: *The Prophets of Israel.*
> W. Robertson Smith: *The Old Testament in the Jewish Church.*
> *The People and the Book* (Essays, ed. Peake).
> *Record and Revelation* (Essays, ed. Wheeler Robinson), with bibliographies.

V. CHAPTERS IV–VI

(A) GENERAL. – The best modern text-book of Greek history is Bury: *History of Greece*. See also, *The Legacy of Greece* (ed. Livingstone), Holm: *History of Greece*, and the yet larger works of Grote and Thirlwall (for the seventh century onwards).

On Greek literature, Mackail: *Lectures on Greek Poetry*; Gilbert Murray: *History of Greek Literature*. On Greek philosophy, the works of Zeller and Burnet; Gomperz, *Greek Thinkers*; and Adamson's *Development of Greek Philosophy*. Translations of the Greek (and Latin) classics will be found in the *Loeb* and *Everyman* Series and in the *Temple Greek and Latin Classics*. In the Loeb and Temple volumes the Greek (or Latin) text and the English translation face one another throughout.

(B) SPECIAL SUBJECTS. – The following works are referred to the part of this book where they will first be found useful. In many cases, they contain matter relevant to later sections.

(1) CH. IV: PART II

> Warde Fowler: *The City-State of the Greeks and Romans.*
> Zimmern: *The Greek Commonwealth.*

PART III

> P. N. Ure: *The Greek Renaissance.*
> P. N. Ure: *The Origin of Tyranny*

PART IV

    Gilbert Murray: *Rise of the Greek Epic*.
    Jebb: *Introduction to Homer*.
    Leaf: *Companion to the Iliad* (in Lang, Leaf, and Myers' translation).
        Translations of the *Iliad* by Lang, Leaf, and Myers, of the *Odyssey*
        by Butcher and Lang, and by Palmer.

PART V

    Burnet: *Early Greek Philosophy*.
    Burnet: *Thales to Plato*.
    Cornford: *Greek Religious Thought*.
    Guthrie: *Orphism*.
    Jane Harrison: *Prolegomena to the Study of Greek Religion*.
    Jane Harrison: *Ancient Art and Ritual* (Home University Library).
    Adam: *Religious Thoughts in Greece*.
    Gilbert Murray: *Five Stages of Greek Religion*.
    Nilsson: *A History of Greek Religion*.
    A. E. Taylor: *Platonism and its Influence*.

(2) CH. V: PART I

The student should not fail to read translations of *Herodotus* (in the *Everyman* and the *Loeb* Series, or by Macaulay) and *Thucydides* (in the *Everyman* Series, or by Jowett); also Plato's studies of democracy (with Athens in his mind) in Books VI and VIII of the *Republic*, and of timocracy (with Sparta in view) in Book VIII. The *Republic* is translated by Jowett (Clarendon Press) and by Davies and Vaughan in the *Golden Treasury* Series. Zimmern's book is excellent on the economic basis of Athenian public life.

PART II

Greek art is far better studied in the galleries of the British Museum than in books about the subject. The cheap and excellent official guide-books will furnish the requisite assistance. A good general hand-book is Fowler and Wheeler: *Greek Archaeology*.

On the drama,
    Haigh: *The Attic Theatre*.
    Ridgeway: *The Origin of Tragedy*.
    Gilbert Murray: *Euripides and His Age*.
    Gilbert Norwood: *Greek Tragedy*.
    Verrall: *Euripides the Rationalist*.

The following translations may be noted as of special value: *Aeschylus* by W. and C. E. S. Headlam, *Sophocles* by R. Whitelaw, *Euripides* (certain plays) by Gilbert Murray, *Aristophanes* by Rogers and (certain plays) by Hookham Frere. Aeschylus' *Oresteia* by E. D. A. Morshead, the *Agamemnon* by Gilbert Murray, Euripides' *Alcestis* by Robert Browning (in *Balaustion's Adventure*). If a selection is desired, the student is advised to begin with Aeschylus' trilogy (the *Oresteia*) and *Prometheus Bound*, Sophocles' *Antigone, Oedipus King, and Philoctetes*, Euripides' *Medea, Hippolytus, Alcestis*, and *Bacchae*, Aristophanes' *Frogs, Clouds, Acharnians, Birds*, and *Wasps*.

On Thucydides, read Cornford: *Thucydides Mythistoricus*.

PART III

On the Sophists and Socrates, Burnet: *Thales to Plato* and Gomperz (vol. ii). Xenophon's *Memorabilia* is well translated by Dakyns. All students should read Plato's *Apology*, *Crito*, and *Phaedo*, which are translated in the *Golden Treasury* Series by Church, under the title *The Trial and Death of Socrates*, and by Jowett.

PART IV

Plato's dialogues have been translated in their entirety by Jowett. In addition to the versions of separate dialogues referred to above, the *Symposium* has been translated by the poet Shelley, and the *Lysis*, *Phaedrus*, and *Protagoras* by Wright (*Golden Treasury* Series). Several dialogues have been issued in English in the *Everyman* Library. It is much to be regretted that no cheap and good version of the *Gorgias* is obtainable.

On Plato's philosophy, see Burnet and Gomperz (vol. iii), A. E. Taylor's *Plato*, Grote's *Plato*, and the essay on *Plato's Theory of Goodness and the Good* in R. L. Nettleship's *Lectures and Remains* (vol. i). The best aids to the study of the *Republic* are the last-mentioned writer's *Lectures on the Republic* and his essay in *Hellenica* on *The Theory of Education in the Republic of Plato*. On Platonism and its history, see A. E. Taylor: *Platonism and its Influence* (*Our Debt to Greece and Rome* Series).

(3) CH. VI: PARTS I–II

On Alexander, Hogarth: *Philip and Alexander*.
On Alexander's successors,
    Bevan: *House of Seleucus*.
    Tarn: *Hellenistic Civilization*.
    Mahaffy: *The Progress of Hellenism in Alexander's Empire*, Holm: vols. iii, iv.

Theocritus is translated by Andrew Lang in the *Golden Treasury* Series.

PART III

On Aristotle, Grote: *Aristotle*, Zeller: *Aristotle and the Aristotelian Schools*, Gomperz: vol. iv. Jaeger: *Aristotle*, Mure: *Aristotle*, J. L. Stocks: *Aristotelianism*.

A translation of the whole of Aristotle's works has been published by the Clarendon Press; a volume of translated selections has been compiled by Sir D. Ross. Students are advised to approach the study of Aristotle through the *Ethics* (translated by Peters, and in the *Everyman* Series by Chase) and the *Politics* (Jowett's translation, ed. Davis – Clarendon Press). Muirhead's *Chapters from Aristotle's Ethics* and the introductory volume to Newman's edition of the *Politics* are also recommended. The beginner may well find in Dante the stimulus to an interest in Aristotle's philosophy, bearing in mind that Dante interpreted Aristotle in the light of many beliefs that were post-Aristotelian.

PART IV

Zeller: *Epicureans and Stoics*, Bevan: *Stoics and Sceptics*, Wallace: *Epicureanism*, Dudley: *Cynics*.

Marcus Aurelius and *Epictetus* have been frequently translated (e.g. in the *Camelot* Series). The former has been translated by Rendall (*Golden Treasury* Series) with a useful Introduction. *Lucretius'* poem (*On the Nature of Things*) has been translated by Munro and by Bailey.

VI. CHAPTERS VII–VIII

(A) GENERAL. – The best short text-book is Pelham: *Outline of Roman History* (a reprint of his article in the *Encyclopaedia Britannica*); among many others, those of Wells, of How and Leigh, and Warde Fowler's *Rome* (*Home University Library*) will be found useful. See also *The Legacy of Rome* (ed. C. Bailey) and H. Stuart Jones: *Companion to Roman History*. Of larger works, Mommsen's *History of Rome* is specially valuable for its interpretation of Roman institutions, law, and civilization. Greenidge: *Roman Public Life*, Heitland: *Roman Republic*, and T. Rice Holmes: *Roman Republic*, may also be mentioned. Montesquieu's *Grandeur et décadence des Romains*, written in the first half of the eighteenth century, is full of acute and pregnant observations.

(B) SPECIAL SUBJECTS

(1) CH. VII: PART I

Warde Fowler: *City-State of the Greeks and Romans*.
Sohm: *Institutes of Roman Law* (tr. Leslie). This work should be consulted on the history and character of Roman law up to the time of Justinian. See also the article *Roman Law* in the *Encyclopaedia Britannica* and Maine: *Ancient Law*.

PART III

Bosworth Smith: *Carthage and the Carthaginians*.
Bosworth Smith: *Rome and Carthage* (*Epochs of Ancient History*)
Church and Gilman: *Carthage* (*Story of the Nations*).
Mabel Moore: *Carthage of the Phoenicians*.

There is much need for a new history of Carthage, and of the Phoenicians, that shall embody the results of recent research. Flaubert's novel *Salammbô*, the scene of which is laid in Carthage after the first Punic war, is based on a close study of the material available in the middle of the last century. On Rome in the East, Bevan: *House of Seleucus*.

PART IV

On Latin literature generally, Mackail: *Latin Literature* and, for fuller treatment of the poets, the works of W. Y. Sellar.

(2) CH. VIII: PART I

Greenidge: *History of Rome from* 133 B.C. (unfinished).
Warde Fowler: *Caesar* (*Heroes of the Nations*).
Warde Fowler: *Social Life at Rome in the Age of Cicero*.

E. S. Shuckburgh: *Augustus*.

Pelham: *Essays in Roman History* (and for the rest of this chapter).

G. Boissier: *The Opposition under the Caesars*.

Jeans: *Select Letters of Cicero* (an admirable translation, with brief explanatory introductions).

T. Rice Holmes: *Caesar's Conquest of Gaul*.

Caesar's narrative of the *Gallic War* can be read in Rice Holmes' translation.

PART II

Mommsen: *Roman Provinces under the Empire* furnishes a brilliant survey up to the time of Diocletian, based largely on the evidence of contemporary inscriptions.

H. Stuart Jones: *Roman Empire* (*Story of the Nations*).

Capes: *The Early Roman Empire* (*Epochs of Ancient History*).

Capes: *The Roman Empire of the Second Century* (*Epochs of Ancient History*).

W. T. Arnold: *Roman Provincial Administration*.

W. T. Davis: *The Influence of Wealth in Imperial Rome*.

Haverfield: *Roman Britain* (a reprint of the article in the *Encyclopaedia Britannica*).

Haverfield: *The Romanization of Roman Britain* (ed. Collingwood).

PART III

The reader is advised to become acquainted with Cicero through his *Letters* (translated by Jeans) rather than through his speeches or other writings. Lucretius has been translated by Bailey and by Munro. The *Aeneid* may be read in Dryden's poetic version or in Mackail's prose translation. Tacitus has been translated by Church and Brodribb; Catullus, Ovid's *Metamorphoses*, Seneca, Quintilian, Pliny's *Letters*, and Boethius' *Consolation* in the Loeb Series; Plutarch by Langhorne. See also H. E. Butler: *Post-Augustan Poetry*, Bossier: *Tacitus and other Roman Studies*.

VII. CHAPTER IX

PART I

The literature dealing with the rise of Christianity is well-nigh inexhaustible, and the arbitrary nature of any brief selection is obvious. In the author's judgement, the most adequate history of the early church is by a French scholar, the late Mgr Duchesne: *Histoire ancienne de l'Eglise* (translated). The following English works will serve as an introduction to the period:

A. C. Headlam: *The Life and Teaching of Jesus the Christ*.

Bigg: *Origins of Christianity*.

Bigg: *The Church's Task under the Roman Empire*.

Burkitt: *The Gospel History and its Transmission*.

Cochrane: *Christianity and Classical Culture*.

Dodd: *Apostolic Preaching*.

Moffatt: *An Introduction to the Literature of the New Testament.*
Stanton: *The Gospels as Historical Documents.*
Harnack: *The Expansion of Christianity in the First Three Centuries.*
Ramsay: *The Church in the Roman Empire.*
Dollinger: *The Gentile and the Jew.*
Hatch: *The Influence of Greek Ideas and Usages upon the Christian Church.*
Hatch: *The Organization of the Early Christian Churches.*

And articles in Hastings' *Dictionary of the Bible*, *Encyclopaedia Biblica*, and the *Cambridge Medieval History*, vol. i (esp. C. H. Turner on *The Organization of the Church*). For the New Testament literature, consult the volumes in the *International Critical Commentary* and Lightfoot: *Epistles of Saint Paul*; for the literature of the subsequent epoch, Lightfoot: *Apostolic Fathers* and translations in the Loeb Series.

PART II

Cumont: *The Mysteries of Mithra.*
Cumont: *Oriental Religions in Ancient Paganism.*
A. S. Geden: *Select Passages illustrating Mithraism* (S.P.C.K.).
Kennedy: *St Paul and the Mystery Religions.*
S. Angus: *The Mystery Religions and Christianity.*
Warde Fowler: *The Religious Experience of the Roman People.*
Warde Fowler: *Roman Ideas of Deity.*
Dill: *Roman Society from Nero to Marcus Aurelius.*
Dill: *Roman Society in the Last Century of the Western Empire.*

On the philosophy of the period, see translations of Marcus Aurelius and of Epictetus (as above) and Renan's volume on *Marcus Aurelius.* Philostratus' *Life of Apollonius of Tyana* is translated in the Loeb Series. There is a very interesting translation of Plotinus by Stephen MacKenna. On Neo-Platonism, Inge: *The Philosophy of Plotinus*, Whittaker: *The Neo-Platonists*, Bigg: *Neo-Platonism*, E. R. Dodds: *Select Passages illustrating Neo-Platonism* (S.P.C.K.). Webb's short *History of Philosophy* (Home University Library) is admirable on this period.

PART III

Harnack: *History of Dogma.*
Hefele: *History of the Councils.*
Both these works are exhaustive studies of the history of doctrine.
Bigg: *Christian Platonists of Alexandria.*
Gwatkin: *Studies of Arianism.*
Bright: *Age of the Fathers.*
Newman: *The Arians of the Fourth Century.*
Figgis: *The Political Aspects of St Augustine's City of God.*

The articles in the *Dictionary of Christian Biography* may be usefully consulted. Translations are to be found in the *Library of Nicene and post-Nicene Fathers.*

VIII. CHAPTER X

(A) GENERAL. – On the Decline and Fall, the great work of Edward Gibbon should form for all readers the basis of study. It has been re-edited with notes by Bury. Students must bear in mind that it was compiled mainly from the literary sources available in the later eighteenth century, and that it reflects throughout the outlook and temper of the age of Rationalism.

> Bryce: *Holy Roman Empire.*
> Davis: *Medieval Europe* (Home University Library).
> The *Cambridge Medieval History*, vols. i and ii (with copious bibliographies).

(B) SPECIAL SUBJECTS

PART II

On ancient agriculture, Heitland: *Agricola.*

PART III

> Hodgkin: *Italy and Her Invaders.*
> Davis: *Charlemagne* (Heroes of the Nations).
> Bury: *History of the Later Roman Empire* (from 395).

On the life and times of Justinian see Procopius (Loeb translation in progress).

PART IV

> Bury: *op. cit.*; and *Eastern Roman Empire.*
> Diehl: *History of the Byzantine Empire* (translated by G. B. Ives).
> Finlay: *History of Greece* (written 1864).

On the Slavs, see the articles by Peisker in the *Cambridge Medieval History*, vol. ii.

On Mohammed and Islam, see the articles by Bevan and by Becker in the *Cambridge Medieval History*, vol. ii, Margoliouth: *Mohammed* (Heroes of the Nations) and *Mohammedanism* (Home University Library), and translations of the *Koran* by E. H. Palmer, Rodwell, and George Sale (ed. Ross, 1921).

PART V

On Justinian's Code, see Gibbon (c. 44), the article in the *Cambridge Medieval History*, and Sohm. On the Monophysites, see Duchesne and Harnack; on the Iconoclastic conflict, Bury: *Later Roman Empire.* On Byzantine civilization, see the *Encyclopaedia Britannica*, esp. the article by Krumbacher on *Greek Literature (Byzantine).*

IX. CHAPTER XI

(A) GENERAL. – As this chapter is of the nature of a supplement to those which precede it, only a few of the most accessible works bearing on points of special significance are mentioned below. Davis: *Medieval*

Europe (Home University Library), gives a brief outline of the mediaeval order of society and history. H. O. Taylor: *The Medieval Mind*, gives a useful and comprehensive survey. On classical learning in the Middle Ages, Sandys: *History of Classical Scholarship*. On the universities, Rashdall: *The Universities of the Middle Ages*.

(B) SPECIAL SUBJECTS

PART II

Webb: *History of Philosophy* (Home University Library) contains an excellent chapter on the subject. No single large history of mediaeval philosophy with outstanding merits is available in English. De Wulf: *History of Scholastic Philosophy* is useful, as also is the mediaeval section in Ueberweg's *History o Philosophy*. R. L. Poole: *Illustrations of the History of Medieval Thought* should certainly be read.

On Aquinas, see Wicksteed: *Reactions between Dogma and Philosophy* (*Hibbert Lectures*, 1916) and E. Gilson: *The Philosophy of S. Thomas* (translated). The *Summa Theologica* and the *Summa Contra Gentiles* have been translated by the English Dominicans.

On the Arabs, see Renan: *Averroès et l'Averroisme*. Dante should be read in the *Temple Classics* edition.

PART III

Pollock and Maitland: *History of English Law*, vol. i.
Vinogradoff: *Roman Law in Medieval Europe*.
Gierke: *Political Theories of the Middle Age* (ed. Maitland, with Introduction).
Poole: *Essays in Medieval Thought*.
Carlyle: *A History of Medieval Political Theory in the West*.
Figgis: *Divine Right of Kings*.
Figgis: *Studies of Political Thought from Gerson to Grotius*.
Jenks: *Law and Politics in the Middle Ages*.

PART IV

On Erasmus, Seebohm: *Oxford Reformers*.
Froude: *Erasmus*.
P. S. Allen: *The Age of Erasmus*.
P. S. Allen: *Selections from Erasmus*.

Mark Pattison's *Life of Casaubon* and *Essays*, Payne's *History of the New World called America* (vol. i) and Miss Haldane's *Life of Descartes* will serve to illustrate other aspects of this part of the chapter.

INDEX

TO VOLUMES ONE AND TWO

*

INDEX

*

Figures in heavier type indicate the most important of the passages referred to. *Passim* = constantly mentioned; *n* = note. Where the reference is both to the text and to the notes on a given page, the page only is indicated, unless the note is of special importance.

Aachen, 411

Abbasid caliphs, 410 *n*, 419, 419 *n*, 420

Abbotsford, 542

Abelard, 443, 448, 452, 456, 467

Absolute, the, 178, 544, 556, 557

Abyssinian church, 429

Academy, academies (*Greek*), 204, 352, 426; *Platonic*, 174–5, 180–1, 217, 446, 449 *n*; *Renaissance*, 204, 485

Accursius, 467

Achaean League, 107, 198

Achaeans, 20 *n*, 36, 96–7, 129 *n*, 183

Achaemenid, 392

Achaia (Roman province of), 252, 287 *n*

Acropolis (*Athens*), 102, 145, 146, 150

Actium, battle of, 276

Acton, Lord, 480

Adonai (*Heb.*), 51 *n*

Adoption (*in Babylonian law*), 26; (*in Roman law*), 233, 233 *n*, 241 *n*, 282, 357 *n*

Adoptionism, 367 *n*

Adrianople, battle of, 397

Aebutian law, 262, 263

Aegean peoples (and early civilization), 19, 20, 33, 34, 35, 36, 96–8, 113; *see also* Crete; Minoan

Aeneid, the, 5–6, 112, 305, 306 *n*, 313–14, 512

Aeolians, 111, 115; (*Aeolic dialect*), 111 *n*

Aeschylus, 112, 117 *n*, 130, 130 *n*, 134, 138 *n*, 139 *n*, 150 *n*, 151, 153–4, 156, 512, 540

Aethelberht, 464

Aetius, 399 *n*, 400

Aetolian league, 107, 198

Africa 7; (*Greek*), 108; (*Roman*), 249, 251, 260, 274, 275 *n*, 281, 380; (*Christian*), 325, 326, 329 *n*, 332, 374, 409 (*Decline and fall*), 399, 402, 405 *n*, 417, 421, 421 *n*

Agamemnon, 576

Agathon, 189

Agesilaus, 191 *n*

Agnates (in Roman law), 230 *n*

Agnosticism, 462–3

Agobard, 465

Agora (*Gr.*), 102, 102 *n*

Agricola, 298 *n*

Agriculture (*Egypt*), 16; (*Babylonia*) 23–4, 24 *n*; (*Hebrew*), 34; (*Persia*), 41 (*Greek*), 103, 134, 161; (*Roman*), 236, 253, 265, 266, 268, 279, 284, 288, 289, 306 *n*, 395 *n*; (*Gaul*) 295; (*Britain*) 297

Ahab, 57

Ahaz, 64 *n*, 65

Ahijah, 56 *n*

Ahriman, 40

Ahuramazda (Ormuzd), 40

Aidos (*Gr.*), 116, 116 *n*

Akaiuasha (Achaeans), 20 *n*, 36

Alaric, 311, 379, 396, 398, 403, 404

Alba, 225, 227

Albert of Cologne (Albertus Magnus), 455 *n*, 491 *n*

Alchemists, 505 *n*

Alcibiades, 107, 144, 166 *n*, 170–1

Alcidamas, 187

Alcmaeon, 123 *n*, 125 *n*

Alcmaeonidae, 136

Alcuin, 411 *n*, 449

Alcman, 255 *n*

Aldhelm, 432

Alemanni, 291, 398 *n*

Alexander (the Great, of Macedon), 12 *n*, 15, 21, 41, 43, 44, 92, 139, 191–201, 204, 205, 206, 215, 223, 224, 252, 276 *n*, 512

Alexander, S., 124 *n*, 506 *n*, 509 *n*

Alexandria (*Graeco-Macedonian*), 21, 193, 195 *n*, 195, 196, 198 *n*, 202–5, 511; (*Jews at*), 80, 94, 363; (*Christian*), 326 *n*, 327 *n*, 329 *n* (*Roman empire*), 345, 388

Alfred, King, 76 *n*, 402

Allegory, Allegorical method, 22, 83 *n*, 220 *n*, 329 *n*, 338, 363, 447, 470, 488

Ambrose, St, 344 *n*, 371 *n*, 374, 385, 385 *n*

Amenhotep IV (Ikhnaton), 19

Ammianus Marcellinus, 400 *n*

Ammon (Canaanite people), 34, 35

Ammon (Egyptian deity), 19

Amos, 57–65

Amphiktyonic league, 107

Amphipolis, 158 *n*

Amraphel, 25 *n*

Analogia entis, 462

Anamnêsis, Platonic doctrine of, 176 *n*, 461–2

Anatomy, 203
Anaxagoras, 125–8, 134
Anaximander, 121, 121 *n*, 122 *n*, 123 *n*, 127 *n*, 156
Anaximenes, 121, 123 *n*, 126
Anchorites, 328 *n*, 343 *n*, 363, 372, 385 385 *n*
Ancyran monument, 276–7
Anglo-Saxons, 234, 298, 402, 408, 420, 432 *n*; (law), 76 *n*, 298
Animalibus, de, 448 *n*
Anselm, St, 444 *n*, 448, 452, 455, 456, 467 469 *n*, 503 *n*, 544 *n*, 557
Antalcidas, peace of, 189
Anthemius (of Tralles), 430
Anthony, St, 363, 372, 385 *n*
Anthropomorphism, 462, 463
Antinous, 285
Antioch, 196, 197, 205, 325, 325 *n*, 327 *n*, 329 *n*, 335 *n*, 367 *n*, 383
Antiochus I, 197 *n*
Antiochus II (Theos), 199 *n*
Antiochus III (the Great), 250–1
Antiochus IV (Epiphanes), 75, 78, 81, 82, 86, 93, 195
Antonine emperors, 283 *n*, 287, 288, 297 *n*, 301, 313, 315, 332; *see also* Marcus Aurelius
Antony, 276
Apelles, 205
Apocalyptic (Jewish), 30 *n*, 71 *n*, 73 *n*, 84–8 and *nn*, 92 *n*, 121 *n*, (Christian), 87 *n*, 323 *n*
Apocrypha, the, 121 *n*
Apollinaris of Laodicea, 428 *n*
Apollo, 97, 127 *n*, 129 *n*, 152 *n*, 153; *see also* Branchidae; Delos; Delphi
Apollo Belvedere, the, 206
Apollonius of Rhodes, 202
Apollonius of Tyana, 337, 337 *n*
Apologists (Christian), 326, 333, 361, 446
Apostles' creed, 329 *n*, 360
Apostolic age, tradition, 323–9, 325 *n*, 329 *n*, 336, 356 *n*, 360–3, 374, 382
Appius Claudius (censor), 241, 263
Apubeius, 308 *n*
Aquinas, St Thomas, 76 *n*, 365 *n*, 368 *n*, 439, 443, 448, 449, 454 *n*, 455 *n*, 456 *n*, 458–64, 470, 471–4, 472 *n*, 477–81, 485 *n*, 490, 491 *n*, 522 *n*, 557, 569, 570, 576
Aquitaine, 294, 398, 419
Arabia, the Arabs, 8, 25, 31, 42, 43, 192, 281, 288 *n*, 417–18, 417 *n*, 418 *n*, 419 *n*, 420, 421 *n*, 446 *n*; (philosophy), 447, 450, 452–4, 504, 513
Archimedes, 180 *n*, 203, 203 *n*
Architecture (*Egypt*), 19, 23; (*Babylonia and Assyria*), 27, 28, 29; (*Crete*), 37;

(*Persia*), 41; (*Greek*), 103, 106, 145–7; (*Hellenistic*), 204–6; (*Gaul*), 296; (*Mithraic*), 341 *n*; (*Byzantine*), 402, 430; (*Renaissance*), 492, 496–7; *also* 521 *n*
Aretē (*Gr.*), 103, 161, 213
Argos, 99 *n*, 99, 145
Ariovistus, 274 *n*, 542
Aristarchus of Samos, 203
Aristarchus of Somothrace, 203
Aristophanes, 134, 141, 151, 152–3, 154–5, 159, 164, 184, 202
Aristotle, 206–17; also (*early Greek philosophers*), 119, 121; (*Sophists*) 162 *n*, (*Socrates*), 165, 168 *n*, 212–13, 213 *n*, 214; (*Plato*), 174 *n*, 175, 181–2; (*Stoics*), 218–19, 220; (*Neo-Platonism*), 214, 334, 352, 353 *n*; mediaeval thought), 209, 211, 212–15, 402, 443–64; 471–8; (*Revival of Learning*), 490–1, 491 *n*; (*art and poetry*), 145–6, 148–50, 156 *n*, 517 *n*, (*women*), 184 *n*, 185; (*slavery*), 187; (chief other references), 103 *n*, 106, 116 *n*, 117 *n*, 137 *n*, 162 *n*, 163 *n*, 364 *n*, 370 *n*, 375, 378 *n*, 458, 461, 463, 469, 503, 530–6, 572
Arius, Arianism, 364 *n*, 366–71, 372, 385, 398 *n*, 400, 409, 427 *n*
Arles, 294, 296
Armageddon (*Har-magedon*), 21 *n*
Armenia, Armenians, 270 *n*, 290, 432; (church), 429
Art, the arts (including mechanical arts), (*China and Japan*), 12; (*Egypt*), 16–19; 23, 204–5; (*Babylonia*) 25, 28, 29; (*Phoenician*), 34; (*Minoan*), 37–8; (*Persian*), 41; (*Greek*), 44, 132, 145–53, 154 *n*; (*Hellenistic*), 23, 201–6; (*Indian*), 193, 206; (*Roman*), 256–7, 295–6; (*Gaul and Britain*), 295–7; (*Jewish*), 514 *n*, 516
Artaxerxes III (Ochus), 43
Arthur, King, 298
Aryan (and Indo-European, Indo-Iranian), 8–9, 32, 38, 39–40, 96, 232, 240, 339, 400, 414 *n*, 415
Ascham, Roger, 493
Ashtoreth (*Heb.*), 53
Asia (*kingdom of*), 92, 249–50; (*Roman province of*), 251, 260 *n*, 270 *n*, 273 *n*, 280, 287, 340; (*Christian*), 322 *n*, 325, 329 *n*, 332–3, 429; (*under Eastern emperors*), 418, 421–2, 429–30, 431 *n*
Asia Minor, 137
Asiarchs, 280
Aspasia, 183
Assemblies (Roman), 258 *n*, 277–8, 282, 299; *see also* Comitia
Asshur, 26, 27, 28

Assouan dam, 16
Assur-bani-pal, 25 n, 27 n
Assyria, Assyrians, 20, 25, 26–8, 29, 40, 61–2, 63, 64, 65, 67 n, 67, 83 n; (Roman province of), 288 n
Astorga, 293
Astronomy (*including* astrology) (*Chaldaean*), 30, 121; (*Greek*), 120, 122, 162, 203, 208, 216 n, 491; (*astrology and Eastern cults*), 337, 341 n; (*mediaeval*), 449 n, 450 n; (*modern*), 486–7, 491
Ataraxia (*Gr.*), 222
Atè (*Gr.*), 118
Athanaric, 404
Athanasian creed, 369 n, 428 n
Athanasius, 364 n, 368 n, 370, 371–3, 374, 375, 381 n, 385
Athens, Athenians, 99, 105, 109, 110, 115, 118, 124 n, 128, 129, ch. v *passim* 189–90, 198, 202, 221, 242 n, 250, 265, 271, 285, 324, 352 n, 426, 432, 509, 511, 512
Atom, the atomists, atomic theory, 125–6, 222, 508
Atonement, doctrine of, 76 n, 323 n, 408, 470 n
Attalus, the attalids, 205, 252
Atteius Capito, 301 n
Attica, 136, 141 n
Attila, 400, 401
Auctoritas (*Lat.*), 231 n, 233, 258
Augustan age, 305–6
Augusti (*Lat.*), 393
Augustine, St (of Britain), 408
Augustine, St (of Hippo), 228, 310, 311, 352, 355 n, 356 n, 365 n, 370, 374–80, 381, 385, 386, 399, 406 n, 408, 444 n, 450–1, 456 n, 472 n, 473, 478, 512, 527, 540; (the *de. civ. Dei*), 379 n, 381, 381 n, 411 n
Augustus Caesar, 242 n, 267, 273, 274, 275 n, 276 n, 276–81, 282, 287 n, 290, 293, 294, 295, 296, 298–301, 305, 305 n, 312, 316, 388, 390, 396, 410, 476, 479 n
Aurelian, 283 n
Ausonius, 296
Austen, Jane, 410 n, 545
Autarkeia (*Gr.*), 352
Authority (mediaeval), 327–8, 447–8, 449, 450, 457, 458, 482; (*principle of authority and Rome*), 9, 227, 232–3, 267–8, 273, ch. XII *passim*, 475 n, 512, 522, 523, 524; (*and ideal life*), 501, 523 n, 524 n, 574
Autun, 296, 296 n
Avars, 403 n, 410 n, 414–15, 416
Averroes (Ibn-Roschd), 453, 456 n, 457–8, 492
Avesta, the, 41 n
Avicebron (Ibn-gebirol), 454 n

Azo, 467

Baal, Baalim, 56, 57, 63
Babel, 29
Babylon, Babylonia, Babylonians (including Chaldaea), 20–21, 23–31, 35, 40, 40 n, 65, 67, 69, 74, 82 n, 94, 95, 121 n, 192, 193, 204, 340
Babylonian captivity (of Israel), 69–73, 224
Bacchanalia, the, 330 n
Bacon, Francis, 216, 481, 491, 493 n
Bacon, Roger, 442 n, 446, 448 n
Bactria, Bactrians, 40
Baghdad, 410 n, 419, 450, 513
Balkan provinces (of Roman empire), 287 n, 288 n, 291, 393; (*see also* Achaia, Macedonia) (*under eastern emperors*), 415, 419, 421–2, 434
Ballantyne, 542
Baptismal confession, 328, 360, 366, 369 n
Barabbas, 9
Barbarian (*barbaros*, *Gr.*), 2, 11, 44, 99, 254, 386, 396, 464
Basel, 495, 496
Basil of Caesarea, 368, 385, 431 n
Basil, the Macedonian emperor, 425
Basilika, the, 425
Bathyrians, 371 n
Beaumanoir, Philippe de, 467
Beauvaisis, Coutume de, 467
Bede, 407, 432, 464
Beethoven, 546, 561
Beirut, 424
Belgae, Belgica, 294, 295, 397
Benedict, St, rule of, 408, 467
Beneventum, 246 n, 403
Bentham, Jeremy, 481, 555; *see also* Utilitarians
Bentley, Richard, 497
Berbers, 419 n
Bergson, M. Henri, 219 n, 460, 503 n, 506 n, 508 n, 513, 562
Berkeley, bishop, 346 n, 364, 494 n
Bernard, St, 467, 504 n
Berosus, 204
Bethel, 58
Bibliolatry, 74, 75, 336, 493, 516
Biology, biological sciences (*Greek*), 121 n, 125 n, 180, 208–9, 210, 215; (*modern*), 487, 488, 505–6
Bismarck, 543
Bithynia (*Roman province of*), 270 n, 287 n, 332
Black Forest, 291, 291 n, 296 n, 397
Blandina, 333
Blood vengeance, 26, 238

Bobbio, 442
Boethius, 311, **402**, 441, 450 n
Boghaz-Keni, 32 n
Bohemians, 415
Bologna (university and law-school), 426, 443, 444 n, 466, 467, 468
Bona fides (Lat. in Roman law), 302 (cf. 262)
Boniface, St, 410 n
Boniface VIII, Pope, 468 n
Book of the Dead, 21
Bordeaux, 296
Boris, King, 416
Boswell, 7 n
Botta, 28
Boulé, 141
Bowman, 571 n
Bracton, 467
Brahma, 40 n
Branchidae, temple of, 20
Breviarium Alaricianum, 465
Breviary of the Roman Empire, 279 n
Britain, British Isles; (*Roman province*), 203, 283, 285, 290, 296–8, 340, 397; (*Anglo-Saxon*), 299, 420, 432, 432 n, 450, 464–5; (*Britain and Rome, analogies*), 232 n, 234, 242–3, 245, 259; (*Christianity in Britain*), 297, 298, 325, 408, 409, 432; (*English law*), 467, 468; (*revival of learning*), 493, 494; (*British India, analogies with Rome*), 247, 251, 270 n, 316, 331, 465
British Commonwealth, 531, 532
British Museum, 27, 29, 147, 340
British Weekly, 534
Brougham, Lord, 548
Browning, Robert, 186 n, 502 n
Brundisium, 225 n, 246 n
Brunhilda, 409
Bruno, Giordano, 487, 493
Brutus, 275
Bulgaria, Bulgars, 392, 412, 414, 415, 416, 419, 432, 435
Bunyan, John, 492 n, 516
Bureaucracy (*Egypt*), 19; (*Assyria*), 27; (*Persia*), 42–3; (*Graeco-Macedonian*), 196, 218; (*Rome, Rep.*), 259–62, 470; (*Rome, Emp.*), 268 ff, 280, 286, 317, 388, 391–5, 422, 426; (*modern*), 502
Burgundy, Burgundians, 296, 371, 397, 399 n, 442 n; (*law*), 464
Burke, Edmund, 243
Burnet, 169 n
Burns, 303
Bury, 44 n
Butler, bishop, 570
Butler, Dom Cuthbert 376 n
Butler, Samuel, 183 n
Byron, 303, 516

Byzantine civilization, 430–2; (*law*), 425; (*empire*), 392, 393–4, 409, 410 n, 412–36; (*art*), 402, 430–1; (*literature*), 430–1; (*philosophy*), 431, 450, 453–4
Byzantium, 198, 393; *see also* Constantinople

Caecilus Africanus, 301
Caerleon, 290
Caesar, Julius, 5, **270–6**, 303, 513, 530, 540, 541, 542, 551, 574; *see also* Augustus Caesar
'Caesar's household,' 288
Caesarea, 93, 369 n
Caesares (*Lat.*), 393
'Caesaropapism,' 427
Calas tragedy, 386 n
Calendar, the, 17, 274
Caligula, 283
Callistus, pope, 328
Calvin, Calvinism, 379, 489 n, 490 n, 493, 533
Cambridge University, 444 n, 495
Cambyses, 21, 42
Campania, Campanians, 88 n, 244, 254
Canaan, Canaanites, 20, 24, 27, 31–5, 51, 52, 53, 63, 66, 191; *see also* Judaea, Palestine
Cannae (battle of), 249
Canon (Old Testament), 75 n; (New Testament), 328; *see also* Scriptures
Canon law, 329 n, 399 n, 408 n, 441, 448 466–9, 471, 472 n, 476 n, 521
Canuleian law, 235, 241
Capitalism, 570
Capitalist (oligarchy), 139 n
Cappadocia, 32, 32 n, 270 n
Cappadocian Fathers, 368, 371, 385, 431 n
Caracalla, 292, 299
Carchemish, 20 n, 32
Caria, Carians, 205
Carlyle, Thomas, 438 n, 502 n
Caroligian Schools, 442 n, 450–1
Carpocrates, 362 n
Carrhae, battle of, 275, 281
Carroll, Lewis, 502 n
Carthage, Carthaginians, 33, 34, 100 n, 108, 139 n, 191, 245, 248–9, 273, 305 333 n, 383, 418–20
Cartesian rationalism, 551
Casaubon, 497
Cassiodorus, 402
Cassius, 275
Catechetical School (of Alexandria), 362
Categories, 463
Catharsis (*Gr.*), 149 n
Catholic Faith, 353 n, 536

Cato (the Elder), 231, 253, 257, 272 *n*, 292, 293
Cato (the younger), 272, 272 *n*
Catullus, 255, 303
Causality, 533 *n*
Celsus (critis of Christianity), 364
Celsus (jurist), 301
Celts, 2, 8, 244 *n*, 291 *n*, 295–8, 341 *n*; see also Gaul; Gauls census, 279, 279 *n*
Census, 279
Centuries (Roman assembly of), 235
Cervantes, 484
Chaeronea, 190, 207, 338
Chalcedon, council of, 426, 428, 429
Chaldaea (name), 28 *n*; see under Babylon, Babylonia
Chance, 531
Charles (the Bald), 451
Charles (the Great), 410–11, 412, 415, 419, 430, 442 *n*, 450, 466
Charles Martel, 409, 410, 419
Chartres, School of, 446, 446 *n*
Chasidim, the (*Heb. – Asidaeans*), 78, 81
Chaucer, Geoffrey, 256, 402
Childeric, 410
China, 12, 224 *n*, 428, 499
Chios, 186, 198
Chorus (in Greek poetry), 111, 114, 115 116
Church Times, 568
Christ, 81, (name) 81 *n*, 84, 535
Christianity, 178
Christianity, ch. IX, *passim*; (name) 197; (*and Judaism*), 3, 50, 66 *n*, 75 *n*, 76 *n*, 84, 84 *n*, 89 *n*, 88–92, 317, 317 *n*, 319–24, 358; (*and Hellenism*), 223–4, 311, 324, 325, 326, 336–57; 380–2, 429–32; (*and Platonism*), 181, 182, 214, 342, 352–5, 362–6; (*and Aristotle*), 188, 214, 215, and ch. XI *passim*; (*and Stoicism*), 218–9, 220–1, 343, 352; (*and Roman empire*), 5, 247, 286, 324–37, 380–7, 406, 407, 408, 409, 423, 423 *n*, 440, 441; (*Spain*), 293–4; (*Gaul*), 295, 296; (*Britain*), 297, 325–6; (*Teutons*), 395, 396–412; (*Slavs*), 415–17; (*Virgil*), 66 *n*, 313, 314; (*Oriental Cults*), 357 *n*, 358, 358 *n*; (*Mohammedanism*), 417 *n*, 417; (*India*), 428; (*and mediaeval thought*), ch. XI *passim*; (*and progress*) 499 *n*, 535, 555, 556, 566, 568, 569, 574; (*philosophy*) 575
Chronology, 15 *n*, 18 *n*, 23 *n*; (*tables*), 46–9
Chrysippus, 220 *n*
Cicero, 237, 261 *n*, 271–2, 276 *n*, 279, 294, 303–5, 308 *n*, 344 *n*, 405, 446 *n*, 479, 493, 496, 525

Cilicia, 32, 191, 199, 204, 220 *n*, 261 *n*, 270 *n*, 275 *n*
Cimabue, 430
Cimmerians, 28 *n*, 39
Citizenship (Roman), 234, 234 *n*, 237 *n*, 247, 247 *n*, 248 *n*, 266, 274, 284, 292, 295, 299, 394
City-state (*Phoenician*), 33, 100 *n*; (*Hellenic Polis*), 5, chs. IV, V, VI *passim*, esp. 98–106, 128–30, 152, 161, 178–82; (*Plato*), 207, 208; (*Aristotle*), 207, 208, 212, 213, 214–5; (*Stoics*), 220, 221, 312, 313, 469, 470, 471, 504 *n*; (*Rome*), 232–3, 246–8, 254, 259, 264–6, 271, 275–6, 383; (*mediaeval*), 439–40
Civilization (*meaning*), 1–2; (*epochs*), 7–8, 486; (*on continuity*), 9–11, 500; (*essentials*), 9, 501, 524
Civil law of Rome, see Law
Civil wars (of Rome), 269–72
Civitas Dei, 386–7, 540, 551
Classics, 493, 494, 496–7, 517–18
Claudian, 388
Claudius (emperor), 290, 291, 295, 296
Cleanthes, 220 *n*, 221, 221 *n*
Clement (of Alexandria), 363, 372 *n*
Cleon, 155, 158 *n*
Cleopatra, 132
Clisthenes, 136, 141
Clive, Lord, 139
Clough, A. H., 111 *n*
Clovis, 397, 398, 464
Clytemnestra, 540
Cnossus, 19, 37
Codex (of Justinian), 422–5, 425 *n*; see also Justinian law
Codex gregorianus, 424 *n*
Codex Hermogianus, 424 *n*
Codi (Provencal), 467
Cognition, 538
Coinage, currency (incl. measures), 26, 31, 39, 247, 298, 398, 422, 486 *n*, 514
Colchester, 292, 297
Coleridge, 150 *n*
Colet, Dean, 494
Collatio legum Mosaicarum, 424 *n*
Collingwood, R. G., 480 *n*
Cologne, 292, 397
Coloni Caesaris, 296 *n*, 395 *n*
Coloni, Colonization (*Phoenician*), 34, (*Greek*), 108–9; (*Roman*), 246–8, 259–61, 268, 273–4, 289, 296
Colossians, epistle to the, 324 *n*, 342 *n*, 356 *n*, 361
Colossus of Rhodes, 206
Columban, Saint, 442 *n*
Columbus, Christopher, 7, 486, 486 *n*, 491
Columella, 293

Comedy (Old Greek), 128, 148 *n*, 149 *n*, 152, 154–5; (*new Greek*), 155, 186, 202, 206; (*Roman*), 254
Commagene, 292, 429
Commerce (*and civilization*), 7, 511, 527 *n*; (*Egypt*), 16–18; (*Babylon*), 24–5, 31; (*Phoenicia*), 33–4; (*Greece*), 108–9, 135, 139–40, 192, 198–201; (*Carthage*), 249; (*Rome*), 252–3; (*Empire in East*), 393, 422; (*Britain*), 297; (*Russia*), 416 (*modern*), 7, 486, 511
Commodus, 333
Commonwealth, British, 568
Communism (*and private property*), 164 *n*, 179, 184–5, 240, 317, 472 *n*, 478 *n*, 567, 571–2, 574
Commenus, 434
Compass, the mariner's, 486 *n*
Comte, Auguste, 555, 567
Conceptualism, 444 *n*
Condorcet, 555, 564, 567
Conrad II (emperor), 467
Conscientious objector, 170
Constantine, 76 *n*, 294, 297, 319, 329, 334, 371 *n*, 384, 389–90, 393–6, 423 432; (*donation of*), 335 *n*, 410 *n*
Constantine VI, 411 *n*
Constantine Palaeologus, 435
Constantinople, 327 *n*, 371, 383, 389, 393–4, 398, 402–4, 407–9, 412–35 *passim*, 453, 484–5; (*council of*), 369 *n*, *see also* Byzantium
Constantius, 372
Constitutions, imperial, 300, 423–6
Consul, consulship, 234, 242, 258, 258 *n*, 398 *n*
Contemplative life, 168, 207, 211, 340, 348, 520–1; *see also* Theoria
Contract, the social, 101 *n*, 438, 472, 479, 507
Contracts (*Roman law*), 239–40, 265 *n*, 301–2; (*mediaeval law*), 467, 472 *n*
Contradiction, principle of, 458 *n*, 458
Copernicus, 203 *n*, 486–7, 505 *n*
Coptic Church, 429
Corcyra, 109 *n*
Cordova, 294, 306, 450, 453, 513
Corinth, 109 *n*, 143, 157 *n*, 250, 273, 324; (*Corinthian style*), 205
Corpus Juris Civilis, 237, 389, 412, 421 *n*, 442, 467, 468 *n*, 479 *n*; *see also* Justinian, law
Cosmic teleology, 576
Cosmological argument, the, 455
Cosmopolitanism, 77, 106, 200, 204, 489, 495, 514; (*Stoic*), 221, 313, 343 (*Roman emp.*), 286, 292, 301, 313, 383 *n*, 394, 468
Councils (of the church), 329 *n*, 384

385 *n*, 466; (*conciliar movement*), 479 *n*, 480
Covenant, book of the, 51, 52 *n*; (*idea of, in religion of Israel*), 53, 68, 68 *n*
Crassus, 270
Creeds (Christian), 328, 329 *n*, 336, 359, 360, 368–9, 369 *n*
Crete, Cretan civilization, 13, 32, 35–8, 96–7; (*Roman*), 269 *n*, 274 *n*; *see also* Aegean, Minoan
Criminal law (*Athens*), 135, 140; (*Rome*) 76 *n*, 233, 238–9, 269, 284, 300
Critias, 169
Croats, 415
Croce, 421 *n*, 506 *n*, 550
Croesus, 29 *n*, 33, 39, 105 *n*
Cromer, Lord, 16
Cromwell, Oliver, 515, 548
Crusades, 434, 439, 453
Ctesiphon, 377 *n*
Curator, 240
Curiatii, the, 227
Curies (*Roman assembly of*), 233, **235** *n*
Cyaxares, 28
Cybele, cult of, 312, 330, 338 *n*, 341 *n*
Cynics, the, 155, 184, 343 *n*
Cyprian, St, 336, 470 *n*, 509
Cyprus, 28, 36, 275 *n*, 321
Cyrenaicism, 81 *n*
Cyrene, 42, 274, 287 *n*
Cyril, 428 *n*, 535
Cyrus, 29, 35, 39, 42, 74, 82 *n*
Czechs, 573

Dacia, 283, 288, 290, 397, 403 *n*
Daedalus, 36 *n*
da Gama, Vasco, 7, 486 *n*
Daemons, 116, 337; (*daimonion of Socrates*), 165
Dalmatia, 325
Damascus, 58 *n*
Damascus, pope, 327 *n*
Daniel, 81 *n*, 86 *n*, 87 *n*
Dante, 92 *n*, 106, 220 *n*, 277, 306, 308, 346, 439, 448 *n*, 450 *n*, 458 *n*, 459, 475–7, 482, 483; (*and Aristotle*), 216, 216 *n*, 470, 471; (*and Neo-platonism*), 346, 349 *n*, 350 *n*, 351 *n*; (*and Rome*), 228, 272 *n*, 275, 311, 335, 475–7, 523; (*and Justinian*), 422, 458 *n*; (*and Virgil*), 314, 523 *n*, 523–4; (*ethics*), 470, 476; (*political theory*), 407, 407 *n*, 473, 475–6, 476 *n*, 477; (*language, rhyme, etc.*), 111 *n*, 406, 431; (*additional references*), 540, 543, 557
Danube, 274, 281, 291, 393
Danubian frontier (of Roman empire),

274, 281, 291, 340, 388, 391, 394, 395–404, 413–4, 415

Dardanians, 36

Darius I (son of Hystaspes), 42–3, 43 n, 137, 138, 193, 426

Darius Codomannus, 191

Darwin, 208, 502 n, 546 n, 558

D'Arcy, Fr, 536 n

Dasgupta, 13 n

David, 2, 33, 35, 70–3, 77 n, 81, 87

Day of Yahweh, 58, 67 n, 70, 81; see also Kingdom of God

Day of Judgement, 349–50 n

Dea Syra, 338 n

Dead, Book of the, 21

Deborah, song of, 53

Debts (in Roman law), 236, 240

Decalogue, 76 n, 516; the older, 52 n

Decius, 334, 335, 366

Declaration of American Independence, 163, 481

Decrees (Roman Imperial), 300

Decretals (papal), 327 n, 467, 468 n

Delian confederacy, 140

Delos, 97, 140

Delphi, Delphic oracle, 43, 100, 109, 138, 167, 168

Demetrius Poliorcetes, 195

Demiurge, 461

Democracy (Greek), 103, 104, 107, 109, 132, 135, 136, 140, 145, 155, 157, 169, 179, 199 n; (Roman), 236, 257, 264, 267–72; (and Christianity) 326 n, 353; (mediaeval), 479–89; (modern), 489–90 n, 506–7

Democritus, 11, 125, 125 n, 126 n, 222

Demosthenes, 138 n, 190, 199, 271, 275, 496

Descartes, 124, 175, 215, 216, 219, 219 n, 222 n, 307, 375, 442 n, 444, 456, 460, 481, 487, 488, 490, 491, 497, 505, 558

Determinism, 530 n

Deuteronomic legislation and writings, 51 n, 52 n, 61 n, 64 n, 66, 67, 70, 74

Dialectic and dialegesthai (Gr.), 171 n

Diaz, Bartholomew, 7

Dictator, dictatorship, 234, 235, 258, 269 270, 272–3, 277

Didactic poetry (Greek), 115–19

Dido, 132

Dies irae, 67 n

Digest (of Justinian), Pandects, 229–30, 262 n, 301, 303 n, 425–6, 425 n, 466, 467, 471, 473; see also Justinian, law

Dioceses, (Roman Imperial), 392

Diocletian, 277 n, 279 n, 282, 291, 298, 334, 335, 383, 388, 390, 391–4, 411, 420, 422

Dionysia, the Great, 285

Dionysius I, of Syracuse, 205; (cf. 180)

Dionysius Exiguus, 466

Dionysius, pseudo, 350 n, 352, 352 n, 362 n, 450 n, 451, 453

Dionysius, Dionysiac religion, 127 n, 129, 150, 152, 154 n

Dispersion (of the Jews) = Gr. diaspora, 70, 93, 322, 511, 513

Disraeli, Benjamin, 514 n

Dithyramb, 149

Divine right, theory of, 408 n, 477, 477 n

Divina Commedia, 214, 543, 545, 547

Docetism, Docetists, 338 n, 339 n, 348

Dodds, C. H., 356

Domitian, 308, 331

Donation of Constantine, see Constantine

Donatism, Donatists, 376, 377

Dorians, 96, 98, 115, 148, 186; (Doric) 145, 205

Drachma, 200

Drama, (Greek), 148–56; (Shakespearian), 148, 148 n; 149 n; (Restoration), 155; (modern), 148 n, 155, 517 n

Druids, 295, 330

Dryden, John, 492 n, 516

Dual Government (at Rome), 242, 278 (cf. 282, 391)

Dualism, (theories of), 40, 173–4, 345–6, 354, 358 n, 361, 362 n, 508; see also Fact and value

Duces (Lat.), 392

Dynamis (Gr.), 211

Ebionites, 322

Ecclesia (Gr.), 141, 155 n

Ecclesiastes, 80 and nn

Eclipses (theory of), 30, 122

Eclogues (of Virgil), 202; (the fourth Eclogue), 66 n, 313

Ecstasy (Gr. ecstasis), 129 n, 130 n, 131, 337, 338, 338 n, 348 n, 356

Eden, garden of, 29, 478, 523 n

Edicts (praetorian), 262–5; (imperial), 300

Edictum, perpetuum, 262; (of Salvius Julianus), 284, 299

Edom, 35

Education (Rabbinical), 70, 74 n; (Greek), 103 n, 104, 106, 112, 112 n, 116 n, 146, 151, 158–9, 159 n, 159–64, 177, 177 n, 180–1, 184, 213; (Roman), 284, 289, 304, 309, 309 n; (Byzantine), 431–2; (mediaeval), 309–10, 399 n, 449, 450 n, 451 n; (Renaissance), 482–3, 484–5, 485 n; (modern), 502 n, 505–7, 518 n, 521; (liberal and practical), 103 n, 162–3 n, 517

Egypt, Egyptians, 15–23, 28, 31, 32, 35,

43, 65, 83 *n*, 92, 94, 97, 108, 120 *n*, 138, 140, 187, 499; (*Graeco-Macedonian*), 191, 195 *n*, 196, 203–4, 252; (*Roman*), 278, 287 *n*; (*under eastern emperors*), 412, 418, 421, 432; (*Christianity*), 328 *n*, 371–2, 385 *n*, 428: *see also* Alexandria

Eidos (*Gr.*), 173 *n*, 209, 210; *see also* **Forms**

Einstein, Dr., 513, 558

Elam, 29 *n*, 30

Elbe, 203

Elegiac poetry (*Greek*), 114, 202

Elephantine (papyri), 52 *n*

Eleusis, (mysteries of), 129, 285, 339

Elgin marbles, 147

Elijah, 9, 57

Eliot, George, 515 *n*

Eliot, Sir John, 496

Eliot, T. S., (*Little Gidding*), 576

Elisha, 57

Elizabeth I, 489 *n*

Elohim (*Heb.*), 51 *n*, 515 *n*; (*Elohistic narrative*), 51 *n*, 52 *n*

Elpis (Gr.), 118

Elvira (council of), 294

Elysium, 130 *n*

Emanation (theory of), 347, 351, 361 *n*

Emerson, 547

Empedocles, 121 *n*, 125, 127, 156, 211 *n*, 499

Empire (*Roman*), ch. VII, VIII, IX, X, *passim; mediaeval*, ch. XI, *passim*

Engels, 567

England, English, 555; *see* Britain

Energeia (*Gr.*), 211

Enneads (of Plotinus), 345

Ennius, 254, 257, 285, 305

Enoch, book of, 87 *n*, 121 *n*

Ephesus, 280, 324, 332, 362 *n*; (councils of), 428

Ephorus, 157 *n*

Ephraim, Ephraimite Kingdom, 27, 35, 52 *n*, 56–8

Epic poetry (Greek), 110–15, 149, 150, 202; (*Roman*), 308

Epictetus, 285 *n*, 333, 343

Epicurus, Epicureans, Epicureanism, 81, 126 *n*, 182, 217–23, 444; (*Roman*), 257, 303, 339

Epimenides, 129

Episcopal jurisdiction, 384 *n*, 395 *n*, 409, 423, 424 *n*, 466

Episcopate, history of, 325 *n*, 328, 329 *n*, 383; *see also* Papacy

Equites, 265, 268, 271, 280, 287 *n*

Equity (*Roman law*), 262 *n*, 300; *see also* **Law**

Erasmus, 365 *n*, 494–6, 511 *n*

Eratosthenes, 202, 203

Ermine Street, 297, 298 *n*

Erôs (*Gr.*), 118, 167

Esarhaddon, 20, 27 *n*, 28

Esdraelon (plain of), 21 *n*

Esdras, 88 *n*

Eternal City, 226; eternal objects, 552

Ethics (*Persian*), 40; (*Jewish*) ch. III *passim*; (*and Greek*), 323 *n*, 324 *n*; (*and Christian*), 323, 381 *n*, 515 *n*; (*Greek*), 115–9, 127, 130, 131, 152–4, 158–81 *passim*, 212–15, 217–23, 343; (*and Christian*), 469; (*Roman*), 307; (*mediaeval*), 468–81; (*general references*), 501–2, 504 *n*, 505, 508

Ethiopia, Ethiopians, 19, 20, 31

Ethos (of the Greek *polis*), 104, 110

Etruria, Etruscans, 226, 233, 244, 246

Eucharist, 325 *n*

Euclid, 124 *n*

Eudaimonia (*Gr.*), 105, 213; (cf. 341, 342, 503, 523)

Eudoxus, 180

Eunapias, 309

Euphrates-Tigris, 13, 20, 23, 24, 26, 192, 193, 196, 275, 281, 290, 391, 396, 417, 426

Euric, 465, 466

Eutychia (*Gr.*), 105 *n*

Euripides, 118 *n*, 134, 151, 153–4, 159, 163 *n*, 184, 186 *n*, 189, 202 *n*

Eusebius, 431 *n*

Evans, Sir Arthur, 38 *n*

Evil (problem of) (*Persian*), 40, 71, 79–81; (*Greek*), 129–30, 168, 176, 213–14, 337, 339 *n*, 346 *n*; (*and Christianity*), 353, 354, 455, 476; (*Christianity*), 358, 365; (*Mithraism*), 340; (*Manicheism*), 358 *n*, 377 *n*; (*mediaeval*), 451, 476

Evolution (*theories of*), 210 *n*, 211 *n*, 347, 499 *n*, 500 *n*, 507, 508, 509 *n*; *see also* **Progress**

Exarchate, exarchs, 403, 410

Exodus, 20

Ezekiel, 59 *n*, 61 *n*, 71 *n*, 71–3, 74, 79, 82, 87 *n*

Ezra, 73, 74, 94, 515

Fact and value, 2, 4, 90, 207, 320, 353–4, 359, 380–2, 506 *n*, 510 *n*, 520, 521, 524–7

Faith and reason, 59–60, 61, 78–81, 126–9, 354–5, 359–62, 445–64, 509–10, 526, 527

Fall of man, 364, 379 *n*, 469, 472 *n*, 476

Family, the (*Greek*), 102, 103, 179, 183, 184, 185; (*Roman*), 227, 229–31, 239, 423, 425

Faraday, 543, 558

Farinata, 540
Fas (*Lat.*), 238
Fascist, 532 *n*, 560, 561
Favorinus, 285 *n*
Federated Europe, 574
Feudalism, 395 *n*, 420, 426 *n*, 439, 479, 481
Ficino, 491
Fictions, legal, 232 *n*, 241 *n*, 374 *n*, 476 *n*
Fielding, Henry, 112 *n*
Fifth symphony, 545
Figgis, 379 *n*, 426 *n*
Finns, 415
Flamininus, 250, 254
Flaminius, 251 *n*
Flavian, 288
Florence (Dante), 106, 459–60, 509
Florence, 511
Form, Forms (Platonic doctrine of), 173–5, 175 *n*, 178–9, 207–15, 349–51, 364 *n*, 380, 451, 455, 461, 556, 563, 565
Formulae (*Roman law*), 236–7, 262–3, 423
Fosse Way, the, 297
Francis of Assisi, St, 439, 504 *n*, 549
France, 555
Franks, 96, 291, 296, 397, 398–9, 404, 409–11, 419, 435, 450, 504
Fraternity, 573–7
Frederick the Great, 515, 546 *n*
Freedmen, 280, 287 *n*, 292 *n*, 299
Freedom, problem of (*Persian*), 40, 41; (*Jewish*), 89 *n*; (*Greek*), 153, 168, 219, 222, 362, 378; (*Christian*), 358 *n*, 364, 378; (*Mediaeval*), 447, 451, 458, 504; (*modern*), 487, 510
Fréjus, 294
French Revolution, 163, 304, 412, 481, 496, 560
Freud, 558
Fueros (*Span.*), 399 *n*
Fulbert of Chartres, 446 *n*
Funeral oration (*of Pericles*), 136 *n*, 142–3, 159 *n*, 182–3

Gabinian law, 270
Gades (= Cadiz), 273, 293
Gaius, 230, 237 *n*, 301, 303 *n*, 423
Galatians (epistle to the), 322, 324 *n*, 361
Galerius, 334
Galilee, 94
Galileo, 215, 442 *n*, 481, 487, 491, 493, 497, 505, 558
Gallen, St, 442 *n*
Gallienus, 291
Gallio, 331
Games (Hellenic), 99, 114, 131, 254
Gassendi, 222 *n*
Gathas, 41 *n*
Gaugamela, battle of, 43, 139, 191

Gaul, Gauls (*in Asia*), 198, 205; (*Roman*), 244 *n*, 248, 251, 268, 270, 271, 273 *n*, 291 *n*, 294–6, 303, 305, 389, 392–3; (*Christian*), 325, 332, 398, 399, 409; (*Germanic kingdoms*), 397; *see also* Celts
Gaul, the Dying, 206 *n*
Gaunilo, 455 *n*
Gaza, 84
Gela, 139 *n*
Gelo, 138
Geneva, 489 *n*, 493, 533
Genius (of Rome and Augustus), 281, 290, 295, 330, 334
Genseric, 380, 399
Gentile, Giovanni, 464, 526 *n*
Geographical Science, 203
Georgics (*of Virgil*) 306
Germany, Germans (*including Teutons, Teutonic tribes*), 2, 8, 31, 268, 274 *n*, 281, 290–2, 291 *n*, 295 *n*, 296 *n*, 388–412 *passim*, 414, 440, 500, 504, 561, 562; (in Middle Ages) ch. XI *passim*
Gibbon, Edward, 76 *n*, 315–16, 373, 388, 393 *n*, 412, 423, 424, 428 *n*, 432 *n*, 438 *n*, 501 *n*, 522
Glossa ordinaria, 467 *n*
Gnósis (*Gr.*) (including *epignôsis*), 356, 356 *n*, 359, 361
Gnostics, Gnosticism, 30 *n*, 326, 358, 361–2, 362 *n*, 367, 378 *n*
Godwin, William, 163, 555
Goethe, 156 *n*, 449, 517 *n*
Goodness, 538–9 (and greatness), 538–53
Gorgias, 139 *n*, 162, 162 *n*
Goshen, 20
Goths, 96, 291, 396–7, 404, 416, 418; *see also* Ostrogoths, Visigoths
Gower, 115
Gracchus, Caius, 268
Gracchus, Tiberius (the elder), 292
Gracchus, Tiberius (the younger), 267, 268
Granicus, battle of the, 191
Gratian, 468, 468 *n*
Greece, Greeks, *see* Hellas, Hellene, Hellenism; 109, 110, 114, 115, 116, 131, 132–3; (*modern Greeks*), 228, 237, 425, 426, 435–6
Green, T. H., 541 *n*
Gregory I, the Great, pope, 408 *n*, 441 466
Gregory III, pope, 409 *n*
Gregory VII, pope, 467, 478 *n*
Gregory IX, pope, 468
Gregory of Nazianzus, 368, 385, 431 *n*
Gregory of Nyssa, 368, 371, 385, 431 *n*
Gregory of Tours, 398 *n*
Grocyn, 494

Grote, George, 162 n
Guillotine, 567
Guthrie, 13 0 n
Gwynne, Nell, 504

Habbakuk, 67 n, 81 n,
Hades, 130 n
Hadrian, emperor, 93, 283–7, 291, 296 n, 299, 313, 315, 322, 330 n, 333
Hadrian I, pope, 410, 466
Haggai, 74 n
Handel, 492 n
Hannibal, 195, 245, 248, 251 n, 259
Hanno (voyage of), 34
Hanseatic towns, 199
Harvey, 488, 505 n
Hasmonaeans, 93; see also Maccabees
Heath, 180 n
Hebraic Chris., 566–75
Hebraism, 576
Hebrew, Hebrews, Hebrew civilization (including Israel, Jews, Judaism), (i, name), 50 n; (ii, stock), 9, 31; (iii, gen. character of civilization), 2–3, 8, 512, 513–16; (iv, history), 19, 20, 26 n, 27, 28, 34–5, ch. III passim, 92–5; (post-exilic), 101, 192 n, 196, 203–4, 286, 322, 323, 324, 513–15; (v, religion), ch. III passim, 499–500, 512, 523; (and Babylonia), 27, 35, 69–70, 71–2, 73; (and Persia), 41; (and Greek philosophy), 60–1, 80–1, 91, 121 n, 169, 217 n, 220, 344 n, 363, 364 n, 381 n, 513, 515; (and Christianity), 76 n, 84, 86–92, 320–4, 330, 331, 353 n, 355, 358, 360–1, 365, 469, 500, 501, 501 n, 515–16; (and Islam), 417 n; (and mediaeval), 73–4, 76n, 92 n, 437, 477 n; (and Khazars), 416; (and Reformation), 492 n; (vi, Mosaic law), 26 n, 51, 69–92 passim (esp. 72–9, 94), 76 n, 320, 322, 331, 361, 365, 469; (vii, Mosaic law and Roman empire), 94–5, 270 n, 286, 330–1, 361; (viii, Hebraism and Hellenism), 44, 75, 80, 81, 93–5, 121 n, 153, 157, 174 n, 175 n, 203–4, 220–1, 224, 321 n, 323 n, 324 n; (ix, Jewish and mediaeval philosophy), 446 n, 446–7, 448, 453, 513–14
Hebrews, epistle to, 76 n
Hecataeus, 156
Hegel, 162 n, 170 n, 201n, 216, 274, 360 n, 369, 369 n, 382, 443, 458 n, 461, 464, 505, 544, 546 n, 548
Heine, 303
Helen, 132
Heliocentric theory, 203
Hellas, Hellenes, Hellenism (i, name), 3,

412 n; (ii, gen. character of civilization), 3–5, 8–9, 44–5, 131–3, 380–2, 512–13; (iii, history of Hellenism), chs IV, V, VI passim; (iv, and Hebraism), see Hebrew; (v, and Rome), 244, 249–57, 265, 270 n, 280, 289, 302, 311–12; (vi, and Christianity), ch. IX passim, 429–32; (vii, under Eastern emperors), 412–36 passim; (viii, and modern education and life), 496, 516–19
Hellenistic civilization, ch. VI passim (esp. 201–6); (name), 201 n; (metaphysics), 458–9
Helots, 186
Helvetii, 274 n
Henry II, of England, 541
Henry of Portugal, 486
Henry VIII, of England, 489 n, 494
Heraclea, 198
Heraclitus, 123, 126, 128
Heraclius, 388, 412 n, 415, 417, 433
Hermes, mutilation of, 115
Herod Agrippa I, 93
Herod the Great, 93
Herodotus (general), 11, 134, 157–8, 160 n, 162 n; (special references), 7 n, 20 n, 24 n, 36 n, 39 n, 41, 67 n, 102 n, 105 n, 113 n, 118 n, 135 n, 138 n
Herophilus, 203
Herrenvolk (policy), 136
Hesed (Heb.), 62
Hesiod, 115, 115 n, 118, 129, 255 n, 498, 499 n
Heth, sons of, 32 n; see also Hittites
Hexameter metre, 111 n, 254–5
Hexapla (of Origen), 363
Hezekiah, 63, 64 n
Hiero, 139 n
Hieroglyphic scripts, (Egypt), 16, 17; (Hittite), 32; (Minoan), 38
Hieros (Gr.), 102 n
Himera, battle of the, 138
Hincmar, 451
Hippias, 162, 163 n
Hippocratian, 132 n
Hippodamus, 160 n
Hiram, 33
Hissarlik, 36
History (conception and treatment of), (name), 10, 157 n, 525 n; (Jewish and Hellenic), 89 n, 156–7; (Greek), 157–8, 311–12; (Roman), 159 n, 254, 255, 305–6, 311–12; (conception of), 11, 490, 490 n, 499 n, 525–7; (and individuality) 506; (as theodicy), 365, 379, 379 n, 380–2, 525–7; (and philosophy), 498–9, 506 n, 525 n
Hitler, 560, 562, 563
Hittites, 19, 32–3, 38, 97 n

Hobbes, 438, 481, 489, 494 *n*, 521, 557
Hogarth, 557
Holiness, holy, 64, 64 *n*, 72; (*Levitical*), 74; (*book of holiness*), 52 *n*
Homer, Homeric poems, 36, 110–15, 128–9, 132, 135 *n*, 193, 194, 203, 493 *n*, 524; (*Homeric culture*), 36, 98, 102 *n*, 111–13, 116, 128–9, 183, 185; *see also* Iliad, Odyssey
Homo-ousios (*Gr.*), 348 *n*, 368
Honorius, 298 *n*, 396, 404
Horace, 255, 257, 279, 281 *n*, 305
Hortensian law, 235, 244, 257
Hosea, 3, 57 *n*, 58 *n*, 59–65, 224
Hosius, 294
Hubris (*Gr.*), 117–9, 122, 144, 158, 249, 520
Humanism (*Renaissance*), 481–96; (*Hellenic*), 517–9; (*idol of*), 566–75 (*modern*), 554–77
Hume, 460, 460 *n*
Huns, 399, 400–1, 404, 414, 416, 421 *n*
Huxley, T. H., 162, 507–8
Hyksos, the, 19
Hylê, 210
Hypocritês, (*Gr.*), 149
Hypostases (*Gr.*), 349–51, 354, 364, 368 427

Iambic metre, 150 *n*, 156 *n*
Iconoclastic controversy, 409, 420, 429, 433
Idealist metaphysic, 464
Ideas, (Platonic theory of), *see* Form, Forms
Ignatius, 325 *n*, 356, 357 *n*, 360 *n*
Ikhnaton, *see* Amenhotep IV
Iliad, 36, 110–13, 183 *n*, 194, 309 *n*, 513
Illyricum, 392; (*Illyrian emperors*), 392–3, 396
Immanence, 55
Immortality, belief in, (*Egypt*), 22, (*Hebrews*), 61, 80, 84–8, 323; (*Greek*), 84 *n*, 129–30, 129 *n*, 130 *n*, 176, 212–13; 222, 348, 365 *n*; (*Virgil*), 314; (*Mithraism*), 340; (*Christianity*), 84 *n*, 314, 321, 323, 323 *n*, 365; (*mediaeval*), 447, 454, 457, 458–9, 504; (*modern*), 458, 509 *n*, 509; *see also* Resurrection
Imperator, (*Lat.*), 273, 277
Imperium (*Lat.*), 230, 232–4, 242–3, 258, 258 *n*, 259 *n*, 261, 264 *n*, 267–8, 270, 273, 277–8, 282
In jure cessio (*Lat.*), 239 *n*
Ina of Wessex, 432
Incarnation, doctrine of the, 355, 364, 364 *n*, 367, 372, 378, 379 *n*, 381 *n*, 427, 459, 534, 535

India, Indian civilization, 8, 12, 13, 24, 206, 224 *n*, 339, 428, 486, 486 *n*, 499 *n*, 502 *n*, 536; *see also under* Britain (analogies with Rome) *and* Religion
Individuality (including *particularism; individualistic theory*), (i, *Jewish particularism*), 50, 60, 68 *n*, 69, 69–92 *passim*, 323; (ii, *and in Greek life and thought*), 3, 106, 118, 120–2, 151, 157, 188, 217, 220, 221, 312, 313, 343, 348, 352–3; (iii, *Roman contrast*), 226–8, 241–3; (iv, *growth at Rome*), 265, 266; (v, *Christianity*), 352–5, 358–9, 375; (vi, *mediaeval*), 440, 448, 475, 476, 476 *n*, 481, 488, 489; (vii, *in modern life and thought*), 476 *n*, 481, 488–9, 506, 508–10
Indo-European races, *see* Aryan
Indo-Iranian races, 8, 39, 40, 339; *see also* Aryan
Indus, 8, 192, 193, 194
Infanticide, 24 *n*, 185 *n*, 328 *n*, 423 *n*
Inheritance (*Roman law*), *see* Testamentary succession
Innocent III, pope, 454
Innocent IV, pope, 476 *n*
Institutes (of Justinian), 229 *n*, 403 *n*, 425; *see also* Justinian, law
Intercessio (*Lat.*), 235
Internationalism (including *international law*), 264 *n*, 265 *n*, 303 *n*, 476, 482; *see also* Law
Interrex (*Lat.*), 232
Ionia, Ionians, 97, 109, 111, 115, 120–8; (*philosophers*), 132, 156, 158 *n*, 224; (*Ionic dialect*), 111 *n*; (*Ionian league*), 97; (*Ionic style*), 145, 205
Ipsus, battle of, 194
Irân, 7, 8, 24, 39, 197, 339
Ireland, Irish culture, 297, 298, 441 *n*, 442 *n*, 451 *n*
Irenaeus, 328, 336, 358 *n*, 383 *n*
Irene, 411
Irnenius, 467
Irony (of Socrates), 167, 167 *n*
Isaeus, 185 *n*
Isaiah, 3, 57 *n*, 60 *n*, 61, 63, 63–6, 66 *n*, 70, 81, 91-*n*, 157, 512
Isaiah, 'second', 82, 82 *n*, 82–4, 86 *n*, 224, 320
Isaurian, Leo the, 433
Isidore of Pelusium, 428
Isidore of Seville, 294
Isidore of Utiletus, 430
Isodore, pseudo-, 466
Isis, 22, 312, 330, 337 *n*
Islam (*name*), 417 *n*; *see* Mohammedanism
Isocrates, 161 *n*, 191

Isonomia (*Gr.*), 135
Israel (*name*), 50 *n; see* Hebrews
Issus, battle of, 139, 191
Italian allies (of Rome), 247, 266, 269, 269 *n; see also* Italy
Italy (*Greek*), 108, 124, 124 *n*, 157, 243, 244, 246–8; (*Roman and mediaeval*), ch. VII–XI, *passim;* (*Roman government*), 259–61, 271, 279–80, 291–2, 391, 392; (*epoch of barbarian invasions*), 396–412; *see also* Renaissance; (additional), 138, 283, 284 ,560, 561, 567

Jacob-el, Jacob-her, 19 *n*
James, Henry, 188 *n*
James, William, 460
Jansenists, 492 *n*
Japan, 12
Jason, 191 *n*
Javan (= *Ionia*), 97
Jehovah (*name*), 51 *n*
Jehovistic narrative, 30 *n*, 51 *n*, 52 *n*
Jehu, 57
Jeremiah, 39 *n*, 60, 67 *n*, 67–9, 81, 534
Jeroboam I, 56 *n*
Jeroboam II, 57, 58 *n*
Jerome, St, 310, 311, 441 *n*
Jerusalem, 28, 63, 66 *n*, 67, 69, 71, 74, 83–4, 93, 191, 192 *n*, 224, 286, 322, 329 *n*, 524
Jews (*name*), 50 *n*
Jezreel, 21 *n*
Joachim (of Flora), 365 *n*
Job, 79, 86
John, St, 378
John of Salisbury, 443, 446 *n*, 477, 477 *n*, 478 *n*
John the Scot, 442 *n*, 443, 444, 451 *n*, 451, 456
Johnson, Dr, 165
Jonah, 83 *n*
Jonson, Ben, 307
Josephus, 295
Josiah, 20, 66, 68 *n*
Judaea, *see* Hebrew
Judah, kingdom of, 27, 35, 52 *n*, 63–6, 69
Judaism, *see* Hebrew
Judas Iscariot, 275
Judas Maccabaeus, 93
Judex, judices (*Lat.*), 239, 262, 263, 268, 300, 301, 423
Julia Domna, 337
Julian, emperor, 371 *n*, 372, 396
Julius Caesar, *see* Caesar
Julius II, pope, 495
Jurisprudence, science of (Roman), 263–5, 298–9, 300–2, 389, 422–6, 466–71; *see also* Law

Jurists (Roman), 221, 241 *n*, 263 *n*, 284, 300, 301 *n*, 303 *n*, 423, 425, 470–1, 475 *n*
Jus, jura (*Lat.*) *see under* Law, II
Justinian, 181, 229, 237, 292 *n*, 301, 303 *n*, 352, 389, 394 *n*, 399, 403, 403 *n*, 413, 421–6, 426 *n*, 427, 431 *n*, 436, 442–3, 465–7, 479 *n*
Justitia (*Lat.*) (mediaeval meaning), 471 *n*
Juvenal, 310

Kadesh, 34
Kant, 160, 216, 219, 456 *n*, 458, 461, 503 *n*, 505, 510, 526 *n*, 542, 546 *n*, 552, 558, 563, 565, 572
Karnak, temple of, 19
Keftiu, 19, 20 *n*
Kempis, Thomas à, 549
Khammurabi, 25, 26, 40
Khazars, 416
Kheta, Khatti, 32 *n; see* Hittites
Khyber pass, 39, 192
Kierkegaard, 535
Kingdom of God, 9, 72, 76, 81–8, 91–2, 320–1, 329, 357, 358, 359, 379 *n*, 411 *n*, 501, 524, 568
Kings (*Roman*), 226, 227, 232–3
Knowledge, its abuse, 556–65 *passim*
Kugler, Father, 30 *n*
Kunstgeschichte, 546 *n*

Labes, 301 *n*
Labyrinth, 36 *n*
Lacedaemon, *see* Sparta
Lactantius, 406
Lampridius, 396
Language (*Egypt*), 17; (*Hittite*), 32; (*Cretan*), 37–8; (*Greek*), 111 *n*; (*Latin*), 293 *n*, 412, 426; (*Byzantine Greek*), 426, 431; (*Latin and mediaeval*), 307, 308, 310–11, 405, 406 *n*, 441, 465; (*Renaissance and ancient language*), 484–5, 488–9, 493–6; (*Greek theories on origin of language*), 164; (*classical language in modern education*), 517–18
Langue d'Oc, 295, 406 *n*
Langue d'Oïl, 295, 406 *n*
Laocoon, the, 206
Lares (and Penates), 229
Latins, Latium, 100, 225–6, 234, 244; (*Latin league*), 225–6, 244, 247, 248 *n*; (*Latin rights*), 237 *n*, 247, 248 *n*, 258, 284, 289, 292 *n*
Laurion, 186
Law: –
  I. (*Babylonian*), 25–6; (*Mosaic*), *see under* Hebrew; (*Greek*), 135, 140,

141, 180, 181, 186, 198; (*Roman*),
6, 10, 228–31, 236–41, 261–5, 273 n,
283–4, **298–303**, 422–6, 521–3;
(*R. and Hellenism*), 237 n, 301; (*R.
and Christianity*), 374 n, 384; (*R.
and mediaeval*), 405, 440, 464–81,
(*Christian*) see Canon law, Episcopal jurisdiction; (*Germani c peoples*)
76 n 397 n, 405, 465–6, 467;
(*courts*), 558

II. *jus*, 230 n, 423, 465, 471; (*and fas*),
238; (*and lex*), 423, 465, 471 n, 472;
jus civile (civil law of Rome), 237,
264, 299, 383, 408 n, 425 n, 448,
457, 466, 467, 468, 470–1, 472 n;
jus gentium (law of nations), 263–4,
299, 301, 302 n, 425 n, 468–9, 470,
471, 472, 479; *jus honorarium*
(praetorian), 264, 425 n; *jus inter
gentes*, 303 n; *see also* International
law; *jus naturae* (*lex naturalis, law of
nature*), 221, 302, 303 n, 344 n, 365,
383, 423, 439, 469–73, 480–1; *jus
positivum*, 472; *jus privatum*, 237 n,
238; *jus publicum*, 230 n, 237 n, 238;
lex divina (*aeterna*), 386, 471–2,
472 n, 473; *lex humana*, 472 n, 472,
473; *lex regia*, 479 n; *lex talionis*,
26, 238, 239

III. *See also* Canon law, Codex,
Corpus juris civilis, Criminal law,
Digest, Episcopal jurisdiction,
Hebrew (mosaic) law, Institutes,
Jurisprudence, Jurists, Justinian,
Novels; and for particular laws of
Rome, the name of the author,
e.g. Aebutian law

Laws (Plato), 187 n
Layard, Sir Henry, 28
League of Nations, 559
Learning (revival of), 481–97 (*esp.* 483–5,
492–7)
Legacy of Greece, 180 n
Legati (*Lat.*), 93, 270, 278
Legion, 245, 251
Leibnitz, 505, 558
Lenin, 567, 570
Leningrad, 101
Leo I, pope, 327 n, 428
Leo III, pope, 408, 410
Leo III the Isaurian, 413 n, 419, 425, 429
Leo XIII, pope, 444 n
Leon, 290
Leucippus, 121 n, 125
Leuctra, battle of, 189
Leviathan, New, 480 n
Lewis, C. S., 110 n, 486 n, 534 n
Lex, leges (*Lat.*), *see under* Law, II. and
III

Liber de Feudis, 426
Liberalism, 568
Liberius, pope, 327 n
Licinio-Sextian laws, 236, 241
Limes (*Lat.*), 286, 291 n, 296 n
Linacre, 494
Lincoln, 297
Literary patronage, 202, 305
Literature (*Egypt*), 22; (*Babylon*), 25, 29;
(*Hebrew*), ch. III *passim*; (*Greek*), 4, 105,
110–19, 147–59, 201–4, 311, 312;
(*Latin*), 112, 254–6, 303–313, 388, 521;
(*Byzantine*), 430–2; (*Renaissance*), 485,
492
Livy, 305, 330n
Locke, John, 215, 481, 494 n, 504 n
Logical Positivists, 460
Logos (*Gr.*), 213, 343 n, 349, 364 n;
(*Christian doctrine*), 343 n, 355, 364 n,
366–7
Lombards, 371, 371 n, 398 n, 403, 403 n,
408–9
London, 297, 298, 340, 494, 502 n, 511 n
Lorenzo de Medici, 491
Lucan, 272 n, 293, 308
Lucian, 223, 339, 339 n, 495
Lucilius, 255, 256 n
Lucretius, 222 n, 303, 499 n
Lugudunum (Lyon), 290, 294, 332, 383
Luther, Lutheranism, 76 n, 310, 489
489 n, 492 n, 495, 496, 515 n
Lybia, Lybians, 19, 28
Lyceum (School of the), 181, 217
Lycurgus, 36 n
Lydia, Lydians, 20, 32, 39
Lyric poetry, (*Greek*), 114–15, 149–50,
155; (*Roman*), 303
Lysicrates (monument of), 205
Lysimachus, 194
Lysippus, 205

Macaulay, 254, 276 n, 521
Maccabees, 81, 93
Macedonia, 43, 80–8, 100, ch. VI, *passim*,
249–51, 433
Machiavelli, 474, 489
Magi, 41
Magistri militum (*Lat.*), 392
Magnesia, battle of, 250
Magyars, 415
Mahomet, 51, 417, 418, 447
Mahomet II (Sultan), 435
Maimonides, (*Moses ben Maimon*), 453
453 n, 513
Majestas (*Lat.*), 284 n
Manah (*Babyl.* = *Gk. mnâ*), 31
Mandates (Roman imperial), 300

Manes, Manichaeism, 341, 358 *n*, 377, 385 *n*

Manetho, 18 *n*, 204

Manilian law, 270

Manumission, (*Roman law*), 299, 328 *n*, 395 *n*, 423 *n*

Manus (*Roman law*), 229 *n*, 231

Marathon, battle of, 137, 138, 154, 158 *n*

Marcion, 358 *n*

Marcomanni, 291

Marcus Aurelius, 291, 332, 333, **342**, 388, 391

Marduk, 25

Maritain, 569

Marius, 268–9

Marlborough, Duke of, 276 *n*

Marriage (*Greece*), 184–5; (*Roman law*), 229–32, 239, 240, 423; (*Christianity*), 328 *n*, 423

Marsilius (of Padua), 479, 479 *n*

Martial, 293

Martin, St, of Tours, 385, 385 *n*

Marx, Karl, 514, 567, 570

Massilia (Marseilles), 198, 290, 294

Mathematics (*Egypt*), 22; (*Greek*), 124, 132, 162, 166, 173, 174, 180, 203, 208, 487, 491; (*mediaeval*), 450 *n*; (*and modern science*), 491, 505–6, 566

Matilda of Tuscany, 467

Matter, theory of, 122–7, 172–5, 209–10, 211, 219, 329 *n*, 346, 353, 361 *n*, 487

Mausoleum, the, 205

Maxwell, Clerk, 558

Mayor of the palace, 410, 410 *n*, 419

Mâya, 12

Mecca, 412, 417

Media, Medes, 8, 28, 40

Mediaeval civilization, etc., *see* Middle Ages

Medici, the, 205, 491, 492

Medicine, 22, 123, 124 *n*, 125 *n*, 311

Mediterranean and Oceanic epochs, 6–8, 96, 264 *n*, 486

Megiddo, 20

Mehemet Ali, 16

Mekran, the, 192

Mela, 293

Melanchthon, 492 *n*

Melkarth, 33

Melos, *Melian dialogue*, 118 *n*, 144, 159 *n*, 163 *n*; (*Venus of*), 206

Memphis, 18, 37

Menander, 183, 202

Mendelssohn, 514 *n*

Menes, 17

Merchant of Venice, 486 *n*

Mercier, Cardinal, 445 *n*

Meredith, George, 256

Merovingians, 398, 410, 410 *n*, 419

Messiah, Messianic prophecy, 72, 81, 87, 87 *n*, 313, 321–3, 357

Metaphysics (*name*), 208, 208 *n*; *see* Philosophy

Metres (*Greek*), 111, 111 *n*, 150 *n*, 156 *n* (*Latin*), 111 *n*, 254 *n*

Micah, 57 *n*, 63, 64 *n*, 83 *n*, 91 *n*

Michael I, 411 *n*

Michelet, 484, 487

Middle Ages, mediaeval civilization, ch. XI *passim;* also (i, *demarcation from ancient and modern history*) 385–7, 405, 437, 441–2; (ii, *and Judaism*), 74, 76 *n*, 92 *n*, 93–5, 437; (iii, *and Roman empire*), 275, 314, and ch. X to 412 *passim, esp.* 407–12; (iv, *and Greek philosophy*), 175, 181, 182, 212, 214–16, 351–2, 443–62, 473–5; (v, *and Roman literature*), 66 *n*, 305–11, 313–14; *see also* Christianity, Education, Law, Philosophy, Universities; and in addition, 554, 557, 566, 575

Middlemarch, 540

Milan, 383

Miletus, 109, 120, 121, 156, 199 *n*

Mill, John Stuart, 560

Millennarianism, 86 *n*

Milner, Lord, 286

Milton, John, 148 *n*, 156 *n*, 202, 449, 478 *n*, 492 *n*, 511 *n*, 516, 524, 540, 545

Minoan civilization, 18, 33, 36–8, 96–8, 108 *n*, 129, 500; *see also* Crete

Mitanni, 19

Mithra, Mithraism, 40 *n*, 41 *n*, 197 *n*, 312, 323 *n*, 330, 334, 337–41, 391

Mithradates III, of Pontus, 270, 275, 340

Moab, 35

Modernism, 353 *n*, 526, 526–7 *n*

Modestinus, 301

Moeris, lake, 16

Moesia (*Roman province of*), 283, 391–2, 397, 415

Mohammedans, Mohammedanism (including *Islam*), 26, 50, 417–20, 433–4, 446–7, 504; *see also* Arabs, Mahomet, Saracens, Turks

Molière, 155

Moloch, 330

Mommsen, Theodor, 253 *n*, 258 *n*, 266 *n*, 269 *n*, 315–16

Monarchy, mediaeval theory of, 472–80

Monasteries, monasticism, 328 *n*, 385, 385 *n*, 402, 429, 439, 444 *n*

Mongols, 377 *n*, 400 *n*, 509

Monism, 463

Monolatry, 52, 83

Monophysite controversy, 427–8, 427 *n*, 428 *n*, 535

Monotheism (*Egypt*), 19; (*India*), 40;

(*Persia*), 41 *n;* (*Jewish and Christian*), 3, 30, 52, 61 *n*, 82–3, 88, 89, 323, 324 *n*, 357, 370, 386, 447, 515; (*Islam*), 417–18, 446–7

Monothelete controversy, 428, 428 *n*, 535

Montaigne, 255, 484, 496

Montanism, 326

Montesquieu, 226, 227, 245 *n*

Morant, Sir Robert, 286

More, Sir Thomas, 494–5

Moses, 34, 51, 54, 76 *n*, 447; (*law of*), *see under* Hebrew

Moslem (Muslim) (*name*), 417 *n; see* Mohammedan

Motion, theory of (*Greek*), 122, 125–6, 175–6, 210–12, 222; (*mediaeval*), 455; (*modern*), 487, 520

Mulvian bridge, battle of, 334

Munda, battle of, 272

Munich, 563

Municipia (*Lat.*) (*Roman rep.*), 247; (*Roman emp.*), 273 *n*, 279, 289, 293 *n*, 297

Mustapha Kemel, 532

Mussolini, 560, 567

Mycenae, Mycenaean culture, 19, 38

Mystery-cults (*Greek*), 127 *n*, 152 *n; see also* Dionysus; (*and Christianity*), 324 *n*, 355, 357 *n;* (*Oriental*), 337, 338 *n*

Nabis, 200 *n*

Nabopolassar, 28

Nahum, 28 *n*, 67 *n*, 81 *n*

Napoleon, 16, 103 *n*, 139, 276 *n*, 317 *n*, 412, 513, 540, 541, 543, 547, 551, 560

Narbo, Narbonese Gaul, *see* Gaul

Nation-state (*modern*), 386 *n*, 439, 478–9, 482, 489, 531–2 and *n*, 555

Nature (*state of*), 379 *n*, 383, 438; (*law of*), *see under* Law, II, 523, 529, 555, 561; (*Roman poetry of*), 255

Naucratis, 20, 108, 120 *n*

Nazareth, 320

Nazi (Germany), 386 *n*, 573

Nazoraeans (= Ebionites), 322

Nebuchadrezzar, 20, 28, 35, 67, 69

Necho, 20

Nemean games, 99

Nemesis (*Gr.*), 117 *n*, 117, 119, 144

Neo-Platonism, Neo-Platonists, 337, 343, 344, 344–55, 442 *n*, 444, 444 *n*, 445; (*and earlier philosophy*), 131, 173 *n*. 174, 214, 218; (*and Christianity*), 345, 347 *n*, 349–55, 369, 377, 504, 522 *n*, 526; (*and mediaeval*), 444, 450–6, 476, 491; *see also* Plato, Plotinus

Nephesh (*Heb.*), 515 *n*

Nereid shrine, the, 205

Nero, 282, 283, 306, 308, 324, 331

Nerva, 308, 315

Nestorius, Nestorians, 385 *n*, 427, 428

Newman, Cardinal, 304, 375, 444, 518 *n*

Newton, Sir Isaac, 386, 497, 504 *n*, 558

Nexum (*Roman law*), 240 *n*

Nibelungs (Saga of the), 399 (cf. 401)

Nicaea, council of, 294, 329 *n*, 369 *n*, 371, 371 *n*

Nicene creed, 369 *n*

Nicias, 186 *n*

Nicolas of Cues, 479, 479 *n*

Nicomedia, 247, 393

Nietzsche, Friedrich, 494 *n*, 499

Nile, 13, 15–16, 23, 192

Nîmes, 290

Nineveh, 26, 28

Nominalism, 444 *n*

Nomos (*Gr.*), 163, 469

Non-resistance (doctrine of), 327, 327 *n*

Northern invaders, 108 *n*

Normans, 234, 420, 434, 468

Nous (*Gr.*), 126, 127, 345, 350, 350 *n*

Novel (*Roman law*), 425; *Roman literature*, 308, 308 *n*

Novgorod, 416

Numa, 227

Numenius, 344 *n*

Numidia, 252, 274

Numinous, 552

Oakeshott, Michael, 567, 568

Oates, Titus, 504 *n*

Obligations (*Roman law*), 302, 552; *see* Contracts

Occupation (*Roman land-law*), 236

Ochus, *see* Artaxerxes III

Octavian, *see* Augustus Caesar

Odoacer, 401, 402, 407

Odyssey, 102 *n*, 110–12, 120, 183 *n*, 185

Officia (*Lat.*), 469

Oligarchy, 110 *n*

Olympian, 99, 100, 155, 189 *n*, 205; (*Olympian gods, cult of*), 3, 38 *n*, 100, 113, 119, 127 *n*, 128, 130 *n*, 152 *n*, 196; (*Olympic Games*), 99, 162

Omar Khayyam, 81 *n*

Omri, 35, 57

Ontological argument, 455

Opera, 492

Oratorio, 492 *n*, 516

Oratory, 159, 161, 255, 303–4, 308, 309 *n*; *see also* Rhetoric

Orchêstra (*Gr.*), 152

Origen, 358 *n*, 359 *n*, 362–6, 371, 374, 446

Ormuzd, *see* Ahuramazda

Orosius, 379, 404 *n*

Orphic brotherhoods, Orphism 129–31, 169, 170 *n*, 176, 499 *n*

Osiris, 21
Ostia, 225, 420 n
Ostrogoths, 311, 371, 393, 398 n, 402;
  see also Germans, Goths
Ottoman Turks, 435
Ousia (Gr.), 209, 350, 368
Ovid, 279, 306, 306 n
Oxford (English Dictionary), 566; (School
  of Law), 467; (Society of Historical
  Theology), 536 n; (university), 443,
  444 n

Pagan (paganus, Lat., paganikos, Gr.),
  385–6, 412 n
Paine, Tom, 163
Palaestra (Gr.), 102, 165
Palestine, 39 n, 50 n, 65, 92, 310, 361, 378,
  431 n; see also Canaan
Panaetius, 220 n
Pan-Athenaic festival, 147
Pandects (of Justinian), see Digest
Pannonia, 402, 403 n
Pantheism, 40, 219 n, 338 n, 350, 451
Papacy, 327, 383, 403, 407–12, 410 n,
  411 n, 468, 521–2; (conflict with em-
  pire), 410–11, 441, 468, 477 n
Papal States, 383, 410
Papia-Poppaean law, 423 n
Papyrus, papyri, 23, 65 n, 203
Parabasis (Gr.), 155
Paris university, 443, 444 n, 445, 454
Parliament, 540, 558
Parmenides, 124, 156, 166 n, 173 n
Parousia (Gr.), 323, 536
Parrhêsia (Gr.), 103 n
Parthenon, the, 147, 446, 512
Parthia, Parthians, 40, 94, 197, 252, 275,
  281, 290, 391, 417
Paterfamilias (Lat.), 229–30
Paternal government, 292, 313, 316, 502
Patria potestas (Roman law), 229–30,
  284, 299, 425
Patricians, 235–6, 251, 259, 259 n; (title
  patrician), 410
Patrimonium Caesaris (Lat.), 288
Patrimony (of St Peter), 409
Patronage of literature, 202
Paul (the jurist), 301, 423
Paul, St, 9, 115, 280, 328, 332, 349 n,
  352 n, 512, 525, 549, 561; (mission to
  Gentiles), 44, 94, 294, 321, 322, 324–5,
  324 n, 327–8; (and Judaism), 90, 322 n,
  324, 361; (and Roman empire and law),
  283, 327, 331, 357 n; (and Christian
  theology), 342 n, 357 n, 358 n, 360 n,
  378, 381 n; (and Stoicism), 221, 307;
  (epistles), 324 n, 564

Paul of Samosata, 367 n
Pavia, 403; (school), 403 n, 466
Pax Romana (Lat.), 6, 523
Peculium (Lat.), 231
Peithô (Gr.), 118
Pekin, 547
Pelagius, Pelageanism, 378–80
Pelasgians, 96
Peloponnesian war, 143–5, 154, 157
Penestae (Gr.), 186
Pentateuch, 51 n, 52 n, 54, 55, 74, 76 n
Pepin, 410
Pergamos, 198, 204, 205, 250
Peri, Jacopo, 492
Pericles, Periclean age, 99, 134, 140–3,
  145–8, 154, 157, 158 n, 159, 182–3, 205,
  224, 265, 512
Perpetua and Felicitas, Saints, 333 n
Persecutions (of Christianity), 331–7; (of
  Jews), 513
Persia, Persians, 7, 8, 29, 39–43, 86, 118,
  137–40, 143, 144, 156, 158, 377 n, 391,
  396, 417, 418, 419 n, 428
Persona ficta (Lat.), 476 n
Personality (divine), 40, 52, 54, 56, 61–2,
  355, 367, 370 n, 427; (human), 4, 70, 77,
  163, 164, 188, 348 n, 353, 358, 370,
  374 n, 440, 447, 455, 456, 458, 477, 480,
  508, 509, 512, 520; see also Individu-
  ality; (corporate), 476 n, 481 n; (private
  and public), 477
Pervigilium Veneris, 310
Peter the Great, of Russia, 190
Peter, St, 324, 328, 405
Petronius Arbiter, 308
Phaleas, 164 n
Phaestus, 37
Phalanx, 190, 192, 245
Pharisees, 78, 321
Pharaoh (name), 18 n
Pharsalia, battle of, 272
Phidias, 134, 145, 147, 155, 524
Philanthropy (Roman imperial), 284, 285,
  288, 289, 307, 315, 395 n; (modern),
  502 n
Philia (Gr.), 188
Philip of Macedon, 43, 189–90, 191, 275
Philippi, 324
Philippians, 564
Philistia, Philistines, 34, 54, 63, 67 n
Philo, 89 n, 174 n, 351 n, 363, 364 n, 442 n,
  513
Philosophy (i, Greek), 4, 101, 105, 105 n,
  380–81; (pre-Socratic), 118–28; (Soph-
  ists and Socrates), 158–70; (Plato),
  170–82; (Aristotle), 206–17; (Stoic and
  Epicurean), 217–23; (Neo-Platonism),
  343–55; (and Greek religion), 126–31;
  (and Judaism), 60, 84 n, 88, 89; (at

Rome), 257, 337–9, 341–5; (*and Christianity*), 336–55; (*Byzantine*), 431–2, 450–1; (ii, *mediaeval*), 439, 443, 444, 463–4, 476, 504–5; (iii, *modern*), 483, 487–90, 494 n, 503–7; (iv, *progress in*), 503–7; (v, *and history*), see under History; (*of religion*), 552–3

Phoenicia, Phoenician, 19, 31, 33–4, 100 n, 199, 293

Phronêsis (*Gr.*), 116 n, 213

Phrygia, Phrygians, 32, 39, 326

Phthonos (*Gr.*), 119 n

Physis (*Gr.*), 122, 122 n, 125, 126, 163 (cf. 187), 219, 469

Piers Plowman, 115

Pietas (*Lat.*), 229, 305

Pilate, Pontius, 93, 288 n, 331

Pindar, 114, 116, 130 n, 139 n, 193

Piraeus, 135, 139, 145

Pisistratus, 109, 135, 224

Place-names (*Britain*), 298

Plataea, battle of, 138

Plato, 170–82; also (*earlier thinkers*), 119, 120, 121, 123, 124, 124 n, 125 n, 126 n, 160–3, 164–7; (*Aristotle*), 206–17; (*Stoics*), 217–21; (*Plutarch*), 338; (*Neo-Platonism*), 344–55; (*Christianity*), 356 n, 363–6; (*mediaeval*), 349, 350, 351, 431, 441, 446, 450, 452–5, 474; (*Renaissance*), 491; (*on ethics and politics*), 103 n, 104 n, 105–6, 107, 116 n, 137, 164, 191, 207; (*on women*), 155, 184–5; (*on slavery*), 187; (*on art*), 146–7, 148 n, 149 n, 151; (*on poets as religious teachers*), 112 n, 113 n, 116 n, 128, 130, 131; (*other references*), 130, 131, 134, 137 n, 139 n, 159, 203, 206, 207, 208, 217, 344, 345, 365, 365 n, 368 n, 369, 375, 377, 378 n, 380, 426, 469, 499 n, 504, 507, 512, 513; (*additional*), 147 n, 373, 461, 551, 556, 563, 564, 565, 574

Plantagenets, 558

Plautus, 155

Plebeians, 234, 235, 251, 259 n

Plebiscites, 560

Pliny (the younger), 247 n, 288 n, 332

Plotinus, 173 n, 338, 345–55, 363, 364 n, 377, 380, 389, 445, 453, 455, 491, 508 n, 526

Plutarch, 220 n, 297, 311–12, 338, 496, 513

Poictiers, battle of, 409, 419, 419 n

Poland, 548

Poles, 573

Polis (*Gr.*), see City-state

Political theory (*Greek*), 101, 105–6, 127, 160–5, 169, 172, 178–9, 180, 207, 213–15, 221; (*Rome*), 232–3, 242–3, 275–6;

(*mediaeval*), 407, 439–40, 468–82; (*modern*), 482–3, 489, 492 n

Polybius (*general*), 100 n, 204, 256 n; (*special references*), 106 n, 137 n, 195, 227 n, 242 n, 245 n, 249 n, 250 n, 253 n, 256 n, 257 n, 258 n

Polycarp, 333

Polygnotus, 145

Pompey, 93, 270–2, 274–5

Pope, Alexander, 444

Porphyry, 345 n, 348 n, 353 n, 363 n, 441

Portrait-painting (*Greek*), 205

Portugal, S., 284

Posidonius, 220 n

Postal service (*Persian*), 42; (*Roman empire*), 284

Potestas (*Lat.*), 229–31

Pothinus, 333

Praetor, praetorship, 234 n, 258 n, 260–4, 299, 300; see also Edicts, Equity Formula

Praxiteles, 205

Prayer-book, English, 117 n

Presbyter, 325

Pre-existence, 130, 130 n, 176, 365

Prefects (*Roman*), 247, 278, 287, 287 n, 301 n, 392, 408, 421

Priestly code, 52 n, 74, 76 n, 77; (*history*), 52 n, 74

Primogeniture, 240 n

Princeps (*Lat.*), 242 n, 277 n, 299

Printing, invention of, 488, 493

Proclus, 347 n, 352 n, 454 n, 491

Proculian law school, 301 n

Proconsul, proconsular *imperium*, 258 n, 278, 278 n

Procopius, 431 n

Procurator, 93, 287

Prodicus, 162 n

Progress of civilization, 498–510

Prophecy, prophets (*in Israel*), 3, ch. III, *passim*; 121 n, 153, 157, 220, 224, 320–1, 323, 365 n, 469, 516; see also under Hebrew

Protagoras, 160, 160 n, 161, 161 n, 162 n, 162, 166 n, 172, 537

Protogenes, 206

Provence, Provençal, 251, 295–6, 406, 466, 467

Providence, belief in, 82, 88, 144, 158 n, 211, 219, 305, 340, 353, 379, 447, 483, 492; also (*in religion of Israel*), ch. III, *passim*

Provinces (*of Roman empire*), 248, 251, 258 n, 259–61, 270 n, 273, 277–81, 287–9, 288 n, 289 n, 290, 391; also ch. VIII, *passim*

Provincia (*Lat.*), 235, 259 n

Provocatio (Lat.), 227, 239 *n*
Psalms, Psalmists, Psalter, 68 *n*, 68, 77–8, 87 *n*, 224, 469, 515
Psellus, Michael, 431, 454 *n*
Psychology, *see* Soul
Ptôchos (Gr.), 326 *n*
Ptolemaic theory, 486
Ptolemy, the Ptolemies, 92, 194–7, 203–6, 513
Publicani (Lat.), 260 *n*
Publilian law, 235
Pulcheria, 428
Punic wars, 245, 248, 292
Punjâb, 12 *n*, 39, 43, 192, 197, 206, 251
Punt, 18
Puritanism, Puritans (*and Judaism*), 3, 76 *n*, 489; (*in New England*), 76 *n*, 418 *n*, 489 *n*, 492 *nn*
Pyramids, 18
Pyrrhus, 195 *n*, 245, 248, 258
Pythagoras, Pythagoreanism, 124 *n*, 124–6, 125 *n*, 130–1, 166
Pytheas, 203
Pythian games, 99

Qoheleth (Heb.), *see* Ecclesiastes
Quadi, 291
Quadrivium, 450 *n*
Quaestiones perpetuae, 239 *n*, 300
Quaestor, quaestorship, 243 *n*, 260
Quintilian, 159 *n*, 255 *n*, 293, 303 *n*, 307 *n*, 308–9, 309 *n*
Quirinal, 225 *n*
Quirites (Lat.), 225 *n*
Quixote, Don, 483

Rabbis, Rabbinical teaching, 70, 75, 321 *n*
Rabelais, 483
Racine, 156 *n*, 492 *n*, 516
Radakrishnan, 13 *n*
Raphael, 207 *n*
Rationalism, age of, 460
Ravenna, 401, 407, 410, 426, 467
Realism (*in mediaeval philosophy*), 444 *n*
Reason, 459, 460 *n*
Recollection (*Plato's theory of*), *see* Anamnêsis
Reformation, the (*including Protestantism*), 75 *n*, 76 *n*, 365 *n*, 376, 386 *n*, 407 *n*, 412, 482, 491, 493, 495, 496, 515, 521
Re-incarnation, 129, 130, 176
Religio licita (Lat.), 330
Religion: –
    I. (i, *Greek*), 3–4, 22, 38 *n*, 84 *n*, 104, 112, 115–9, 126–31, 152–4, 155 *n*, 206, 337–9, 344, 351–5; (ii, *Roman*), 5, 227, 256, 381; (*under empire*), 280–1, 312, 329–30, 333–41, and ch. IX, *passim*; (*and Oriental cults*), 286, 312, 337, 338; (iii, *Minoan*), 38 *n*; (iv, *Egypt*), 21–3, 44, 330, 337; (v, *Babylon and Assyria*), 25, 27, 29, 44, 69, 70, 340; (vi, *Persia*), 40–1, 44, 86, 339–40; (vii, *India*), 12–13, 40, 339, 377 *n*; *see also* Christianity, Hebrew, Mithraism, Mohammedanism, Monotheism, also 570–2
    II. (*religion and morality*), 378–9 504 *n*; (*and mediaeval philosophy*), 444–64; (*and philosophy generally*), 526–7; *see also* Persecution, Toleration. (*Additional*), 570–3
Rembrandt, 513, 542, 573
Renaissance, the, 109, 154 *n*, 205, 304, 306, 307, 442, 443, 481–96, 505, 554
Renan, Ernest, 286, 344, 453, 453 *n*
Rescripts (*Roman imperial*), 284, 300, 301
Responsa prudentium (Roman law), 263 *n*, 301, 423
Resurrection (*belief in*), 80, 84–6, 87, 321, 323 *n*, 340, 353, 358, 360, 365 *n*; *see also* Immortality
Revelation, 459, 459 *n*, 460
Rheims, 295
Rhetoric, 159, 161, 204, 304, 308, 309 *n*
Rhind papyrus, 22 *n*
Rhine frontier (*of Roman empire*), 271, 274, 281, 291, 292, 296 *n*, 388, 391, 394
Rhodes, 198, 202, 204, 250
Ricimer, 396
Richelieu, 546 *n*
Ritschl, Albrecht, 526, 526 *n*
Roads (*Persian*), 42; (*Graeco-Macedonian*), 197 *n*; (*Roman*), 6, 246, 246 *n*, 289, 293; (*in Britain*), 297, 298, 383 *n*; *see also* Via for special roads
Romaioi, 412
Roman church, ch. IX, 325–6, and *passim*, 374, 521–3, 558; *see also* Papacy
Romance languages, 295, 307 *n*, 406, 439, 465
Romanos, 431 *n*
Romans, epistle to the, 322 *n*, 324 *n*, 361
Romanticism, 517 *n*
Rome, ch. VII–X, *passim*; (*general character of civilization*), 5–9, 226–9, 304, 305, 306, 314–17, 380–1, 389–90, 512, 520–4; (*function in history*), 6, 237, 244, 252, 390, 547; (*mediaeval view of*), 275, 314, 406, 441; *see also under* Britain, Christianity, Church, Hebrew, Hel-

lenism, Jurisprudence, Language, Law Literature, Middle Ages, Religion

Romulus, 227

Romulus Augustulus, 401, 411 *n*

Rosetta stone, 16

Ross, Dr, 541

Rossetti, D. G., 28 *n*, 114

Rothanis, 403 *n*

Roumanians, 406, 435

Rousseau, 163, 476 *n*, 507, 542

Rubicon, the, 272

Rufinus, 396

Rule of faith (Christian), 329 *n*, 336, 360

Rûm (kingdom of), 434

Ruskin (John), 162

Russell (Lord), 506 *n*, 510 *n*, 555, 566

Russia, Russians, 101, 190, 414 *n*, 414–15, 432, 435, 514 *n*, 515 *n*, 536, 561

Sabellius, Sabellianism, 365 *n*, 367, 368 *n*

Sabines, 225 *n*

Sabinian law school, 301 *n*

Sacerdotalism (*Jewish*), 76 *n*, 81 *n*, 321 *n*, (cf. 70–3); (*Christian*), 76 *n*, 325 *n*, 329,

Sacra (*Lat.*), 229, 233 *n*

Sacramentum (*Lat.*), 266 *n*, 340 *n*

Sadducees, 321 *n*

St Albans, 297

Sais, 20

Salamanca university, 444 *n*, 492

Salamis, battle of, 138

Salerno university, 444 *n*

Salic law, 397 *n*

Salvius Julianus, edict of, 299

Samaria, Samaritans, 35, 63, 67, 75

Samnites, 244, 245, 522 *n*

Samos, 140

Sanhedrin, 94

Sancta Sophia, church of, 421 *n*, 430

Sappho, 114

Saracens, 294, 389, 390, 399, 404, 409, 413, 418–19, 420, 429, 434, 501 *n*, 504

Saragossa, 293

Sarapis, 22

Sardica, council of, 327 *n*

Sardis, 31, 42 *n*, 138

Sargon of Akkad, 24

Sargon of Assyria, 27, 27 *n*, 35

Sassanid, 392

Satan, 41 *n*, 323

Satire (*Greek*), 114; (*Roman*, satura, *Lat.*), 254–5, 308 *n*, 310; (*modern*), 492 *n*

Satrap, satrapy, 42, 192

Saturnian metre, 254 *n*

Saul, 34, 56, 513

Sayce, Prof. A. H., 32 *n*

Scaevola, Q. C., 301

Scaevola, Q. M., 300

Scaliger, 493 *n*, 497

Scandinavians, 2, 8, 96, 401, 416, 440

Schliemann, Heinrich, 36, 113

Scholê (*Gr.*), 103 *n*

Science (*Egypt*), 22; (*Babylon*), 30; (*Greek*), 45 *n*, 120–31, 160–2, 172, 173, 180, 181, 192, 203, 203 *n*, 210 *n*, 211 *n*. 215–17, 222; (*mediaeval*), 306, 448 *n*, 449 *n*, 454; (*modern, rise of*), 462, 480, 485–6, 486–93, 497, 557, 558, 562, 563, 564; (*scope of term*), 490 *n*, 575; (*progress in*), 504–7; *see also* Astronomy, Biology, Mathematics, Medicine, Philosophy

Scipio Aemilianus, 256 *n;* (*circle of*) 204, 256 *n*

Scipio Africanus, 251 *n*

Scopas, 205

Scot, John the, 443, 450 *n*, 451, 451 *n*, 454 *n*

Scot, Michael, 448 *n*

Scott, Sir W., 545

Scribes, Jewish, 67, 70, 74

Scriptures, the, 75 *n*, 77, 112, 310, 320, 323, 363, 447, 466, 469, 472, 476, 488, 493, 515–16; *see also* Canon, Septuagint, Vulgate

Sculpture (*Egypt*), 19, 23; (*Assyrian*), 27; (*Minoan*), 37; (*Greek*), 125 *n*, 145–7, 204–6, 524; (*Roman*), 285; (*mediaeval*), 145, 296, 443

Scythians, 28 *n*, 39 *n*, 67 *n*, 197 *n*

Seba'oth (*Heb.*), 58

Seleucia, 197 *n*

Seleucids, the, 92, 93, 196–9, 195 *n*, 206, 250–1, 270 *n*, 275; *see also* Asia, Syria

Seleucus I, 194, 195 *n*

Seleucus (astronomer), 204

Seljuk Turks, 434

Semites, (*stock*), 8, 17–20, 25, 26–9, 31–5; (*and religion*), 44, 50, 220; *see also* Hebrew, Mohammedan

Senate, 232, 257–8, 267–73, 277, 282, 299–300, 410; (*at Constantinople*), 421

Senatus consulta (*Lat.*), 258 *n*, 299

Seneca, 219 *n*, 293, 293 *n*, 306–8, 307 *n*, 308 *n*, 344 *n*, 368 *n*

Sennacherib, 20 *n*, 27, 27 *n*, 63, 64 *n*, 65

Septuagint, 94, 203, 204 *n*, 363

Serbia, Serbs, 391, 415, 435

Sertocius, 293

Servant of Yahweh (songs of the), 82 *n*, 82, 83, 84, 320

Servetus, 493

Servius Tullius, 226

Severus, 283 *n*, 296, 301 *n*, 363

Severus Alexander, 301, 335 *n*, 396, 425 *n*

Sext, the, 468 *n*

Shakespeare, 105 *n*, 148, 256, 276, 307 *n*

312, 370 *n*, 484, 492–3, 496, 511 *n*, 517 *n*

Shalmaneser IV, 27, 27 *n*

Shelley, 4, 132 *n*, 149 *n*, 151–2, 156 *n*, 167 *n*, 202, 351 *n*, 460, 508 *n*

Sheol (*Heb.*), 61, 84 *n*, 85, 85 *n*

Sheshonk I (*Shishak*), 20 *n*

Shiloh, 67

Sicily (*Phoenicians*), 33; (*Minoans*), 36; (*Greek*), 108, 124 *n*, 138, 149, 155, 202; (*Athenian expedition to*), 115 *n*, 118 *n*, 144, 155, 159, 170; (*Roman province*), 248, 251, 259 *n*, 273 *n;* (*epoch of Decline and Fall*), 403, 420, 421, 434; *see also* Syracuse

Sidon, 33

Siger of Brabant, 456 *n*

Silchester, 297, 298 *n*

Simeon, Song of, 84

Simonides, 110, 114

Sinai, 18, 34

Sirmium, 393

Slavery, 66 *n*, 113, 154, 164, 185, 185–8, 253, 284, 299, 302, 303 *n*, 328 *n*, 383, 386, 391, 395 *n*, 425, 478, 478 *n*, 496

Slavs, 389–90, 398 *n*, 412, 413–16, 421 *n* 432, 435

Slovenes, 415

Smith, Edwin, 22 *n*

Smyrna, 199, 332

Societas (*Lat.*), 476 *n*, 478

Socrates, 105, 125 *n*, 126 *n*, 128, 144, 153 *n*, 155, 164–70, 531, 541, 559, 569; (*and Pythagoreans*), 130 *n*, 166; (*and Plato*), 170–2, 176; (*and Aristotle*), 166

Solomon, 20 *n*, 33, 35, 56

Solon, 22, 105 *n*, 162 *n*, 224

Son of Man, 87, 87 *n*

Sophia (*Gr.*), 131, 161, 214

Sophists, the, 125 *n*, 158, 159–64, 165, 187, 197 *n*

Sophocles, 118 *n*, 118, 119 *n*, 134, 151, 153, 154, 163 *n* and 183 *n*, 517 *n*

Sophrosyné (*Gr.*), 116, 119

Sothic year, 17 *n*

Soul (*including psychology*), (*Hebrew*), 85, 515 *n;* (*Greek*), 125 *n*, 129–30, 129–30 *nn*, 168–9, 217, 219–23; (*Plato*), 130, 173–7; (*Aristotle*), 175, 213–14; (*Neo-Platonists*), 347–9; (*Christianity*), 358 *n*, 374 *n;* (*mediaeval*), 446–7, 455; (*modern*), 488; (*Descartes*), 505–6, 506 *n;* (*world-soul, soul universal*) 174 *n*, 175 *n*, 175–6, 219, 338 *n*, 339 *n*, 344–5, 346, 347, 349–50, 452, 569

Sovereignty (theories of), 101, 233, 473–80, 492

Soviet, 531–2

Spain (*Roman*), 94, 246 *n*, 248, 249, 260;

(*province of*), 251, 268, 270 *n*, 287 *n*, 289, 290, 292–4, 369 *n*, 389, 393; (*epoch of Decline and Fall*), 397, 399, 409, 410 *n*, 421; (*Arabs*), 409, 418, 419, 453

Sparta, Spartans, 98, 99 *n*, 104, 114, 136, 138–45, 159 *n*, 169, 184, 186, 189, 198, 415

Spartianus, 285, 286

Spencer, Herbert, 162 *n*

Spinoza, 345, 348 *n*, 451, 453, 464, 513, 538, 545, 546 *n*, 570; (*Ethics*), 545; (*and time*), 13 *n*

Spoletum, 403

Stane Street, 298 *n*

Stasis (*Gr.*), 106, 185

State, 556–7, 567, 574

Statius, 92 *n*, 308

Stilicho, 396

Stipendium, 243 *n*

Stoa poikilê (*Gr.*), 220

Stoics, Stoicism, 217–21; (*ethical ideal*), 181, 182, 222, 223, 312, 343, 565; (*cosmopolitanism*), 77, 106, 200, 313; (*slavery*), 188; (*the logos*), 364 *n*; (*Roman*), 257, 333; (*Seneca*), 307; (*Marcus Aurelius*), 342–3; (*Roman law*), 302, 470; (*Neo-Platonism*), 349, 352; (*Christianity*), 224, 343, 343 *n;* (*general*), 223, 339, 378, 444, 447, 499 *n*

Strabo, 197 *n*

Stratêgiai (*Gr.*), 421

Suarez, 492

Subjective idealism, 346 *n* (cf. 173–5)

Subordinationism, 364

Subsistence, 552

Substance (concept of), 173–4, 209–11, 368, 370, 374 *n; see also* Ousia

Suebes, 371, 396, 399

Suetonius, 283

Sulla, 239 *n*, 269–72, 293, 300

Sumer, Sumerians, 25

Superman, the, 163

Susa, 25, 42 *n*, 137, 192

Swinburne, A. C., 119 *n*, 156, 156 *n*

Syagrius, 398 *n*

Sybaris, 109

Symbolon (*Gr.*), 336

Syracuse, 9, 99, 109, 138, 144, 180, 186 *n*, 198, 202, 205

Syria, Syrians, 19, 24, 27, 28, 31–5, 39 *n;* (*Graeco-Macedonian kingdom*), 197, 250; (*Roman province*), 93, 270 *n*, 275, 281, 287 *n*, 321, 338 *n;* (*under Eastern emperors*), 412, 418, 421, 432; (*Christian*), 428–9

Syro-Roman law book, 424 *n*

Synagogue (*the Jewish*), 77, 323, 324, (cf. 70)

Tacitus, 197 *n*, 279 *n*, 283, 295 *n*, 298 *n*, 305 *n*, 310, 331, 405

Talmud, 286

Tarentum, 198, 244

Tarquins, the, 226 *n*, 484

Tarraco, 293

Tarshish, 33

Tarsus, 204, 221, 321

Tartars, 400, 414–15, 501 *n*

Taxation (*Roman*), 243, 260, 273 *n*, 279, 288, 292 *n*, 392, 422

Technai (*Gr.*), 161

Tekoa, 58

Teleology (*in Greek philosophy*), 126 *n*, 176, 209, 210, 220; (*mediaeval and modern*), 486–7, 488, 505, 510 *n*, 519, 526

Tell-el-Amarna letters, 19 *n*

Temple (Jewish), temple-worship, 66, 69–70, 74, 77

Ten Thousand, retreat of the, 190

Tennyson, 111 *n*, 313, 502 *n*

Terence, 155, 256 *n*

Tertullian, 266 *n*, 326, 360 *n*, 374, 374 *n*, 441 *n*, 456 *n*, 470 *n*

Testamentary succession (*Roman law*), 240, 265 *n*, 284, 423

Teutons, *see* Germans

Thales, 121, 121 *n*, 122, 373

Theatre, the Greek, 149, 150

Thebes (*Egypt*), 18, 37; (*Greece*), 99 *n*, 189, 190, 193

Themistocles, 107, 134, 138, 139 *n*

Theocracy (*Jewish*), 69–76, 81 *n*, 82 *n*, 93; (*mediaeval and later*), 411 *n*, 489 *n*, 492 *n*

Theocritus, 202, 202 *n*

Theodicy, 86 *n*, 378–9, 379 *n*, 381, 507, 525

Theodore, 393

Theodore of Tarsus, 432

Theodoric the Ostrogoth, 311, 402, 403

Theodoric the Visigoth, 400

Theodosius the Great, 371 *n*, 385 *n*, 393, 398, 412

Theodosius II, 385 *n*; (*code of*), 423 *n*, 424, 464

Theaetetus, 464

Theognis, 110, 115, 183

Theology, 462

Theophrastus, 24 *n*, 209

Theôria (*Gr.*), 124 *n*, 131, 211, 520; *see also* Contemplative life

Theotokos (*Gr.*), 427 *n*

Thermopylae, battle of, 114

Thessalonica, 246 *n*, 324, 430

Thessaly, 97, 111, 189

Thothmes III, 19

Thrace, 43, 96, 129, 137, 140, 190, 287 *n*, 419, 421

Thracian conquests, 137

Thrasymachus, 162 *n*, 163, 163 *n*

Thucydides (*general*), 134, 144, 157–9; (*special references*), 36, 109 *n*, 115 *n*, 118 *n*, 136 *n*, 141 *n*, 142–4, 143 *n*, 144 *n*, 182

Thurii, 157, 160 *n*, 205

Tiberius, 93, 279 *n*, 281 *n*, 299, 310, 331

Tiglath-Pileser III, 27 *n*

Timur, 435

Tiryns, 36–8

Titus, emperor, 93, 322

Toleration, religious (*Rome*), 270 *n*, 329–30, 338; (*Christian*), 384–5; *see also* Persecution

Tolma (*Gr.*), 354 *n*

Tolstoi, 179

Torah, the (*Heb.*), *see under* Hebrew (*Mosaic law*), 217 *n*

Toscanelli, 491 *n*

Totalitarianism, 573

Toulouse, 398, 444 *n*

Town-planning (*Greek*), 160 *n*, 205

Tractatus de Intellectus Emendatione, 570

Trafalgar, 545

Tragedy (*Greek*), 148–56; (*Roman*), 306–7

Trager, 565

Trajan, 247 *n*, 283, 288 *n*, 290, 293, 308–10, 313, 315, 332, 411, 425 *n*

Transcendence, divine, 89 *n*, 350 *n*, 364, 369 *n*, 370 *n*, 370, 451 *n*, 456, 552, 553 *n*

Trasimene, lake, battle of the, 251 *n*

Trèves, 295, 393

Tribes, Roman assembly of, 235 *n*

Tribonian, 424

Tribune, tribunate, 235, 268, 272, 277, 282

Trinity, doctrine of the, 351, 364, 364 *n*, 366–71, 373, 379, 427, 452; (*and the Incarnation*), 459

Trivium, the, 450

Troy, the Trojan war, 36, 97

Troyes, battle of, 400

Truth in art, 132

Tsar, 416 *n*

Tudor monarchy, 489, 489 *n*; *see also* Henry VIII, Elizabeth

Turks, 390, 400 *n*, 412, 418 *n*, 429, 434–5, 484

Tutor (*Roman law*), 240

Twelve Patriarchs, Testament of the, 92 *n*

Twelve Tables, the (*Roman law*), 235, 236–41, 261, 263, 265 *n*

Tyranny (*Greek*), 107, 109, 117, 129 *n*, 135, 157; (*Tarquins*), 226 *n*; (*mediaeval view of*), 473

Tyre, 33, 57, 191, 366

Ulfila, 398 *n*
Ulpian, 301 *n*, 302 *n*, 303 *n*, 423, 441
Ummayyad caliphs, 410 *n*, 419, 453
United States, 568
Unities, dramatic, 148 *n*, 517 *n*
Universals, problem of, 209, 210, 444,
    444 *n*, *see also* Forms
Universities (*ancient*), 180, 220 *n*, 284,
    296, 309 *n*, 362, 383 *n*; (*mediaeval*),
    439, 443, 444, 444 *n*, 485; (*modern*),
    162 *n*, 494, 511 *n*, 517
Utica, 33, 272
Utilitarians, British, 494 *n*, 502; (*School
    of Bentham*), 555

Vacarius, 467
Valens, 397–8
Valentian III, 423, 464
Valentinus, 362 *n*
Values (and facts), *see* Facts; *also* 528,
    528 *n*, 538–40, 564, 565
Vandals, 294, 371, 380, 396, 399–400,
    401, 421 *n*
Varro, 248
Varus, 281
Vegetius, 245 *n*
Venice, Venetians, 401, 403, 434–5, 511;
    (*ambassadors' reports*),   422;   (*St
    Mark's*), 430
Vesalius, 488, 505 *n*
Vespasian, 281 *n*, 296 *n*, 308
Via (*Lat.*) (*Aemilia, Appia, Domitia,
    Egnatia, Latina*), 246 *n*, 251 *n*
Via remotionis (*Lat.*), 350 *n*, 455
Victorian age, 501
Victorinus, 377
Virgil, 132, 281 *n*, 285, 303 *n*, 305, 306,
    308, 310, 313–14, 496, 512; *also*
    (*Roman spirit*), 5, 226, 228, 232 *n*,
    279, 305, 381; (*love of nature*), 255;
    (*Homer*), 112, 493 *n*; (*Theocritus*), 202;
    (*Cato*), 272 *n*; (*Christianity*), 66 *n*,
    313–14, 381 *n*; (*Dante*), 314, 524
Virgin, the, 427 *n*
Virtus (*Lat.*), 227, 470
Visigoths, 294, 296, 369 *n*, 371, 379, 393,
    397, 398, 401, 404, 464
Vitale, S., 422 *n*
Vitellius, 288 *n*

Voltaire, 156 *n*, 160, 339, 386 *n*, 412, 496,
    510 *n*, 517 *n*, 546 *n*
Vulgate, 310, 442 *n*

Wall of Severus, 296
Watling Street, 297, 298 *n*
Wells, H. G., 555
Wessell, John, 490
Whitehead, Dr, 538, 552, 558, 566
William of Moerbeke, 454 *n*, 485 *n*
William of Occam, 445
William I (the Norman), 448
Wills (*Roman law of*), *see* Testamentary
    succession
Wisdom, 131
Wisdom literature (*Jewish*), 81, 81 *n*
Women, status of, (*Babylon*), 26; (*Greece*),
    113, 155, 164, 182–5; (*Rome*), 229–32,
    284, 425; (*Mithraism*), 340 *n*, 341 *n*;
    (*Christianity*), 320, 386; (*mediaeval*),
    182
Wordsworth, 460, 508 *n*
World-soul, see under Soul
Wren, Sir Christopher, 521 *n*
Wright, Dr, 32 *n*
Wroxeter, 297

Xenophanes, 128
Xenophon, 158 *n*, 163 *n*, 164 *n*, 168 *n*,
    182 *n*, 186
Xerxes, 138, 158 *n*, 191
Ximenes, Cardinal, 488

Yahweh (*Heb.* = Jehovah), 51, 51 *n*
York, 297

Zacharias, pope, 410
Zechariah, 74 *n*
Zeit-geist, 531
Zeller, 546 *n*
Zeno, emperor, 402
Zeno, paradoxes of, 125 *n*, 166 *n*
Zeno, Stoic, 220
Zephaniah, 39 *n*, 67 *n*, 81 *n*
Zeus, 36, 99, 153, 155
Zoology, 208
Zoroaster, Zoroastrianism, 41, 86
Zulueta, de (*Legacy of Rome*), 238 *n*,
    263 *n*, 467 *n*
Zwingle, 491